SO-AFE-422

TEACHING AGAINST GLOBAL CAPITALISM AND THE NEW IMPERIALISM
A Critical Pedagogy

Peter McLaren and
Ramin Farahmandpur

ROWMAN & LITTLEFIELD PUBLISHERS, INC.
Lanham • Boulder • New York • Toronto • Oxford

ROWMAN & LITTLEFIELD PUBLISHERS, INC.

Published in the United States of America
by Rowman & Littlefield Publishers, Inc.
A wholly owned subsidiary of The Rowman & Littlefield Publishing Group, Inc.
4501 Forbes Boulevard, Suite 200, Lanham, Maryland 20706
www.rowmanlittlefield.com

PO Box 317, Oxford, OX2 9RU, UK

Copyright © 2005 by Rowman & Littlefield Publishers, Inc.

All rights reserved. No part of this publication may be reproduced, stored in a
retrieval system, or transmitted in any form or by any means, electronic, mechanical,
photocopying, recording, or otherwise, without the prior permission of the publisher.

British Library Cataloguing in Publication Information Available

Library of Congress Cataloging-in-Publication Data

McLaren, Peter, 1948–
   Teaching against global capitalism and the new imperialism: a critical pedagogy /
Peter McLaren and Ramin Farahmandpur.
      p. cm.
   Includes bibliographical references and index.
   ISBN 0-7425-1039-5 (cloth : alk. paper) — ISBN 0-7425-1040-9 (pbk. : alk. paper)
   1. Critical pedagogy—United States. I. Farahmandpur, Ramin, 1966– II. Title.
LC196.5 .U6M355 2005
370.11'5—dc22

                                                                        2004009291

Printed in the United States of America

∞™ The paper used in this publication meets the minimum requirements of American
National Standard for Information Sciences—Permanence of Paper for Printed Library
Materials, ANSI/NISO Z39.48-1992.

£ 30.95

TEACHING AGAINST GLOBAL CAPITALISM AND THE NEW IMPERIALISM

To the memory of my mother, Frances Bernadette Teresa McLaren, and to Peter Hudis, whose extraordinary work, along with that of Kevin Anderson and others, has charted out a new direction for the future of revolutionary struggle.

Peter McLaren

To my parents, Amir and Mehrangiz;
my sister, Ladan;
and finally, to my critical friends, Swapna, Brian, and Carla.

Ramin Farahmandpur

Contents

Foreword   ix
Roberto Bahruth

Acknowledgments   xiii

Introduction   1

1   Reconsidering Marx in Post-Marxist Times:
A Requiem for Postmodernism?   13

2   Freire, Marx, and the New Imperialism:
Toward a Revolutionary Praxis   38

3   Critical Pedagogy, Postmodernism, and the Retreat from Class:
Toward a Contraband Pedagogy   68

4   Critical Multiculturalism and the Globalization of Capital:
Some Implications for a Politics of Resistance   97

5   Globalization, Class, and Multiculturalism:
Fragments from a Red Notebook   120

6   Teaching against Globalization and the New Imperialism:
Toward a Revolutionary Pedagogy   159

7   Educational Policy and the Socialist Imagination:
Revolutionary Citizenship as a Pedagogy of Resistance   192

8   Teaching in and against the Empire:
Critical Pedagogy as Revolutionary Praxis   227
With Gregory Martin and Nathalia Jaramillo

9   Critical Revolutionary Pedagogy at Ground Zero:
    Renewing the Educational Left after September 11   257

Afterword   281
    Juha Suoranta

Index   285

About the Authors   299

Foreword

THIS LATEST OFFERING by Peter McLaren, coauthored with Ramin Farah-mandpur, provides a critical synthesis of the most pressing issues in the world today. Their analyses of relevant dimensions of Marxist theory in application to a critique of globalization—as a euphemism for imperialism—are useful to concerned citizens who are engaged in the struggle for global justice and world peace. The call for critical revolutionary pedagogy should be heeded by educators, and they should be alarmed by the many examples provided of First Amendment violations of the rights of teachers and students across America in the name of patriotism. Linkages between terrorism and American foreign policy enlighten and respond to the question posed by those who were shocked by 9/11 and left wondering, "Why do they hate us?" If corporate media had been doing their jobs, we would have seen it coming and perhaps might have applied more democratic pressure to our government to express the will of its many citizens rather than to support the pillage of the world by a greedy few.

This is an important text that makes significant contributions to the field of critical pedagogy in relation to globalization. McLaren and Farahmand-pur make new connections between capitalism, globalization, and state-sponsored terrorism while providing powerful pedagogical recommendations. Across the chapters, they move from Marxist theory to critical revolutionary pedagogy to recommendations for applications of a "contra-band pedagogy" in public schools and especially in colleges of education. The connections made to specific dimensions of globalization and U.S.

foreign policy are strong, and the work is thoroughly supported by other scholars in the field.

Herein, McLaren and Farahmandpur pose embarrassing questions to the status quo to illustrate its inability to address the human dilemmas provoked by a capitalism constantly in crisis. Such questions provide us with the ontological clarity to focus and to continue our efforts to struggle over history toward a social democratic resolution rather than to resign ourselves to the "death of history" myths of those who see capitalism as the highest expression of humanity despite the tomes of counterevidence in the form of human and environmental catastrophes.

In an age where the corporate media—no longer representing the fourth estate—has perfected the science of "manufacturing consent," the courage and criticality of a civilization's thinkers become vital, essential, and desperately necessary. Two major problems exist in the academy, where the epitome of intellectualism is supposedly alive and well. First, it is evident that a great many of the professors come from the elite class and are themselves influenced by and invested in the dominant ideology of their received culture, which is reified and promoted by the corporate media. Funding holds many others hostage to silence. An even more pernicious silence comes when those who are critically aware of the propaganda that deliberately confuses patriotism with conformity remain silent out of fear of repercussions. We have all witnessed in history the horrors that result from silence and conformity as people look out only for their immediate and personal interests. Schmidt (2000) reminds us, "The individual is obliterated not by confronting the system, but by conforming to it" (252).

In the long history of Peter McLaren's career, and in the emerging scholorship of his coauthor, Ramin Farahmandpur, the consistency of their ability to read the word and the world critically and the courage to speak out against the oppression and social injustices cultured in the petri dish of capitalism—and now globalization—are evident. One might conjecture that, in McLaren's case, this tenacity in the face of hegemony is because of and bolstered by his working-class roots. Giroux once referred to himself as "an historical, academic accident" since he also entered the academy from a working-class background. I would insist that the true patriot is not the one who floats the river of conformity where rich rewards await those who are willing to sell their souls to the highest bidder but the one who is willing to struggle "in order to form a more perfect union, establish justice, insure domestic tranquility, provide for the common defence, promote the general welfare, and secure the blessings of liberty to ourselves and our posterity" (Constitution of the United States), not just for those who are citizens of the

United States but for human beings everywhere. As Samuel Johnson indicated so long ago, "Patriotism is the last refuge of a scoundrel." Countless scoundrels would have us wrap ourselves in the flag, while the liberties it pretends to represent are shrinking under the pressure of the rhetorical "patriot act."

As Nader (1992) has so eloquently clarified for those who have been confused by the distortions of patriotism promoted by those who are pillaging the present as they mortgage the future, "a democracy is a society where less and less courage and risk are needed of more and more people to spread justice and the blessings of liberty throughout the land" (vi).

It is not surprising that there is such heated debate over education in America. In a Jeffersonian sense, public education holds the potential for an enlightened citizenry. It is under siege precisely for this reason. Education holds an equal potential to transform as it is now being used to produce conformity. The present climate of standardization, accountability, and the myth of objective, "scientifically based research" represses teachers while it ideologically imposes on the vocation of teaching. As Adrienne Rich (1994, 3) points out, "Objectivity has been little more than male subjectivity." This is apparent in the ways that patriarchy continues to delimit a female-dominated profession. According to Aronowitz,

> It might be possible to show that the virtual abandonment, by today's educational leaders, of the goal of providing for society a layer of critical intellectuals is a response to the upsurges of student activism in the 1960s. In this light, the turn toward vocationalization and toward a reduced conception of learning may be part of an effort, openly urged by many on the right, to make sure the 1960s never happen again. (2000, 172)

Professors of labor studies, sociology, anthropology, political science, and business and especially those in colleges of education would be negligent to ignore the critical issues raised here and the powerful suggestions offered to engage in the struggle for humanity in their respective fields. Community activists can profit from the specific recommendations offered to prevent the "divide and conquer" effects of fighting individual causes while overlooking class struggle as a unifying factor across all other "isms" incited in the name of democratic capitalism. Statistics on greed and the exploitation of defenseless children around the world, in the pursuit of profit, should awaken us to the horrors of runaway multinational corporations.

Roberto Bahruth, Ph.D., 2004

References

Aronowitz, S. 2000. *The knowledge factory.* Boston: Beacon Press.

Nader, R. 1992. Foreword. In *Civics for democracy: A journey for teachers and students,* ed. Katherine Isaac. Washington, D.C.: Essential Books.

———. 1991. *Preamble: The Constitution of the United States of America.* Thirteenth Edition. Washington, D.C.: Commisssion of the United States Constitution.

Rich, A. 1994. *Blood, bread, and poetry: Selected prose 1979–1985.* New York: Norton.

Schmidt, J. 2000. *Disciplined minds.* Lanham, Md.: Rowman & Littlefield.

Acknowledgments

We would like to acknowledge the publishers and organizations who granted us permission to reprint revised versions of our essays in this book.

Chapter 1 is a revised version of Peter McLaren and Ramin Farahmandpur's "Reconsidering Marx in post-Marxist times: A requiem for postmodernism?" *Educational Researcher* 29, no. 3 (April 2000): 25–33.

Chapter 2 is a substantially revised version of Peter McLaren and Ramin Farahmandpur's "Freire, Marx, and the new imperialism: Toward a revolutionary praxis," in *The Freirean Legacy: Educating for social justice*, ed. J. J. Slater, S. M. Fain, and C. A. Rossatto, 37–56. New York: Peter Lang, 2002.

Chapter 3 is a substantially revised version of Peter McLaren and Ramin Farahmandpur's "Critical pedagogy, postmodernism, and the retreat from class: Towards a contraband pedagogy," in *Postmodern excess in educational theory: Education and the politics of human resistance*, ed. D. Hill, P. McLaren, M. Cole, and G. Rikowski, 167–202. London: Tufnell Press, 1999.

Chapter 4 is a substantially revised version of Peter McLaren and Ramin Farahmandpur's "Critical multiculturalism and the globalization of capital: Some implications for a politics of resistance," *Journal of Curriculum Theorizing* 15, no. 4 (1999): 27–46.

Chapter 5 is a revised version of Peter McLaren and Ramin Farahmandpur's "Globalization, class, and multiculturalism: Fragments from a red notebook," in *Global learning*, ed. M. Singh, 55–94. Altona, Victoria, Australia: Common Ground Publishing, 2002.

Chapter 6 is a revised version of Peter McLaren and Ramin Farahmandpur's "Teaching against globalization and the new imperialism: Towards a revolutionary pedagogy," *Journal of Teacher Education* 52, no. 2 (2001): 136–50.

Chapter 7 is a substantially revised version of Peter McLaren and Ramin Farahmandpur's "Educational policy and socialist imagination: Revolutionary citizenship as a pedagogy of resistance," *Educational Policy: An Interdisciplinary Journal of Policy Practice* 15, no. 3 (2001): 343–78.

Chapter 8 is a revised version of Peter McLaren, Gregory Martin, Ramin Farahmandpur, and Nathalia Jaramillo's "Teaching in and against empire: Critical pedagogy as revolutionary praxis," *Teacher Education Quarterly* 31, no. 1 (2004): 131–53.

Chapter 9 is a revised version of Peter McLaren and Ramin Farahmandpur's "Critical Revolutionary Pedagogy at Ground Zero: Renewing the Educational Left after 9/11." The original version is copyright 2003 from *Education as enforcement: The militarism and corporatization of schools* by K. J. Saltman and D. A. Gabbard. Reproduced by permission of Routledge/Taylor & Francis Books, Inc.

Introduction

Empire or Imperialism?

THE GRAND IMPERIALIST DESIGN OF THE U.S. ruling elite has ribboned itself through the labyrinth of contemporary history like military maneuvers on a colonial war map. While the most ambitious of imperial destinies for the United States was penned by a fanatical cabal of Cold War warriors associated with the Project for the New American Century years before George W. Bush came to power, the forces that have set in train the present course of imperialism and its undiluted reign that have been so explosively impacting the world have taken place over numerous generations. This book does not pretend to be a comprehensive account of how we have arrived at this tragic state of affairs but attempts, if only modestly, to explore some of the central characteristics of U.S. imperialism and to situate these characteristics within a specific problematic that has been our province of research for a number of years, that of developing a philosophy of praxis that has gone by various descriptions: critical pedagogy, socialist pedagogy, and revolutionary critical pedagogy being among the most prominent.

There is no question that the topics of imperialism and empire have attracted considerable notice, occasioning the requisite premonitory warnings about the demise of civilization but also promoting vigorous debates in the academy over recent years. Perhaps the most significant of these involves the best-selling book, *Empire* by Michael Hardt and Antonio Negri.

Hardt and Negri's (2000) *Empire* has been hailed by many leftist scholars (as well as grassroots activists) as a conceptual tour de force that unlocks the

---

boneyard secrets of capital and uncoils the mysteries of empire. Many have applauded the book for its meticulous mapping of the past, present, and future trajectories of capitalism. The book's thesis on empire fervently claims to have surpassed Lenin's (1977) theory of imperialism, in which imperialism was understood as the highest stage of capitalism. We do not have space here to rehearse, instance by instance, Hardt and Negri's thesis on empire; we do, however, offer a brief overview of the major arguments they make in their book as a means of distinguishing our own contrasting position.

In *Empire*, Hardt and Negri announce the arrival of postimperialism. They proclaim that empire is what follows imperialism. While Hardt and Negri do not go as far as dismissing Lenin's theory of imperialism in its entirety, their mainly Kautskyian analysis of capitalism (while we reject Kautsky's fatalistic Marxism that views the laws of the development of society as acting independently of human volition, inevitably assigning to the mass of working-class individuals a specific form of consciousness, we do not mean to dismiss all of the insights of "the renegade Kautsky," sometimes known as the "pope of Marxism") does signal the demise of interimperialist rivalries and global competitions. Hardt and Negri make the dubious claim that we have entered an era of "peaceful capitalist coexistence." They identify the rise of empire with Bush *padre*'s announcement of a New World Order, the defeat of U.S. imperialism in the Vietnam War, the expansion of nongovernmental organizations (NGOs); the diminishing role of the welfare state, the increasing influence of multinational corporations, and the overwhelming power of supranational organizations such as the WTO and the IMF. However, as Bashhir Abu-Manneh (2004) correctly points out, a cardinal weakness in Hardt and Negri's analysis is that they fail to account for one of the three major contradictions of capitalism, namely, its "combined and uneven development." Abu-Manneh (2004) writes that interimperialist rivalries, which arise from the "combined and uneven development," constitutes one of capitalism's inescapable contradictions. Lenin recognized that in the era of interimperialist competition, "uneven development" could only intensify, and that "there can be no permanent joint exploitation of the world" (Abu-Manneh 2004). A brief outline of Lenin's theory of imperialism below will elucidate our point.

Lenin (1977) referred to imperialism as "moribund capitalism" because it was impregnated by the contradictions of capitalist social relations of production. He identified three major contradictions in capitalism. The first contradiction is the contradiction between labor and capital; that is, between the working classes and the ruling classes. This antagonistic relationship holds true both in national and international contexts in which workers are exploited by multinational corporations. The second contradiction is the one that exists among multinational corporations and those imperialist countries (i.e., United States, Europe, and Japan) that compete with each other over the control of the world's natural resources and frequently engage in military warfare over territorial conquests. The third is the contradiction between Western industrial countries and so-called Third World and developing nations. This contradiction arises from the fact that in order to exploit these (often colonial or neocolonial) nations, imperialist countries must industrialize them by building railroads, factories, and commercial centers. In the course of their economic development, new revolutionary classes of proletariats and intelligentsia emerge that challenge the colonizers and occupiers.

We agree with Abu-Manneh (2004) that Lenin's theory of imperialism as the highest stage of capitalism unassailably provides a much needed analysis and framework that sheds important light on the latest developments of capitalism and continues to have relevancy for organizing revolutionary proletarian struggles as we press forward into the twenty-first century. Our major disagreement with Hardt and Negri is with their stubborn insistence that state power has become obsolete or that its role has significantly diminished. In contrast, we believe that the state continues to play a key role in advancing the U.S. imperial project of global dominance by means of two interlocking processes: globalization and neoliberalism.

At the time of the Cold War, the United States relied on a "double containment" strategy to maintain its global supremacy and dominance. On the one hand, such a strategy prevented the spread of communism from spilling over from the Soviet Union and Eastern bloc countries into Third World countries and also suppressed the rise of nationalist inspired movements in the former colonies that posed a serious challenge to its geopolitical interests. Bill Blum (2004) writes:

> From the late 1940s to around the mid-1960s, it was an American policy objective to instigate the downfall of the Soviet government as well as several Eastern European regimes. Many hundreds of Russian exiles were organized, trained and equipped by the CIA, then sneaked back into their homeland to set up espionage rings, to stir up armed political struggle, and to carry out acts of assassination and sabotage, such as derailing trains, wrecking bridges, damaging arms factories and power plants, and so on.

Of course, the Reagan administration would like to take most of the credit for the breakup of the Soviet Union. In fact, Reagan's tough anticommunism no doubt delayed the breakup since in all likelihood the extreme militarization of American policy strengthened hard-liners in the Soviet Union and worked against those Soviet reformers who, independently of the United

States, had been working for change within the Soviet Union ever since Stalin (Blum, 2004). Blum puts it thusly:

> [W]hat were the fruits of this ultra-tough anti-communist policy? Repeated serious confrontations between the United States and the Soviet Union in Berlin, Cuba and elsewhere, the Soviet interventions into Hungary and Czechoslovakia, creation of the Warsaw Pact (in direct reaction to NATO), no glasnost, no perestroika, only pervasive suspicion, cynicism and hostility on both sides.
>
> It turned out that the Russians were human after all—they responded to toughness with toughness. And the corollary: there was for many years a close correlation between the amicability of US-Soviet relations and the number of Jews allowed to emigrate from the Soviet Union. Softness produced softness.

On the other hand, the United States also used the fear of communism as part of its overall foreign policy strategy to keep in check its main imperial rivals, Europe and Japan. However, by the early 1990s, with the collapse of the Berlin Wall and the breakup of the Soviet republics and eastern European satellite states, the United States faced a "crisis of legitimacy." It could no longer rely on the "communist threat" to stave off its potential imperial rivals. In an effort to reestablish its legitimacy in the international arena, U.S. imperialism targeted and attacked a number of countries, most notably Iraq and the former Yugoslavia. Under the "humanitarian" pretext of putting an end to the ethnic wars that had swept the former Yugoslavian republics, and with the help and the intervention of NATO forces, the United States was able to secure a more visible role and active military presence in Europe. The same is true in the more recent case of the Middle East. After having lost its legitimacy as the protector of the ruling monarchy in Saudi Arabia against Saddam Hussein's territorial ambitions for a greater Iraq (which included the failed annexation of Kuwait in 1991), the United States decided to invade and occupy Iraq under cover of a series of carefully stage-managed lies that led the U.S. public to believe that a connection existed between the September 11 attacks and Saddam Hussein's regime. With the help of the CIA and the corporate-run media machine, the Bush administration orchestrated a propaganda campaign that accused Saddam Hussein of hiding an extensive supply of Weapons of Mass Destruction. Of course, neither the missing link between Saddam Hussein's regime and al Qaeda nor the Weapons of Mass Destruction were found. It was not until the tragic events of September 11, 2001, and the full-blown "war on terrorism," that the United States was able to find the political and ideological justification to maintain and expand its imperial dominance, which included the military occupation of Iraq and Afghanistan. Of course, as we all know by now, the main objective of the U.S. occupation was to establish a strategic geopolitical presence in the Middle East and to secure the oil fields in Iraq, which are the second-largest oil reserves in the world after Saudi Arabia. Thus, in his address to a joint session of Congress and the American people, Bush's jackhammer statement—"Every nation, in every region, now has a decision to make. Either you are with us, or you are with the terrorists"—was a molten warning to all nations that the United States had decided to pursue a foreign policy of "unilateralism" that positioned it as the one and only uncontested imperial power in the world. Of course, imperialism requires a strong military, and the United States depends on a volunteer army. Which is why members of the U.S. military—all four branches—are offered free breast enlargements, face-lifts, liposuction, and nose jobs. This ensures that soldiers will look good when they visit the Moonlight Bunny Ranch, a legal Nevada brothel that offers free sex to American GI's returning from Iraq.

Lite Fascism as Democracy

As Boaventura de Sousa Santos (2004) and others have argued, in recent history, society's claims on the state needed to be controlled because the pressures put on the state by historical actors demanding rights and inclusion have been too powerful to contain by a centralized government. Hence, we have seen a major move toward decentralization and a withdrawal of the state from social and economic sectors via privatization, marketization, and liberalization. This has led to a condition that Santos describes as one of indirect rule by powerful economic actors who hold tremendous control over the basic livelihoods of people, ushering in a period that is politically democratic but socially fascistic. Debates have proliferated in the academic literature as to whether or not the United States has transformed itself into a fascist state. While we are not in a position to evaluate these debates, we readily admit that the latent conditions for the actualization of fascism are everywhere in evidence, something that could be called a dormant fascism waiting to erupt. Anis Shivani (2002) warns that

> America today is seeking a return to some form of vitalism, some organic, volkisch order that will "unite" the blue and red states in an eternal Volkgemeinschaft; is in a state of perpetual war and militaristic aggression targeting all potential counters to hegemony; has been coercing and blackmailing its own victims and oppressed (justified by anti-political correctness rhetoric) to return to a mythical national consensus; has introduced surveillance technology to demolish the private sphere to an extent unimaginable in the recent past; and fetishizes technology as the futuristic solution to age-old ills of alienation and mistrust.

Fascism consists of, but at the same time exceeds, the following multitude of factors: intolerance toward opposition by means of ruthless repression, the glorification of militarism and war, a hatred for liberalism and communism, the creation of a nationalist authoritarian state, a mixing of romanticism and mysticism, the co-optation of a populist-revolutionary antiestablishment rhetoric as a means—paradoxically—to restore order, the destruction of working-class organizations, the proliferation of racism and fear of difference, exhibiting scorn for the weak, promulgating the view that dissent is a betrayal of the homeland and that pacifism is tantamount to aiding and abetting the enemy, the trivialization of mass death (i.e., Iraqi deaths don't matter because the Iraqis are subhuman), the glorification of random violence and the elevation of brutality to the art of the sublime (witness talk radio hosts in the thrall of bliss as they so adoringly extol the torturing of Iraqis at Abu Ghraib prison, even entreating the torturers to inflict greater pain and punishment, including mutilation and execution). Fascism is also a call to consensus building, to enlisting the masses with appeals to the ideal of the new Christian warrior (Shivani 2002). Shivani writes,

> America today wants to be communal and virile; it seeks to overcome what is presented by propagandists as the unreasonable demands for affirmative action and reparations by minorities and women; it wants to revalorize nation and region and race to take control of the future; it seeks to remold the nation through propaganda and charismatic leadership, into overcoming the social divisiveness of capitalism and democracy.

We would be remiss to dismiss the transformation of the United States that we are currently witnessing under the Bush administration as merely a form of low-carb fascism, when there may, in fact, be something considerably more potent brewing.

Critical Revolutionary Pedagogy in the Age of Imperialism

As U.S. imperialism sinks its claws deeper into the rich oil fields of the Middle East, foreign policy pundits in the White House brandish the bragging rights of belonging to the one and only uncontested imperial power of the twenty-first century. In the wake of the recent invasion, occupation, and brutish colonization of Iraq, not to mention Afghanistan and Haiti, there has been an unforgiving yet understandable reluctance on the part of some educators in graduate schools of education and teacher education programs to engage in political and ideological debates over the current social, political, and economic crisis of capitalism (which Marxists claim are dangerously moving us closer to a fatal collision course with capitalism's own internal contradictions). Fewer still have seen fit to inquire into and oppose the baleful erosion of human rights that have been provided by the Constitution. They have justified their inaction in the name of fighting a permanent war on terrorism.

Under the false pretense of research "objectivity" and "neutrality," many educators are reluctant to take a public stance, let alone rally against the blood-soaked ambitions of the American empire. Protected by the ivory towers of academia, educators routinely resort to a discourse of objectivity and neutrality as a tactic to avoid facing the political and ideological nature of their work (hooks 2004). In some cases, the discourse of neutrality and objectivity allows educators to distance themselves from the larger set of social and political contradictions and antagonisms that are generated by capitalist social relations of production. It also enables them to reduce the risks of having their fellow colleagues criticize them for lacking collegiality. Of course, for tenured professors who sport $120 Tommy Bahama's T-shirts and are waiting for their retirement benefits to kick in, there is little to worry about. But for a number of untenured Marxist educators, who have opened up a new front in university classrooms by teaching against global capitalism and the new imperialism, it has become increasingly dangerous to *problematize* let alone *unmask* the relationship between imperialism and education.

Within the academy in general, there exists too little genuine discussion or debate over the globalization of poverty, the exploitation of labor in Third World countries, or the Wal-Martization of the American workforce in the domestic frontiers. Given that most universities are now under corporate board-style management, this comes as little surprise. That a significant amount of scholarship churned out of graduate schools of education across the United States continues to operate from within the parameters drawn by capitalist social relations of production is simply restating a truism that holds for most of the academy. But what disturbs us is that this situation equally holds true for much of today's radical and progressive scholarship, which has largely failed to offer a lucid and incisive criticism of capitalism.

This is because *naming* let alone *questioning* the social, political, cultural, and economic arrangements under capitalism constitutes a form of political intervention and activism that for many educators is simply too risky. Instead, many engage in a form of "soft-radicalism" that scantly scratches the surface of the mechanisms of the dominant ideology. Here, protests reverberate like distant eructations from the bar stools of the local pub. Other colleagues may hide their class and race privileges in an obscure political and ideological discourse and language that leaves little room for actually addressing the material needs of those in our society who permanently live on the margins and the periphery.

Oftentimes, educators divorce political and ideological questions from pedagogical questions and reduce pedagogy to a congerie of prescribed methods and techniques that sacrifice theory and reflection at the altar of the high priests and prophets of practice. Here we are referring to those self-proclaimed practitioners who advocate concrete applications of teaching and learning over theory and self-reflection. We do not deny the importance of practice. In fact, we believe that theory must serve practice, and vice versa, for questions raised in practice must be answered by theory, which underscores the dialectical relationship between theory and practice. However, the theoretical and the practical dimensions of pedagogy can never be reduced to each another. This is because they exist in dialectical tension. In the absence of a theoretical understanding of the world, or a conceptual framework where we can reflect upon our experiences, or a discourse that enables us to examine our positionalities, or an opportunity to explore and rethink the ways in which we interact and relate to the world, practical tools and applications of pedagogy work only to reproduce and maintain capitalist social relations of production.

In many instances, teacher education programs have failed to engage students in dialogues about class exploitation and oppression. Oftentimes, class power is sanitized and its powerful effect on the life chances of working-class students is denuded or made invisible. As Paul Lauter (1998) has cogently expressed:

> Class . . . remains that unaddressed member of that now-famous trio "race, gender, class." Over the last two decades, there has been far more widespread acknowledgment of and open discussion of race and gender in the classroom, while class has generally remained the silenced subject. In fact, in classrooms, people have seemed afraid to talk about class. They often don't know [how] to acknowledge economic difference and economic privilege—with their entourage of conflicting social and cultural forms.

Regrettably, many progressive teacher education programs too often divorce the causes of cultural, racial, and gender oppression from class oppression. As a result, the struggle for social justice oftentimes is reduced to a truncated and dogmatically fatalist strategy of attrition that fails, in the main, to challenge and expose the mechanisms responsible for reproducing capitalist hegemony. In fact, such programs serve as a recipe for inaction.

Educators in our view need to shoulder the courage to question and to problematize the intensification of class antagonisms, the reproduction of the sexual division of labor, and the stubborn persistence of institutional racism that nourishes the ever-decaying roots of capitalism in its latest metabolic stage, namely, the new imperialism. As educators, we need to take the moral and ethical responsibility to question why the United States, as the wealthiest nation on the planet, continues to have the highest child poverty rate among Western industrialized countries. We need to question why 34.6 million Americans are living in poverty. We need to question why 43.6 million Americans are lacking any access to health insurance. And why is the combined income of the three wealthiest individuals on the planet equal to the combined national income of the poorest forty-nine countries? A historical comparison by Mathew Fox may shed some light on the issues. Fox (2004) notes that "in the 1960s, the overall income of the richest 20 percent of the world's population was thirty times that of the poorest 20 percent. Today, it is 224 times larger! In the 1960s, the richest 20 percent held 70 percent of the world's revenues; in 1999 it was 85 percent"(42).

Those of us who teach in graduate schools of education, and whose work is informed and guided by the principles of critical pedagogy, feel a sense of urgency in drawing attention to the growing class inequalities. Take for example, access to higher education, which now more than ever is beyond the reach of working-class high school graduates. In a recent issue of *BusinessWeek*, Jessi Hempel (2004) notes that in a study of the country's top 146 colleges and universities, only 3 percent of the student body came from families in the bottom quarter of wage earners. A more disturbing trend is the growing number of entering freshman who are from families earning $100,000 or more. Hemple writes that in the nation's top forty-two state universities, the number of entering freshman in this category jumped from 32 percent to 40 percent in less than five years.

How do we organize teachers and students against domestic trends such as these and also enable them to link these trends to global capitalism and the new imperialism? What pedagogical discourses and approaches can we use? The foundational principles of a renewed and revamped approach to critical pedagogy that we adumbrate throughout this book parallels the five pillars of popular education articulated by Deborah Brandt (1991). First, critical pedagogy must be a *collective process* that involves utilizing a dialogical (i.e., Freirean) learning approach. Second, critical pedagogy has to be *critical*; that is, it must locate the underlying causes of class exploitation and economic oppression within the social, political, and economic arrangements of capitalist social relations of production. Third, critical pedagogy must be profoundly *systematic* in the sense that it is guided by Marx's dialectical method of inquiry, which begins with the "real concrete" circumstances of the oppressed masses and moves toward a classification, conceptualization, analysis, and breaking down of the concrete social world into units of abstractions in order to reach the essence of social phenomena under investigation. Next, it reconstructs and makes the social world intelligible by transforming and translating theory into concrete social and political activity. Fourth, critical pedagogy should be *participatory*. It involves building coalitions among community members, grassroots movements, church organizations, and labor unions. Finally, critical pedagogy needs to be a *creative process* by integrating elements of popular culture (i.e., drama, music, oral history, narratives) as educational tools that can successfully raise the level of political consciousness of students and teachers. In our view, critical pedagogy must be animated by a passionate and critical-minded optimism. In the chapters that follow, we attempt to expand on this approach to pedagogy as a means of challenging current social relations of production and incarnations of imperialism worldwide.

When U.S. citizens look at the map of the world, many only see a surface of obviousness and miss the palimpsest known as history staring back at them. A critical education can help them look beneath the surface and notice the faint borders of nations at very different times, boundaries brought into existence by those who had the military power to redraw them. They would notice that the borders have been created by the victors. Here in the United States those borders were once those of the great Indian nations before they were mercilessly slaughtered by colonial armies. And while today many of the borders being rewritten are electronic ones that map the fault lines of stock and bond trading, and the trajectories of finance capital, futures, and derivatives, there are also borders still being redrawn by the scarcity of natural resources such as oil and natural gas. Both types of borders have very much to do with the new imperialism that we are facing today.

We write this introduction as the body of one of the world's most famous Cold War ideologues, Ronald Reagan, lies in state, with hundreds of thousands of mourners reverentially jostling to catch a glimpse of his coffin. As a response to the egregious and ongoing scandals of the George W. Bush administration, the country appears to be rallying around the historical charade of the Reagan legacy, finding succor in a shameful history of imperialism that rivals the George W. Bush presidency in its deception and loathsome disregard for human life. The corporate media are busily doing their assigned jobs: covering up the real history of the Reagan presidency and helping to circulate the myth of America as the land of freedom and democracy, which of course is the proper function of the corporate media in "democratic" nation states such as the United States. Curiously, many of our leftist colleagues have expressed surprise over the extent of the fanfare and media spectacles surrounding the Reagan legacy. But is it, we ask, really so surprising that a country would honor with such elegiac paeans of gratitude and feverish odes to the Gipper, a man in charge of a regime that during the 1980s sponsored and directed brutal military regimes in Guatemala, El Salvador, and Honduras that repressed, tortured, and murdered thousands of their own citizens using military weapons and training directly from the United States? Is it so surprising that a country would praise a leader whose administration operatives became notorious for channeling millions of dollars to the Contras in Nicaragua—whom Reagan referred to as "Freedom Fighters"—much of it illegally obtained by selling arms to Iran and crack cocaine to disaffected youth in poor urban communities? Is it so surprising that the panegyrical media spectacle featuring the encomiastical blubbering of newscasters paying final tribute to the Great Communicator made no mention of the Reagan administration's sale of chemical weapons of mass destruction to Saddam Hussein? The answer, of course, is "no" to anyone who thinks hard about the way imperialist states behave or who would consider the fact that U.S. citizens have never been able to face their country's own history of imperialism. They haven't been able to face it because they have never been taught it.

We hope that this book is one small contribution to this teaching, and to the cumulative process of trying to refashion a critical revolutionary pedagogy adequate to these precipitous times.

References

Abu-Manneh, B. 2004. The illusions of empire. *Monthly Review* 56(2). www.monthly review.org/0604abumanneh.htm (accessed June 1, 2004).

Blum, B. 2004. The myth of the Gipper: Reagan didn't end the Cold War. *Counterpunch.* www.counterpunch.org/blum06072004.html (accessed June 10, 2004).

Brandt, D. 1991. *To change this house: Popular education under Sandinistas.* Toronto: Between the Lines.

Fox, M. 2004. Mel Gibson's Passion and fascism's piety of pain. *Tikkun* 19(3): 41–43.

Hardt, M., and A. Negri. 2000. *Empire.* Cambridge, Mass.: Harvard University Press.

Hempel, J. 2004. College tuition? Gumption won't cover it. *BusinessWeek* May 31: 68.

hooks, b. 2004. *Teaching community: A pedagogy of hope.* New York and London: Routledge.

Lauter, P. 1998. Interview with Paul Lauter by Leo Parascondola. *Workplace: The Journal for Academic Labor* 1(2). www.workplace-gsc.com/workplace2/lauter.html (accessed June 2, 2004).

Lenin, V. 1977. *Imperialism: The highest stage of capitalism.* New York: International Publishers.

Santos, B. de Sousa. 2004. Governance: Between myth and reality. Unpublished paper.

Shivani, A. 2002. Is America becoming fascist? *Counterpunch.* www.counterpunch.org/cptxhd2.gif (accessed June 3, 2004).

Smith, C. 1996. *Marx at the millennium.* London and Chicago: Pluto Press.

1

Reconsidering Marx in Post-Marxist Times: A Requiem for Postmodernism?

Capital is dead labor which, vampire-like, lives only by sucking living labor, and lives the more, the more labor it sucks.

—Karl Marx

The Fin-de-Siècle Millennium and the Vertigo of Global Capitalism

AS WE CROSS THE MINE-SOWN THRESHOLD of a new era of capitalist globalization, we can hear the earth groaning behind us. The Greek gods are now sporting seersucker suits and outsourcing the industries of Mount Olympus. Maquiladores decorated with red, white, and blue party favors are sprouting up in the eternal summer lands of Elysium. The world of mortals has long been abandoned to its own devices and its own "miracles" of the market. The portal through which the human race has dragged itself over the past few centuries is ominously decorated with the blood-soaked trophies of capital: slavery, racism, sexism, homophobia, starvation, genocide, imperialist conquest, war, disease, unemployment, alienation, and despair. These historical reminders should reveal to current generations that the Lords of Commerce—the newly ordained saviors of civilization—are nothing more than paper saints, contemporary Lords of the Flies. We've seen their likes before. From the turbulent revelations in past decades of U.S. complicity in supporting death squad politics in Latin America, of the covert overthrow of democratically elected governments by the CIA, to the more recent gunboat democracy campaigns in Afghanistan and Iraq—all of which have been scalded into our historical subconscious like seared Arab flesh from a U.S. military bombing run—we are no longer strangers to the gifts bestowed on us by those who rule us by the "noble lie." We courier our wedding gifts of democracy to the rest of the world by F-16 fighter jets. Unfortunately, we still mistake the disease (free-market capitalism) for the cure (liberty and freedom). Such persistent misrecognition, mutatis mutandis, brings to the fore a world-historical dilemma: will we continue to interpret our defeats as victories, to reaffirm our hegemonically reproduced and ideologically conditioned reflexes, or will we finally see the writing on the wall?

President Bush has recently congratulated Secretary of Defense Donald Rumsfeld for the wonderful job he has been doing even as it becomes clear that Rumsfeld helped create the conditions that enabled the torturing of Iraqi prisoners at Abu Ghraib and elsewhere to take place. The media is facilitating an orgy of delirium for the legacy of Ronald Reagan, who, after his death, is being praised throughout the country as one of the world's great leaders. Not named is Reagan's legacy as a war criminal; his government-sponsored assassination manuals; his financial support to the Contra terrorists in Nicaragua who purposely slaughtered men, women, and children; his financial support to the Guatemalan military as it ruthlessly exterminated 200,000 Mayan peasants; and his million-dollar-a-day-in-aid gift to the Salvadoran government that ultimately assisted the death squads who murdered 70,000 citizens. Yet there is no mass public outcry because the history of U.S. war crimes has been hidden from the people and because the media render the U.S. public hypnagogic more often than critical when it comes to evaluating leaders who have achieved popular iconic status, even leaders like Reagan, who believed that nuclear missiles were recallable twenty minutes after launch and who considered tomato ketchup to be a vegetable. Even as we learn that the Pentagon wasted as much as $100 million on commercial airplane tickets that were never used between 1997 and 2003, nobody is talking about how this wasted money could have been used to fight disease, feed the hungry, and build infrastructure for social programs.

As social scientists argue over the vexing question of whether imperialism has all but disappeared, critical educators are engaged in the arduous task of reintroducing the term into the breezy lexicon of progressive education, where it has been languishing since the days of the Cold War. Especially after the recent invasion of Iraq, it has become clearer that U.S. imperialism is not a fractional blip on the progress reports of civilization but rather the very heartbeat of globalized capital.

Marx's description of capitalism as the sorcerer's dark power that has now become uncontrollable is even more apt today than it was in Marx's time despite the fact that Marxism has been relegated by the postmodernists to the Icarian status of failed aspirations. No other individual has been able to analyze the Frankensteinian dimensions of capital accumulation with the same intensity and foresight as Marx (1959), who wrote, "If money . . . 'comes into the world with a congenital blood-stain on one cheek,' capital comes dripping from head to foot, from every pore, with blood and dirt" (760). Never before has a Marxian analysis of capitalism been so desperately needed than at this particular juncture in history, especially since the global push toward finance and speculative capital. It is becoming increasingly clearer that the quality of life in capitalist nations such as the United States is implicated in the absence of freedom in less developed countries. Global carpetbaggers profiteering on human suffering and bargain-basement capitalists with a vision of transforming the environment into Planet Mall are bent on reaping short-term profits at the expense of ecological health and human dignity and drawing ever more of existence within their expanding domain, cannibalizing life as a whole.

Capitalism, according to Terry Eagleton (1999), has a "built-in dynamic to universalize itself" and "is bound to ensnare itself in its own strength, since the more it proliferates, the more fronts it breeds on which it can become vulnerable" (37). Marx's prophetic warning against capitalism is no less true for those of us who work in schools of education, where the logic of privatization abounds and where postmodernism has more than encroached on leftist educational discourse; it has taken up permanent residence.

The resignation produced by the seeming inevitability of capitalist society and its attendant relations of exploitation digs like a spur into the flesh of everyday consciousness, rendering us sick from exposure to too much reality. But, as Marx argues, capital is a historically produced social relation that can be challenged (most forcefully by those exploited by it). A renewed engagement with and challenge to capital by means of Marxist theory fibrillates our social imagination, which largely has been flatlined since the ascendancy of Ronald Reagan and Margaret Thatcher and their evisceration of Keynesian welfare state capitalism. The advance of contemporary Marxist scholarship (Cole 1998; Hill 2001; Hill and Cole 2001; Rikowski, 2001a 2001b), critical theory (Giroux 1981, 1983), and a rematerialized critical pedagogy (McLaren 2000) in the field of education—although still modest glimmerings—is, in our view, sufficient enough to pose a challenge not only to neoliberal free market imperatives but also to post-Marxist solutions that most often take the form of social movements grounded in identity politics.

The treacly term "neoliberalism" hides its more invidious characteristics. Neoliberalism ("capitalism with the gloves off" or "socialism for the rich") refers to a corporate domination of society that supports state enforcement of the unregulated market, engages in the oppression of nonmarket forces and antimarket policies, guts free public services, eliminates social subsidies, offers limitless concessions to transnational corporations, enthrones a neomercantilist public policy agenda, establishes the market as the patron of educational reform, and permits private interests to control most of social life in the pursuit of profits for the few (that is, through lowering taxes on the wealthy, scrapping environmental regulations, and dismantling public education and social welfare programs). It is undeniably one of the most dangerous politics that we face today. As described by Robert McChesney (1999), neoliberalism is "the immediate and foremost enemy of genuine participatory democracy, not just in the United States but across the planet, and will be for the foreseeable future" (11). So much has been made of the wonders of the U.S. economic model, yet its so-called success can be measured in its complete rejection of social and environmental capital for the short-term gains of investors and consumers. As McMurtry (2000) remarks,

> Cheaper goods and costs come by the loss of tens of millions of secure domestic jobs. Real lower taxes for upper income brackets are achieved by stripping social assistance programs for the poor and unemployed. Equity values are increased by non-productive mergers, laundered drug billions, Internet stocks with no earnings, and leveraged debt and asset-flip money. Low unemployment figures are achieved by massive increases in part-time and starvation-wage jobs and a staggering 2,000,000 citizens in prison off the employment rolls (over 12 times the number of US citizens caged as in 1968, and about six times the Western European rate). The new regime rules the globe behind bars of money and iron. (10)

That Marxism appears to have lost its epochal footing and does not yet enjoy a new refunctioned status as the official opponent of neoliberalism and the downsizing of democracy does not mean that educators should remain inactive until history is suddenly served by a wake-up call that will make Marxism relevant again. History has already been punched in the solar plexus by the current crisis of capitalism and educators are not taking this warning sitting down. It remains for them to decide how they are going to exercise their political agency. The globalization of capital has occasioned what Mészáros (2001) describes as the "downward equalization of the differential rate of exploitation" (109) where workers all over the world—including those in advanced capitalist countries such as the United States—are facing a steady deterioration of working conditions because of the structural crisis of the capitalist system, a crisis of fast-track, pushcart capitalism of the "grab-the-profits-and-run" variety.

Yet at the same time, capitalism has never been so blindly infatuated with its own myth of success. Corporate leaders in the United States and dominant media have inured us into accepting the capitalist marketplace as the only possible social reality. Walter Mosley (2000) puts it thus: "The juggernaut of capitalism, having broken the bonds of its imprisonment—national borders—exacts its toll in an equal opportunity manner. It is the nature of capitalism to apply its value system to everything" (11). David McNally (1999) writes, "Having vanquished all challengers, having apparently tamed labor, anti-imperialist, and radical social movements, [capitalism] can now calmly go about the business of making us all rich" (134). McNally traces the current capitalist triumphalism to the antihistorical character of bourgeois ideology. He also notes that contemporary procapitalist ideology "betrays a remarkable amnesia about capitalism itself: it forgets its bloody past, its recurrent crises; it denies everything that hints at the historically specific limits of the capitalist mode of production" (135). To wit, it naturalizes the exploitation of the world's poor and powerless, reducing workers to the market price of their sweat and blood.

The Charge of the Lite Brigade

Radical theorists such as Paulo Freire and Antonio Gramsci have been disinterred from Marxist soil, where they first drew breath, and their graves now sprout the saplings of postmodern theory. It is all part of the postmodernization of the Left and its accompanying retreat from class struggle and latent support of laissez-faire evangelism. This is not to say that postmodernism has been a complete disaster. Far from it. Even in its nascent state, postmodern theory has made a significant contribution in helping educators grasp the politics that underwrite popular cultural formations, mass-media apparatuses, the technological revolution's involvement in the global restructuring of capitalism, the ideological machinations of the new capitalism from Schumpeter to Keynes, and the reconceptualization of schooling practices in the interest of making them more related to (racial, gender, sexual, and national) identity formation within postcolonial geopolitical and cultural spaces. However, its ability to advance (let alone sustain) a critique of global capitalism, corporate anorexia (downsizing and outsourcing), and the contemporary reign of money has been severely compromised. Too eager to take a wide detour around political economy, postmodern educators have been hampered by a number of factors: (1) by their tacit—and often overt—acceptance of a market economy, (2) by their joining in the chorus of post-Marxists celebrating the death of universalism and grand narratives, (3) by their impatience to strike a novel posture in the theater of educational transgression, (4) by their predilection for allowing their politics to be distracted by their postcolonial cultural performances of dissent, and (5) by their failure to recognize that, in the words of Robin D. G. Kelley (1999), "We are hardly in a 'postcolonial' moment. The official apparatus might have been removed, but the political, economic, and cultural links established by colonial domination still remain with some alterations" (18). Teresa Ebert (1996) goes so far as to argue that within postmodern theory, the "assumption of the deimperialism of the center is an act of concealed imperialism" (285).

Although postmodern "masters of suspicion" have managed to deftly map the semiotic fault lines of the contemporary *fracture social,* have uncovered the necessity hidden under the appearance of contingency, have challenged stable genres of discourse, have ruptured the Eleatic cohesiveness of master narratives, have transgressed hidebound and sacred binarisms and rent them apart, and have brazenly and percipiently challenged the right-wing philippics of William Bennett–style cultural brokers, they have failed in the main to challenge in any deep or sustained way the engineered misery of neoliberal fiscal regimes and— more important—capitalist relations of exploitation. Consequently, the post- modern Left remains hostage to its own strategic ambivalence about capital. Not only have postmodern theorists been woefully remiss in explaining how cultural representations and formations are indentured to capitalism, they have often confused socialism with, at worst, the history of Stalinism and, at best, the welfare state reformism often associated with Scandinavian countries such as Denmark and Sweden. As James O'Connor (1998) notes,

> The theory of capital accumulation and crisis, pioneered by Marx and fine- tuned by three or four generations of Marxist economists, is the baby thrown out with the dirty bathwater of totalitarian socialism. Just at the moment that capi- tal triumphs globally, the greatest theorist of capital is relegated to the status of a wrongheaded 19th-century ideologue. . . . This irony, or anomaly, is so perva- sive today that we are forced to turn one of Hegel's most famous lines on its head. The great dialectician wrote that "the owl of Minerva spreads its wings only at dusk," meaning that only after a particular historical event or change is it possible for reason to apprehend what has happened and why. (281)

Mocked as a "modernist" form of outmoded phallomilitary and "totalizing" demagoguery, Marxism is now relegated to history's cabinet of lost revolu- tionary dreams, where it is abandoned to those romantic images of guerrillas of the Sierra Maestra. While elegiac hymns to Che Guevara still abound in the courtyards of the diminishing Left, this should not detract from the fact that, when read sharply against Guevarian challenges to imperialism and Marxist challenges to social relations of production and global regimes of capitalist ex- ploitation, postmodernist theory frequently collapses into a form of toothless liberalism and airbrushed insurgency.

While to its considerable credit, postmodern theory—especially through the insights of its pantheon of progenitors such as Nietzsche, Toynbee, Hei- degger, C. Wright Mills, Horkheimer, and Adorno—has troubled the primary status of the colonizer, peeled back the horizon of culture to reveal the trace marks of the antipodal, broken the semiotic gridlock of reigning binarisms, prevented the authoritative closure that serves to reenlist alterity into the ranks of Western imperialism, and revealed how temporal structures of dislocation constitute rather than describe our geographies of identity, it has often reconfirmed as much as contested capitalist relations of exploitation. Although it is important to follow postmodernists in introducing subaltern readers of texts, such texts need to be acknowledged as speaking through the ventriloquism of Western epistemologies linked to imperialist and capitalist social relations. Progressive educators need to ask, How does the semiotic warfare of the postmodern or postcolonial critic reinscribe, repropose, and recohere capitalist social relations of production through decentering and rerouting cultural representations? This is a central question that postmodernists routinely sidestep, and to do so at this current historical conjuncture of titanic capitalist forces is, to say the least, perilous. As the dust finally settles, we are troubled by the fact that much of what is called postmodern education is freighted with insoluble contradictions that unwittingly push radical critique toward the center.[1]

Capitalism and democracy share a forced intimacy; their marriage has been arranged so that the families of the global ruling class can consolidate their power and set limits on how and what questions concerning equality and emancipation can be raised and in what contexts. The preservation of capital remains entombed within postmodernism's own ineffable logic and "conceals the true contradictions of advanced capitalist societies" (Larrain 1995, 288). This remains the case even though some postmodernists like to imbibe the miasmically iconoclastic aura of Marx without, we might add, necessarily engaging in radical (let alone revolutionary) politics. As postmodernists look amusingly at what Charlie Bertsch and Joe Lockard (1999) call "the widely successful repackaging of *The Communist Manifesto* as a pricey fetish object for the upwardly mobile" (3), they can play out their cathartic fantasies of the *guerrillero/a* while continuing to trash the politics that underlies revolutionary praxis.

In many instances, postmodernists have dismissed Marxism as a form of ideological Neanderthalism or as a crusted-over antediluvian memory and have disabused educators of the notion that there are practical and workable alternatives to capitalism worth considering. In their less generous moments, they recycle Marxist theory as contemporary farce (see Lather 1998). We don't want to deny the crimes against humanity committed by regimes who claimed to be the heirs of Marx, to ignore the problems associated with Eastern and European Communist parties in their unregenerate Stalinist aspects, or to defend what in certain cases could be called Marxism's recidivistic retreat into bureaucratic authoritarianism, dogmatism, and economic determinism. Nor do we wish to defend what Eagleton (1999) calls "the long tragedy of class-society" (35), corporate governance, the ill-gotten gains of financial profiteers and speculators, and the history of imperialism and international terrorism committed by Western "democracies." On the other hand, we don't believe that Marxism should be dismissed because it appears to have reached its apex in the decades before the collapse of the Soviet Union and the appearance of Russia's new gangster capitalism, red bourgeoisie, and forms of primitive accumulation. We admit that Marxist theory may be out of fashion, but it has not run out of conceptual fuel for providing the kind of analysis urgently needed at this point in the history of capitalism. Although marked by a depleted vitality in educational research and criticism, Marxist theory is not yet sounding its death rattle. In fact, it appears to be making a comeback, as it is increasingly summoned to the service of the political present. We are confident that Marxist analysis will have a roborant effect on critical pedagogy.

The Postmodern Promise

Postmodernism has done more than ensorce the art students; it has made impressive advances in helping educators map the hidden trajectories of power within the processes of representation (especially the political optics of mass media), enabling teachers as cultural workers to strip back the epistemological scaffolding that props up essentialist claims to authenticity and to peel away layers of ideological mystification that shroud the assertion of truth and validity made by positivists within the empirical sciences. Postmodern theory's articulations of the epistemic subject have been, for the most part, invigorating and innovatory. In this regard, postmodernism has offered up a veritable cornucopia of research tools for the analysis of identity and has helped uncover ways in which universal narratives are based on masculinist and heteronormative practices of exclusion. Furthermore, postmodern educators have mediated successfully between the group identities of marginalized peoples and universal moral claims.

Despite its successes, postmodern dissent is symptomatic of the structural contradictions and problematic assumptions within postmodern theory itself. By too often displacing critique to a field of serial negation without fully grasping its prefigurative or emancipatory potential, postmodern criticism frequently traps intelligibility and meaning internally, that is, *inside* the texts of culture. In revealing the inconsistencies, aporias, and contradictions within the text of culture, postmodernism often fails to connect the significance of these contradictions, inconsistencies, and equivocations by comprehending their necessity. As a consequence, it often blunts an understanding of contemporary society and unwittingly agitates for a reenactment of the fate of society that constitutes the object of its critique. This line of fracture is emblematic of the problem that has plagued the postmodern Left over the past several decades. At this moment, we are compelled to ask, Is the practice of ignoring these contradictions and inconsistencies of culture structurally advantageous to capitalist relations of exploitation? Do such contradictions left conspicuously unaddressed merely—or mainly—provide ballast to reigning hegemons and the international division of labor? Postmodernists appear loathe to raise such questions yet continue unrepentantly to dismiss an analysis of the so-called economic "base" in favor of the cultural "superstructure." While postmodernists encourage an examination of the cultural discourses of capitalism as open-ended sites of desire, Marxists, by contrast, treat discourses not as sanctuaries of difference barricaded against the forces of history but as always an interpretation naturalized by the libidinal circuits of desire wired into the culture of commerce and historically and socially produced within the crucible of class antagonisms. Marxist criticism uncoils the political economy of texts by remapping and rethinking systems of signification in relation to the material and historical practices that produce them (McLaren 2000), thus valorizing the "structural endurance of histories" over the "contingent moment" (Ahmad 1995, 15). In doing so, it examines not the present's lack of coincidence with itself or its lack of self-identity but rather its ability to surpass its own limitations.

The shift toward a postmodernism[2] layered with a thin veneer of cultural Marxism, scaffolded by identity politics and postsocialist ideology, sprayed by aerosol terms such as "difference" and "indeterminancy," and dipped in the gurgling foam of Jacuzzi socialism and window-dressing democracy, has witnessed the categories of cultural domination and oppression replace those of class exploitation and imperialism as capitalism's reigning antagonisms. At the same time, a politics of representation has deftly outflanked the issue of socioeconomic redistribution (Fraser 1997). The postmodernist and postsocialist assumption that culture has suddenly found ways of winning independence from economic forces and that somehow the new globalized capitalism has decapitated culture from the body of class exploitation by constructing new desires and remaking old ones in ways that are currently unmappable and unfactorable within the theoretical optics of political economy has not only contributed to the crisis of Western Marxism but also effectively secured a long-term monopoly for capitalist market ideology. Gospelized and accorded a sacerdotal status in the temple of the new postsocialist Left, postmodern theory has failed to provide an effective counterstrategy to the spread of neoliberal ideology that currently holds educational policy and practice in its thrall. In fact, it has provided neoliberalism with the political stability it needs to reproduce its most troublesome determinations.

Our purpose here has not been to establish, evidentially, instance by instance, or in toto, the dilemmas, pitfalls, and shortcomings of postmodern theory but rather to sound a rather basic caution with respect to its potential for mounting an effective counterhegemonic project against global capitalism and its discontents. In doing so, we raise the following questions echoed by the epigones of the modernist project: Does returning to Marx reveal the ultimate sources of the patriarchal and colonizing venture of the West's master narratives? Will reembracing Marxism somehow summon a new coherent identity for the patriarchal West? Is Marxism a quixotically romantic quest for liberation that can serve only as a stimulant for the passion of the Western master narrative? Can Marxist writings today be anything more than a dirge on the death of the communist dream? Will engaging the writings of Marx only exacerbate the theoretical megrims already inflicting the anti-intellectual educational left?

The position we take on the issues raised by these questions is unambiguous. We believe that Marxist analysis should serve as an axiomatic tool for contesting current social relations linked to the globalization of capital and the neoliberal education policies that follow in its wake. Educational researchers ignore Marxist analyses of globalization and the quotidian poetics of the everyday at their peril. At the same time, we admit that Marxist theory constitutes a social system of analysis that inscribes subjects and is seeped in the dross of everyday life. As such, it must continually be examined for its underlying trajectories. We believe that a critical reflexive Marxist theory—undergirded by the categorical imperative of striving to overthrow all social conditions in which human beings are exploited and oppressed—can prove foundational in the development of current educational research traditions as well as pedagogies of liberation.

Postmodern Politics

Following tectonic shifts in the geopolitical landscapes of the 1980s and 1990s, postmodern social and political theory—with its preening emphasis on language, culture, and identity—has become the de rigueur conceptual attire among social scientists attempting to make sense of contemporary social life within late capitalism. Mining the terrain of identity politics, consumer fetishism, and privatopia has become a central academic activity and is now considered theoretical chic. In contrast, Marxism has been mummified along with Lenin's corpse, and its scholarly exercise has been likened to tampering with historical relics.

The joint ambition of uncovering the hidden ideologies secreted within Western representations of the "Other" and refashioning the antifoundational self has disposed postmodern theorists to dampen their euphoria surrounding social transformation at the level of relations of production and to heighten their regard for reforming and decentering dominant discourses and institutional practices at the level of cultural transactions. According to Sam J. Noumoff (1999), postmodern politics attempts (1) to separate culture from ideology, (2) to employ culture as a construct that diminishes the centrality of class, (3) to insert a neoliberal political system of intelligibility and policy agenda, (4) to perpetuate the belief in the ultimate futility of the socialist project, and (5) to promote an assortment of "post" concepts—such as poststructuralism, postmodernism, posthistory, and postideology—as a way of limiting the theoretical direction of inquiry and preempting socialist challenges to new objective realities brought about by the globalization of capital. Hilary Wainwright (1994) rightly asserts that much of what passes as postmodern politics not only lacks a coherent social and political vision with which to actively challenge the radical Right but also endorses a number of the Right's main tenets in progressive and radical discourses. She writes that postmodernism does not "provide adequate tools to answer the radical right . . . the tools of postmodernism produce only a more volatile version of the radical right. . . . Postmodernism cuts the connection between human intention and social outcome" (100).

Postmodern theory's stress on micropolitics transforms what are essentially social struggles into discursive struggles that overvalue economies of desire at the expense of political economy and a philosophy of praxis. Many postmodernists refute the idea that any particular social group or class is capable of transforming the existing social relations of production under capitalism. At the same time, however, they fail to lay the conceptual foundations for building necessary political alliances among oppressed and marginalized social groups. John Ehrenberg (1998) underscores this vividly:

> It will not do to claim that knowledge is local, "identity" and "difference" are the key categories in modern social life, human relations are constituted by language and "discourse," "culture" is the site of struggle, and no single agent of human liberation can even be theorized. The inexorable concentration and centralization of capital stand in eloquent opposition to the claim that fragmentation and discontinuity have eliminated all possibilities for collective action toward a common end which can cut across the multiple, shifting and self-defined "identities" that make up the social world. (43)

While postmodern politics tends to focus on particular forms of oppression, the irrefragable power of Marxist theory resides in its ability to reveal how all forms of social oppression under capitalism are mutually interconnected (Ebert 1996; Hennessey 1993; McLaren and Farahmandpur 1999; Wood 1996). While both Marxism and postmodernism address the "interlocking triumvirate" of race, class, and gender, Marxist theory attempts to reveal how all of these forms of oppression are linked to private ownership of the means of production and the extraction of surplus labor. In other words, they are not coprimary.

It is a cardinal position in postmodernism to place under suspicion master narratives, universalism, and objectivity on the grounds that they are particular epistemological and moral discourses camouflaged under the guise of universal discourses. Enlightenment ideals come under fire as well since they putatively aim at creating homogeneous discourses that are based on scientific progress associated with European economic, social, and political dominance (Thompson 1997). Postmodernists additionally dismiss the Enlightenment's claim and appeal to universalism by associating it with European imperialism and colonialism, which, in their view, aided the Spanish, Portuguese, and British conquest of the "New World." However, history demonstrates that prior empires did not rely on specific universal discourses similar to the Enlightenment ideas to justify their atrocities, genocide, and territorial conquest. On the contrary, Enlightenment thinkers frequently stressed the significance of other cultures' moral and ethical commitments by comparing and contrasting them to their own European origins. According to Willie Thompson (1997),

> The Spanish conquistadors did not require the Enlightenment to commit genocide upon the populations of the Caribbean, Mexico and Peru and subject the remnant to slavery, nor Genghis Khan to do similar things in Central Asia during the earlier period. These acts were committed by cultures with no pretensions to universalism (unless Christianity is to be regarded as such, in which case the root of all evil has to be sought a lot further back). (219)

The New Social Movements? A Hit-and-Miss Proposition

The new social movements in the 1980s and 1990s signaled the decline of class politics and the rise of social struggles existing outside the economic sphere and based on "extraeconomic identities" of individuals and groups (Laclau and Mouffe 1985). As a result, social struggles became diversified around the particular interests of social groups such as environmentalists, feminists, gays and lesbians, and peace activists. While there is much to praise in the work of these new social movements, our celebration of their practices is not unqualified or unreserved. Only a minority of these social movements have been class based. Many lack a common focus such as socialism and are organized primarily around the interests of the middle class (Croteau 1995; Wood 1996).

We would also like to point out that capitalism is not necessarily endangered by the ethnic, racial, gender, or sexual identities of the social groups that it seeks to exploit. Capitalism can survive antiracist and antisexist practices because it is a social system based on economic exploitation and the ownership of private property (Wood 1996).[3] Of course, antiracist and feminist struggles *can* help bring capitalism down, but they are necessary and not sufficient struggles. In order to lead the struggle against oppression, they need to situate racial and gender antagonisms within the larger capitalist totality. We believe that in its failure to recognize capitalism as a fundamental determinant of social oppression, and in its focus on racism, sexism, and homophobia delinked from their attachment to white patriarchal epistemologies, the law of value, and the international division of labor, identity politics falls prey to a facile form of culturalism.

In our opinion, certain contexts arise in which identity politics tends to hamper and weaken working-class struggles. In some instances, for example, by blaming only whites for the oppression of blacks, men for the oppression of women, and heterosexuality for the oppression of gays and lesbians, identity politics fails to situate white racializing and racist practices, as well as patriarchal and heteronormative practices, as *conjunctional practices* within the wider context of capitalist relations of exploitation.

The accusation of some postmodernists (such as Lather 1998) that classical Marxism leaves virtually untroubled the issue of gender ignores the contributions of Marxist feminists and multiculturalists, not to mention Marxist revolutionaries (Ebert 1996; Hennessey 1993). We refer to the programmatic documents on the oppression of women produced by the Fourth International. Trotsky, for example, argued for the liberation of women from unpaid domestic labor as part of the advance toward socialism. And in his criticism of the effects of the Stalinist counterrevolution on the family, he wrote,

> How man enslaved women, how the exploiter subjected them both, how the toilers have attempted at the price of blood to free themselves from slavery and have only exchanged one chain for another—history tells us much about this. In essence, it tells us nothing else. But how in reality to free the child, the woman, and the human being? For that we have as yet no reliable models. All past historical experience, wholly negative, demands of the toilers at least of all an implacable distrust of all privileged and uncontrollable guardians. (Cited in Kelly, Cole, and Hill 1999, 13)

Some postmodern feminists have argued that classical Marxism is shrouded in claims to universal truth and has overlooked the specificity of women's labor. They assert that historical materialism is reductive because it reduces all types of oppression into class exploitation, ignoring racism, sexism, and homophobia (Lather 1991, 1998). Carol Stabile (1994) responds by describing this attack on Marxism as underwritten by what she calls "theoretical essentialism." Stabile argues that the end to sexual domination does require ending class exploitation. She notes,

> Without considering class position and its centrality for capitalism, socialist-feminism ceases to exist. Only economic analyses can force academic and similarly privileged feminists to confront the unevenness of gender oppression and undermine its methodological centrality. Only along the frictionless plane—a location where social relations and class antagonisms hold little or no critical purchase—can the category of class be so easily dismissed. (157)

Jane Kenway (1997) astutely recognizes that in the work of negotiating among competing discourses in pedagogical processes and practices, materialist feminists are more attentive to extradiscursive (that is, economic) factors than are postmodern feminists. She writes,

> University and schools can be seen to consist of fragile settlements between and within discursive fields and such settlements can be recognized as always uncertain; always open to challenge and change through the struggle over meaning, or what is sometimes called the politics of discourse; that is, interdiscursive work directed towards the making and remaking of meaning. Materialist feminists participate in this struggle over meaning but recognize more fully than do postmodernist feminists that this struggle is overdetermined by the distribution of other resources. It is neither naïve nor voluntaristic. (141)

By focusing on identity politics, postmodernists tend to lose sight of the determinate character of global capitalist relations. The challenge posed by theorists like Judith Butler (1993, 1997)—to see identity as performance and as a corporeal exhortation to mobilize against oppression—is undeniably important but must be accompanied by a critique of the cultural formations in which performance as a material practice is produced within existing social relations of production. Otherwise, postmodern performance as a "practice of the self" always remains at the level of the cultural disruption of existing discourses instead of the transformation of relations of production—that is, the transformation of the exploited labor power of the proletariat and private ownership of the means of production.

Hybridity and Postmodern Multiculturalism

In their attempts to proclaim the hyphenated immanence of all identity, postmodern theorists in the metropolitan academy have too often self-styled hybridity as the prerogative of the Anglo border crosser, failing to answer why some immigrants end up heading multinational corporations and others end up in the sweatshops of East Los Angeles or living in cardboard condominiums not far from City Hall. According to Arif Dirlik (1999), "Globalism is uncompromising in its desire, and to answer such uncompromising desire with a negotiation of hybridity only nourishes its appetite for conquest" (184). In their articulations of identity politics, hyperindividualism is conjugated with consumerism and becomes a default politics. In contrast, Marxist theory calls for a collective politics of resistance against capitalist relations of exploitation.

The postmodern illusion that harmony is somehow achieved through hybridity and heterogeneity has deflected important attention away from the persistence of neocolonialist practices (Libretti 1999). This amounts to the Euro-American Great Delusion—the belief that racial oppression has been overthrown.

Despite the pronouncements of the postmodern Left that we are all "postethnic multiculturalists" or "hybrid subjects" living in a "postcolonial" society, it remains the case that official U.S. history suppresses the fact that racialized minorities still exist as internally colonized political subjects within the Anglosphere, contained by contemporary practices of institutionalized racism. One need only witness the recent efforts by the U.S. government to demonize and falsely imprison Puerto Rican activists (such as education professor Jose Solís Jordán) who seek independence for Puerto Rico from the jaws of U.S. imperialism (McLaren and Solís Jordán 1999).[4] While it is one thing (and a good thing at that) to advocate a politics of difference, it is another to forget that despite all our racialized and culturalized differences, we remain standardized by the logic of capital and the (white supremacist) values and ideals that shape U.S. culture, including those of economic and cultural imperialism.

Cultural imperialism provides access to a borderless world of capitalist markets where cultural practices are maddeningly commodified. As Giroux (1992) argues, the concept of critical pedagogy as a postmodern form of border crossing needs to be dramatically reconfigured by observing how cultural practices are produced and reproduced to serve the interests of capital. This means recognizing how border crossing constitutes an unequal and uneven exchange of both social labor and cultural practices of, for example, workers in the maquiladoras.[5] In this instance, the politics of border crossing utilizes commodity fetishism to transform Mexicano/a cultures into consumable tastes, images, clothing, and attitudes for middle-class Americans, while the working-class are locked inside the maquiladoras panoptimexes (after Foucault's use of "panopticon") near the U.S./Mexican border, unable to cross the social, political, and economic barriers that their "free trade" labor was designed to overcome (Alamada 1999). Thus, capital has the power to cross the same race, class, gender, and geopolitical barriers that keep the workers walled in (Kincheloe 1998).

American democracy, whose dramatic ideal and conceptual underpinnings accompanied the emergence of market exchange in the West, admits marginalized groups into the ranks of the enfranchised only when they are politically depotentiated, that is, when they are subdivided off or otherwise separated from other subaltern or oppressed groups or when "the rights, responsibilities and powers they were struggling for have become de-valued or in effect unimportant as tools for actually challenging the social structure and initiating social transformation" (Allman 1999, 128). The violent exporting of democracy to Iraq by means of "shock-and awe" bombing, the "lighting up" of innocent civilians at military checkpoints, and the widespread humiliation and torture of Muslim prisoners at detention centers in Iraq, Afghanistan, Guantanamo Bay, and elsewhere signal the hypocrisy of the "world's greatest democracy," which defines itself as being underwritten by the principles of freedom and self-determination. We all know that the Iraqi people will only be permitted by the United States to determine their future as long as it coincides with the corporate interests of the transnational ruling elite, an elite overpopulated by the intentions of the U.S. financial aristocracy. The coupling of markets and democracy will never bring about social justice because in order for real equality to occur, the market economy must be severely ruptured and eventually overturned in favor of a socialist alternative.

Marxist theory[6] does not retire the discourses of race, class, gender, and sexual orientation to the conceptual mausoleum but rather reanimates these categories by interrogating how they are refracted through material relations of power and privilege and linked to relations of production. Marxist theory can reveal how race, class, gender, and sexual orientation—as structural positions within the symbolic order that pre-date the existence of the subject—are implicated in the social division of labor and enmeshed in relations of production. We do not follow postmodernists in arguing that traditional Marxist theory be quarantined away until it is fully "cured" of its masculinist or economistic discourses or until it complicates its teleological trajectories. Nor do we argue that it be exempt from serious feminist and multiculturalist critique. We do maintain, however, that Marxism bears serious reexamination in an era where globalization appears depressingly resilient. It should not be placed on the lexical back burner or in history's bottomless dustbin but rather given center stage in an effort to challenge the current reign of globalized capital and the corporatization and privatization of education. The key here is for members of the working class to achieve a generalized consciousness of class, a recognition of their common condition or location within the totality of capitalist social relations (such as having to sell their labor power in order to survive), an understanding of their emplotment in the division of labor, and an awareness of the historical role of the working class.

It is urgently important that we remain attentive to the ways in which "difference"—racial, ethnic, and gender difference—is variously insinuated in the production/reproduction dialectic of capital that is mainly responsible for the gross inequalities and unjust distribution of resources (that disproportionately affect high percentages of people of color who become trapped in the lower rungs of domestic and global labor markets). Women of color especially provide capital with its superexploited labor pools. We disagree unequivocally with those who claim that the extraction of surplus value is merely one of many dominations and oppressions. Our position—simply stated—is that capitalism is a universal system of domination that integrates and coordinates and ultimately subsumes all other forms of oppression to its brutal commodity logic and privileging hierarchies of exploitation.

It is a disquieting truth that racism and sexism are necessary social relations for the organization of contemporary capitalism and forms of traditional and emergent imperialisms. We reject the lamentably misleading race/class/gender triptych—the holy trinity of post-Marxist progressives—that has served as a defining framework for postmodern educators. In our view, the social category of class is directed at highlighting the ways in which the social relations of production mediate relations of exploitation among individuals and groups within a global division of labor and polarization of wealth. The racialized and gendered modalities in which class relations are lived mandates the creation of a multiracial, multigendered, and international working-class struggle. What is of signal importance is that phenomena and their determinations are historicized contextually and relationally within any given social field. Our decidedly Marxist position differs from the dominant Weberian perspective on class. Unlike Weber, who argues that economic classes constitute only one way that power is distributed among groups, Marx stresses the economic conflict between the bourgeoisie and the proletariat.

In contrast to Weber, who views class action as contingent and circumstantial, Marx understands classes to display an objective existence and to possess their own objective existence (even if they don't understand what those interests are). How resources are deployed in the market is what, for Weber, distinguishes between economic classes. By contrast, Marx posits the point of production as the engine that produces value and where surplus value is produced (Hickey 2000).

It is worth remembering that, unlike Weber, Marx does not conceive of exploitation as an artifact of greed and an attempt to acquire and display power through the actions of a profit-thirsty employer. Rather, for Marx, all employers, including the most responsible and fair, are exploiters since all surplus value or profit, large or small, is achieved through the extraction of surplus value from the direct producer. Capitalists may be highly successful or grievously unsuccessful exploiters, but they are nonetheless all exploiters (Hickey 2000).

Postmodern Theory in Education

In response to postmodernism's triumphant announcement of the death of Marxism and its claims about the impoverishment of Marxist theory, there has been a measured resurgence of Marxist theory in education (McLaren and Farahmandpur 1999). To cite one example, Marxist educationalists in England

(Cole, Hill, and Rikowski 1997; Green 1994) have mustered a spirited response to the recent criticisms made by postmodern theorists against the call for a renewed consideration of Marxist theory in the terrain of critical pedagogy. Cole et al. (1997) reject many of the claims of postmodern social and political theory by identifying it as a "theoretical virus which paralyses progressive thought, politics, and practice" (187). They provide a powerful critique of "resistance postmodernism" by arguing convincingly that postmodern theory does not offer a radical break in educational practices since its origins can be traced to antifoundationalism. They go on to offer a more critical position that endorses a structuralist analysis of capital, the state, and educational institutions.

In addition, Cole et al. (1997) make a convincing case that, by prematurely celebrating the exhaustion of and the end to socialist discourses, postmodern politics assists the political agenda of the radical Right and is used (quite unwittingly but nevertheless frequently) as an ideological tool to paralyze the development of a viable coalitionary politics of radical social and economic transformation. Postmodernism's endorsement of antifoundationalism and its refutation of master narratives too often is accompanied by a less-than-coherent set of common social and political goals. The postmodern project frequently culminates in vague and self-negating narratives (Cole and Hill 1995). By this account, it seems highly unlikely that a "postmodernism of resistance"—that is, one that advocates multiple voices, agency, and personal autonomy—can develop into an effective political coalition against global capitalism and the New Right's pernicious neoliberal political agenda.

Andy Green (1994) criticizes those postmodern progressives who have abandoned Marxist social theory altogether and suggests that the dangers that lie within postmodern educational theory lurch it toward an "individualistic educational consumerism" that closely resembles the New Right's ideology of free market economics. In postmodernism's quest to liberate and empower marginalized social groups, there exists an overemphasis on pluralism and choice in education (McLaren 1997).

Consumption or Production?
Class Struggle and Postmillennial Consciousness

Postmodern theory's shift from production practices toward consumption practices removes labor and class as the central categories of social organization and instead replaces them with discourses stressing the politics of desire and consumption. Likewise, postmodern theory has replaced discourses on economic production and the objective interests of the working class with the subjective interests of the bourgeoisie. We follow Zavarzadeh

(1995) in claiming that "class is the repressed concept in all theories of post-ality" (42).

Like graffiti sprayed adventitiously across the tropes and conceits of bleached-out modernist narratives, postmodern theory remains a soft form of revolt. It constitutes a transgression of the "already said" in the name of the poetics of the "unsaid." Slouching under the Promethean hubris of the metropolitan cognoscenti, postmodern theorists privilege the poetics of the sublime over the drab flux of quotidian existence, evanescent immateriality over the raw materiality of lived experience, the imponderability of representations over the historically palpable concreteness of oppression, the autonomy of cultural and political practices over the political and economic determinations of capitalism, fashionable apostasy and academic outlawry over the collective ideals of revolutionary struggle from below (*bas materialisme*), the salubriousness of aesthetic subversion over the physical dangers of civil disobedience, the bewitchment and exorcism of signs over the class struggle that shapes their epistemological character, and transgressive pedagogy of reform over the pedagogy of social and economic revolution.

Homespun Domination and the Global Reach of Power

The presence of capitalism floats in the air like the avuncular aroma of pipe tobacco wafting through your bedroom window from a neighbor's veranda. It tickles the nostrils with a mixture of familiarity and security. It instills a capitalist nostalgia, a deep yearning for a time when success appeared inevitable, when progress was assured, when hunger and disease would be wiped out by the steady advance of industrial wealth and technological prowess. Mesmerized by the scent of money, we willfully ignore the ramifications of capitalism's current capital flight; its elimination of multiple layers of management, administration, and production; and processes such as deindustrialization, the ascendancy of financial and speculative capital, the expansion of transnational circuits of migrant workers, and the casualization of the labor force. We ignore the monopolies, the oligopolies, the cartels, the new corporate carpetbaggers, the prophets of privatization, the Wal-Martization of the global lifeworld, and the transfer of capital investments to cheaper markets offering higher rates of exploitation. We pretend we don't see the reduced social expenditures in health, education, and social services; the business counterattack against labor; the state's growing indebtedness to corporate bondholders; the privatization of municipal services; the assault on trade unionism; and the draconian attacks on the social safety net. We want to believe all of this will soon pass, leaving us once again curled up beside the glowing hearth of the American Dream.

Marx's utopian vision of a democratic society has much to offer today's educators as it does the world's exploited classes. Its task has been "less to imagine a new social order than to unlock the contradictions which forestall its historical emergence" (Eagleton 1999, 35). We would do well to consider Ian McKay's (1995/1996) reminder:

> Marx . . . presents us with a vista of human beings struggling toward an infinite horizon of freedom as a manifestation of their humanity: he affirms a deontological ethic of freedom, even a freedom which, although it cannot be realized on earth, is nonetheless held before us as a regulatory ideal. (43)

Though Marx admired capitalism for its creativity, global reach, and material benefits, he condemned it for its human costs and casualties and its reduction of human beings to their "exchange value." Capitalism was the debris from which socialism would be built (Berman 1999).

What is desperately needed today is a "basic armory of Marxian concepts" to make sense of both old and new types of instabilities in the capitalist marketplace. It is imperative, in our view, that critical pedagogy expand its lexicon of Marxian categories, deepen its Marxist analysis, and renew its commitment to class struggle. But a repudiation of capitalism does not constitute either its elimination or our escape from it. Consequently, critical educators would be wise to respond to the "explosions of popular militancy" that we have seen recently in India, Korea, Colombia, Venezuela, Puerto Rico, and Seattle, Washington. A revolutionary pedagogy must teach that private property, capitalist accumulation, the extraction of labor surplus, and the search for profits are not natural facts of life but socially conditioned practices that hinder the development of self-production as praxis and that block the free development of individuals. We don't know where praxis will take us once we have overcome the travails of capital since human nature is historically produced and never guaranteed in advance. The agent of revolutionary struggle works toward the abolition of capitalist exploitation as well as the abolition of whiteness, keeping in mind the realization that there can be no positive identity premised on the racialization of class hierarchy that grew out of the Virginia plantocracy (McLaren 1997).

The unforeseeable future of leftist educational practice is, in part, linked to the outcome of the following questions: Can a renewed, retooled, or conceptually redrawn Marxism—absent in its most vulgar and dogmatically rigid trappings—provide the epistemological machinery for explaining and transforming the complex determinations and indeterminacies of culture, as well as theorizing the gap between empirical contingencies and eternal structures, better than a depoliticized and depleted postmodernism can? Can educational theorists escape the vulgarities that compromise the emancipatory potential of Marxism? Can Marxists sufficiently salvage a form of "totalizing" thought within the Marxian optic in such a way that does not forfeit empirical complexity by means of a reductive synthesis? Can educators excise from the grid of casual determination a Marxism that escapes a generalized formalism and monolithic idealism? We believe that these questions can be answered resoundingly in the affirmative. We believe that critical educators can surmount the crisis of credibility of the socialist project. Establishing the conditions of possibility for the restoration of historical materialism will not be easy, but the hermeneutical expansion of Marxism that is already taking place in some precincts of the academy is promising (Cole et al. 1997; Ebert 1996; Hennessy 1993; Jameson 1991). We share a guarded optimism about the extent to which educators can become tactically prepared and ideologically predisposed to carry out a "war of position" on sequestered fronts, waged in the interest of building oppositional cultures of revolutionary workers.

The all-embracing social revolution of which Babeuf, Marx, Lenin, Luxemburg, Trotsky, and others so eloquently spoke is exceedingly relevant today despite the interminably changing social conditions facing us. History undoubtedly will point us further in the direction of a socialist future, but whether we will have the will and the courage to bring it about is quite another story. Capitalism doesn't come equipped with air bags. On its collision course with history, vast numbers of human fatalities are a certainty. No one escapes injury, especially the exploited classes. The answer is not to acquire customized protection for the masses against the ravages of capital but to create a different historical trajectory altogether by cutting capitalism off at the production line. The alternative is to wait for capitalism to drive the human race over the cliff.

Marx and Engels (1956) write that "history does nothing, 'it possesses no immense wealth,' it 'wages no battles'" (125); history is the concrete activity of men and women pursuing their various goals in the contextual specificity of their daily life. It all comes down to the question of how we choose to live our lives. All of our lives have meaning, but not all of us live meaningfully. For educators, this challenge should have a special urgency.

Notes

1. There are exceptions to this, most notably the work of Henry Giroux and Joe Kincheloe (see Giroux 1983; Kincheloe 1998).

2. We acknowledge that there are many "postmodernisms" just as there are many "Marxisms." Our criticism is directed against postmodern theories that do not sufficiently contest capitalist relations of production. Our approach to Marxism could be described as classical in that we argue that the root of exploitation is directly connected to private property and the extraction of surplus labor from workers by the capitalist class. Texts that address the topic of postmodern education include Stanley Aronowitz

and Henry Giroux (1991), *Postmodern Education*; Patti Lather (1991), *Getting Smart: Feminist Research and Pedagogy With/In the Postmodern*; William Doll Jr. (1993), *A Post-Modern Perspective on Curriculum*; Joe Kincheloe (1993), *Towards a Critical Politics of Teacher Thinking: Mapping the Postmodern*; Robin Parker Usher and Richard Edwards (1994), *Postmodernisms and Education*; Andy Hargreaves (1994), *Changing Teachers, Changing Times*; and Richard Smith and Philip Wexler (1995), *After Postmodernism*.

3. Our position as Marxist theorists is not to privilege class over race, gender, or sexual orientation but to see class relations as dealing with the process of producing, appropriating, and distributing surplus value. As such, it is the strongest totalizing force that lies at the very roots of racism and sexism.

4. The Federal Bureau of Investigation brought up Professor Jose Solís Jordán (formerly of DePaul University and now at the University of Puerto Rico) on trumped-up charges of planting two bombs in a military recruitment center, and he was sentenced to a lengthy prison term (see McLaren and Solís Jordán 1999).

5. Third World factories of the transnational corporations.

6. We adopt a classical Marxist position insofar as we recognize class and the forces of production as largely determinant of the social. Unlike postmodernism, which often conceptualizes the social as radical heterogeneity driven by desire and detached from labor and human need, classical Marxism understands difference as determined primarily in relation to private property and to the means of production.

References

Ahmad, A. 1995. The politics of literary postcoloniality. *Race & Class* 36(3): 1–19.

Alamada, F. 1999. Marxing across the border. *Bad Subjects*, no. 45. www.eserver.org/bs/45/alamada.html (accessed November 30, 1999).

Allman, P. 1999. *Revolutionary social transformation: Democratic hopes, political possibilities and critical education.* Westport, Conn.: Bergin and Garvey.

Aronowitz, S., and H. Giroux. 1991. *Postmodern education.* Minneapolis: University of Minnesota Press.

Berman, M. 1999. *Adventures in Marxism.* New York: Verso.

Bertsch, C., and J. Lockard. 1999. Marx without monsters. *Bad Subjects*, no. 45. http://english-www.hss.cmu.edu/bs/45/editors.html (accessed November 30, 1999).

Butler, J. 1993. *Bodies that matter: On the discursive limits of sex.* London: Routledge.

———. 1997. *Excitable speech: A politics of the performative.* London: Routledge.

Cole, M. 1998. Globalization, modernisation and competitiveness: A critique of the New Labour Project in Education. *International Studies in Sociology of Education* 8(3): 315–32.

Cole, M., and D. Hill. 1995. Games of despair and rhetorics of resistance: Postmodernism, education and reaction. *British Journal of Sociology of Education* 16(2): 165–82.

Cole, M., D. Hill, and G. Rikowski. 1997. Between postmodernism and nowhere: The predicament of the postmodernist. *British Journal of Educational Studies* 45(2): 187–200.

Croteau, D. 1995. *Politics and the class divide: Working people and the middle-class Left.* Philadelphia: Temple University Press.

Dirlik, A. 1999. Place-based imagination: Globalism and the politics of place. *Review* 22(2): 151–87.

Doll, W., Jr. 1993. *A post-modern perspective on curriculum.* New York: Teachers College Press.

Eagleton, T. 1999. Utopia and its oppositions. In *Socialist register 2000,* ed. L. Panitch and C. Leys, 31–40. Suffolk, U.K.: The Merlin Press.

Ebert, T. 1996. *Ludic feminism and after: Postmodernism, desire, and labor in late capitalism.* Ann Arbor: University of Michigan Press.

Ehrenberg, J. 1998. Civil society and Marxist politics. *Socialism and Democracy* 12(1–2): 15–46.

Fraser, N. 1997. *Justice interruptus: Critical reflections on the "postsocialist" condition.* New York: Routledge.

Giroux, H. 1981. *Ideology, culture and the process of schooling.* Philadelphia: Temple University Press.

———. 1983. *Theory and resistance in education: A pedagogy for the opposition.* South Hadley, Mass: Bergin and Garvey.

———. 1992. *Border crossings.* New York: Routledge.

Green, A. 1994. Postmodernism and state education. *Journal of Education Policy* 9(1): 67–83.

Hargreaves, A. 1994. *Changing teachers, changing times.* New York: Teachers College Press.

Hennessy, R. 1993. *Materialist feminism and the politics of discourse.* New York: Routledge.

Hickey, T. 2000. Class and class analysis for the twenty-first century. In *Education, equality and human rights,* ed. M. Cole, 162–81. London: Routledge/Falmer.

Hill, D. 2001. State theory and the neo-liberal reconstruction of schooling and teacher education: A structuralist neo-Marxist critique of postmodernist, quasi-postmodernist, and culturalist neo-Marxist theory. *British Journal of Sociology of Education* 22(1): 137–57.

Hill, D., and M. Cole. 2001. Social class. In *Schooling and equality: Fact, concept and policy,* ed. D. Hill and M. Cole, 137–59. London: Kogan Page.

Jameson, F. 1991. *Postmodernism or the cultural logic of late capitalism.* Durham, N.C.: Duke University Press.

Kelley, R. D. G. 1999. A poetics of anticolonialism. *Monthly Review* 51(6): 1–21.

Kelly, J., M. Cole, and D. Hill. 1999. Resistance postmodernism and the ordeal of the undecidable. Unpublished paper presented at the meeting of the British Educational Research Association, September 2–5, 1–23.

Kenway, J. 1997. Having a postmodern turn or postmodernist angst: A disorder experienced by an author who is not yet dead or even close to it. In *Education: Culture, economy, society,* ed. A. H. Halsey, H. Lauder, P. Brown, and A. S. Wells, 131–43. Oxford, U.K.: Oxford University Press.

Kincheloe, J. 1993. *Towards a critical politics of teacher thinking: Mapping the postmodern.* Westport, Conn.: Bergin and Garvey.

———. 1998. *How do we tell the workers? The socioeconomic foundations of work and vocational education.* Boulder, Colo.: Westview Press.

Laclau, E., and C. Mouffe. 1985. *Hegemony and socialist strategy: Towards a radical democratic politics.* London: Verso.

Larrain, J. 1995. Identity, the other, and postmodernism. In *Post-ality: Marxism and postmodernism*, ed. M. Zavarzadeh, T. Ebert, and D. Morton, 271–89. Washington, D.C.: Maisonneuve.

Lather, P. 1991. *Getting smart: Feminist research and pedagogy with/in the postmodern.* New York: Routledge.

———. 1998. Critical pedagogy and its complicities: A praxis of stuck places. *Educational Theory* 48(4): 487–98.

Libretti, T. 1999. Leaping over the color line: Postethnic ideology and the evasion of racial oppression (Paper no. 5). *Working papers series in cultural studies, ethnicity, and race relations*, 1–20. Pullman: Department of Comparative American Cultures, Washington State University.

Marx, K. 1959. *Capital* (vol. 1). Moscow: Foreign Languages Publishing House.

Marx, K., and F. Engels. 1956. *The holy family: Or critique of critical critique.* Moscow: Foreign Languages Publishing House.

McChesney, R. W. 1999. Introduction. In *Profit over people: Neoliberalism and global order*, ed. N. Chomsky, 7–16. New York: Seven Stories Press.

McKay, I. 1995/1996. The many deaths of Mr. Marx: Or, what Left historians might contribute to debates about the "crises of Marxism." *Left History* 3(2)/4(1): 9–84.

McLaren, P. 1997. *Revolutionary multiculturalism: Pedagogies of dissent for the new millennium.* Boulder, Colo.: Westview Press.

———. 2000. *Che Guevara, Paulo Freire, and the pedagogy of revolution.* Boulder, Colo.: Rowman & Littlefield.

McLaren, P., and R. Farahmandpur. 1999. Critical pedagogy, postmodernism, and the retreat from class: Towards a contraband pedagogy. *Theoria*, no. 93, 83–115.

McLaren, P., and J. Solís Jordán. 1999. The struggle for liberation! La lucha continua! Jose Solís Jordán's fight for justice. *International Journal of Educational Reform* 8(2): 168–74.

McMurtry, J. 2000. A failed global experiment: The truth about the US economic model. *Comer* 12(7): 10–11.

McNally, D. 1999. The present as history: Thoughts on capitalism at the millennium. *Monthly Review* 51(3): 134–45.

Mészáros, I. 1999. Marxism, the capital system, and social revolution: An interview with István Mészáros. *Science and Society* 63(3): 338–61.

———. 2001. *Socialism or barbarism: From the "American Century" to the crossroads.* New York: Monthly Review Press.

Mosley, W. 2000. *Workin' on the chain gang: Shaking off the dead hand of history.* New York: Ballantine.

Noumoff, S. J. 1999. *Globalization and culture.* Pullman: Washington State University Press.

O'Connor, J. 1998. *Natural causes: Essays in ecological Marxism.* New York: Guilford Press.

Rikowski, G. 2001a. After the manuscript broke off: Thoughts on Marx, social class and education. Paper prepared for the British Sociological Association, Education Study Group Meeting, King's College London, June 23.

———. 2001b. *The battle in Seattle: Its significance for education.* London: Tufnell Press.

Smith, R., and P. Wexler, eds. 1995. *After postmodernism.* London: Falmer Press.

Stabile, C. A. 1994. *Feminism and the technological fix.* Manchester, U.K.: Manchester University Press.

Thompson. W. 1997. *The Left in history: Revolution and reform in twentieth-century politics.* London: Pluto Press.

Usher, R. P., and R. Edwards. 1994. *Postmodernisms and education.* London: Routledge.

Wainwright, H. 1994. *Arguments for a new Left: Answering the free market Right.* London: Blackwell Publishers.

Wood, E. M. 1996. *Democracy against capitalism: Renewing historical materialism.* Cambridge, U.K.: Cambridge University Press.

Zavarzadeh, M. 1995. Post-ality: The (dis)simulations of cybercapitalism. In *Post-ality: Marxism and postmodernism,* ed. M. Zavarzadeh, 1–75. Syracuse, N.Y.: Maisonneuve Press.

2

Freire, Marx, and the New Imperialism: Toward a Revolutionary Praxis

The Triumph of Capitalism

THE DEFEAT OF SOCIALIST REGIMES in Eastern Europe and the former Soviet Union, followed by the blue wave of pinstriped warriors from Wall Street, armed with translucent laptops, and taking up positions in Red Square where steely-eyed statues of Lenin once stood, leaves little doubt as to who won the major ideological battle of the twentieth century.

The capitalist world is gloating, and free marketeers and global carpetbaggers from the advanced capitalist nations are vastly expanding its role, disrupting—but not eliminating—the capacity of nation-states to manage the interface between transnational corporatism and the politics of everyday life. Neoliberal reformers and regional integrationists have launched a frontal, no-holds-barred attack on social justice, accelerating the incapacity of individuals to recognize capital's internal logic of accumulation and diminishing the power of individuals to counter the pressure of vested corporate interests and the politics of the capitalist class while at the same time mystifying the entire process by linking democracy to the so-called natural pulsations of the market. What is deliberately occluded in this process are the market's internal relations of production, exploitation, alienation, and feral politics of surplus value extraction from the direct producers (Ollman 1998a).

The methods used by corporations have, to a large extent, devolved beyond legal boundaries and government control. Corporate power and state repression have become an intertwined dynamic as corporations and governments collude in ways that overwhelmingly serve the interests of the ruling class. The outcome is a community of mutual interests—a countervailing and mutually reinforcing coalition that legitimizes itself through an appeal to geopolitical correctness. As we have defined it, geopolitical correctness is a process of paying lip service to the internationalization of profit making in the interest of stabilizing national and domestic markets while willfully overlooking the benefits of uneven resources that favor the global ruling class.

Global Capitalism as the New Imperialism

Sociologists and political scientists have studied the phenomenon of globalization extensively and have pronounced it a discomfiting inevitability for some but a powerful, life-enhancing economic tonic for many. In our opinion, globalization represents an ideological facade that camouflages the manifold operations of imperialism. In fact, the concept of globalization has effectively replaced the term "imperialism" in the lexicon of the privileged class for the purpose of exaggerating the global character of capitalism—as an all-encompassing and indefatigable power that apparently no nation-state has the means to resist or oppose. Furthermore, it deceitfully suggests that capitalism no longer needs the protection of the nation-state. This position hides the fact that a large portion of production in western European countries takes place within national boundaries. Moreover, the globalization thesis maintains that whereas state power can be used in the interests of the large multinational corporations, it cannot be employed in the interest of the working class.[1]

"Globalization" is a term that we unconditionally reject. We do so because it skillfully avoids dealing with social relations of production within the larger totality of global capitalism. Hence, we use terms such as the "globalization of capital" or "capitalist globalization" in order to stress what the term "globalization," left on its own, fails to do. According to Martha E. Gimenez (2002), "'globalization' is simply the reified, fetishized way of talking about the effects of capitalist development without having to talk about capitalism itself and without having to acknowledge, therefore, the capitalist material basis of the phenomena lumped under the label" (85–86). Globalized capitalism is, of course, a particular unfolding of capitalism's potentials, but its particularity is an effect and a precondition of its universality (Gimenez 2002). As such, we urge readers to heed the warning set forth by Gimenez (2002):

> To take globalization as the starting point of the analysis, to attribute to globalization all the problems that currently afflict direct producers all over the world, or to marvel at its accomplishments and qualified transformations in consciousness, communications, and scientific and technological achievements is simply to

worship a fetish, unless its historically specific roots in the capitalist mode of production are elucidated. Once it is acknowledged that the so-called new era of globalization is simply the unfolding of capitalism's potentials, it becomes possible to develop a more sober assessment of its nature, its positive and negative aspects, and the conditions for effective political resistance to its social, economic, cultural, political, and environmental effects. (85–86)

We are tracing the term "imperialism" here to Lenin (1951), who refers to the merging of industrial capital via cartels, syndicates, and trusts with banking capital, the result of which is *finance capital.* To call globalization a form of imperialism might seem a rhetorical exaggeration. But as rebarbarative as it might seem, we believe that this identification is axiomatic because the term "globalization" is calculated by bourgeois critics to render any radical politicization of it extreme. The ideology of this move is invisibly to enframe the concept of globalization within a culturalist logic that reduces it to mean a standardization of commodities (that is, the same designer clothes appearing in shopping plazas throughout the world). By contrast, we see the process as inextricably tied to the politics of neoliberalism, in which violence asserts itself as stability through a recomposition of the capital–labor relationship. Such a recomposition entails the subordination of social reproduction to the reproduction of capital (Dinerstein 1999), the deregulation of the labor market, the globalization of liquid capital, the outsourcing of production to cheap labor markets, and the transfer of local capital intended for social services into finance capital for global investment.

The "new" imperialism to which we refer is a combination of old-style military and financial practices as well as recent attempts by developed nations to impose the law of the market on the whole of humanity itself, not to mention their reluctant subjugation to the will of the United States in its quest for world domination. Having obscured the distinction between the sacred and the profane, the global aristocracy's new world order has set out to expand the free market in the interest of quick profits, to increase global production, to raise the level of exports in the manufacturing sector, and to intensify competition among transnational corporations. It has also benefited from part-time and contingent work, reduced the pool of full-time employment, and accelerated immigration from Third World and developing countries to industrial nations (Bonacich and Appelbaum 2000). In addition to our description of globalization as imperialism, we might add the following: imperialist military intervention primarily disguised as humanitarian aid or the overthrow of "evil" rogue states that have become enemies of freedom and democracy, the submission of international institutions such as the United Nations to the social and economic demands of imperialist conquest (witness the recent subservience of the United Nations to the demands of the United States, first in the context of weapons inspections in Iraq and second in the context of helping to choose Iraq's interim government), and the instigation of ethnic and nationalistic conflicts to weaken nations refusing to submit to the rule of the market (Azad 2000).

While we agree that capitalism has, since its inception, always functioned as a world economy, we also want to stress what we see as a powerful new movement in contemporary capitalist production and global relations of power. This movement provides the groundwork for a more centralized and unitary regulation of both the world market and global power relations that tend toward "a single supranational figure of political power" and that introduce "a new inscription of authority and a new design of the production of norms and legal instruments of coercion that guarantee contracts and resolve conflicts" (Hardt and Negri 2000, 9). But we stress here, in contrast to Hardt and Negri, that these movements are today only tendencies—not a paradigm shift.

In fact, in contrast to Hardt and Negri, we believe that concepts such as "center" and "periphery" are not outdated. Not only are these terms serviceable, but they are essential concepts with which to frame the current global map of power. We reject the notion that the world market has made imperialism obsolete through its deterritorialized and uncoded homogeneous flows and the global expansion of the internal constitutional project. Clearly, in our view, the recent occupation of Afghanistan and Iraq have demonstrated that U.S. global hegemonic imperialism as part of a larger project of unilateralist world domination continues to employ its standard fare of deceit, deception, and military muscle in order to achieve its objectives, even if its overall goal is world rule through the use of client states and proxy governments rather than permanent occupation.

According to Samir Amin (2001), historically there have been three stages of imperialism: the European conquest of the Americas, the colonial subjection of Asia and Africa during the industrial revolution, and the intervention of the Triad (the United States, western Europe, and Japan) in situations where "rogue nations" interfere with democracy and the free market. The first stage of imperialism saw the rise of the mercantilist system of Atlantic Europe coincide with the genocidal destruction of native American civilization as well as its Hispanicization/Christianization. The second stage resulted from what could be described as the creation of a "second Europe" by the United States by means of the advances brought about by the industrial revolution. It marked the opening up of global capitalist markets and a seizure of the world's natural resources. In this stage, inequality grew from a maximum ratio of 2:1 (around 1800) to around 60:1 today. The third stage in Amin's model is underwritten by a justification of any military aggression useful to the United

States and the quest for international markets and the unimpeded opportunity to loot the earth's natural resources. It also involves the superexploitation of the labor reserves of the peripheral nations. The third stage of imperialism is also marked by the perceived "convergence" of democracy (modern management of political life) and the market (capitalist management of economic activity). Amin argues that, in reality, democracy and the market are divergent but that this divergence is progressively concealed as democracy continues to be emptied of all its content that is dangerous for the smooth functioning of the market.

A symptom of a new stage of imperialism can be seen in the arena of recent international military conflicts involving the North Atlantic Treaty Organization (NATO) and its allies. For instance, Hardt and Negri (2000) trace the Gulf War (and we would also include the bombing of Kosovo in this category) to the concept of *bellum justum,* or "just war," whose genealogy can be traced all the way back to the biblical tradition. Today the concept of *jus ad bellum* (the right to make war) has been both reduced and banalized to the status of police action or routine police repression and sacralized as an ethical instrument used against an "absolute" enemy. And though the concept repeats ancient or medieval notions, it also represents a shift in practice: since it is no longer an activity of defense or resistance but an activity *that is justified in itself* (Hardt and Negri 2000).

Contrary to popular opinion, wealth depletion among developing nations is not rescued by capital from the imperialist activities of advanced capitalist countries. This is because transnational corporations drain the local capital from the open economic veins of poor countries rather than bring in new transfusions of capital. Because their savings are often low, banks in developing countries would rather lend to their own subsidiary corporations (who send their profits back to advanced nations) than to struggling local businesses in developing nations. Faced with low prices for exports, high tariffs on processed goods, and a lack of capital and rising prices, local businesses are locked into entrenched impoverishment because of structural adjustment measures to balance the budget. Such measures are financed through drastic cuts in spending for human development (Imam 1997). The World Trade Organization does not permit poor countries to prioritize fighting poverty over increasing exports or to choose a development path that will advance the basic interests of the countries' own populations. By 1996, the resulting concentration of wealth had "the income of the world's richest individuals . . . equal to the income of 52 percent of humanity" (Imam 1997, 13). Big business moved swiftly to secure control of the government and to cash in on the theft of the White House by George Bush *hijo.*

Bush's "appointment" as president of the United States (this chapter is being written before the 2004 presidential elections) has made a mockery of the idea that you can reform capitalism through the existing electoral process. And this White House *caudillismo* has made it clear that helping the poor and powerless is not on the agenda at all. Why should the Bush White House have anything but disdain for the poor and the powerless when we have arrived at a juncture in our political history where General Motors is bigger than Denmark in wealth, Daimler Chrysler is bigger than Poland, Royal Dutch/Shell is bigger than Venezuela, and the United States basically is dedicated to serve profits rather than its citizens. We need to stand back and take a deep breath, asking ourselves who, as citizens of the world's poster-child democracy, we really serve and for whose benefit. In 1990, the sales of each of the top five corporations (General Motors, Wal-Mart, Exxon, Mobil, and Daimler Chrysler) were bigger than the gross domestic products of 182 countries.

John McMurtry notes that on December 12, 1991, the chief economist of the World Bank wrote in a leaked memorandum that his colleagues in the least developed countries should strive to achieve a "welfare environment" by increasing the migration of "dirty industries" and "toxic waste" to their societies. McMurtry is devastatingly accurate in summarizing the baneful logic of the World Bank's top ideological warlord. According to the logic of the World Bank, it posed a comparative advantage to Third World countries for them to pollute their environment by storing toxic wastes. Because the "demand for a clean environment" has "very high income elasticity"—meaning that money demand for clean air varies with people's income—the rational thing to do where the consumption of clean air is nontradable is to import polluted air by means of dirty industries and wastes. Such a move would vastly increase their financial revenues on their "welfare environment." The chief economist's conclusion that the "economic logic" of dumping toxic wastes into the developing countries was "impeccable " is, McMurtry notes, exactly in accordance with the money-sequence chain of life-destructive, annihilative, and morally grotesque rationality. And, of course, McMurtry is absolutely correct. He writes,

> Life itself in this calculus is conceived as being of worth only to the extent of its price, and with no price received it is counted as being worthless. Disease and death are of no concern except as they cost money. Pollution and toxic wastes are not to be prevented, but assigned a money value to increase the output of the money-sequence. The poor are to be poisoned by the richer for their own welfare of more revenue, which they now lack. Health and life themselves are to be sacrificed to a higher good, an advanced place in the money order of worth. (323)

However, even with the retreat of socialism, capitalism's post–Cold War II victory has created a number of fundamental structural challenges to its global domination. For example, it has caused new interimperialist competition among various capitalist camps (the United States, Germany, and Japan), in addition to growing social and economic disparities between the rich and the poor in Western industrial countries, in particular the United States. As an article in *The Economist* (2000) reports,

> Never in the history of human wealth-creation has so much been pocketed so quickly by so many. The United States now boasts 300 billionaires and 5m millionaires, with Silicon Valley adding 64 new millionaires every day. Nine million Americans have household incomes above $100,000 a year, up from just 2m in 1982. If Great Britain was the first country to produce a mass middle class, the United States is the first country to produce a mass of upper class. (42)

During the 1970s, capitalism successfully averted a deepening economic crisis primarily caused by the falling rate of profit. It achieved this feat because profiteers were able to take advantage of the technological revolution (that is, computer technology and automation) to cheapen labor. Marx (1977) recognized that technology in the service of capital has a disposition toward both "cheapening" commodities and labor while simultaneously raising productivity and profitability. Similarly, current employment patterns in the United States have shifted toward a service-based economy caused, in part, by the transferring of the skills and knowledge of workers to computerized and automated machinery (Bello 1999). Thus, an army of low-skill, low-wage, "keypunch" laborers has emerged.

Western industrial countries have also benefited from economic structural adjustments, including the exporting of manufacturing jobs to developing countries and expanding the service and retail sector of the economy. Since the late 1960s, part-time employment in the United States has increased threefold. Declining full-time employment has followed in the wake of a widespread corporate trend of reducing wages and benefits and abolishing overtime pay. In the service-related industries of the "new economy," full-time employment is no longer acknowledged as forty hours per week. In Wal-Mart, for instance, full-time employment is twenty-eight hours per week, while at the GAP clothing company, full-time employment is limited to thirty hours per week (Klein 1999).

The global economy is increasingly relying on low-wage, part-time jobs comprised of an army of "contingent," "disposable," "temporary," and "footloose" laborers. The current expansion of the service and retail sector represents 75 percent of the overall workforce in the United States (Klein 1999). More important, education in the new economy is no longer heeded as a significant factor in securing higher wages for high school and college graduates. For instance, the average real wages for men declined from $14.60 in 1989 to $13.65 in 1996, while for women it decreased from $13.17 to $12.20.

According to Persuad and Lusane (2000), the new methods employed in capital accumulation are part of the "dual regime of accumulation." On the one hand, capital greatly depends upon the "absolute surplus value exploitation" of a growing class of unskilled and semiskilled laborers in the service sector of the economy. On the other hand, capital relies on the "relative surplus value extraction" of a new class of educated professionals in the knowledge industry. Persuad and Lusane (2000) also suggest that the two regimes of accumulation enjoy a symbiotic relationship. While relative surplus value depends on the intensification of the rate of exploitation, absolute surplus value rests on the breadth of the rate of exploitation.

These social and economic readjustments have been followed by persistent attacks on labor unions and a reduction of workers' wages and benefits mainly by employing flexible and informal methods of production. On the one hand, flexible methods of production permit corporations to tap into to cheap, contingent, and temporary labor markets. In addition, they allow transnational corporations to move to cheaper labor markets. On the other hand, informal methods of production allow for the expansion of sweatshops in garages where workers are paid by piece rates in slavelike conditions (Wichterich 2000). Although these structural changes have temporarily suspended the arrival of an economic crisis, they have nevertheless failed to offer long-term solutions to capitalism's structural contradictions. In fact, capitalism relies on the exploitation of labor more than ever.

We follow Marx (especially his value theory of labor) in asserting that the primary antagonism in capitalist economies exists between labor and capital, between the owners of the means of production and workers who are forced to sell their labor in exchange for wages. These contradictions are further visible in the yawning disparities between the wealthy and the poor. Consequently, the failure to find long-term solutions to the existing contradictions within the capitalist mode of production has shifted the political terrain to the Right. Bahman Azad (2000) summarizes this shift as follows:

> The global contradiction between labor and capital; the contradiction between a handful of imperialist states and the rest of humanity; the ever-widening gap between wealth and poverty in the world, which increasingly manifests itself in the gap between over-production by transnational monopolies, on one hand, and lack of purchasing power for these same products among the great majority of the world population, on the other; the economic bankruptcy of a great majority of the "third world" countries and their inability to repay their heavy international debts—all these are increasingly causing great problems for the

financial and banking systems of the imperialist countries. The loss of credibility and the ever-increasing economic and political bankruptcy of "social democratic" policies aimed at "resolving" the problems and contradictions of the capitalist system from within the system itself has led to a continuous shift of the social democracies to the right, the ascendancy of various right-wing bourgeois parties to power, revocation of most social protection plans, and the widening gap between the rich and the poor in all of the advanced capitalist countries. (27–28)

What distinguishes this new phase of imperialism from the old imperialism of the earlier part of the twentieth century? Ellen Meiksins Wood (2003) suggests that under the present stage of imperialism, there is an absence of any direct transfer of surplus labor from labor to capital. In other words, the extraction of surplus value is invisible and goes largely undetected. This is because the relationship between workers and capitalists today is "mediated" through market forces. What makes capitalism stand out from previous modes of production is that in the current incarnations of imperialism, capitalists need not rely on coercive measures to extract surplus value from workers. The simple and overwhelming reason is that capitalism is based on property relations, and unlike peasants in the feudal model of production, workers neither have control over the means of production nor possess property. Hence, they are compelled to sell their labor power in exchange for wages.

Understanding the "new imperialism" requires grasping the oftentimes contradictory and intricate relationship between economic forces and extraeconomic forces, or what has been referred to by traditional Marxists as the relationship between the base (economic foundations of society) and the superstructure (judiciary, political, and military institutions of a society). Unlike the feudal mode of production where landlords and the feudal nobility depended largely on extraeconomic forces (military, church, and political institutions) to exploit peasants and maintain and reproduce property relations, capitalism relies on economic forces—that is, market mechanisms—to extract surplus value from workers. The market allows capital to separate economic power from extraeconomic power, making it feasible for capitalism to rely less on extraeconomic forces and more on market forces to maintain and reproduce class relations between workers and capitalists.

As Wood (2003) correctly points out, there exists a contradictory but also complementary relationship between economic and extraeconomic forces. Extraeconomic forces such as the state continue to play an important role in securing and reproducing capitalist hegemony. Hence, we agree with Wood's (2003) critique of globalization theorists who have argued that the state has been weakened as a result of capital moving beyond the boundaries of the nation-state and thus no longer plays a vital role in capitalist economies. In contrast to globalization theorists who celebrate the demise of the state, Wood (2003) maintains that the current stage of globalization is governed by a "global system of multiple states," under which nation-states cooperate with one another to maintain and secure control over the local markets. Of course, this collaboration does not always serve the political and economic interests of all major capitalist nations.

Finally, Wood (2003) reminds us that the major contradictions under capitalist nations resides in the relationship between economic and extraeconomic forces. While capitalism relies less on extraeconomic forces and more on market force to exploit workers, it continues to depend on the state to secure its economic interests and its need to expand and penetrate other markets outside its sphere of influence. This is because capitalism is a social system that relies on the overaccumulation of capital and thus is increasingly territorial. The current historical bloc led by the United States maintains a widely shared worldview and imposes corresponding global practices and forms of state control and domination through the World Bank, the International Monetary Fund, neoliberal politics, and military superiority (NATO or unilateral strikes or wars by the United States). The transnational capitalist class in each state helps secure general acceptance of this situation that favors disproportionately the interests of leading capitalist countries, such as the United States, Western Europe, and Japan (with the United States in a position of dominance), through coercion (bribery, international legal enforcement, economic blackmail, and military threat) and consent (via media and culture that celebrates social democracy), creating a situation of trilateral transnational hegemony (Minkkinen 2004).

Given the current militaristic adventurism of U.S. imperialism in recolonizing and redrawing the geographical boundaries of the world (most notably in the Balkans) coupled with the economic stagnation of capitalist economies as a result of overproduction and overcapacity of goods (most noticeably in the technology and manufacturing sectors of the economy), the question that remains unanswered for many Marxist critics of imperialism is whether these signs are any indication of the declining power of U.S. imperialism. One prominent Marxist critic, James Petras (2003), who cannot abide the spectacle of progressive pundits announcing the dissolution of U.S. economic power, warns against simplistic and monocausal explanations offered by some theorists on the Left who view the current economic crisis of capitalism as a sign of the decline of the U.S. empire. Petras is equally guarded against leftist theorists who see the overextension of the U.S. empire as a precursor to its demise. Petras believes that neither of these factors alone will cause the downfall of the U.S. empire. Petras also criticizes hegemony theorists for underestimating coercive measures used by the U.S. imperialists, such as military force, in their analysis of the current stage of imperialism. For instance, the weakness Petras finds in the work of world-system theorists such as Wallerstein (who centers his analysis on the division of the world into center, periphery, and semiperiphery in explaining the workings of global capitalism) is that it completely lacks historical specificity. In addition, it fails to underscore the importance of class antagonisms and the role played by the state in maintaining and reproducing capitalist hegemony.

To refute the claims of Marxist and leftist critics of imperialism who overstate the significance of the economic crisis or the overextension of the empire, Petras (2003) suggests that we examine multinational corporations as a measure of the empire's economic strength or weakness. He emphasizes that 48 percent of the leading 500 multinational corporations worldwide are located in the United States. Of the top fifty largest corporations, 66 percent are based in the United States. Narrowing the number of the largest corporations down to the top twenty, 70 percent are U.S. owned. Finally, eight of the top ten multinational corporations exist in the United States. This offers overwhelming evidence for the superiority of U.S. economic power over its rival capitalist nations in Europe and Asia. Contrary to many critics of imperialism, Petras concludes that the U.S. empire is not declining. In fact, a symbiotic relationship exists between the dominant economic power of the United States and its overwhelming military dominance worldwide (with military bases in over 120 countries). Consequently, the thesis of overextension of the empire constitutes "ahistorical speculation" that does not correspond to the concrete historical facts of imperialism (although clearly in our view there are limits to U.S. power that its warlords need to respect).

Furthermore, Petras (2003) notes that within the current stage of capitalism, there are no major signs of interimperialist rivalries among the leading capitalist nations. On the contrary, most European and Asian capitalist countries have decided to collaborate with the United States and, for the most part, accept its role as a dominant hegemonic power. In exchange, they can enjoy the spoils of the recolonization of the globe. Take, for example, the presence of the 40,000 occupying European forces in the Balkans that operate under the supervision of the U.S. military. Petras maintains that the expanding role of U.S. militarism around the world is not adversely affecting its economic empire–building ambitions. He offers three compelling reasons for this. First, as we have already mentioned, the majority of the top 500 multinational corporations are based in the United states, which is a testament to the relative strength of its economic power. Second, the United States has secured control over major oil fields around the world, most notably in the Middle East. Finally, at the present moment, no large-scale organized oppositions from within the United States against the ruling classes or against the expansion of the U.S. empire exist.

Despite Petras's (2003) bleak outlook for the development of any immediate or sustained social and political movements against the "new imperialism," he does offer a number of conditions that may seriously challenge the U.S. empire. He identifies four contradictions in the social, political, and economic sphere of the U.S. empire that may weaken the pillars that support it. The first contradiction arises from the struggle between Latin America's organized rural and urban populations and the U.S. imperialists in the region. These include the guerrilla movement in Colombia, the Bolivarian circles in the urban slums of Caracus, the landless peasants of Brazil, the cocoa farmers of Bolivia, Mexico's Zapatistas, and finally the unemployed and semiemployed urban working class in Peru and Argentina. Second, Petras (2003) points to the expansionist policies of the empire and to the decline of the republic, which illustrate the extent to which capital is being siphoned off and redirected from the domestic economy to support the imperial ambitions of the United States. The third contradiction exists between the territorial occupation of Third World countries (as in the case of Iraq and Afghanistan) and the increasing anticolonial and nationalistic resistance movements in these regions. Petras identifies the fourth contradiction as one that exists between the growing military empire on the one hand and the failure to extract profits from oil and other natural resources in the colonized regions of the world on the other. He notes that the major weakness of empire is in its long-term occupation of recolonized territories. This is clearly the case in the failure of the U.S. military to fend off daily attacks by the growing resistance and guerrilla movements in Iraq against its soldiers, key military installations, and the oil pipelines. In response, the United States has been forced to request the United Nations to play a larger role in Iraq.

The (Un)response of the Educational Left

In recent years, a large body of literature has been written on the growing convergence of corporate interests and public education in the United States. Yet very little work has been advanced by critical educators that attempts to develop a concerted and programmatic counteroffensive to the corporate takeover of our educational institutions. The field of critical pedagogy has been moderately successful in providing symptomatic readings of the current privatization and commercialization of public education. Yet educators in the field of critical pedagogy have not attempted to situate the current crisis of education within the historically persistent struggle between capital and labor, particularly in relation to the expanding low-skill, low-wage service economy.

A certain complacency has grown up around matters of capitalist exploitation and class struggle. Much of the work being done in critical pedagogy has focused on criticizing the corporate-sponsored curricula and the exchange of free technological equipment. Considerable attention has been given to uncovering the relationship between the commercialization of public education and the growing erosion of civil society presently excluding working-class and minority participation in the social and political sphere (Boggs 2000). In fact, many of these efforts evidence support for an antistatist capitalism or antiegalitarian relativism or else unconsciously reposition themselves within a liberal, capitalist-inclined discourse of social justice, all under the banner of critical pedagogy. Paulo Freire foresaw these developments as domesticating and vulgarizing radical efforts at educational reform.

Today, even among some of the most progressive accounts by critical educationalists, class struggle has remained an ambiguous, indistinct, and undigested place. The twilight existence suffered by Marxist educational reformers can be traced to the fact that class struggle has been perceived as anodyne or has been banished as a primordial category in critical pedagogy following the collapse of the Soviet Union and the Eastern European bloc regimes. The disappearance of class politics from the ramparts of history has coincided with the growing interest in identity politics, which has assumed a prominent place in the agenda of the postmodern educational Left. Surfing hybrid identities within spaces opened up by furious clashes in the fight clubs of culture has been a primary pursuit of postmodern educationalists (see McLaren and Farahmandpur 1999a, 1999b, 2000). Yet such a pursuit has consistently ignored the role played by the forces and relations of production. While attention is given to controlling capital in the interests of a democratic redistribution of wealth, postmodern educationalists have so far failed to recognize the importance of labor as the source of all value and the substance of all value (abstract labor); thus, they have failed to argue for the uprooting of the basis of value production itself, which is the abolition of capitalist social relations and capital itself.

Beyond Capitalist Schooling

Capitalist schooling participates in the production, distribution, and circulation of knowledge and social skills necessary for reproducing the social division of labor and hence capitalist relations of exploitation. As consumers of school knowledge, students as citizens-in-the-making are beholden largely to the physics of capitalist accumulation.

Capital is a force that colonizes the entire social universe. Within this social universe, the workers and capitalists are in objective conflict with each other. The workers are exploited by the capitalists whether the workers subjectively know it or not or whether they like it or not (Hill 2001). The capitalist class owns the means of production. This reality obtains today in much the same way as it did during capitalism's infancy. While it is possible to identify a transition from a mass production (Fordist) to a specialized (post-Fordist) economy, such changes are limited to certain areas of the world; furthermore, these changes are relatively superficial. The relationship of workers to the means of production is essentially the same. To argue that there has been a shift from relations of production to an emphasis on consumption patterns works to obscure the relations of exploitation of the capitalist class who own the means of distribution and exchange. From the standpoint of capital, education is considered a commodity with quantifiable and measurable outcomes that helps increase the efficiency and the productivity of workers. Working-class students partake of particular knowledges, skills, and social capital that prepare them as workers to produce surplus value for capital accumulation.

Recognizing the "class character" of education in capitalist schooling and advocating a "socialist reorganization of capitalist society" (Krupskaya 1985) are two fundamental principles of a socialist pedagogy. Following Marx (1973), we argue that it is imperative that teachers recognize the contradictions of "free" and "universal" education in bourgeois society and question how education can be "equal" for all social classes. Education can never be "free" or "equal," as long as social classes exist. We believe that the education and instruction of working-class students must be linked to productive labor and also to social production. Thus, we envision a working-class pedagogy that pivots around a number of key linkages: the production of critical knowledge and productive work, the organization and management of critical knowledge and the organization and management of production, and the utilization of critical knowledge for productive consumption (Krupskaya 1985).

Furthermore, the severing of workers from the products of their labor under the capitalist mode of production mirrors in a number of basic instances the separation of the production and consumption of knowledge among students. For instance, in public schools today, theoretical knowledge is seldom linked to labor practices. Our vision of a socialist schooling, on the other hand, consists of teaching students how knowledge is related historically, culturally, and institutionally to the process of production and consumption.

Revolutionary critical pedagogy, in our view, should focus on problematizing the production of value through work experience even in instances where
we are clearly referring to the information economy and immaterial labor.
This should include but not be limited to four relations that lie at the center
of the work experience in U.S. society. Marx described these four relations as
constituting what he termed "alienation." These are summarized by Ollman
(2001) as follows:

> (1) the relation between the individual and his/her productive activity, in which
> others determine how it is done, under what conditions, at what speed, and for
> what wage or salary, and even if and when it is to begin and end; (2) the relation
> between the individual and the product of that activity, in which others control
> and use the product for their own purposes (making something does not confer
> any right to use what one has made); (3) the relation between the individual and
> other people, particularly, with those who control both one's productive activity
> and its products, where each side pursues their own interests without consider-
> ing the effects of their own actions on the other (mutual indifference and com-
> petition become the characteristic forms of human interaction); and (4) the re-
> lation between the individual and the species, or with what it means to be a
> human being. (111)

According to Marx, capitalist production and consumption constitutes a
totality of interconnected social relations that can be divided into productive and unproductive consumption. While productive consumption satis-
fies the physical, spiritual, and social needs of individuals, unproductive
consumption (its antithesis) appropriates and transforms the surplus value
of labor into capital. Thus, it is imperative that teachers and students question how knowledge is produced and ask the following: Who produces it?
How it is appropriated? Who consumes it? How is it consumed? In what
sense is it productive? In what sense is it unproductive? In whose interests
does such labor serve? Working-class pedagogy gives priority to the struggle
between labor and capital, to the relationship between the forces of production and the means of production, and to the relationship between nature
and society.

In the space that follows, we attempt to sketch out in broad strokes the key
characteristics of a socialist working-class pedagogy that attempts to move
beyond current liberal and Left-liberal efforts at making capitalist schooling
less barbaric and more democratic. The democratic working-class pedagogy
that we envision here agitates on behalf of pedagogical practice connected to
a larger socialist political project. This struggle includes the struggle not only
against the globalization of capital but also against capital itself (Mészáros
1995).

Responses to the Rule of Capital: Freirean Pedagogy

Paulo Freire's critique of capitalism, in particular his critique of class exploitation, has largely been ignored by critical educationalists operating within the precincts of postmodern theory and cultural studies. This is a lamentable situation, especially given Freire's totemic status among progressive educators and the fact that his writings serve as the railhead of the critical educational tradition. In his early work especially, Freire (1978) positioned education as an ideological and political activity that is intimately linked to social production. Critical education, he argued, empowers students and workers to organize and classify knowledge by differentiating between bourgeois ideology and working-class ideology, bourgeois culture and working-class culture, and ruling-class interests and working-class interests.

As an offspring of Freirean pedagogy, critical pedagogy seeks to reclaim these distinctions identified by Freire as well as to transcend the existing antagonisms between manual and mental labor, theory and practice, teaching and learning, and what is known and what can be known. In this respect, Freire (1978) raised important questions regarding the relationship between education and social production, such as, "Why is anything produced? What should be produced? How should it be produced?" (107). We join Freire in arguing that, as part of a larger concerted effort of educating workers and students, critical pedagogy must also address the following questions: "What to know? How to know? In benefit of what and of whom to know? Moreover, against what and whom to know?" (100).

Following Freire's (1978) lead, critical pedagogy supports the practice of students and workers reflecting critically not only on their location *in* the world and *against* the world but also on their relationship *with* the world. Freire maintained that productive labor is the basis for critical knowledge and vice versa. Subsequently, a critical analysis of schooling begins by examining the relationship between productive labor and critical knowledge. That is, critical education is associated with productive labor, with labor that privileges use value over exchange value.

While capitalist schooling provides students with basic knowledge and skills that increase their productivity and efficiency as future workers and that subsequently reproduce class relations, critical pedagogy works toward the revolutionary empowerment of students and workers by offering them opportunities to develop critical social skills that will assist them in gaining an awareness of—and a resolve to transform—the exploitative nature of capitalist social and economic relations of production.

Worker and student empowerment requires teachers in urban schools to acknowledge and exploit critically the dialectical unity between theory and practice and action and reflection (Freire 1978). Reflection on one's own social practice means being attentive to the concrete social and economic issues in the workplace and in schools. It further stipulates that workers and students gain a critical purchase of their social location. Freire referred to this as achieving a "radical form of being," which he associated with "beings that not only know, but know that they know" (24).

The revolutionary character of Freire's approach is lucidly reflected in Bertell Ollman's description of what constitutes a "dialectical understanding" of everyday life. Ollman (1998b) argues that a dialectical understanding of social life is "more indispensable now than ever before" (342) because he believes that the current stage of capitalism is characterized by far greater complexity and much faster change and interaction than at any time in human history. In tracing the social, economic, and political antagonisms under capitalism, Marxist dialectics conceives of capitalism to be constituted by

> intersecting and overlapping contradictions. . . . Among the more important of these are the contradictions between use-value and exchange-value, between capital and labor in the production process (and between capitalists and workers in the class struggle), between capitalist forces and capitalist relations of production, between competition and cooperation, between science and ideology, between political democracy and economic servitude, and—perhaps most decisively—between social production and private appropriation (or what some have recast as the "logic of production vs. the logic of consumption"). (350)

Ollman (1998b) captures the essence of the Marxian dialectical process when he writes, "Marx's dialectics views reality as an internally related whole with temporal as well as spatial dimensions. Things that are separate and independent . . . cannot be in contradiction, since contradiction implies that an important change in any part will produce changes of a comparable magnitude throughout the system" (349).

In exposing the underlying contradictions inherent in the capitalist mode of production, socialist pedagogy encourages critical educators to employ a dialectical understanding of the social world in their classroom by creating conditions for students to explore how class exploitation, racism, and sexism constitute a set of complex social, cultural, political, and economic relationships in which every individual is implicated (Ollman 1978). In underscoring the significance of the concept of "relations," Ollman (1978) remarks,

> The relations that people ordinarily assume to exist between things are viewed here as existing within (as a necessary part of) each thing in turn, now conceived of as a relation (likewise, the changes which any "thing" undergoes). The peculiar notion of relation is the key to understanding the entire dialectic, and is used to unlock the otherwise mysterious notions of totality, abstraction, identity, law, and contradiction. (227–28)

Ollman (1998b) articulates a dialectical method that he breaks down into six successive moments. The *ontological moment* has to do with the infinite number of mutually dependent processes that make up the totality or structured whole of social life. The *epistemological moment* deals with how to organize thinking in order to understand such a world. The *moment of inquiry* appropriates the patterns of these internal relationships in order to further the project of investigation. The *moment of intellectual* reconstruction or *self-clarification* puts together the results of such an investigation for oneself. The *moment of exposition* entails describing to a particular audience the dialectical grasp of the facts by taking into account how others think. Finally, the *moment of praxis* uses the clarification of the facts of social life to act consciously in and on the world, changing it while simultaneously deepening one's understanding of it. These acts, versed repeatedly over time, bear a striking similarity to the pedagogy of Freire.

Ollman (1993) maintains that a dialectical understanding of the social world is both critical and revolutionary. It is revolutionary because it makes connections among past, present, and future histories. This allows educators to examine past social revolutions and, by using the present as a point of departure, to explore the possibilities for future revolutionary transformation of society. Dialectical understanding of the social world is also critical because it allows educators to recognize their common class interests with the working class and, in effect, act as revolutionary agents of class struggle. Consequently, by linking theory to practice, a dialectical understanding of the social world illuminates both the limitations and the possibilities for the revolutionary transformation of society. Finally, a dialectical understanding of the social world shows class struggle to be an amalgamation of the existing sociohistorical contradictions between capital and labor. For educators, this translates into either being active participants or passive spectators in revolutionary struggle. Therefore, educators need to address the pressing question: Where do we wish to stand? On the side of the oppressed or the oppressors?

We agree with radical educationalist Paula Allman (2001) that teaching practices that are grounded in a theoretical synthesis of the ideas of Freire, Gramsci, and Marx can indeed work in formal contexts in public educational institutions. Allman's discussion and analysis of her own teaching is highly illuminating. Her perspicacious grasp of Freire is especially welcome, given the often grave misperceptions about Freire's pedagogy that have proliferated over the past several decades, following in the wake of what has been a steady domestication and embourgeoisement of his work.

Following in the footsteps of Freire, Allman (2001) successfully activated in her classroom a pedagogical site that facilitated the development of critical consciousness, a mode of dialectical engagement with everyday life that disposed her students to reflect upon their own historical experiences. They achieved this through the act of decoding everyday life and in the process were liberated to deal critically with their own reality in order to transform it. Students learned that they do not freely choose their lives and that their identities and their objects of consumption were adaptive responses to the way that the capitalist system manipulates the realm of necessity. With a perceptive understanding that Freirean pedagogy is decidedly prescriptive and that Freirean educators are unwaveringly directive, she created the context for her students to name their world and through dialogue come to creatively reshape their historical reality. She carefully delineates Freirean pedagogy from its imitators who would turn the teacher into a passive facilitator; she does this by asking the following questions: Is it not prescriptive that we should ask students to "read the world" critically in order to transform it in a way that will foster humanization? Is it not also prescriptive to demand that the world need transforming and that education should play a critical role in this effort? Furthermore, shouldn't educators use the authority that comes from their own critical reading of the world and their understanding of Freire's philosophy of education? Isn't the most facilitative, nonprescriptive, and nondirective form of progressive teaching doubly prescriptive in the sense that it is a prescription for nonprescription as well as for political domestication and adapting successfully to the social universe of capital and the law of value? Of course, Freirean educators direct and prescribe, but in a way redolent of humility and in a spirit of mutuality, dialogical reciprocity, and self-respect.

Toward a Socialist Pedagogy

One of the fundamental principles of socialist pedagogy is the revolutionary empowerment of working-class students. Empowering working-class students means having them explore the complex linkage among sexism, racism, and the exploitation of labor. This requires a decidedly dialectical grasp of everyday social relations.

Challenging the causes of racism, class oppression, and sexism and their association with the exploitation of labor demands that critical teachers and cultural workers reexamine capitalist schooling in the contextual specificity of global capitalist relations. Critical educators recognize that schools as social sites are linked to wider social and political struggles in society and that such struggles have a global reach. Here the development of a critical consciousness enables students to theorize and critically reflect upon their social experiences and also to translate critical knowledge into political activism.

A socialist pedagogy actively involves students in the construction of working-class social movements. Because we acknowledge that building cross-ethnic/racial alliances among the working class has not been an easy task to undertake in recent years, we encourage the practice of community activism and grassroots organization among students, teachers, and workers. Yet we believe that the task of overcoming existing social antagonisms can be accomplished only through class struggle—the road map out of the messy gridlock of historical amnesia.

Remaining Skeptical

We are not altogether convinced that we have entered into a postindustrial economy where production can be moved with frictionless ease from advanced capitalist countries in the North to developing countries in the South. As Kim Moody (1997) has noted, most production still occurs in the North, and most foreign direct investment is still controlled by the North. In fact, 80 percent of this investment is invested in the North itself. While it is true that northern industries are being transplanted to the South to take advantage of the cheaper labor markets, the North merely modernizes its economic base while making it more technologically sophisticated. We don't believe that the state has withered away under the onslaught of an information economy or information-based capital. In fact, we have not seen a qualitative rupture in capitalist relations of production. We still live within monopoly capitalism or late capitalism, and internationally the struggle between capital and labor as part of the practice of imperialism has not seen a qualitative change or shift in direction. For this reason, we still regard the working class as the privileged agent for fundamental social change with the state still serving as the central target of the revolutionary struggle of the masses. This is because the state is still the main agent of globalization, it continues to maintain the conditions of accumulation, it undertakes a rigid disciplining of the labor force, it flexibly enhances the mobility of capital while ruthlessly suppressing the mobility of labor, and it serves as a vehicle for viciously repressing social movements through the state apparatuses of the police, the military, the judicial system, and so on. That the state is still the major target of working-class struggle should be made clear in the recent mass political strikes in France, South Korea, Italy, Belgium, Canada, Panama, South Africa, Brazil, Argentina, Paraguay, Bolivia, Greece, Spain, Venezuela, Haiti, Colombia, Ecuador, Britain, Germany, Taiwan, Indonesia, Nigeria, and elsewhere (Holst 2001).

We remain skeptical of the new social movements dedicated to "transforming the world without taking power" and democratizing civil society but leaving the state apparatuses largely untouched. We are not interested in ways to democratize civil society if that means (and it usually does) that capitalism will be strengthened in the process. Many of the new social movements mistakenly believe that industrial production has declined in relevance, engage in a self-limiting radicalization of the public sphere, struggle largely on behalf of bourgeois rights for the petite bourgeoisie, fail to consider the state as a unitary agent of intervention and action in promoting structural reform, and eschew the goal of revolutionary Marxists of taking over the state and the economy. In fact, Holst (2001) notes that at a time when segments of the Left have embraced a politics of discursive struggle and fragmentation, capitalism as a world economic system has become more universal and unified.

Finally, we support a socialist pedagogy that follows Marx's lifelong struggle of liberating labor from its commodity form within relations of exchange and working toward its valorization as a use value for workers' self-development and self-realization (Eagleton 1999).

Conclusion

What might constitute the main pillars of a revamped, retooled, and oxygenated Marxist pedagogy? What can Marxist educational theory offer educators in the wake of the dictatorship of the financial markets, in which, in the words of Robert Went (2000), the "invisible hand" of the market is mercilessly and ruthlessly obliterating the lives of millions of working-class men, women, and children? How do we liberate creative human powers and capacities from their inhumane form, namely, capital?

We believe that a revolutionary critical pedagogy must begin by reaffirming its commitment to the struggle for emancipating humanity from its own inhumanity. For Marxist educationalists, the challenge of critical pedagogy is intimately linked to the following questions (following the conviction that a good question is half the answer): What does it mean to be human? How can we live humanely? What actions or steps must be taken to be able to live humanely? We believe that these questions, along with others, can be answered in the course of revolutionizing educational practices in the context of class struggle (Hill and Cole 2001).

Our vision of a revolutionary critical pedagogy is informed by Marx's historical materialist method of social inquiry. To engage in Marxist analysis and praxis does not mean plumping for the standard bearers of the Second International. We do not agree with post-Marxists who continue to criticize—often adventitiously and carelessly—Marx's historical materialist method of inquiry as dogmatic and mechanically reductive (which is not to say that all examples of historical materialism claiming to be derived from Marx's writings escape dogmatism and/or economic reductionism). However, we believe that Marx's approach to historical materialism is, in the main, a human science that can restore humanity to human society (Smith 1996). For Marx, the question of what it means to be human was not bound to or constrained by an eternal or fixed concept of human nature. Rather, Marx maintained that the question of what it means to be human was conditioned by the specificity of the sociohistorical conditions and circumstances of human society, particularly the social relations of production. Marxism is not used here as a codicil of revolutionary amendments to the radical literature on education, as a collection of unchallengeable postulates enjoined on the faithful, or as an ideology used to target constituencies of the masses; rather, Marxism as a practice hews closely to its notional starting point in dialectical analysis. We are using Marxism not as a radical critique of society but, more important, as a negative theory against capitalist society. As John Holloway (1993, 1994) puts it, Marxists are not bent on understanding social oppression as much as they are determined to unmask the fragility and vulnerability—that is, the contradictions—of capitalism.

The contradictions of capitalism do not exist independently of class struggle. This is because capitalism relies on human labor while human labor does not rely on capitalism. Using negative categories to understand capitalism from the standpoint of noncapitalism, Marxists such as Holloway view the objective conditions of class struggle as alienated expressions of the power of labor. As long as capital is dependent on the power of labor, the powerless can realize their power through class struggle. In this view, Holloway notes that there is no room for the concept of historical necessity. This is because, when we view the world as continuous struggle, we must evacuate the notion of certainty and historical determination. Following Marx, we believe that the purpose of education is to enable people to realize their powers and capacities. Whereas liberal approaches to education and self-development attempt to liberate individuals *from* the social, revolutionary critical pedagogy attempts to help individuals liberate themselves *through* the social, through challenging, resisting, and transforming commonly held discourses and practices. Thus, the objective of revolutionary critical pedagogy is the liberation of both consciousness and labor from the shackles of capital and the creation of a society in which each person participates according to his or her abilities for the benefit of his or her needs.

How can teachers recognize the important role they play in the battle between labor and capital? How can they develop a revolutionary ideology? Part of the answer to these questions will depend on the ability of teachers to cultivate the potential of schools as sites for capacity building and democratization and for fostering a spirit of popular activism and socialist militancy. And while it is true that teachers take part in reproducing class relations (pedagogically), they can at the same time utilize their pedagogical skills and expertise to resist and to challenge capitalist schooling. And even if it is true that "a single, homogeneous working-class of the type described in the works of traditional Marxists does not exist . . . anywhere" (Kagarlitsky 2001, 64), a class movement is nevertheless possible in the form of a popular front.

What Paula Allman (2001) calls a "revolutionary critical pedagogy" is grounded in an analysis of capitalist society that is untethered from the comprised language of identity politics associated with many educational postmodernists, such as Patti Lather, a language whose nomenclature and systems of intelligibility remains tributary to anticapitalist struggle. It is a pedagogy that is underwritten by a unified struggle over collective needs in contrast to the individual's right to compete in the marketplace and become rich beyond the imagination. A revolutionary critical pedagogy is premised on a socialist commitment to an egalitarian distribution of economic power and exchange and a mutually beneficial division of labor coupled with a realization that you "simply cannot have private property in the means of production, finance, exchange and communication and at the same time have an unalienated, socially just, and democratic social order" (Panitch and Gindin 2001, 199). It is a Marxist-driven pedagogy that revises the hidebound and doctrinaire Marxism of the Second International, so the anti-Marxist gaggle need not expect a tongue-wagging Joseph Stalin to spring out behind every mention of class struggle.

Panitch and Gindin (2001) argue for bringing a new conceptual layer to Marxism by developing the concept of capacities and potentials. Here they refer to capacities and potentials as new productive forces, such as "the collective capacities to govern democratically everyday life, the economy, civil society, and the state" (196). Panitch and Gindin wish to utilize the study of capacities as a way to help us "to inhabit capitalism while building bridges to those individuals/institutional capacities to get socialism on the agenda" (196–97). Socialism, as we conceive it, means the creation of a vibrant life economy. According to John McMurtry (2002), "A functioning life economy consciously selects for life goods, rather than against them. At the most basic, it selects for life capital—means of life that produce more means of life . . . all life is a process and this process always follows the pattern of the life sequence of value" (139). Life capital is wealth that produces more wealth, with wealth in this instance referring to "*life capabilities and their enjoyments* in the individual, the bio-regional, or the planetary form" (139). Life capital is the "*life-ground in its economic form*" (142), and in capitalist society it is subjugated to money-sequence capital.

In a provocative discussion, David Harvey (2000) argues that Marx did not openly support the concept of social justice because he believed that the struggle for social justice was limited to the redistributive characteristics of the capitalist mode of production. For Marx, a redistribution of wealth and income merely addresses one of the several "moments" or dimensions of the mode of production that includes production, exchange, distribution, and consumption, all of which constitute the elements of an "organic totality." Emphasizing one "moment" while ignoring other moments does little to advance the elimination of exploitation. However, this does not mean that Marxists should abandon the *idea* of social justice. Far from it. Critical educators must work toward liberating the concept of social justice from its liberal and Left-liberal roots, which has, for the most part, operated from within the boundaries drawn by capitalist social relations of production.

In a particularly insightful passage in *Capital*, Marx (1977) declares, "A spider conducts operations which resemble those of a weaver, and a bee would put many a human architect to shame by the construction of its honeycomb cells. But what distinguishes the worst architect from the best of bees is that the architect builds the cell in his mind before he constructs it in wax" (284). In other words, the fundamental distinction between humans and other species is that humans are endowed with a social imagination, one that operates as a tool for transforming their social conditions. (This is not an argument for speciesism, as we believe in animal rights, and that we need to prevent the suffering of animals and to grant them moral consideration.) Marx believed that while consciousness is conditioned by social and economic structures, it continues to remain a powerful mediating force in transforming the existing social and economic structures that constrain it. This is especially true of a critical consciousness minted in the service of revolutionary praxis, a praxis that is not limited to, in the words of Marx and Engels (1850), "the smoothing over of class antagonisms but the abolition of classes, not the improvement of existing society, but the foundation of a new one." In this regard, revolutionary critical pedagogy is designed to dispel the necessary misrecognition of the inner structure of antagonisms informing capital, to peel away its occult quality, and to reveal to the light of day capital's subterranean connection to alienation and exploitation.

Panitch and Gindin (2001) remind us that the current pessimism that surrounds us can be broken by "drawing inspiration from the continuity between the utopian dream that predates socialism and the concrete popular struggles in evidence around the world as people strive, in a multitude of diverse ways, to assert their humanity. . . . [A]bove all, it means apprehending that the very power of capital is inadvertently proclaiming as it overruns, subordinates, and narrows every aspect of our lives: that capitalism is 'the wrong dream' and that only an alternative that is just as universal and ambitious, but rooted in our collective

liberating potentials, can replace it" (199).[2] Here what we call revolutionary critical pedagogy can take flight on the wings of a new political imaginary and as-
cend toward an imaginative socialist empyrean. Samir Amin (2001) makes an
important point when he argues that neither modernity nor democracy has
reached the end of its potential development. This is why he prefers the term "democratization," "which stresses the dynamic aspect of a still unfinished process,
to that of democracy, which reinforces the illusion that we can give a definitive
formula to it" (12). In our view, democracy can be deepened by its engagement
with revolutionary critical pedagogy and vice versa. By challenging the rule of
capital, we simultaneously engage in a revolutionary process of democratization.

Critical revolutionary educators speak truth to power not by attempts to
expand the parameters of liberal democracy but by challenging the very core
of liberal democracy. Slavoj Žižek expands on this idea in his discussion of
Lenin's role in Soviet and world history. According to Žižek, Lenin understood
that liberal democracy is a vehicle that gives ballast to capitalism rather than
capsizes it. In fact, Lenin was all too aware that liberal democracy was an
otiose development as far as economic equality was concerned and had become the political arrangement that best facilitated capital's ongoing survival.
Žižek (2002) argues that challenging liberal democracy today represents
Lenin's "ultimate lesson" since "it is only by throwing off our attachment to
liberal democracy, which cannot survive without private property, that we can
become effectively anti-capitalist" (23). Žižek (2001) notes that "actual freedom of thought means the freedom to question the predominant, liberal
democratic, 'postideological' consensus—or it means nothing" (194). For instance, to believe that land distribution in Russia in 1917 could have been accomplished through parliamentary means is, notes Žižek (2002), the same as
believing that "the ecological threat can be avoided by applying market logic
(making polluters pay for the damage they cause)" (10).

Žižek (2001) argues that from Lenin we can learn to escape the "lure" that
"one can undermine capitalism without effectively problematizing the liberal
democratic legacy which (as some leftists claim), although engendered by capitalism, acquired autonomy and can serve to criticize capitalism" (196). Žižek
describes this lure as "a rhizomatic monster/vampire that deterritorializes and
swallows all—indomitable, dynamic, ever rising from the dead, each crisis
making it stronger, Dionysis-Phoenix reborn" (196). Lenin's historical lesson
avoids what Jacques Lacan refers to as the "narcissism of the lost cause"
whereby pseudo-leftists can participate in struggles against the state that are
perceived by the public as too extreme and thus are always already doomed to
fail. Pseudo-leftists depend upon having a failed politics so they don't have to
encounter "the extreme violence of the real." This sounds a lot like the plight of
today's postmodernists who have toe-tagged the project of social transforma-

tion before engaging it. The narcissism of the lost cause prevents an authentic "explosion of emancipatory potential" brought about by true spontaneity" (see Žižek 2002, 16) that Žižek believes rests at the center of any true liberatory politics and what he feels Lenin's politics best exemplifies. Žižek emphasizes that Lenin "was fully aware that true spontaneity is very rare: in order to achieve it, one must get rid of false, imposed ideological spontaneity" (23). Lenin's challenge, Žižek (2001) proclaims, is how to "invent the organized structure that will confer on this unrest the form of the universal political demand" (197). Lenin's lesson can be summed up thusly: "politics without the organizational form of the party is politics without politics" (198). According to Žižek, then, Lenin's criticism of liberals could be pitched as follows:

> They only exploit the working classes' discontent to strengthen their position vis-à-vis the conservatives, instead of identifying with it to the end. Is this also not the case with today's left liberals? They like to evoke racism, ecology, workers' grievances, and so forth, to score points over conservatives without endangering the system. (198)

We therefore need to retrieve what Žižek calls the "Lenin-in-becoming." We do not want to recapture the old Lenin in a gesture of nostalgia; rather, we wish, in Žižek's terms, to "repeat Lenin." To repeat Lenin is to admit that the old Lenin is dead and to advance the notion that we must act within the field of possibilities that he opened up but could not succeed within. Žižek (2001) writes that to repeat Lenin

> is thus to accept that "Lenin is dead"—that his particular solution failed, even failed monstrously, but that there was a utopian spark in it worth saving. To repeat Lenin means that one has to distinguish between what Lenin effectively did and the field of possibilities that he opened up, the tension in Lenin between what he effectively did and another dimension, what was "in Lenin more than Lenin himself." To repeat Lenin is to repeat not what Lenin did but what he *failed to do*, his missed opportunities. (198)

Repeating Lenin means that we must not only take an anticapitalist position but also problematize capitalism's political form, which, as Žižek reminds us, is the liberal, parliamentary, democratic consensus. There is a split between pure politicians who have abandoned the economy as the site of struggle and the economists who preclude the possibility of a political intervention into the global economy. This split must be overcome.

Lenin chose to go a different path than those who want to wait endlessly until the moment is ripe for revolution, according to the necessity of historical evolution, or those who wish to seize the moment that emerges since there is no historically proper time to revolt. Lenin's achievement was a prolonged explosion of utopian energy that should be christened "The Event of Lenin." Of course, we believe that there is more to appreciate in Lenin than "Lenin as an Event" or "utopian spark" since his writings constitute some of the most important analyses of the state and the politics of imperialism ever produced. But Žižek's point on the importance of Lenin's praxiological moment is well taken, if not conceptually overdrawn.

We seek a politics where we can be both disciplined and compassionate, where we can be moved by the sound of Beethoven's Appassionata or carried away by Nathalie Cordone singing "Hasta Siempre" without forfeiting our daily commitment to a rigorous engagement with revolutionary praxis. It is a politics where we can remain steadfast to anticapitalist struggle without being dogmatic or inflexible and without sliding inexorably toward the political swindle of pragmatic compromise that follows from today's postmodern/postpolitical premise that universal forms of emancipatory praxis can only lead to problems greater than the ones that they are attempting to transform.

Notes

1. As Kim Moody (1997) has noted, most production still occurs in the North, and most foreign direct investment is still controlled by the North. In fact, 80 percent of this investment is invested in the North itself. While it is true that northern industries are moving to the South to take advantage of the cheaper labor markets, the North merely modernizes its economic base while making it more technologically sophisticated. The state hasn't dramatically withered away under the Silicon Valley onslaught of an information economy or the derealized character of information-based capital. In fact, he and other socialist adult educators argue that, if anything, we have witnessed not the diminution of state power but rather its augmentation. We have not seen a qualitative rupture in capitalist relations of production since World War II. We still live within monopoly capitalism or late capitalism, and internationally the struggle between capital and labor as part of the practice of imperialism has not recorded any seismic shift that warrants world-historical reconsideration. Consequently, the privileged agent for fundamental social change must remain the working class, with the state still serving as the central target of their revolutionary struggle. This is because the state is still the main agent of globalization, continues to maintain the conditions of accumulation, undertakes a rigid disciplining of the labor force, flexibly enhances the mobility of capital while ruthlessly suppressing the mobility of labor, and serves as a vehicle for viciously repressing social movements through the state apparatuses of the police, the military, the judicial system, and so on. That the state is still the major target of working-class struggle is evidenced by the recent mass political strikes in France, South Korea, Italy, Belgium, Canada, Panama, South Africa, Brazil, Argentina, Paraguay, Bolivia, Greece, Spain, Venezuela, Haiti, Colombia, Ecuador, Britain, Germany, Taiwan, Indonesia, Nigeria, and elsewhere.

Contrary to the opinion of many mainstream social and political theorists, who support the globalization thesis, the power and influence of the state in regulating the capitalist economy has not diminished or rendered the state an appendage of transnational capital. Though the role of the state in providing basic social services for the working poor, children, women, and the elderly has been noticeably curtailed by capital, the state continues to play a number of fundamental functions in maintaining capitalist social relations of exploitation. For example, the state continues to be the guardian of property rights. It also regulates and overlooks currency exchange rates and oversees international economic trade agreements. In short, it provides a base for the legitimate operation of multinational corporations and friction-free operation of capital accumulation.

References

Allman, P. 2001. *Critical education against global capital: Karl Marx and revolutionary critical education.* Westport, Conn.: Bergin and Garvey.

Amin, S. 2001. Imperialism and globalization. *Monthly Review* 53(2): 6–24.

Azad, B. 2000. *Heroic struggle!—Bitter defeat: Factors contributing to the dismantling of the socialist state in the USSR.* New York: International Publishers.

Bello, W. F. 1999. *Dark victory: The United States, structural adjustment, and the global poverty,* 2nd ed. London: Pluto Press.

Boggs, C. 2000. *The end of politics: Corporate power and the decline of the public sphere.* New York: Guilford Press.

Bonacich, E., and R. P. Appelbaum. 2000. *Behind the label: Inequality in the Los Angeles apparel industry.* Berkeley: University of California Press.

Dinerstein, A. 1999. The violence of stability: Argentina in the 1990s. In *Global humanization: Studies in the manufacture of labor,* ed. M. Neary, 47–76. London: Mansell.

The Economist. 2000. The country-club vote. May, 5.

Eagleton, T. 1999. *Marx.* New York: Routledge.

Freire, P. 1978. *Pedagogy as process: The letters to Guinea-Bissau.* Translated by C. St. John Hunter. New York: Seabury Press.

Gimenez, M. 2002. The global fetish. *Latin American Perspectives* 29(4): 85–87.

Hardt, M., and A. Negri. 2000. *Empire.* Cambridge, Mass.: Harvard University Press.

Harvey, D. 2000. Reinventing geography. *New Left Review,* no. 4 (2nd ser.), 75–97.

Hill, D. 2001. State theory and the neo-liberal reconstruction of schooling teacher education: A structuralist neo-Marxist critique of postmodernist, quasi-postmodernist, and culturalist neo-Marxist theory. *British Journal of Sociology of Education* 22(1): 137–57.

Hill, D., and M. Cole. 2001. Social class. In *Schooling and equality: Fact, concept and policy,* ed. D. Hill and M. Cole. London: Kogan Page.

Holloway, J. 1993. The freeing of Marx. *Common Sense: Journal of Edinburgh Conference on Socialist Economics,* no. 14: 14–21.

———. 1994. The relevance of Marxism today. *Common Sense: Journal of Edinburgh Conference on Socialist Economics,* no. 15: 38–42.

Holst, J. 2001. *Social movements, civil society, and radical adult education.* Westport, Conn.: Bergin and Garvey.

Imam, H. 1997. Global subjects: How did we get there? *Women in Action,* no. 3: 12–15.

Kagarlitsky, B. 2001. The road to consumption. In *After the fall: 1989 and the future of freedom,* ed. G. Katsiaficas, 52–66. New York: Routledge.

Klein, N. 1999. *No logo: Taking aim at the brand bullies.* New York: Picador.

Krupskaya, N. 1985. *On labour-oriented education and instruction.* Moscow: Progressive Publishers.

Lenin, V. 1951. *Imperialism: The highest stage of capitalism.* Moscow: Foreign Languages Publishing House.

Lenin, V. I. 1965. A great beginning. In *Collected Works.* Vol. 29. Moscow: Progressive Publishers.

Marx, K., and F. Engels. 1850. Address of the Central Committee to the Communist League, London. www.marxists.org/archive/marx/works/1847/communist-league/1850-ad1.htm (accessed June 1, 2003).

Marx, K. 1973. *Critique of the Gotha program.* New York: International Publishers.

———. 1977. *Capital: A critique of political economy: Vol. 1.* (Translated by B. Fowkes). New York: Vintage Books.

McLaren, P., and R. Farahmandpur. 1999a. Critical multiculturalism and globalization: Some implications for a politics of resistance. *Journal of Curriculum Theorizing* 15(3): 27–46.

———. 1999b. Critical pedagogy, postmodernism, and the retreat from class: Towards a contraband pedagogy. *Theoria,* no. 93, 83–115.

———. 2000. Reconsidering Marx in post-Marxist times: A requiem for postmodernism? *Educational Researcher* 29(3): 25–33.

McMurtry, J. 1998. *Unequal freedoms: The global market as an ethical system.* West Hartford, Conn.: Kumarian Press.

———. 2002. *Value wars: The global market versus the life economy.* London: Pluto Press.

Mészáros, I. 1995. *Beyond capital.* New York: Monthly Review Press.

Minkkinen, P. 2004. New imperialism and beyond: Why the new imperialism will fail and unseat the Bush administration. *Revista Electronica Historia actual on-line* Ano II, no. 4, Primavera 2004. www.hapress.com/prn.php?tp=61 (accessed June 1, 2004).

Moody, K. 1997. *Workers in a lean world: Unions in the international economy.* London: Verso.

Ollman, B. 1978. On teaching Marxism. In *Studies in socialist pedagogy,* ed. T. M. Norton and B. Ollman, 215–53. New York: Monthly Review Press.

———. 1993. *Dialectical investigations.* New York: Routledge.

———. 1998a. Market mystification in capitalist and market socialist societies. In *Market socialism: The debate among socialists,* ed. B. Ollman, 81–121. New York: Routledge.

———. 1998b. Why dialectics? Why now? *Science and Society* 62(3): 338–57.

———. 2001. *How to take an exam and remake the world.* Montreal: Black Rose Books.

Panitch, L., and S. Gindin. 2001. Transcending pessimism: Rekindling socialist imagination. In *After the fall: 1989 and the future of freedom,* ed. G. Katsiaficas, 175–99. New York: Routledge.

Persuad, R. B., and C. Lusane. 2000. The new economy, globalisation, and the impact on African Americans. *Race & Class* 42(1): 21–34.

Petras, J. 2003. Empire building and rule: U.S. and Latin America. www.rebelion.org/petrasenglish.htm (accessed June 15, 2003).

Smith, C. 1996. *Marx at the millennium.* London: Pluto Press.

Went, R. 2000. *Globalization: Neoliberal challenge, radical responses.* London: Pluto Press.

Wichterich, C. 2000. *The globalized woman: Reports from a future of inequality.* Translated by P. Camiller. London: Zed Books.

Wood, E. M. 2003. *Empire of capital.* London: Verso.

Žižek, S. 2001. Have Michael Hardt and Antonio Negri rewritten the Communist Manifesto for the twenty-first century? *Rethinking Marxism* 13(3/4): 190–98.

———. 2002. Seize the day: Lenin's legacy. *London Review of Books.* www.autonomedia.org/article.pl?sid=02/08/04/2214225&mode=nested (accessed June 10, 2003).

3

Critical Pedagogy, Postmodernism, and the Retreat from Class: Toward a Contraband Pedagogy

A S WE LEAN INTO THE GUSTY WINDS of the millennium's final exhale, squaring our shoulders and lowering our heads against an icy unknown, we discover much to our surprise that the future has already arrived, that it has silently imploded into the singularity of the present. We are lost in a crevice in the "wrong side" of history, in a furious calm at the end of a century-old breath, doing solitary confinement in the future anterior. We are lodged in the lungs of time, compressed into shadowy, ovaloid specters out of the horror classic *Nosferatu*. Capitalism has authored this moment, synchronizing the heartbeat of the globe with the autocopulatory rhythms of the marketplace, deregulating history, downsizing eternity.

Contemporary global capitalism signals the revival of idolatry in an Urlandscape of crusaders and über Christian claques who worship the gods of profit at the helm of the *Novus Ordo Seclorum*. Capitalism's sacerdotal power is derived, in part, both from the vulnerability of the worker within the new forces of globalization and from the capitalist's unslakable thirst for power and profit. Capitalism has become a surrogate for nature and a synecdoche for progress. Having confuted the socialism and Marxian optic of the Eastern bloc nations with a triumphaliant "end of history" mockery, capitalism has found its most exalted place in the pantheon of quintessential bourgeois virtues celebrated by the apostolate of that great factory of dreams known as "America." Monopoly captialism did not appear as a result of capital's cumulative overindulgence, like the "flabalanche" on an aging CEO. It was planned. The 1944 Bretton Woods conference at the now famous Mt. Washington Hotel in Bretton Woods, New Hampshire (a conference that created the World Bank, the International Monetary Fund, and, shortly after, the General Agreement on Tariffs and Trade), established the framework and political architecture necessary for the United States to acquire free access to the markets and raw materials of the Western Hemisphere, the Far East, and the British Empire (Korten 1996). The vision that emerged from this historical meeting laid the groundwork for the lurid transmogrification of the world economy into a global financial system overrun by speculators and "arbitrageurs" who act not in the interests of world peace and prosperity and the needs of real people but for the cause of profit at any cost (Korten 1996).

As the world's "mentor capitalist nation," the United States not only has become detached from the struggles of its wide-ranging communities but also betrays an aggressive disregard for them. Of course, capitalism has not brought about the "end of history" as the triumphalist discourse of neoliberalism has announced. Historically, capitalism has not carried humankind closer to "the end of ideology" or "end of history." Rather, as Samir Amin (1996) comments,

> in spite of the hymns to the glory of capital, the violence of the system's real contradictions was driving history not to its end as announced in triumphalist "belle époque" proclamations, but to world wars, socialist revolutions, and the revolt of the colonized peoples. Re-established in post–First World War Europe, triumphant liberalism aggravated the chaos and paved the way for the illusionary, criminal response that fascism was to provide. (3)

As social agents within a neoliberal capitalist regime, one whose link between international competitive forces and neoliberal state policy tightens as market forces gain strength (Moody 1997), we seem to lack substance. Capitalism's history appears to have written us out of the story, displacing human agency into the cabinet of lost memories or into the white bejewelled hands of the nouveau riche glitterati. The world shrinks while difference swells into a forbidding colossus, bringing us face to face with all that is other to ourselves. Global capitalism has exfoliated the branches of history, laying bare its riot of tangled possibilities and hacking away at those roots that nourish a socialist latency. As capital reconstitutes itself *à la discrétion*, as traditionally secure factory work is replaced by the feckless insecurity of McJobs, as the disadvantaged are cast about in the icy wind of world commodity price fluctuations, as the comprador elite expands its power base in the financial precincts of the postmodern necropolis, and as the White House redecorates itself in the forms-fits-function architectonic of neoliberalism, capitalist hegemony digs its bony talons into the structure of subjectivity itself. Communications networks—the electronic servomechanisms of the state—with their propulsions and fluxes of information that have grown apace with capitalism make this hegemony not only a tenebrous possibility but also an inevitability as they ideologically secure forms of exploitation so furious that every vulnerability of the masses is seized and made over into a crisis. Neoliberalism is not simply an abstract term without a literal referent. The current corporate downsizing, outsourcing, and deregulation and the poverty it has left in its wake is neoliberalism in flagrante delicto. Look at the faces of the men and women who line up for food stamps in South Central and East Los Angeles; the slumped shoulders of the workers lining up at the gates of the *maquiladoras* in Juarez, Mexico; and the wounded smiles of children juggling tennis balls, breathing fire, and washing car windows in the midst of a traffic jam in Mexico City, and you will have come face to face with the destructive power of neoliberalism.

The global death rattle that announces this fin-de-siècle moment joltingly alerts lost generations whose subjectivities have been melded into capitalist forms of such pure intensity that time and history do not seem necessary. We are always already shaped by the labyrinthine circuits of capitalist desire, a desire that hides catachrestically behind the veiled dystopianism of postmodern bourgeois rhetorics. It is a desire so ruthless that it thirsts even for the tears of the poor. Accumulation in the name of profit has become the *acta sanctorum* of the age of desire.

Over the past several decades, the social, economic, and political metamorphoses in Western industrial nations and developing Third World countries have culminated in an increasing interest in Marxist social theory within various critical traditions of educational scholarship. While some critical educators are rediscovering Marxism, recognizing its rich historical and theoretical contribution to social theory and acknowledging its invaluable insights into the role of schooling in the unequal distribution of skills, knowledge, and power in society, others are riding the fashionable currents of the postmodern *soi-disant Quartier Latin* (see McLaren 1998a, 1998c, 1999).

Among educational scholars, there has been a growing interest in melding various strands of postmodern social theory with elements of Marxist theory, a project that would be too otiose to summarize here. However, many theorists who straddle the postmodernist–Marxist divide have failed to formulate a sustained and convincing critique of the prevailing social and economic inequalities within advanced Western industrial capitalist nations. Too often such attempts have witnessed social relations of production becoming buried in the synergistic swirl of theoretical eclecticism.

We believe that it is an urgent task to locate educational theory more securely within a Marxist problematic than we have done in the past in order to explain in more accurate and convincing fashion the dynamic mechanisms that ensure the production and reproduction of capitalist social and economic relations as well as to unravel the complex ways in which schools participate in the asymmetrical distribution of technical knowledge and skills. This is not an argument against eclecticism per se but rather a cautionary reminder that much conceptual ground already covered can get lost in the laboratory of theory when trying to meld models into some grand synthesis in an attempt to reveal what has been hidden.

The intensification of international competition among multinational corporations under the flagship of neoliberal economic policies has the threatening tendency of colonizing everyday life. It has created conditions in which declining living standards and increasing wage inequalities between the poor and the wealthy have become the norm. The new global economy is regulated by the growing service and retail industry that relies significantly on the exploitation of unskilled immigrant labor in the Western industrial nations and workers in Third World countries. As a means of decreasing production costs, manufacturing jobs are exported abroad to Third World developing countries where a combination of cheap labor markets and weak labor unions create a ripe mixture for a massive accumulation of capital in a frictionless, deregulated industrial milieu. As one example of this, we refer to Coca-Cola FEMSA in Colombia, which not only "pressures" workers from the assembly lines but supports paramilitary terror that so far has resulted in nine workers being murdered and sixty-seven being placed under death threat. The "Kmarting of the labor force" has yielded unprecedented record profitability for transnational corporations, especially in Third World countries (Zukin 1991). Kim Moody (1997) reminds us that today's transnational corporations "are clearly predators waging class war to expand their worldwide empires and restore the legendary profit-rates of decades ago" (287).

The replacement of the U.S. manufacturing industry by low-wage employment in the service and retail industry has contributed in no insignificant way to the increasing social and economic inequalities and has witnessed 10 percent of the population taking ownership of more that 90 percent of the nation's wealth. Much of the recent evisceration of social programs and the vicious assaults against trade unions by the neoliberal comprador elite can be traced to the 1980s, when the capitalist class was given a dose of corporate Viagra through massive deregulation policies. According to Robert Brenner (1998),

> Capitalists and the wealthy accumulated wealth with such success during the 1980s largely because the state intervened directly to place money in their hands—enabling them to profit from their own business failure through lucrative bailouts, offering them massive tax breaks which played no small part in the recovery of corporate balance sheets, and providing them with an unprecedented array of other politically constituted opportunities to get richer faster through fiscal, monetary, and deregulation policies—all at the expense of the great mass of the population. (207)

Of course, after the initial surge, the economy went flaccid, which put lie to the myth of deregulation. Brenner (1998) remarks,

If, after more than two decades of wage-cutting, tax-cutting, reductions in the growth of social expenditure, deregulation and "sound finance," the ever less fettered "free market" economy is unable to perform half as well as in the 1960s, there might be some reason to question the dogma that the freer market, the better the economic performance. (238)

Moody (1997) reports that at a global level, we are witnessing the production of a transnational working class. He warns that "the division of labor in the production of the world's wealth is more truly international that at any time" (308). While the postmodern academics are busy decentering dominant regimes of signification, they need to be reminded from time to time that of 4.5 billion residents of so-called Third World countries, one-third have no access to drinkable water and slightly fewer are homeless and have no access to medical assistance. In tandem with these economic shifts has been the unceasing virulence of neoliberal attacks against social programs, educational opportunities, and the civil rights of working-class women and minorities. The globalization of national economies (something that is not really new but is as old as capitalism itself; see Marx 1977), through deregulation, free marketization, and privatization, has become an open-door policy to the unrestricted movement of finance capital from national to international markets, creating flexible arrangements suitable for capitalist exploitation. As globalization has dramatically intensified over the past several decades, its lack of an ethical foundation or warrant has never been so apparent. Michael Parenti (1998) writes,

Capitalism is a system without a soul, without humanity. It tries to reduce every human activity to market profitability. It has no loyalty to democracy, family values, culture, Judeo-Christian ethics, ordinary folks, or any of the other shibboleths mouthed by its public relations representatives on special occasions. It has no loyalty to any nation; its only loyalty is to its own system of capital accumulation. It is not dedicated to "serving the community"; it serves only itself, extracting all it can from the many so that it might give all it can to the few. (84–85)

The growing numbers of undocumented immigrants in Los Angeles and throughout the southwestern United States is being examined by the general public as the probable result of miserable social, political, and economic conditions in so-called Third World countries. What the media persistently fail to report is that the root of this situation can be traced to the downgraded manufacturing sector in the United States and the growth of new low-wage jobs in the service sector where the growth industries—finance, real estate, insurance, retail trade, and business services—come equipped with low wages, weak unions, and a high proportion of part-time and female workers. These workers are more than likely to be immigrants who are forced to work for low pay, have little employment security, and possess few technical skills and little knowledge of English (Sassen 1998). Of course, the growing high-income professional and managerial class in the major metropolitan centers has created a need for low-wage service workers—restaurant workers, residential building attendants, preparers of specialty and gourmet foods, dog walkers, errand runners, apartment cleaners, child care providers, and others—who work in the informal economy "off the books" (Sassen 1998).

In the face of the changing dynamics of world capitalism, Moody (1997, 296–97) argues that there is persistent continuation of three aspects of today's economic, social, and political world that resembles the world of a century ago. First, there is no existing social system that competes with capitalism for the future, whether precapitalist regimes or bastions of postcapitalist, communist, bureaucratic collectives. Second, capitalism has retained its market-driven form to create uneven development on a world scale. Third, the state and institutions of capitalist politics have been captured by neoliberal/conservative movements and politicians; and the objective power of international markets continue to impose severe limits on reform projects for those unwilling to struggle.

While much remains the same about capitalism, there does exist a profound difference. Social provisions within the working class have worsened, and resistance to the regime of wage labor is much more difficult than at any other historical moment. David Harvey (1998) reminds us that

> the barriers to that unity are far more formidable than they were in the already complicated European context of 1848 [publication of the *Communist Manifesto*]. The workforce is now far more geographically dispersed, culturally heterogeneous, ethnically and religiously diverse, racially stratified, and linguistically fragmented. The effect is to radically differentiate both the modes of resistance to capitalism and the definitions of alternatives. And while it is true that means of communication and opportunities for translation have greatly improved, this has little meaning for the billion or so workers living on less than a dollar a day possessed of quite different cultural histories, literatures and understandings (compared to international financiers and transnationals who use them all the time). Differentials (both geographical and social) in wages and social provisions within the global working class are likewise greater than they have ever been. (68)

Addicted to its own self-induced adrenaline rush, capitalism's reckless gunslinging frontierism and goon-squad financial assaults on vulnerable nations has brought itself into a naked confrontation with its own expanding limits, the ne plus ultra extremity of accumulation, turning it on itself in a cannibalistic orgy of self-destruction. The collapse of the former Soviet Union and Eastern European state-sponsored bureaucratic socialism, following in the wake of a speeded-up process of globalization and its unholy alliance with neoliberalism,[1] has fostered hostile conditions for progressive educators who wish to create coalitions and social movements that speak to the urgent issues and needs inside and outside our urban schools. These include growing poverty, racism, and jobless futures for generations of increasingly alienated youth.

Confronted by the fancifully adorned avant-garde guises worn by postmodernists as they enact their wine-and-cheese-party revolution, the education Left is hard pressed to make a case for Marx. It has become exceedingly more difficult to mobilize against capital, which is conscripting the school curriculum and culture into its project of venerating eternal accumulation.

Postmodern theory has made significant contributions to the education field by examining how schools participate in producing and reproducing asymmetrical relations of power and how discourses, systems of intelligibility, and representational practices continue to support gender inequality, racism, and class advantage. For the most part, however, postmodernism has failed to develop alternative democratic social models. This is partly due to its failure to mount a sophisticated and coherent opposition politics against economic exploitation, political oppression, and cultural hegemony. In its celebration of the aleatory free play of signification, postmodernism exhibits a profound cynicism—if not sustained intellectual contempt—toward what it regards as the Eurocentric Enlightenment project of human progress, equality, justice, rationality, and truth, a project built on patriarchal master narratives that can be traced to seventeenth-century European thinkers (Green 1994). Perry Anderson (1998), paraphrasing Terry Eagleton, aptly describes the phenomenon of postmodernism as follows:

> Advanced capitalism . . . requires two contradictory systems of justification: a metaphysics of abiding impersonal verities—the discourse of sovereignty and law, contract and obligation—in the political order, and a casuistic of individual preferences for perpetually shifting fashions and gratifications of consumption in the economic order. Postmodernism gives paradoxical expression to this dualism, since while its dismissal of the centered subject in favor of the erratic swarming of desire colludes with the amoral hedonism of the market, its denial of any grounded values or objective truths undermines the prevailing legitimations of the state. (115)

Challenging such ambivalence is one reason that Marxism has come under trenchant assault in recent years by postmodernist theorists of various stripe. Postmodernists have taken Marxism to task for its perceived lack of attention to issues of race and gender.[2] Leaning heavily on the idea of the incommensurability of discourses, some intellectual apostles of postmodernism, such as Patti Lather (1998), offer a tired and hidebound caricature of Marxism as a patriarchal totalizing discourse in order to reinvent the all-too-familiar assertion that Marxist educational theory is quintessentially hostile to feminist theory. This is, of course, a gross overstatement, ignoring much that has gone within Marxist theory over the past several decades (see Cole and Hill 1995; Cole, Hill, and Rikowski 1997; Ebert 1996; McLaren 1995, 1997a, 1997b). For

Lather, the so-called subsumption of Marxism under the superior model of deconstruction has not been a *crève-coeur*. Contrary to Lather's grievous misapprehension that links Marxism to modernism's boys' club, Marxism recognizes that the greatest threat to equality on the basis of race, class, gender, and sexual orientation is capitalism itself.[3] As Aijaz Ahmad (1998) notes,

> Marxism is today often accused of neglecting all kinds of difference, of gender, race, ethnicity, nationality, culture, and so on. But it is not Marxism that recognizes no gender differences. These differences are at once abolished by capitalism, by turning women as much as men into instruments of production. These differences are also maintained through cross-class sexual exploitation, not to speak of the differential wage rate, in which women are paid less than men for the same work, or the direct appropriation of women's labor in the domestic economy. Similarly, it is not communism that sets out to abolish nationality. It is abolished by capitalism itself, through imperialism, through circulation of finance and commodities, through the objectivity of the labor process itself, while nation-states are maintained simply as mechanisms for the management of various units of the world capitalist economy in the context of globally uneven and unequal development. Finally, the bourgeoisie is already a universal class, transnational in its operations and with a culture that also tends to be globally uniform. (22)

Martha E. Gimenez (2004) similarly notes that the problems faced by women, while linked to the ideological ways in which women construct their identities, need to be addressed from the perspective of how women's forms of consciousness are linked to a common location in capitalist structures of oppression: to the universal element of capitalism and the historically specific constellation of kinship and racial, ethnic, and religious inequalities as they play themselves out in capitalist social formations. Bourgeois critics who condemn Marxism as too "deterministic" often advance an ideology of unfettered capitalism that is even more deterministic. Samir Amin (1997) remarks,

> It is rather amusing to see managerial types who dismiss Marxism as unduly deterministic proffering this rather vulgar absolute kind of determinism. Moreover, the social design they seek to defend with this argument, namely the market-based management of the world system, is utopian in the worst sense of the term, a reactionary, criminal utopia, doomed in any case to fall apart under the pressure of its own highly explosive charge. (151)

Bourgeois liberal educational theorists in the United States have enjoyed a long-standing apostolic advantage to Marxist scholars who for the most part are characterized as political extremists, idealists, untrustworthy and intransigent intellectuals, and rogues and renegades. The works of Marx and his heirs have been placed on the *librorum prohibitorum*. Regrettably, too few

Marxist analyses are published in U.S. education journals, and even fewer works by Marxist educators appear in the syllabuses of teacher education programs in the United States. With the exception of works by a handful of Marxists, very few social and cultural theorists in the field of education appear to recognize the extent to which political economy shapes curriculum and policy decisions. Although we acknowledge many of the inherent weaknesses in the reproduction and correspondence theories and models of schooling that surfaced in the 1970s and early 1980s (see, for example, Cole 1998), we nevertheless believe that, mutatis mutandis, schools still wittingly and unwittingly participate in reproducing social and economic inequalities in the name of freedom and democracy. Further, they function in the thrall of capital more overwhelmingly today than at any time in history. Acknowledging the brute and intractable reality of capitalist schooling, Carol Stabile (1997) asserts that

> capitalist education is organized and has a purpose, which is held in place by a number of other institutions and their ideologies. In a word, the educational system in the United States reproduces and maintains division between capitalists and workers, thereby producing . . . capitalist relations of production. This organization and purpose are manifest in the historical link between educational institutions and industry, with the former being directed by the needs and interests of the latter. (209)

We apologize to those conservative postmodernists, neo-Nietzscheans, deconstructionists, Gallo-poststructuralists, and the like who find this observation too crude for their academic taste. We follow our apology with a historical materialist alternative.

The Naughtiness of Postmodernism

Globalization binds people together through the economic–political machinery of new technology, the media, and new circuits of production, distribution, and consumption within the culture industry. Yet globalization also creates new divisions and hierarchies of difference, style, and taste. To be sure, consumer culture industries have intensified "sign value" and exchange value through the processes of commercialization. Following in the wake of the globalization of capital is the globalization of culture, a process that creates as many new differences as it does patterns of sameness. Noting that 60 percent of the revenues of all feature films are made in overseas mass markets, Disney has brought Henry Kissinger to Hollywood to advise on its projects in China (with all its potential moviegoers). If there is already a McDonald's near

Tiananmen Square, why not envision a movie theater in the Great Hall of the People (Gardels 1997)?

Yet it would be a mistake to agree with the postmodernist claim that sign value has superseded use value. Such a claim rests on a mistaken realist assumption and truncated conception of use value that argues that use values have been replaced with exchange values, meaning with money, and human needs with profit (Fornäs 1995). We claim that all capitalist commodity production rests on the production and reproduction of needs and use values. Specific needs and desires have been inflected in certain directions—a process that is certainly visible in the aesthetic surfaces of everyday consumer culture. But Marx anticipated the heterogenization of needs in his commodity theory. We need to stress that sign value does not exceed use value but rather is constitutive of it. What we regard on the new postmodern empire of signs actually belongs to the material reality of use value, even though we concede, as did Marx, that the relationships between needs and use values have been historically and intersubjectively defined. While the aestheticization of everyday life gives the illusion that sign values are epiphenomena of use values, this is decidedly not the case. As Johan Fornäs (1995) has put it, "symbols and aesthetics are more than simple effects of commodification and more than a secondary aura above a firm material base" (220).

Under the impact of rapid technological innovations over the past half century in computers and communications devices, some ludic postmodernists have argued that the hierarchical distinctions between reality and its representations have been erased (Green 1994). Teresa Ebert (1996) identifies two variants of postmodernism: "ludic" and "resistance" postmodernism. Ludic postmodernism celebrates the free-floating articulation of signifiers in the construction of lifestyle discourses that are viewed for the most part as decapitated from external determinations. Resistance postmodernism draws on poststructuralist advances in understanding signification but views language as the product of history and links signification to class struggle through the formalist linguistics of Mikhail Bakhtin and V. N. Volosinov and a sociological analysis of language associated with Lev Vygotsky and G. Plekhanov. Ebert explains that while ludic postmodernism is the result of material and historical contradictions inherent within capitalist social relations of production, resistance postmodernism exposes those contradictions by linking social, political, and cultural phenomena with the existing asymmetrical social and economic relations. Resistance postmodernism and critical postmodernism reveal that the base and superstructure are not independent of one another as ludic postmodern thinkers such as Baudrillard, Derrida, and Lyotard are wont to argue.

Jean Baudrillard's faux pas begins with the belief that a Marxist emphasis on production is no longer relevant in a consumer-driven capitalist culture.

Baudrillard's "spectral superstructuralism" privileges cultural production (that is, images, texts, and simulations) over economic production. While postmodern theory swimming in the currents of Baudrillard's renegade vanguardism dismantles the production of meaning and desire in brilliant and manic flashes of hypertheorizing, it too often ricochets off anticapitalist critique, angling toward a politics of representation whose progressive inertia eventually logjams in a centerless cesspool of floating signifiers.

Postmodernists refute metanarratives and participate in an unequivocal rejection of universal truths (Cole and Hill 1995). However, critics of postmodernism point out that decentering grand narratives and rejecting universalism in favor of heterogeneity and a plurality of truths are feasible only if postmodernism constitutes itself as a totalizing narrative. As Rick Joines (1997) comments,

> One of the founding principles and shibboleths of the postmodern academic left is the disavowal of totalizing master narratives (which are coded as "totalitarian") and the conjoined belief that Marx's so-called predictions have failed as the world of class struggle becomes a world of discursive representations and linguistic play. This discourse, which cannot admit its own totalizing, has abandoned thinking about labor and exploitation in favor of textuality and body: desire is hot—economics and class struggle are not. (30)

We agree with Amin (1998b) when he asserts that modernism has not been surpassed by the fictional period known as "postmodernism." Rather, modernism has yet to be finished:

> Modernity is still unfinished, and it remains so as long as the human race continues to exist. Currently, the fundamental obstacle setting its limits is still defined by the social relationships specific to capitalism. What the postmodernists refuse to see is that modernity can progress further only by going beyond capitalism. (103)

We are not suggesting that the Marxist problematic that informs our work cannot greatly benefit from criticism by postmodernist, feminist, or critical race theorists. We continue to advocate for feminist theory and antiracist and antihomophobic perspectives as an extension and as a deepening of many aspects of the Marxist project. This is far different, however, from the current postmodernist abandonment of the Marxist project *tout court* in favor of identity politics.

Surely it is undeniably a good idea to follow antiessentialism[4] in disbanding, dispersing, and displacing the terms that claim to represent us in a shared field of representations premised on the mutual imbrications of "us" and "them" that we give the term "Western identity." Antiessentialism has, above all, enabled researchers to criticize the notion of the unsullied position of enunciation, the location of interpretation free of ideology, what Vincent Crapanzano refers to as a "lazy divinity . . . contemplating its creation in order to observe it, register it, and interpret it" (cited in Da Cunha 1998, 243). Yet identity politics grounded in an antiessentialist position has not focused sufficiently on the material preconditions for liberated ethnic identities that have been undermined by the dramatic intensity of historical events irrupting across the landscape of advanced capitalism. While displacing our historical selves into some new fashionably renegade identity through a frenzied spilling over of signifiers once lashed to the pillars of conventional meanings might reap benefits and help soften the certainty of the dominant ideological field, such postmodern maneuvers do little to threaten material relations of production that contribute to the already hierarchically bound international division of labor. In the United States, for instance, the money that has been spent on Iraq could have provided medical insurance for every uninsured child for the next twelve years.

We are not against the development of self-reflexivity directed at issues in popular culture or cultural criticism in general. We are interested in finding common ground between cultural criticism and the movement for a transformation of productive relations. Our position is that postmodern cultural criticism—that addresses mainly specific logics of noneconomic factors—for the most part has not addressed the liberation of humankind from economic alienation linked to capitalist economic logics that serve as the motor for transnational oligopolies and the reproduction of established social relations as well as wars for empire. Samir Amin (1998b) sets forth a noneconomic–determinist interpretation of Marxism that, while not without its problems, is particularly insightful on this issue. In Amin's model, the capitalist mode of production is not reduced to the status of an economic structure. In other words, the law of value governs both the economic reproduction of capitalism and all the aspects of social life within capitalism. Unlike the concept of "overdetermination" famously articulated by Althusser, Amin counterposes the concept of "underdetermination," in which the determinations of economics, politics, and culture each possess their specific logic and autonomy. There is no complementarity among logics within the systems of underdetermination; there exist only conflicts among their determining factors, conflicts that allow choice among different possible alternatives. Conflicts among logics find solutions by subordinating some logics to others. The accumulation of capital is the dominant trait of the logic of capitalism and provides the channels through which economic logic is imposed onto political, ideological, and cultural logics.

Precisely because underdetermination rather than overdetermination typifies the conflictual way in which the logics governing the various factors of social causation are interlaced, all social revolutions must of necessity be cultural revolutions. The law of value, therefore, governs not only the capitalist mode of production but also the other social determinants. In order to move beyond—to overstep—contemporary capitalism that is defined by its three basic contradictions of economic alienation, global polarization, and destruction of the natural environment, Amin charts out social transformation that would initiate, through its political economy, its politics, and its cultural logics, a social revolution bent on reducing these contradictions rather than aggravating them. Amin convincingly argues that postmodern criticism for the most part capitulates to the demands of the current phase of capitalist political economy in the hope of making the system more humane. Marxists perceive the humanization of capitalism to be a contradiction in terms. Efforts such as those by Bill Clinton to create a "third way" have rightly been dismissed as "neoliberalism with a smiley face" (Ehrenreich 1998, 13).

Within the precincts of postmodern theorizing and in the absence of universal criteria for evaluating the validity of truth claims, we are forced to accept politically ambiguous positions when confronting the privileging hierarchies of capitalist social relations. In our view, concepts such as universal rights are central to the development of a democratic society and should not be placed in philosophical quarantine as the postmodernists believe. While we may agree with those postmodernists who claim that truth does not have a predetermined or fixed meaning, embedded as it is within the specificity of social, political, and historical contexts, this in no way implies the validity of every truth claim, since truths claims conceal asymmetrical social and economic relations. Teresa Ebert (1996) elaborates on this idea:

> The question of knowing the "truth" is neither a question of describing some "true" metaphysical or ontological "essence" nor a matter of negotiating incommensurable language games, as Lyotard suggests. Rather it is a question of dialectical understanding of the dynamic relations between superstructure and base: between ideology—(mis)representations, signifying practices, discourses, frames of intelligibility, objectives—and the workings of the forces of production and the historical relations of production. Crucial to such a dialectical knowledge is ideology critique—a practice for developing class consciousness. (47)

Conservative postmodernism—epitomized by that *bien-aimé* of postmodern pseudotransgressors, Jean Baudrillard—leaches attention away from the messy, conflictual, and power-sensitive materiality of everyday life by refusing to differentiate between image and reality, surface and depth, discourse and ideology, and fact and fiction. Postmodern epistemology is not so much based on critical inquiry in which "objectivity" is pursued but rather is constructed in relation to the tropicity and rhetoricity of discourse. The fixed dualism of reality versus fiction does not apply. Carl Boggs (1997) captures this absence of any substantive counterhegemonic agenda beneath conservative postmodernism's facade of avant-garde bohemianism:

In politics as in the cultural and intellectual realm, a postmodern fascination with indeterminacy, ambiguity, and chaos easily supports a drift towards cynicism and passivity; the subject becomes powerless to change either itself or society. Further, the pretentious, jargon-filled, and often indecipherable discourse of postmodernism reinforces the most faddish tendencies in academia. Endless (and often pointless) attempts to deconstruct texts and narratives readily become a façade behind which professional scholars justify their own retreat from political commitment . . . the extreme postmodern assault on macro institutions severs the connections between critique and action. (767)

Sardar (1998) makes the cogent claim that postmodernism suffers from a "paradoxical dualism" or double coding. It claims that nothing is real, yet it also claims that reality represents something real: simulated images. Postmodernists view history as a collection of necessarily fragmented narratives where the notion of determinate relations is made anemic by the hemorrhaging of signifiers and their bleeding into each other (Eagleton 1996; Green 1994; McLaren 1995). Historical events are too often transformed into a Disneyesque theme park of fantasy and play where the distinction between fact and fiction is barely—if at all—perceptible. History is sequestered away in a grammatologist's laboratory where it can conjure a metaphysics of disappearances and invent reality as a nightmare where all attempts at objectivity suffer the fate of Dr. Frankenstein and his monster.

And what about the postmodernist aversion to master narratives that guide global struggles for liberation? We find that the postmodernist alternative—the stress on local struggles and regional antagonisms—often subverts the anticapitalist project necessary to bring about social democracy. The totalizing development of world capitalism as an imperializing force, as a means of subjugating labor, as a system of unequal and combined development, and as a means of superexploitation and the repression of democratic aspirations needs more than monadic local efforts at improving resource allocation and warning the public against excessive consumptive practices. Local efforts fail to take advantage of reform at the level of the state. The fact that the state is more dependent on capital than ever before suggests that it could potentially serve as an instrument in reform efforts if these are organized with broad national support. According to Ahmad (1998),

The currently fashionable postmodern discourse has its own answer: it leaves the market fully intact while debunking the nation-state and seeking to dissolve it even further into little communities and competitive narcissisms, which sometimes gets called "multiculturalism." In other words, postmodernism seeks an even deeper universalization of the market, while seeking to decompose "social humanity" even further, to the point where only the monadic individual remains, with no dream but that of, in Jean-François Lyotard's words, "the enjoyment of goods and services." Or, to put it somewhat differently: the postmodern utopia takes the form of a complementary relationship between universalization of the market and individualization of commodity fetishisms. This, of course, has been a dream of capitalism since its very inception. (21–22)

According to Amin (1998b), postmodernism gives theoretical legitimacy to a retreat from revolutionary momentum. He further claims that

> these retreats go exactly counter to the sincere wishes of the postmodernists for a strengthening of democratic practices in the administration of everyday affairs. They give fodder to conformity and hatred, contempt for democracy, and to all sorts of chauvinisms. . . . Postmodernism, therefore, is a negative utopia (in contradistinction to positive utopias, which call for transformation of the world). At bottom, it expresses capitulation to the demands of capitalist political economy in its current phase, in the hope—the utopian hope—of "humanly managing the system." This position is untenable. (101)

Postmodernists rarely elevate facts from anecdote to history, a practice that is commensurate with following the latest top-of-the-line designer narratives. At the same time, they ritualistically weave together post-Marxist and end-of-history claims into a seamless genealogy in an attempt to mummify historical agency and seal the project of liberation in a vault marked "antiquity." It is worth quoting Sardar (1998) again:

> In designer history any choice can be fitted with a tradition by associating it with a chosen historical pattern of ideas or events or characters that are selectively assembled. History returns not to its fictional, putative father—Herodotus—as he was constructed by nineteenth century historians, but to the spirit that moved the civilisation that produced him: history becomes myth-making. (86)

An antifoundationalist cynicism surrounding the telos of human progress often leads ludic postmodernism to reject narratives about history's inevitability that have emerged out of the Marxist tradition. However, Marxism's emphasis on teleology is nonteleological; it arches toward a universal eradication of social injustice, poverty, racism, and sexism while recognizing that history is mutable and contingent. We must emphasize that Marx did not believe history was altogether progressive. He understood that historical progress is never secured or guaranteed but rather moves in and between contradictory and conflicting social spaces and zones of engagement. Alex Callinicos (1989) explains this further by arguing that

> historical materialism is a non-teleological theory of social evolution: not only does it deny that capitalism is the final stage of historical development, but com-

munism, the classless society which Marx believed would be the outcome of so-cialist revolution, is not the inevitable consequences of the contradictions of capitalism, since an alternative exists, what Marx called "the mutual ruination of the contending classes." (36)

Contrary to the criticism of Marxist teleology advanced by some postmodern critics, "Marx doesn't describe the overthrow of capitalism as marking the end of history but rather the end of the *prehistory* of human society" (Callinicos 1995, 39).

Terry Eagleton (1996) similarly confirms Marx's opinion that historical regression is more probable than historical progression since the outcome of historical progress depends on the development of social forces and so-cial relations of production. Moreover, he adds that the "point for Marx is not to move us towards the telos of History, but to get out from under all that so that we may make a beginning—so that histories proper, in all their wealth of difference, might get off the ground" (65). Postmodern theory too often discounts class struggle and underestimates the importance of addressing economic exploitation for fear of succumbing to an implicit teleology of progress. At the same time, it continues to recite the satanic verses of capitalist ideology represented by free-market economics and po-litical neoliberalization, which is fast becoming the governing ethos of our time.

We want to be clear that we are not trying to privilege class relations over those of gender, race, ethnicity, or sexual orientation. We remain aware, how-ever, that the law of value under capitalism plays a formidable role in coordi-nating these relationships and their interrelations. We acknowledge the complex and mutual constitutiveness of race/ethnicity, gender, and sexual orientation as an ensemble of social practices that, while not coprimary, are nevertheless in-terconnected, and to a certain extent constitute different logics. Our point is to underscore the ways that the state makes use of "difference" and "diversity" and the militant antagonisms that play out in the theater of identity politics in order to break up the unity of popular forces.

Postmodernism's apostasy is Delta Force landing in Panama in 1989 and putting a pair of Noriega's red bikini underwear on a goat. It is the equiva-lent of transgressing capital's proprietary norms without challenging the ex-traction of surplus value. Postmodernism's petit bourgeois–driven move-ment away from a "represented exterior" of signifying practices renders an anticapitalist project not only unlikely but also firmly inadmissible. Not withstanding the slippage between Marxist categories and some poststruc-turalist categories, we believe that postmodernist theories, in effectively delinking identity politics from class analysis, have damagingly relegated the category of class to an epiphenomena of race/ethnicity, gender, and sexuality. Class solidarity has often been replaced by ethnic solidarity and an uncritical rehabilitation of difference that defines ethnicity and race in essentialist ways (see Gilroy 1991). This does not mean that we take the position that history is shaped by the infallible laws of economics. Far from it. Amin (1997) rightly argues that history "is the product of social reactions to the effects of these laws, which in turn define the social relations of the framework within which economic laws operate" (103). History in this view becomes more than an effect of a specific logic inherent in the accumulation of capital; in fact, it is given shape by the refusal to subordinate society to the absolute needs of economic laws. Such a politics of refusal admittedly takes many forms, including struggles involving gender, race, ethnic, and sexual liberation. Yet we believe, along with Amin, that "the postmodernist critique, pitched short of the radical perspectives attained by Marxist thought, fails to provide the tools needed to transcend capitalism" (137). Despite postmodernism's ability to deconstruct the metaphysical nature of post-Enlightenment bourgeois discourse and socialist thought and to reveal its economistic rationality while exposing its teleological prejudices, Amin argues that its

> penchant for the uncritical adulation of difference and the glorification of empiricism make it quite compatible with conventional, economistic management practices designed to perpetuate capitalist practices, still considered the definitive, eternal expression of rationality. That leaves the way open for neoconservative communalist ideologies of the kind common in Anglo-Saxon traditions of social management. In extreme cases, it may also lead to nihilistic explosions. Either way, the result is an ideology compatible with the interests of the privileged. (137)

The cultural critique that today predominates in cultural studies and post-Marxist "new times" critical exegesis and that assails Marxist theory for privileging social class over race, gender, and identity often constitutes a veiled essentialism. In contrast to such an accusation, Marxism emphasizes that racism, sexism, and heteronormativity are mutually informing relations and integrally linked to one another, yet they always need to be theorized *in relation to* social and economic inequalities. For antisexist and antiracist struggles to move beyond the rhetoric of identity politics and take on a transformative rather than reactive role within the public sphere, they need to consider beyond simple head-nodding gestures the global shifts in the social relations of production and international division of labor. For this reason, it is important to move beyond "political standpoints that view class, gender, race, and ethnicity as discrete, mutually exclusive phenomena" (Gimenez 1995, 262).

Furthermore, a closer examination of relations of class reveals, for example, how the feminization of poverty and the oppression of women are linked with world-consolidating forces within capitalist social relations, patriarchy, and other catechism of the market. Carol A. Stabile (1996) illuminates the relationship between gender and class by arguing that reinstating "class as a central category of analysis for feminism emphasizes the relationality of structures of oppression in politically powerful ways" (289). She further adds that "this move does not mean relinquishing the theoretical and practical gains following from feminists' analysis of gender and race; instead, it provides a much more nuanced and complicated understanding of the manner in which oppressions are structurally intertwined" (289). The meanings that follow from socially constructed concepts of race, gender, sexuality, identity, and ethnicity are never fixed but rather are historically constructed and interwoven *with* social relations of production. Martha Gimenez (1995) emphasizes this idea, arguing that in order to "attain a fuller grasp of the relevance of gender divisions and struggles for the political future of the working class, it is necessary to leave behind the notion of gender as being primarily an individual attribute and to examine it, instead, as the observable effect of underlying social relations of physical and social reproduction" (258).

While the success of socialist and left-wing progressive movements in Western industrial and Third World countries in forming effective anticapitalist revolutionary alliances has been detained (we hope only temporarily) by the lack of convincing alternatives to global capitalism, postmodern social theorists continue to regard themselves as the primary animateurs of an egalitarian new world order—those who will provide an aesthetic education for the *profanum vulgus* while leaning on the ideological backbone of the multinational corporations. Having dismissed Rosa Luxemburg's alternative of "socialism or barbarianism" as a quaint blot on the horizon of social struggles, postmodern apostles are codifying in their vulgate discourses of transgression primarily linked to an aesthetic problematic that in turn is grounded in the often extempore apostatizing pretensions of the metropolis. The conservative nature of postmodern politics has remained largely undetected, helping to keep the ideology of free enterprise, individualism, and privatization the only real game in town.

Since postmodern theorists have been unable to offer convincing accounts of existing class inequalities, a shroud of suspicion surrounds their political motivation, and a jaundiced eye is cast on their social and political objectives by the Marxist Left. Postmodernists have the appearance at least of rejecting a unified political commitment to social change and transformation. Samir Amin (1998a) has offered a cogent description of the way in which neoliberal economics underwrites the political philosophy of postmodernism (see also Cole and Hill 1995; Habermas 1990). He asserts that

empty economics has its pale complement in the enfeebled social and philosophical theses of "postmodernism, " which teach us to be happy and to cope
with the system on a day-to-day basis, while closing our eyes to the ever more
gigantic catastrophe which it is cooking for us. Postmodernism thus legitimizes,
in its own way, the manipulative practices required of political managers for
whom democracy must be reduced to the status of "low intensity" activity even
as it treats the attachment of a society to its own identity as something neurotic,
empty, and impotent. (38)

The treatment of class as yet another arbitrary floating signifier among
race, class, and identity, and the taboo usage of concepts such as "base" and
"superstructure" has led postmodernists to expunge the notions of capitalist exploitation and imperialism from their lexicon and replace them with
more politically benign discourses of "difference" and "identity politics."
Even self-proclaimed progressive postmodernists fare no better in articulating a persuasive critique of capitalism. Roslyn Wallach Bologh and Leonard
Mell (1994) remark that "the best that this tradition can offer is a re-
arrangement of the existing distribution of power—ideally, some kind of
vague hope for egalitarianism or radical democracy" (85). Because postmodern politics has failed to develop a sustained critique of class inequalities, racism, sexism, and economic inequality are thus framed superficially
within fragmented discourses articulated around the holy trinity of race,
class, and gender. Bologh and Mell culminate their argument with the assertion that "if postmodernism wants to confront colonization and the production of otherness, it must confront capital. If it wants to deconstruct
universal categories, it might begin with the categories of political
economy—as did Marx. Those are the most universal categories in which
power resides" (86). It follows that we need to critically examine and rearticulate from a Marxist perspective the dynamic mechanisms that allow capitalist social relations of exploitation to persist.

Developing and envisioning an anticapitalist pedagogy requires a common yet open-ended historical materialist framework of equality and social
justice. The meaning of equality and justice are not predetermined, nor do
they float freely in some effervescent semiotic ether; rather, they are embedded within the specificity of social, economic, and political relations. In
fact, historical specificity of the concept of equality denies neither its universal quality nor its objective significance. Rather, it is a standard by which
we are able to judge political arguments or social practices, and it is a measure by which we can objectively gauge historical and social progress (Malik
1996).

The antiessentialism and antiuniversalism of conservative postmodernism
considers race, class, and gender to be indeterminate and relatively unstable

identities by which we represent ourselves. However, race, class, and gender are not merely fashionable costumes we wear in our daily social relations but constitute historically grounded social practices within the material relations of production. As Ahmad (1998) explains at length,

> There is the idea of *discreteness* of identities, cultural, ethnic, or national; a kind of remorseless differentiatialism, whereby I am not permitted the claim that I may understand your identity but I am supposed to simply respect whatever you say are the requirements of your identity. In this ideology, any number of people celebrate hardened boundaries between self and other, denounce, what they understand as the "universalism" of the enlightenment, rationalism, and so on, while also fully participating in the globalization of consumption patterns and the packaging of identities as so many exhibits. At the same time and often from the same people, we also have the propagation of the idea of infinite hybridity, migrancy, choice of alternate or multiple identities, as if new selves could be fashioned in the instant out of any clay that one could lay one's hand on, and as if cultures had no real historical density and identities could be simply *made up*, *sui generis*, out of the global traffic and malleability of elements taken from all over the world. (103)

In sum, we need to fashion identities that partake of a universal commitment to social equality. This also means that an ethics of social justice must more clearly underwrite the current work being done in identity politics (Malik 1996; McLaren 1997a, 1997b).

We need to identify radical elements within the postmodern movement and not simply ignore postmodernism since there exists conservative, liberal, and critical variants of it. This does not imply, as many critics of postmodernism would prematurely argue, a defeatist or assimilationist position. On the contrary, we believe that while class exploitation is the condition of possibility of multiple forms of oppression in capitalist societies, class struggle by itself cannot be the driving force for social change. This is not to argue that class is no longer central in developing a revolutionary praxis. What it does suggest is that we need to expand our struggles by way of culture, language, and discourse in order to contest the contemporary triad of social, economic, political oppression. And the scope of our struggle must be international. On this issue, Michael Parenti (1998) writes,

> Our task is not to wage a class war but to realize that class war is being waged against us constantly. More international cooperation between labor unions, progressive organizations, and other popular movements is necessary. The ruling classes have taken the struggle to the international level and we must meet them there to prevent our standard of living, our sovereignty, our rights, and indeed our planet, from being sacrificed to a rapaciously profit-driven, monopoly capitalism. (94)

Class analysis needs to be deepened along the lines of its Marxist predecessors in order to explain its contemporary connections among race, class, gender, and disability. This is, however, a far cry from the postmodern claim that "class" is just one of the many identities by which people represent themselves. Douglas Kellner (1995) reminds us that "it would be wrong to ignore the centrality of class and the importance of class politics, [however] a radical politics today should be more multicultural, race and gender focused, and broad-based than the original Marxian theory" (37). This is not an endorsement of the radical democracy of Ernesto Laclau and Chantal Mouffe (1985), nor is it a call for a commitment to nonviolent negotiation at all costs. If war is being waged on the working class, we support the working class in their attempts to fight back. Our concern is to create the conditions for the defeat of capitalism and in so doing define the real stakes and challenges. Samir Amin (1996) poses one of the biggest challenges in the form of the following question: "How are we to create conditions that allow the genuine advance of universalist values beyond their formulations by historical capitalism?" (8). Certainly the answer is not to be found in the postmodernist's call for local, specific struggles over more global ones. This strategy only plays into the hands of a culturalist, communalist solution resulting in political fragmentation. Rather than contributing to a resistance to exploitation, such culturalism itself becomes part of the problem. As Amin (1996) notes in the case of European capitalism,

> The European project itself is conceived in these terms as the communal management of the market and no more, while beyond its borders maximum fragmentation (as many Slovenias, Macedonias, Chechnyas as possible) is systematically sought. Themes of "democracy" and "peoples' rights" are mobilized to obtain results that cancel peoples' capacity to make use of the democracy and rights in whose name they have been manipulated. Praise of specificity and difference, ideological mobilization around ethnic or culturalist objectives, are the engine of impotent communalism, and shift the struggle onto the ground of ethnic cleansing or religious totalitarianism. (9–10)

In sum, "class" needs to be broadly theorized and class struggle needs to be reconsidered taking into consideration the complexity of its contradictory and shifting meaning within global capitalism. As Julie Graham and Katherine Gibson (1996) remark,

> Because class is understood as a process that exists in change, the class "structure" constituted by the totality of these positions and sites is continually changing. Projects of class transformation are therefore always possible and do not necessarily involve social upheavals and hegemonic transition. Class struggles do not necessarily take place between groups of people whose identities are constituted by the objective reality and subjective consciousness of a particular

location in a social structure. Rather, they take place whenever there is an attempt to change the way in which surplus labor is produced, appropriated, or distributed. (59)

If we can conceive of class as the process of producing, appropriating, and distributing surplus value (which is not to displace or deny the importance of property and power in the structure of contemporary society) and if we can also consider class as types of groupings in terms of how persons perform, appropriate, or receive distributed shares of surplus labor, we will notice that allocations of power and property follow from the different relationships one has to the production and appropriation of surplus labor (Wolff and Resnick 1986). If the class process defines the performers (productive laborers) and the appropriators (capitalists) of surplus value as the fundamental class process, we will also notice that there exist two subsumed classes: distributors and recipients of surplus value. Nonclass processes also need consideration because such processes can at times and under certain circumstances compromise the conditions of existence of the fundamental capitalist class process.

Nonclass processes involving race and gender relations can provide the changes necessary for a transformation of the class processes of Western capitalist societies. Using gender as one example, Wolff and Resnick (1986) remark that

> specific changes in social processes concerned with gender relationships would provide conditions for a change in the class processes of Western capitalist societies today. A change in popular consciousness about what "male" and "female" means (i.e., a change in certain cultural processes) alongside a change in the authority distribution process within families (a change in political or power processes) might combine with a change as women sell more of their labor power as a commodity (a change in the economic process of exchange) to jeopardize capitalist class processes. With other changes in still other social processes—which our class analysis seeks to identify—such altered gender relationships might provide the conditions of existence for a revolutionary change to a new social system including a different class structure. (120)

It follows that our agenda for revolutionary social change does not subsume gender relations or relations involving race, ethnicity, disability, or sexual orientation beneath the class process. Rather, we are trying to call attention to the possibility of using nonclass relations as part of a larger anticapitalist revolutionary project, not by analytically isolating nonclass relations but by bringing them *into conversation* with class relations.

As a counterpraxis to capital, we envision a type of social movement union-ism discussed by Kim Moody (1997). Social movement unionism uses the power of organized workers to mobilize the poor, the casualized workers, and the unemployed as well as neighborhood organizations. This is a far cry from the old business-union service model that is often seen as just another labor aristocracy that remains largely circumscribed by what goes on within the fac-tory gates. Social movement unionism attempts to mobilize the less well-organized sectors of the working class. Here the members participate in shap-ing the union's agenda and democratic workplace organization, fighting to eliminate racial and gender inequalities in job sites, and struggling to ensure social justice for the disabled. Unions must fight for common demands among workers in all countries. In fact, common cross-border activities must be designed to destroy transnational markets. What is important about Moody's vision of social movement unionism is its emphasis on becoming part of a transnational worker network.

Social movement unionism is an approach that significantly moves beyond mere reformism, as in the standard reformist attempts to overcome the frag-mentation of the working class through a stress on diversity through a reform of the old mass party system. Unions must continue to defend welfare mea-sures, health care provisions, employment benefits, existing public services, and the gains of women, ethnic minorities, the disabled, and gays and les-bians. At the same time, it should be recognized that the counterforce to cap-ital's job-destroying tendencies is length of working time. An effective cam-paign for shorter work time must have a global reach and, as Moody (1997) asserts, must resist de facto wage cuts. Hourly wages must be increased pro-portionately as hours are reduced. Moody is at pains to point out that the so-cial movement unionism that he endorses is critical of liberal-populist "stake-holder" capitalism that emphasizes a social contract between capital and "civil society" or the "third sector" of nongovernmental organizations.

We agree with Moody that leftist alternatives such as stakeholder capitalism and civil society/third-sector counterforce movements are not enough. We need an approach that prefigures a deeper and more international socialist politics, such as social movement unionism. The new socialism needs to be more international, as Che Guevara envisioned, and should contribute ac-tively to the recomposition of regional groupings capable of opposing the in-ternationalism of people to that of capital. We need focus on the differentia-tions occurring in the process of capitalist expansion, precisely at the interface between the global and the national aspects of this reality, and on the tension between general struggles and particular, regional efforts.

In order to place liberation on the agenda of history again, we need to reen-chant the project of critical educational theory. As educationalists whose work is underwritten by critical pedagogy (McLaren 1995, 1997b), we need to conscript such a rethinking into the development of a critical pedagogy that is capable of devising a transition beyond capitalism. The stakes in the debate are considerable. In order to make possible the type of dialogue needed for strategizing within today's global arena, the advancement beyond capitalism and toward universal socialism requires some important choices for the Left. Samir Amin (1997) has suggested some important directions: charging the World Trade Organization with planning access to the use of major natural resources of the globe and with planning targets for interregional trade in industrial products, improving the incomes of disadvantaged workers, and reconciling general competitiveness with distributional criteria favoring disadvantaged regions of the globe. In addition, excess finance must be channeled toward productive investment in peripheral countries, accompanied by a rethinking of the international monetary system in the direction of regional monetary systems that guarantee the relative stability of exchange rates and so on. A prerequisite requires that the bourgeois Left—largely inconscient of its own reactive theoretical moves—confront the contradictions inherent in the politics of its own theorizing.

The inexorably downward spiral toward dystopian resignation brought about by the postmodernist assault on material reality and any radical attempts to change it must be confronted by radical hope. It must be confronted by a "contraband pedagogy" that conjugates hope with revolutionary struggle in the search for an alternative to capitalist social relations of exploitation. One primary objective should be the translocation of past socialist struggles into the corridors of our historical imagination as a condition of possibility of transformative change and a necessary prelude to our own history-making activity. Such an objective would be to overcome despair in the face of capital's destructive and imperializing force by outbidding it with an affirmation of socialist solidarity.

While mainstream pedagogy has conjured away the idea that education should play a central role in the struggle for social justice, contraband pedagogy rests on the twin notions that the macrostructural frameworks of capitalism do not fully annihilate possibilities for resistance and revolution and that modernity has not been fully consummated. Contraband pedagogy is not reconciled to the postmodern insight that authentic agency has been eclipsed by the systems of symbolic mediation that create desires that can be only false or always already alienating. We still remain loyal to the conviction that the responsible, self-reflecting subject can exist and that self-knowledge can lead to self-determination and eventually revolutionary praxis. Contraband pedagogy does not seek to help individuals empower themselves. Empowerment is a liberal option that enables people to gain control over the conditions of their daily lives. Contraband pedagogy is not about gaining control of the "always already" but is about struggling and transforming the conditions that delimit the horizons of the daily life and prohibit the acquisition of the material necessities that would enable a decent and just livelihood for all the toilers of the world.

Contraband pedagogy's deployment as a weapon in the fight against globalization can benefit from an engagement with the new wave of Marxist educational scholarship in Britain, particularly the work of educationalists Mike Cole, Tony Green, Dave Hill, and Glenn Rikowski. While lacking the tradition of Marxist scholarship that has benefited education scholars in Great Britain, the educational Left in the United States can nevertheless begin to revitalize educational reform efforts by assessing the limitations of prevailing leftist paradigms built around postmodernist forms of cultural critique. Given the exacerbating contradictions of capital—seen in the growing numbers of homeless in the streets of major U.S. cities, the increasing vulnerability of the middle class, and the growth of the militarized, gated communities of the ruling class—a socialist alternative may not seem as far-fetched as it does today among the vast majority of struggling U.S. workers.

Like many other educators and activists, we face a daunting challenge. In Los Angeles, where we live and labor, we face a bourgeois-driven apathy from many of our colleagues as an overwhelmingly active despair has been exacerbated by the entrenched belief that the ideological hegemony and social practices of the U.S. capitalist class is impossible to resist (even though at some level most people recognize that all forms of hegemony are leaky). Outraged by the vainglorious attempts of politicians to propagate the myth that the United States represents the best of all possible worlds and disgusted by the swelling numbers of U.S. citizens who are following in the ideological footsteps of Christian fundamentalist politicians such as Jerry Falwell (who claimed that the terrorist attacks of September 11 were the result of Americans turning to the evils of fornication and homosexuality) or Pat Robertson (whose televised address to millions of U.S. citizens included a warning that a gay activist event held in Florida could provoke God to send an asteroid to destroy the earth and joins similar condemnations of public schooling as an un-American socialist enterprise that is antifamily and that teaches students to reject God and the marketplace in favor of the perils of drugs, sexual promiscuity, homosexuality, and union membership), our students are becoming more actively politicized, as much if not more so than during the latter years of the Vietnam War. While it is true that our own pedagogical work is taken more seriously in the Third World than it is in the hallowed halls of the North American academy, we believe that efforts to dismantle the exploitative relations of transnational capitalism have to begin here. As one Central American campesino activist, Elvia Alvarado (1987), puts it,

> It's hard to think of change taking place in Central America without there first being changes in the United States. As we say in Honduras, "*Sin el perro, no hay rabia*"—without the dog, there wouldn't be rabies.
>
> So you Americans who really want to help the poor have to change your own government first. You Americans who want to see an end to hunger and poverty have to take a stand. You have to fight just like we're fighting—even harder. You have to be ready to be jailed, to be abused, to be repressed. And you have to have the character, the courage, the morale, and the spirit to confront whatever comes your way.
>
> If you say, "Oh, the United States is so big and powerful, there's nothing we can do to change it," then why bother talking about solidarity? If you think like that, you start to feel insignificant and your spirit dies. That's very dangerous. For as long as we keep our spirits high, we continue to struggle.
>
> We campesinos are used to planting seeds and waiting to see if the seeds bear fruit. We're used to working on harsh soil. And when our crops don't grow, we're used to planting again and again until they take hold. Like us, you must learn to persist. (144)

We are hard pressed to find a better clarion call for the contraband pedagogy we are advocating.

Notes

1. Our claim is that while globalization is not a new phenomenon, its temporal character has been affected by instant financial transactions.

2. See Aronowitz and Giroux (1991); Doll (1996); Giroux and McLaren (1994); Hargreaves (1994); Kincheloe (1993); Lather (1991); Smith and Wexler (1995); and Usher and Edwards (1994).

3. For powerful developments of Marxist feminist approaches, see the work of Ebert (1996), Hennessy (1993), and Stabile (1996). See also McLaren (1998a).

4. Antiessentialism and antifoundationalism can be characterized as a postmodern philosophical position that criticizes the notion that reality exists as an entity independent of appearances.

References

Ahmad, A. 1997. Issues of class and culture: An interview conducted by Ellen Meiksins Wood. In *In defense of history: Marxism and the postmodern agenda*, ed. E. M. Wood and J. B. Foster, 97–111. New York: Monthly Review Press.

———. 1998. The *Communist Manifesto* and the problem of universality. *Monthly Review* 50, no. 2 (June): 12–38.

Alvarado, E. 1987. *Don't be afraid Gringo: A Honduran woman speaks from the heart.* Translated and edited by M. Benjamin. New York: Harper and Row.

Amin, S. 1996. Imperialism and culturalism compliment each other. *Monthly Review* 48(2): 1–11.

———. 1997. *Capitalism in the age of globalization.* London: Zed Books.

———. 1998a. Spectres of capitalism. *Monthly Review* 50(1): 36–39.

———. 1998b. *Spectres of capitalism: A critique of current intellectual fashions.* New York: Monthly Review Press.

Anderson, P. 1998. *The origins of postmodernity.* London: Verso.

Apple, M. W. 1993. *Official knowledge: Democratic education in a conservative age.* New York: Routledge and Kegan Paul.

———. 1996. *Cultural politics and education.* New York: Teachers College Press.

Aronowitz, S., and H. Giroux. 1991. *Postmodern education: Politics, culture, and social criticism.* Minneapolis: University of Minnesota Press.

Boggs, C. 1997. The great retreat: Decline of the public sphere in the late twentieth century. *Theory and Society* 26: 741–80.

Bologh, R. W., and L. Mell. 1994. Modernism, postmodernism, and the new world (dis)order: A dialectical analysis and alternative. *Critical Sociology* (20) 2: 81–120.

Brenner, R. 1998. The economics of global turbulence. *New Left Review* 229: 1–264.

Brosio, R. A. 1994. *A radical democratic critique of capitalist education.* New York: P. Lang.

Callinicos, A. 1989. *Against postmodernism: A Marxist critique.* New York: St. Martin's Press.

———. 1995. *Theories and narratives: Reflections on the philosophy of history.* Durham, N.C.: Duke University Press.

Cole, M. 1998, ed. *Bowles and Gintis revisited: Correspondence and contradictions in educational theory.* London: Falmer Press.

Cole, M., and D. Hill. 1995. Games of despair and rhetorics of resistance: Postmodernism, education and reaction. *British Journal of Sociology of Education* 16(2): 165–83.

Cole, M., D. Hill, and G. Rikowski. 1997. Between postmodernism and nowhere: The predicament of the postmodernist. *British Journal of Educational Studies* 45(2): 187–200.

Da Cunha, O. M. G. 1998. Black movements and the "politics of identity" in Brazil. In *Cultures of politics: Politics of culture: Re-visioning Latin American social movements,* ed. S. E. L. Alvarez, E. Dagnino, and A. Escobar, 220–51. Boulder, Colo.: Westview Press.

Doll, William, Jr. 1996. *A post-modern perspective on curriculum.* New York: Teachers College Press.

Eagleton, T. 1996. *The illusions of postmodernism.* Malden, Mass.: Blackwell Publishers.

Ebert, T. L. 1996. *Ludic feminism and after: Postmodernism, desire, and labor in late capitalism.* Ann Arbor: University of Michigan Press.

Ehrenreich, B. 1998. Beyond Monica—The future of Clinton's past. *The Nation* 267(7): 13–14.

Fornäs, J. 1995. *Cultural theory and late modernity.* London: Sage Publications.

Gardels, N. 1997. Globalization with a human face. *New Perspectives Quarterly* 14(4): 48–49.

Gibson-Graham, J. K. 1996. *The end of capitalism (as we knew it): A feminist critique of political economy.* Malden, Mass.: Blackwell Publishers.

Gilroy, P. 1991. *There ain't no Black in the union Jack: The cultural politics of race and nation.* Chicago: University of Chicago Press.

Gimenez, M. E. 1995. The production of divisions: Gender struggles under capitalism. In *Marxism in the postmodern age: Confronting the new world order*, ed. A. Callari, S. Cullenberg, and C. Biewener, 256–65. New York: Guilford Press.

———. 2004. Connecting Marx and feminism in the era of globalization: A preliminary investigation. *Socialism and Democracy* 18(1): 85–105.

Giroux, H. A. 1988. *Teachers as intellectuals: Towards a critical pedagogy of learning.* South Hadley, Mass.: Bergin and Garvey.

———. 1992. *Border crossings: Cultural workers and the politics of education.* New York: Routledge.

Giroux, H. A., and P. McLaren. 1994. *Between borders: Pedagogy and the politics of cultural studies.* New York: Routledge.

Green, A. 1994. Postmodernism and state education. *Journal of Education Policy* 9(1): 67–83.

Habermas, J. 1990. *The philosophical discourse of modernity: Twelve lectures.* Translated by F. Lawrence. Cambridge, Mass.: MIT Press.

Hargreaves, A. 1994. *Changing teachers, changing times.* New York: Teachers College Press.

Harvey, D. 1998. The geography of the Manifesto. In *Socialist register: The Communist Manifesto now*, ed. L. Panitch and C. Leys, 49–74. New York: Monthly Review Press.

Hennessy, R. 1993. *Materialist feminism and the politics of difference.* New York: Routledge.

Joines, R. 1997. The academic left today. *Political Affairs* 76(6): 29–33.

Kellner, D. 1995. The end of orthodox Marxism. In *Marxism in the postmodern age: Confronting the new world order*, ed. A. Callari, S. Cullenberg, and C. Biewener, 33–41. New York: Guilford Press.

Kincheloe, J. 1993. *Towards a Critical Politics of Teacher Thinking: Mapping the Postmodern.* Westport, Conn.: Bergin and Garvey.

Korten, D. C. 1996. The mystic victory of market capitalism. In *The case against the global economy and for a turn toward the local*, ed. J. Mander and E. Goldsmith, 183–91. San Francisco: Sierra Club Books.

Laclau, E., and C. Mouffe. 1985. *Hegemony and socialist strategy: Towards a radical democratic politics.* Translated by W. Moore and P. Cammack. London: Verso.

Lather, P. 1991. *Getting smart: Feminist research and pedagogy with/in the postmodern.* London: Routledge.

———. 1998. Critical pedagogies and its complicities: A praxis of stuck places. *Educational Theory* 48(4):487–498.

Malik, K. 1996. Universalism and difference: Race and the postmodernists. *Race & Class* 37(3): 1–17.

Marx, K. 1977. *Capital.* Vol. 1. New York: Vintage Books.

McLaren, P. 1995. *Critical pedagogy and predatory culture: Oppositional politics in a postmodern era.* London: Routledge.

———. 1997a. *Life in schools: An introduction to critical pedagogy in the social foundations of education.* 3rd ed. New York: Longman.

———. 1997b. *Revolutionary multiculturalism: Pedagogies of dissent for the new millennium.* Boulder, Colo.: Westview Press.

———. 1998a. Beyond phallogocentrism: Critical pedagogy and its capital sins: A response to Donna LeCourt. *Strategies: Journal of Theory, Culture, and Politics* no. 11/12: 34–55.

———. 1998b. The pedagogy of Che Guevara: Critical pedagogy and globalization— Thirty years after Che. *Cultural Circles* 3: 28–103.

———. 1998c. Revolutionary pedagogy in post-revolutionary times: Rethinking the political economy of critical education. *Educational Theory* 48(4): 431–62.

———. 1999. Traumatizing capital: Pedagogy, politics, and praxis in the global marketplace. In *An introduction to new perspectives in education,* ed. M. Castells, R. Flecha, P. Freire, H. Giroux, D. Macedo, and P. Willis, 1–36. Boulder, Colo.: Rowman & Littlefield.

Moody, K. 1997. *Workers in a lean world: Unionism in the international economy.* London: Verso.

Parenti, M. 1998. *America besieged.* San Francisco: City Lights Books.

Sardar, Z. 1998. *Postmodernism and the other: The new imperialism of Western culture.* London: Pluto Press.

Sassen, S. 1998. *Globalization and its discontents.* New York: New Press.

Smith, R., and P. Wexler, eds. 1995. *After postmodernism.* London: Falmer Press.

Stabile, C. A. 1996. Feminism without guarantees: The misalliances and missed alliances of postmodernist social theory. In *Marxism in the postmodern age: Confronting the new world order,* ed. A. Callari, S. Cullenberg, and C. Biewener, 283–91. New York: Guilford Press.

———. 1997. Pedagogues, Pedagogy, and Political Struggle. In *Class Issues,* ed. Amitava Kumar, 208–20. New York: New York University Press.

Usher, R. P., and R. Edwards. 1994. *Postmodernism and education.* London: Routledge.

Whitty, G. 1985. *Sociology and school knowledge: Curriculum theory, research and politics.* London: Methuen Books.

Whitty, G., D. Halpin, and S. Power. 1997. *Devolution and choice in education: The school, the state and the market.* Buckingham, U.K.: Open University Press.

Wolff, R., and S. Resnick. 1986. Power, property, and class. *Socialist Review* 16(2): 97–124.

Zukin, S. 1991. *Landscapes of power: From Detroit to Disneyland.* Berkeley: University of California Press.

4

Critical Multiculturalism and the Globalization of Capital: Some Implications for a Politics of Resistance

Liberation is a historical act and not a mental act, and it is brought about by historical conditions.

—Karl Marx and Friedrich Engels (1995, 61)

Capital is a controlling force, you cannot control capital, you can do away with it only through the transformation of the whole complex metabolic relationships of society, you cannot just fiddle with it. It either controls you or you do away with it, there is no halfway house between.

—István Mészáros (1996, 55)

Revolution, then, is the way out through history.

—E. San Juan Jr. (1997, 21)

It is 1992, and Los Angeles is on fire. Half a millennium after the arrival of Columbus, the Mesoamerican prophecies are being fulfilled. The enslaved have taken to the streets, burning down the conqueror's golden cities. A decade-long plague that attacks the very immune system upon which our survival depends assumes pandemic proportions. There is famine and worldwide dislocation. People are living in refrigerator boxes on the streets of Aztlán. Earthquakes jolt the California coastline with increasing regularity. And with such violent movement, our ancient codices have predicted, this era—"El Quinto Sol"—will be destroyed. The temple has been toppled and is falling into flames. This is the American destiny. There is a dark patch on the faces of the children. They are crying.

—Cherríe Moraga (1992, 20)

Despite the historic defeat of communism and constant attempts by so-called progressive educators to exorcize any residual Marxist discourse from the literature on multiculturalism, the contradictions of capital playing themselves out in the theater of contemporary social relations are beckoning Marx's specter to return and further trouble those theories proclaiming that the "end of ideology" is upon us and that all we need to do in order to rescue humanity is to heed the clarion call of diversity. Too often overlooked in the debates over multiculturalism at present engulfing the academy are the myriad ways in which globalization is shaping how race, class, gender, and sexuality are being defined and lived. This is especially true in an era in which the global marketplace is becoming alarmingly depoliticized just as the conditioning of deceit among the ruling class is becoming more systematic. We wish to sketch out in broad strokes some of the implications that result from challenging the disarticulation of capitalism from its position in the discourse of traditional multiculturalism and transcoding it within an approach we call "revolutionary multiculturalism" by reposing the issue of globalization and capitalist exploitation in relation to the debates over identity and difference.

The Limits of Global Capitalism

At the dawn of the second millennium and the conclusion of yet another tumultuous and chaotic chapter in the history of class struggle, we are once again confronted with escalating social, economic, political, and environmental crises causing an unimaginable and immeasurable degree of human pain and suffering. The retreat of socialism and the fragmentation of multiracial, multiparty, anticapitalistic struggles in the 1980s and 1990s have led to the bitter yet triumphant revival of capitalism from the economic crisis of the 1970s to the social and economic inequalities and disparities in the 1990s that followed from the dismantling of the welfare state under Presidents Reagan, Bush, and Clinton. We must question whether the inherently contradictory social and economic relations of production within capitalism are sustainable much longer before we experience a deepening global crisis with tragically irreversible consequences.

The United States has no large-scale platform for resisting or even daring to imagine resistance to the steady onslaught of capital accumulation and its concomitant ideology of neoliberalism. As Ostendorf (1996) remarks, "With the disappearance of Socialism as a political inspiration or as a combative alternative, the laws of capitalism have become part of nature again" (41). Yet this situation has not prevented what remains of the U.S. Left from analyzing how capitalism's social and economic system unwittingly contradicts that which it claims in such lofty cadences to defend: freedom, democracy, peace, and social equality. It is becoming quite clear to liberals and radicals alike that capitalism's "expanding power and reach—geographical, cultural, psychological—bring it into collision with human drives for autonomy and meaning, creating a hunger for understanding and alternatives" (Resnick 1997, 12). Capitalism's survival depends on the reproduction of the asymmetrical social relations of production through the barbaric overaccumulation of wealth and the economic and cultural exploitation of working-class and minority groups in Third World countries as well as in Western industrialized and postindustrialized nations, forcing a deepening moral and ethical decadence on a global scale. It is worth quoting Dalla Costa (1996) at length:

> Social reproduction today is more beset and overwhelmed than ever by the laws of capitalist accumulation: the continual and progressive expropriation (from the "primitive" expropriation of the land as a means of production, which dates from the 16th century in England to the expropriation, then as now, of all the individual and collective rights that ensure subsistence); the continual *division* of society into *conflictual hierarchies* (of class, sex, race, and nationality, which pit the free waged worker against the unfree waged worker, against unemployed worker, and the slave laborer); the constant production of *inequality and uncertainty* . . . the continual *polarization* of the production of *wealth* (which is more and more concentrated) and the production of *poverty* (which is increasingly widespread). (111–12)

In an unpredictable and unstable global market economy, the future of billions of men, women, and children is currently at the mercy of transnational corporations that, in an unstoppable feeding frenzy, suck the very marrow out of the bones of society's most vulnerable populations and continue the polarization and proletarianization of the working class. István Mészáros (1998) argues that

> by reducing and degrading human beings to the status of mere "cost of production" as "necessary labor power," capital could treat even living labor as nothing more than a "marketable commodity," just like another, subjecting it to the dehumanizing determination of economic compulsion. (28)

Multinational corporations such as General Electric, Disney, Nike, McDonald's, Microsoft, and Intel are among the new robber barons of the informational age, having replaced the Rockefellers, Morgans, Fords, and Vanderbilts of the early twentieth century. The globalization of capital has re-created conditions similar to the social and cultural crises at the turn of the twentieth century when monopoly capitalism, imperialism, and Fordism emerged as the dominant social and economic modes of production in Western industrialized nations. Social, economic, and political boundaries are shifting at a time when "Western bourgeois democracies are fragmenting in an orgy of rampant postmodernization" and when the neoliberalization of social, economic, and political organization is occurring on a global scale (Ostendorf 1996, 45).

The globalization of capitalism is also causing profound structural readjustments in Third World nations that are mirroring the changes in more developed countries. Giri (1995) notes that

> contemporary economic restructuring, which has emerged in advanced industrial societies in the context of economic and political crises, is now in a phase of global diffusion. Facilitated by the revolutionary manifestation of new technologies in the wake of a post-industrial transformation, it is characterized by the breakdown of the standardized regime of mass production and the rise of "flexible specialization," by a fundamental stress on increasing production and enhancing efficiency, and by globalization of production, distribution, and exchange. (194)

Characterized by a neoliberal ideology of privatization, "outsourcing," and "downsizing," the relationships between human capital and citizenship practices are now orchestrated in the executive boardrooms of transnational corporations as much as they are by the regulative mechanisms of the state. Corporations are viciously attacking public education, social security, and welfare programs for poor working-class Americans, immigrants, and minorities. And the movement of capital beyond national boundaries has created a scenario where multinational corporations are increasingly dictating the social, political, and economic policies of state governments; capital has in some sense become stateless and boundaryless.

With the advent of new deregulatory policies of free marketization and the orgy of corporate mergers that has taken place during the 1980s and 1990s, capital frantically seeks cheap labor and new consumer markets. Since the late 1970s, hundreds of thousands of jobs in the manufacturing industry have been relocated to Third World countries as part of a corporate downsizing trend. In exchange, many Americans in the 1980s and 1990s are working in the retail/service industries with lower wages and benefits than in the previous two decades. As Resnick (1997) remarks, "All of us live and experience a central paradox on a global scale: vastly expanding technological and productive power, great riches being produced, yet most people getting poorer, less secure, more anxious, and the environment more threatened" (12). In addition, the gradual integration of the economic markets of Eastern European countries and the former Soviet Union into the world capitalist economy has been followed by the evolution of a new capitalist class in Russia, China, and Eastern Europe and the frenetic growth of organized crime. In Eastern Europe and the former Soviet Union, the clarion calls of freedom and democracy are sounding in unison with Western values and beliefs in individualism, mass consumption, and privatization.

But the economic, political, and social upheavals in the former communist countries are by no means a manifestation of the demise of revolutionary movements and popular struggles around the world or of the arrival of the end of ideology as predicted by conservative intellectuals such as Francis Fukuyama. The economic and cultural transition toward globalization has been met by local, national, and international resistance. The emergence of new revolutionary movements around the world—such as the Zapatistas in Chiapas, Mexico; the Tupac Amaru Revolutionary Army in Peru; the Intifada in the occupied territories of Palestine; and the continuing working-class labor struggles in South Korea—is testimony to the persistence of liberationist and anticapitalist movements fighting against neoliberalism and globalization.

We do not believe that the free-market system enables the pursuit of democracy, nor do we hold that globalization is innocent of political machinations. Neoliberalism barely exceeds a robber-baron mentality and works in the interest of eviscerating the public sphere and civil society and shredding the social fabric of solidarity and community. We follow Wood (1997), who calls for class unity and coalition building by arguing that "in the face of a 'totalizing' capitalist system, the main organizational energies of the left must more than ever before be devoted to constructing a unified class politics on the local and national level" (28). We also follow Mészáros's (1995) suggestion that our social and political struggle for social equality must be directed not only at the eradication of capitalism but also at the very foundation on which capitalism rests: capital itself.

Globalization and Institutional Multiculturalism

During the past three decades, the expanding economic, political, and cultural phenomenon of globalization has signified the "transnationalization of capitalism, the breakdown of national economies, and the creation of a more interconnected world economic system" (Jusdanis 1996, 141). The breakdown of social and cultural boundaries has been facilitated by the movement of ideas, information, capital, and commodities and their development into a distinct global culture (Jusdanis 1996). The global consumer market, under the leadership of multinational corporations, has helped further the creation of cultural homogeneity by identifying the values and beliefs of specific cultures with commodities and brand names. The paradoxical nature of consumer culture is that

> on the one hand consumer culture offers its products as the source for overcoming alienation and social fragmentation, and . . . it thrives by perpetuating an

unmirroring phase wherein the consuming subject is fated only to (mis)recognize his or her insufficiency, his or her noncorrespondence with the idealized image. (Brown 1997, 30)

Institutional multicultural ideology plays a part in the production of a unified national identity by fusing diverse cultures into one common national culture (Davies and Guppy 1997; Giroux 1996; Lassalle and Perez 1997; Mitchell 1993).

Schools serve as companions to the process of globalization in their attempts to foster compliant citizen–consumers who identify with discourses and practices of nationalism, patriotism, and individualism. Both national and local school reform efforts are for the most part aimed at developing a monocentric school curriculum emphasizing skills and knowledge that can provide society with efficient, productive, and replaceable workers. As Davies and Guppy (1997) argue, "Educational homogeneity is leading to a 'monolithic structure of education'" (449), propagating dominant ideologies and cultural values instrumental in reproducing social and economic inequalities.

The Neoconservative Restoration and the Backlash against Multiculturalism

In the 1980s and 1990s, right-wing and conservative organizations, working on behalf of corporate interests, developed a highly complex web of financially powerful political institutions aimed at attacking social programs designed for poor ethnic minorities and working-class U.S. citizens. The attacks on welfare programs, bilingual education, affirmative action, multicultural education, and civil rights—to name only a few—have functioned to revise history and delete our historical memories of racism, discrimination, prejudice, oppression, and atrocities committed by the guardians of U.S. global interests putatively on behalf of democracy, freedom, and individualism.

More than a century and a half ago, Marx and Engels (1995) noted that the ruling class maintains economic privilege by creating a universal ideology linked to its control of the means of production:

> The class which has the means of material production at its disposal, has control at the same time over the means of mental production, so that thereby, generally speaking, the ideas of those who lack the means of production are subject to it. The ruling ideas are nothing more than the ideal expression of the dominant material relationships, the dominant material relationships grasped as ideas; hence of the relationships which make one class the ruling one, therefore, the ideas of its dominance. (64)

In his book *The Disuniting of America*, Schlesinger (1993) calls for the furious creation of "unifying ideals" that will foster in America a "common culture" and a national identity without which "an individual is deprived of and memory becomes disoriented and lost" (45). He notes that "history becomes a means of shaping history" (46) and further states, "The purpose of history is to promote not group self-esteem, but understanding of the world and the past, dispassionate analysis, judgment, and perspective, respect for divergent cultures and traditions, and unflinching protection for those unifying ideas of tolerance, democracy, and human rights that make free historical inquiry possible" (99). Yet in his patrician advocacy of history as the preservation of values, he attempts to sanitize the historical exploitation and oppression of marginalized social groups by foregrounding the American ideals of "tolerance," "democracy," and "freedom" and concealing past and present economic and social inequalities. He attacks radicals by labeling them militants who are attempting to revise and rewrite history in order to selfishly attain their own political goals, as if somehow Schlesinger is miraculously able to write about history in a heroically disinterested manner.

Schlesinger (1993) believes that we should "teach history for its own sake" (137). However, we believe that history does not have an independent existence from its present actors. We are not talking about platonic shadows on the wall or abstract Kantian universals. History is produced in the act of daily human struggle, not in a domed stadium on top of Mount Olympus, and as a "civilizing mission" it must be inclusive of the lived experiences of oppressed people.

Schlesinger (1993) also attacks bilingual education since it threatens traditional American values and beliefs. He believes that bilingualism "nourishes self-ghettoization, and ghettoization nourishes racial antagonisms" (108). He further suggests that "monolingual education opens doors to the larger society" (108), while bilingualism inhibits the education of minority students. He does not appear to be aware that in today's global society, multilingualism is a necessary tool for communicating ideas, values, and beliefs. Schlesinger's unwavering belief in a "common American identity," which is equivalent to equal opportunity and the right to the ownership of private property, contrasts dramatically with Marx's stress on economic equality and the abolition of private means of production, which is the source of the economic and cultural exploitation of the working class.

Conservative talk show host Rush Limbaugh (1996, 1997), who closely echoes the political sentiments of the McCarthy era of the 1950s, is pushing a platform to transform the education system in order to meet the economic interests of large corporations. Limbaugh associates multiculturalism with "anti-American victimology" and stands in firm agreement with one of the architects of neoliberal economies, Milton Freidman. Limbaugh (1997) attacks public education by stating that "schools teach socialist values, because the educational system is a socialist system. Which is why they are naturally anti-capitalist, anti-business, anti-achievement. If we want schools . . . to reflect traditional American values, we need to introduce educational competition. The solution: school choice" (15).

Attacks on multiculturalism by right-wing conservatives are politically calculated and motivated strategies for promoting a uniform American culture linked to the ascendancy of capital. They are underwritten by a smugly self-satisfied sectarianism that exercises vicious attacks against anything liberal but spares no flummery when it comes to extolling the virtues of right-wing politicians. This ideology of "Americanization" guarantees the preservation of the power and privilege of the dominant social classes. Giroux (1994) reminds us that "the deadly paradox in the conservative offensive is constructed around a politics of difference that attempts to depoliticize politics while simultaneously politicizing culture" (58). The persistent onslaught against multiculturalism by neoconservatives is also articulated by James (1996), who warns that the "conservative backlash against multiculturalism is tied to an attempt to salvage Eurocentrism's hegemony as part of the general campaign against anti-racist and multicultural society" (199).

Neoconservatives wish to preserve racial differences because, as Marable (1996) explains, "racial-identity politics essentially serve to reinforce conservative solutions to poverty, employment and social problems" (xviii). Dinish D'Souza's book *The End of Racism* (1995) is a clear yet cunning attempt to neutralize race as a political and social issue by blatantly rewriting history. His book, funded by the John M. Olin Foundation, a branch of the Olin Chemical and Munitions Company and a frequent supporter of right-wing organizations such as the American Enterprise Institute, argues that racism no longer exists in American society and states that multiculturalism is a "liberal" species of antiracism that has its deepest roots in cultural relativism. He further suggests that slavery cannot be considered a racist institution because it has existed all over the world in various periods; he legitimizes slavery by stating that not all blacks were slaves and that Africans and Indian tribes also owned slaves. D'Souza retains the image of the United States as a harmonious society where democracy is synonymous with equal opportunity, individual pursuit of freedom, happiness, and property. His discourse of democracy privileges individual rights by refusing to reveal how these rights are inherited through class and racial privileges.

Decentering Whiteness

Institutional racism has helped to historically diffuse and fragment the political efficacy of various ethnic groups, preventing them from successfully forging a multiethnic political front against capitalist exploitation. On this point, Hamilton (1996) argues that "racism obscures class distinctions and similarities and at the same time provides a source of cultural belonging for Europeans whose culture has been lost" (173).

Marable (1996) describes "whiteness" as "a power relationship, a statement of authority, a social construct which is perpetuated by systems of privilege, the consolidation of property and status" (6). Winant (1997) uncovers the constituent characteristics of whiteness by arguing that it "may not be a legitimate cultural identity in the sense of having a discrete, 'positive' content, but it is certainly an overdetermined political and cultural identity nevertheless, having to do with socioeconomic status, religious affiliation, ideologies of individualism, opportunity, and citizenship, nationalism, etc." (48). In short, the construction of whiteness as a racialized discourse and set of material practices preserves the political and economic privilege and power of the capitalist class.

The concept of whiteness was introduced in modern history beginning with the Spanish conquest of the "New World" in the early sixteenth century and later reinforced with the practice of slavery in the United States. We need to remember that racial concepts are historically embedded in the specificity of social relations of capitalist production, a point Schiller (1997) articulates clearly, stating that "the construction of race is the product of particular relations of domination in particular places, periods of time, and social locations" (449). Complementing Schiller's position, Winant (1997) suggests that "like any other complex beliefs and practices, whiteness is imbedded in a highly articulated social structure and system of signification; rather than trying to repudiate it, we shall have to rearticulate it" (48). However, the question still remains: how can a racial category be rearticulated?

We believe that the rearticulation of the concept of whiteness can be attained only by its eradication (McLaren 1997), which itself can occur only if accompanied coterminously by the transformation of those capitalist social relations on which the concept is premised (McLaren 1997). This is because the social construction of whiteness is always articulated from a position of privilege and power in relation to marginalized ethnic groups. Schiller (1997) asserts that the abolition of the concept of race is a necessary first step toward the eradication of racism(s):

> Race is a construction that is lived, structuring society and the daily experiences, possibilities, perceptions, and identity of each individual; it is not about people socially defined as black or of color. To the extent that race structures society, all people are "raced," and there is no blackness without the construction and experiences of whiteness, no Indian without a white man, no mulatto without a system of deciding who is truly white. (449)

Following Theodore W. Allen (1994, 1997), Jonathan Scott (1998), and McLaren and Muñoz (2000), we support the claim that whiteness is, first and foremost, a "sociogenic" (having to do with social forces and relations) rather than a "phylogenic" (having to do with phenotype or skin color) phenomenon and is fundamentally linked to the practice of Anglo-European and U.S. colonialism. For instance, in colonial Virginia, roughly between 1676 and 1705, there existed no distinction in status between "black" and "white" bond laborers. Whiteness was a status position introduced by the seventeenth-century Anglo-American and U.S. ruling class—largely the oligarchy of owners of large colonial plantations—who for purely political and economic purposes endowed indentured Europeans (at the time de facto slaves) with civil and social privileges that greatly exceeded those of their fellow African bondsmen.

Within New England's progressive system of equitably distributed small landholdings, freedom for bond laborers (six thousand Europeans and two thousand African Americans) would have effectively ended the plantocracy's superexploitation of the African and European bond laborers and transformed the colony into a diversified smallholder economy. This would have been ultimately disastrous for the tobacco monoculture, which essentially depended on chattel or bond labor. However, the small landholders of colonial Virginia had begun to oppose changes in Virginia land policy, and more and more landless laborers began to fight against their chattel bond servitude. In Bacon's Rebellion, Africans and Europeans fought side by side against the plantation bourgeoisie who would routinely punish runaway laborers by adding years to their servitude and who ordered severe restrictions on corn planting and a ban on hunting for food in the forests so that the rebelling chattel bond laborers would starve to death.

The aim of the Anglo-American continental plantation bourgeoisie was to prepare the ground for a system of lifetime hereditary bond servitude. But the "confederation" of African American and European bond laborers possessed a military power too strong for the bourgeoisie to defeat with its small force of only 500 fighters. The white race had thus to be invented by the colonial bourgeoisie in order to diffuse the potential threat to ruling class hegemony; indentured Anglo-Americans—who had no social mobility and were thus a constant threat to the plantocracy—were recruited into the middle classes through anomalous white-skin privileges that acknowledged their loyalty to the colonial land and property-owning class.

In summary, the invention of the white race was a political and economic maneuver designed to secure control of the plantocracy by homogenizing the social statuses of Anglo-European tenants, merchants, and planters. Later, with the rise of the abolitionist movement, racial typologies, classification systems, and criteriologies favoring whiteness and demonizing blackness became widespread in order to justify and legitimize the slavery of Africans and ensure the continuation of lifetime chattel bond servitude. Today, "whiteness" has become naturalized as part of our "commonsense" reality.

The key question today according to Michael Ignatiev (2004) is why "some members of the working class act in the interests of a group rather than the interests of a *class*, that is, as *whites* instead of as proletarians" (228). Why do white workers cling to a notion of themselves as a group with distinct interests? Ignatiev (2004, 231) supports Theodore Allen's definition of racial oppression (which he summarizes as "a particular form of oppression in which a portion of the exploited class is enlisted in maintaining the rule of the dominant class through a system of privileges that elevate the most degraded member of the privileged group above *any* member of the oppressed group").

Ignatiev (2004) writes that white supremacy in the United States is the American counterpart of European social democracy, "a compact between the ruling class and a portion of the working class" (234). He expands on this idea as follows:

> U.S. political stability has traditionally depended on a majority held together by racial definition. Whiteness has served as a sort of disaster insurance for the ruling class. Of course, some groups occupy immediate positions, sociologically: everyone knows that European-American ethnic groups vary in wealth and status; what makes them all white is their access to things from which others are excluded *by racial definition*. The U.S. may be multi-*ethnic*, but the traditional mode of class rule demands two *races* and no more, the racially oppressed and the racially privileged. The day California or some other state develops a racially oppressed majority is the day the Rodney King rebellion becomes permanent. (2004, 232–33)

White supremacy is being challenged by the existence of a desegregated multiracial propertied class and its not as easy today for the white race to function as effectively as in the past as a means of social control. There are more possibilities today for preventing "the most degraded white man [to] feel himself socially superior to any person of color who walks the earth" (233).

Beyond Whiteness: Toward a Critical Multiculturalism

The dominant ideology of multiculturalism, associated with liberal—and in some instances, Left-liberal—political positions, participates in acknowledging, tolerating, and in some cases celebrating marginalized cultures. However, we believe that such inclusiveness should imply not only recognition of the historical contribution of minority cultures in the building of U.S. society, but also active participation in the reconstruction of U.S. culture and history. Critical multicultural education recognizes both the contributions of marginalized groups and the importance of their political participation in the production of social and cultural meaning. Critical multiculturalism is an oppositional multiculturalism designed to challenge and transform the "authorizing" forces of monocentric U.S. culture. As McLaren (1993) argues,

> A critical multiculturalism as part of a pedagogy of difference seeks not simply to invert dependent hierarchies of domination but rather to inflect the central categories and assumptions of Western rationality towards a displacement of their oppressive political effects. Conflict is not described as a monolinear struggle between the oppressed and the oppressors but as a struggle for spaces of hegemonic rupture out of which new democratizing possibilities may be won and new articulations of identity may be constructed. Since hegemony is not seamless, we must ask: What is the stuff of agency that escapes the act of interpolation? Is it the subject of history? And, if so, whose history is being written and for whose benefit? (286)

Cultures consist of negotiated, contested, and socially constructed spaces of meaning-making activities as well as structured silences. They are conflictual arenas where meanings produced within economic, political, and social relations are constantly struggled over. Cultures not only produce constitutive possibilities for the production of tradition but also create spaces for the remembrance and renewal of the roots of a people's history, customs, beliefs, symbols, spiritual values, and practices. A social group without culture is one without a deepening awareness of its own history, frozen in time and space, unable to challenge or change the oppressive conditions in which it finds itself. For Turner, "Remembering is not merely restoring some past intact but setting it in living relationship to the present" (cited in Mermain 1997, 49).

Unlike Eurocentric ideology, which perceives and produces culture as static, unchanging, dissonant, and wholly dependent on the past, critical multiculturalists view culture as changing, dynamic, and reciprocal: shared among individuals and groups of people. Critical multiculturalism is politically committed to social and economic justice (De La Torre 1996; McLaren 1995; Segal and Handler 1995; Sleeper 1991) and the abolition of asymmetrical social relations embedded in class, race, and gender inequalities; as Phillips (1997) asserts, it deals with "different ways of thinking about morality and religion, different traditions of resolving political conflict, different assumptions about the roles of men and women" (58).

Critical multiculturalism struggles against cultural homogeneity, advocating instead a cultural heterogeneity uniting people of different classes, ethnicities, and genders. It battles the commodification of values and beliefs of subordinate cultures in a consumer-driven society, refocusing on issues related to social inequality (Davis 1996; McLaren 1995, 1997) by encouraging the formation of multiracial, transethnic alliances. By creating conditions in classrooms for minority groups to question the social, economic, and political relations in which they have been historically situated, critical multiculturalism threatens the social and economic interests of the privileged classes who retain their status and power through ideologies that ensure their reproduction. McLaren (1995) asserts that "multiculturalism and multilingualism are seen as threats to the social, political, and cultural stability of this country. In these times of economic crises, as support for the wave of anti-immigrant legislation increases, it becomes even more critical to understand how these sentiments manifest themselves in school policies and practices, in classroom instruction" (157).

We believe that in order to mount any effective social, political, and economic struggle against capital, we must first locate, identify, interrogate, and transform the ideological sites of oppression in the form of a unified multiracial/ethnic oppositional politics. This suggests making ideology critique a fundamental component of multicultural education. As Harris (1994) suggests, "The first move towards countering or demystifying ideological construction would be to recognize the nature, and then to begin to pick out the details, of one's own (and others') constitution as an ideological subject living within the experiential context of such construction" (61).

The social and economic inequalities reproduced by privileged social groups who attempt to preserve them in the past and relive them in the present so as to secure their reproduction in the future can best be challenged through critical pedagogical practices and political activism. This underscores why we believe that any "official" U.S. history must be decentered and ideologically ruptured, thereby opening social and political spaces for marginalized groups to reconstruct their own histories—histories not bleached of oppositional power and tailored to be European-friendly and accommodating to the power elite but rather written from below in order to break the structured silence surrounding the determinate causes of exploitation and to challenge those responsible for it. The struggle must encourage multiracial and transcultural political alliances, for unless a multiracial counterhegemonic political coalition consisting of feminist groups, workers, environmental groups, and other progressive sectors is able to develop sufficient power to contest the power of existing repressive and ideological state apparatuses, the public sphere will continue to diminish in spectacular fashion under the attack of right-wing and conservative forces. And along with the dramatic erosion of the public sphere, we will continue to witness an exacerbation of race, gender, and class antagonisms.

Polycentric social and political spaces can be created by deconstructing the center/periphery and dominant/marginalized dichotomies that underwrite many critical approaches to social reform. The idea is not to move marginalized voices from the periphery to the center since behind this move marginalized voices are no more "authentic" than dominant voices and are vulnerable to reinscription into the "centrist" ideologies of the neoliberal capitalist state. And while the view of marginalized groups is fundamental in providing the initial counterstatement to the dominant ideology, it is not necessarily less distorted than the view of those who occupy the center. Yet a political commitment to social change and equality gives marginalized groups more political urgency and saliency. Flores and McPhail (1997) explain thusly:

> By simply replacing "dominant" voices with "marginalized" voices, critics can perpetuate notions of identity that presume an essential authenticity, subscribe to monolithic notions of race, gender, or ethnicity, or privilege a particular position with "the community." These voices can become as constraining and as counterproductive as those they are intended to replace, often even excluding people within those communities whose voices are ostensibly represented, but who are not being heard. Such voices can also shut down any move toward empathic dialogue. We therefore cannot assume that the marginalized voice is the liberatory voice. (115)

What is required in order to move toward an emancipatory and transformative framework is a critical consciousness accompanied by critical self-reflexivity (McLaren 1997). Self-reflexivity is a process that identifies the source of oppression, both from the outside and from within, through participation in a dialectical critique of one's own positionality in the larger totalizing system of oppression and the silencing of others. Again it is worth quoting Flores and McPhail (1997) in detail:

> While self reflection is an important step in the process of liberation, of asserting and affirming one's own identity, it is insufficient in-and-of-itself for moving from the deconstruction of domination and oppression of social intercourse and interaction. The next step, which is profoundly more difficult, entails the recognition of one's implication in oppression. If we refuse to take this second step and choose to ignore our implicature, emancipatory and reconstructive efforts will quickly reach a dead end. (116–17)

Cameron McCarthy (1993) makes two important arguments with respect to the development of a critical multiculturalism. First, he underscores the fact that unless multiculturalists engage in a systematic critique of Western culture, the strategy of adding diversity to the dominant school curriculum only serves to reproduce the reigning hegemony. He writes,

> The multiculturalist strategy of adding diversity to the dominant school curriculum serves paradoxically, to legitimate the dominance of Western culture in

educational arrangements in the United States. Multiculturalists have simply failed to provide a systematic critique of the ideology of "Westernness" that is ascendant in curriculum and pedagogical practices in education. Instead, proponents articulate a language of inclusion. (294)

McCarthy also notes that a critical multiculturalism must be inherently *relational*. For instance, students pursuing an antiracist agenda must begin to understand how the differential and asymmetrical construction of social groups in the United States is linked to global relations of development and underdevelopment, including relations of imperialism and capitalist exploitation in Latin America, Asia, and elsewhere. McCarthy remarks,

A critical approach to multiculturalism must insist not only on the cultural diversity of school knowledge but on its inherent relationality. School knowledge is socially produced, deeply imbued with human interests, and deeply implicated in the unequal social relations outside the school door. A critical multiculturalism should therefore be more reflexive with respect to the relationship between different social groups in the United States and the relationship of developments in the United States to the rest of the world. This would mean, for instance, that we begin to see the issue of racial inequality in global and relational terms. (295)

Mestizaje Multiculturalism

As McLaren (1997) has argued, some members of the educational Left have championed the term *"mestizaje"* as a metaphor for underscoring the complexity of identity (as distinguished from modernist conceptions of the self as static, monolithic, and fixed) and as a means of constructing an ideal image of the democratic, self-reflexive citizen or cultural worker as a "border crosser." To be a mestizo is to live a deessentialized identity of many cultural, linguistic, and geopolitical contexts. Gloria Anzaldúa (1987), Cherríe Moraga (1992), Emily Hicks (1991), and José David Saldívar (1997), as well as educators such as Giroux and McLaren, have offered in-depth discussions of *mestizaje* identity, drawing attention to its potential for rupturing the static, Anglocentric concept of a unified, monocentric identity. *Mestizaje* identity relies as much on the idea of a "bridge consciousness" that allows individuals to utilize a double vision as both insider and outsider as it does on the concept of a displaced subject who inhabits the borderlands of multiple discourses that exist along the extended U.S.–Mexico *frontera*. Mestizo cultural identity is composed of the fragments, tropes, pastiche, and conceits: the *culturas híbridas* of the borderlands. Here we see the importance of what Saldívar (1997) calls a "transfrontera contact zone" for developing oppositional identities, whether based on *veteranos* preserving more traditional forms of *Chicanismo* or the forging of new spaces of crosshatched subjectivities resulting from the intersection of many "standpoint" positionalities.

We believe that a counterpraxis capable of challenging both local and globalized forms of white supremacist patriarchal capitalism needs to be linked to what Anzaldúa has called "*la conciencia de la mestiza.*" Sandoval (1998) has refined and extended such a notion in new discussions of *oppositional mestizaje*. Sandoval notes that oppositional *mestizaje* relies on *la facultad*—"a set of principled conversions . . . that requires differential movement through, over, and within any dominant system of resistance, identity, race, gender, sex, class, or national meanings: The differential strategy is directed, but it is also a 'diasporic immigration' in consciousness and politics enacted to ensure that ethical commitment to egalitarian social relations enters into the everyday political sphere of culture" (360). Sandoval's concept of oppositional *mestizaje* is both a tactical form of U.S. Third World feminist practice and a differential strategy driven "by the imperatives of social justice that can engage a hermeneutics of love in the postmodern world" (361). Organized around five points of resistance to U.S. social hierarchy—the assimilationist, or liberal, mode; the revolutionary, or insurgent, mode; the supremacist, or cultural-nationalist, mode; the separatist mode; and the mestiza, or "third force," mode—Sandoval has developed a form of oppositional *mestizaje* that is useful for intervening in and transforming the dominant social relations of exploitation and oppression. She emphasizes that neocolonial forces that organize postmodern global economies now require a "fluidity of identity." Yet this fluidity of identity must be made oppositional in the service of creating a new utopian and coalitional postcolonial state. The development of a coalitional consciousness is central to Sandoval's oppositional practice. She writes,

> Oppositional *mestizaje* occurs when the unexplored affinities inside difference attract, combine, and relate new constituencies into a coalition of resistance. Any such generalized and politicized coalitional consciousness, however, can only occur on the site of a social movement that was once overlooked because it was perceived as limited, restricted by gender, sex, or race identity: U.S. third world feminism; a feminism developed by U.S. women of color and by Chicana feminists under the sign of "la conciencia de la mestiza." That is, coalition can only take place through the recognition and practice of a "U.S. third world feminist" form of resistance that is capable of renegotiating technologies of power through an ethically guided, skilled, and differential deployment—a methodology of the oppressed that is only made possible through *la conciencia de la mestiza*. (362)

In addition to the multidimensional typography of subjectivity emphasized by Sandoval—one that we believe is in keeping with Stuart Hall's (1996) "diaspora-ization"—we need to recognize that we can see the world collectively without claiming to be each other. And while Sandoval argues that it is imperative to rely on differently situated knowledges and to conjoin perspectives from different positionalities as a basic principle of oppositional practice, we must be careful not to lose sight of the reality of the accumulation of capital in terms of the ways in which situated knowledges get defined and framed. *Mestizaje* practices and their renegotiation of technologies are linked to the global material technologies of the laws of motion of capital. This can be more clearly understood if we see the relationship among the social relations of production, the consumer ethos driving U.S. culture, and the struggle for identity as one that is linked to the production of subjectivity. For instance, while the feminist political subject has become "fragmented along every conceivable axis of difference" (Gimenez 2004, 101), we need to focus on the "underlying material conditions, common to all propertyless women" (101). In other words, we need to be attentive to the political subject as an ensemble of social relations.

As we argued at the beginning of this chapter, in the current historical interregnum—that deadening lull between the modernist quest for certainty and the postmodern celebration of uncertainty—we face a seismic shift in global capitalist relations. Capital acceleration and the social transformation that has followed in its wake have had devastating consequences for the poor. The self-propelling character of contemporary goon-squad capitalism has been dramatically enhanced by neoliberal policies that have savaged those already vulnerable and powerless. It is in the context of the historical development of capitalism that one of the most urgent struggles over subjectivity takes place. It is in this context that we have to examine the pressing question of a generation who is asking, In what ways has society produced me that I now wish to reject?

Subjectivities are framed by—not dominated by—capital. In a manner of speaking, they constitute the fingerprints of capitalism, a place where capitalism leaves its identifying marks in ways unique to each person and society. Subjectivity is not "a mere internal template of economic process" (Kovel 1998, 107). It occurs in the dialectical interplay of internal and external worlds. Subjectivities are produced conjuncturally, structurally, institutionally, and interpersonally. They are produced conjuncturally in that they are related to specific times and places in rapidly changing and unstable geopolitical arenas not of our own making, where racialized nationalisms proliferate and neocolonial formations interlock as part of a globalizing fortification and symbiosis of capitalism and imperialism. They are produced structurally, within the theater of transnational capitalism and under the control of global carpetbaggers and corporate gangsters. They do not escape the devastating social consequences of the free market that create complex and uneven dispersals of power within the larger social field of capitalist social relations.

Subjectivities are also produced institutionally through the imperializing racist formations that make up our government institutions and administrations where democracy has become an impossible possibility, an empty signifier for a range of attributes by which the oppressed measure their own disempowerment socially, culturally, and politically. Finally, subjectivities are also formed interpersonally, at the fault line that separates needs and desire, through the tenacious colonial tropologies that mystify the history of social relations in which they have been produced and that direct the terrified gaze of the Euro-American toward bodies with brown and black skin who occupy the frayed margins of social life. All these registers of subjectivity share common articulations.

Subjectivities cannot escape the narratives and rhetorics of Western systems of intelligibility that are displaced onto a nonwhite ontological Other. They cannot escape the propensity of the capitalist class to adduce reasons why the poor and powerless in our communities should be held responsible for their own poverty and powerlessness. While anything can be made to bear witness to the promise of diversity, no manner of celebrating diversity or hybridity in a no-holds-barred global economic order can bring about a postborder culture; there are always political borders that barricade against transgression. Dismantling these borders can be accomplished only with the dismantling of capitalist relations of exploitation and the systems of racial, sexual, and gender classification that promote them.

By focusing on the margins rather than the hegemonic center of the neoliberal Anglosphere, mainstream multiculturalists have airbrushed the most vexing dilemmas in the liberal humanist call for diversity and have left uncontested the ever-present discourses of liberal democracy and the workability of capital—discourses that naturalize events so that their outcome no longer seems open to debate. By championing the values of a well-tempered democracy, liberal multiculturalists have also left unchallenged the social relations of production. Latent in the spectrality that has been disclosed by the discursive and representational practices of mainstream multiculturalism is the continuing advance of white supremacist logic and social practices. Ghosted into the ideas of mainstream multiculturalists is a promiscuous fascination with difference and epistemological exoticisms and the return of the erstwhile eclipsed Other. Mainstream multiculturalism remains permeated by the capitalist mode of production through structures of class, race, gender, and sexual domination.

Critical multiculturalism emphasizes the collective experiences of marginalized people in the context of their political activism and social mobilization. We distinguish critical multiculturalism from the dominant ideologies of multiculturalism that seek to legitimize the social order through racial harmony and a national identity based on the "Americanization" of marginalized cultures. As a framework for developing a pedagogical praxis, critical multiculturalism opens up social and political spaces for the oppressed to challenge the various forms of class, race, and gender oppression that are produced and reproduced by dominant social relations. We believe that by using their lived experiences, histories, and narratives as tools for social struggle (McLaren 1995), subaltern groups can interpret and reconstruct oppressive social conditions into meaningful social and political action (McLaren 1995, 1997). Critical multicultural pedagogy encourages marginalized groups and communities to forge political alliances and in so doing to eradicate cultural homogeneity by interpreting and (re)constructing their own history (McLaren 1995). As part of a concerted effort of anticapitalist struggle, critical multiculturalism seeks to establish social and economic equality in contrast to the conservative and liberal ideology of "equal opportunity" that masks the existing unequal distribution of power and wealth.

A democratic multicultural curriculum in the classroom encourages students to interrogate the multiple meanings of race, class, gender, and sexuality in a society that playfully and seductively inverts and reverses the true meaning of social equality. In our view, critical multiculturalism has the potential of pressuring democracy to live up to its name by putting bourgeois liberal egalitarianism on the witness stand of history. Cruz (1996) argues that we must refuse the entrapment of the empty promises of bourgeois democracy by

> bringing into political discourse the promises dangled in the ideology of a longer equality enshrined at the core of bourgeois liberal democracy, by giving groups a sense of place in society and in history, by offering the comfort that comes (tendentiously) in being able to say something about who they are, by attempting to rethink morally and reconstruct institutionally the meanings behind egalitarianism, and by insisting that social power be truly empowering, enhancing, and protecting for all. (32–33)

Here we follow Joel Kovel in struggling not only against economic conditions but also against the delimiting of the self by capital's conversion of labor power into a commodity; that is, against the adherence to bureaucratic rationalization, possessive individualism, and consumerist desire. As Kovel (1998) notes, "It follows that capital must be fought and overcome, not simply at the micro level but as it inhabits and infests everyday life through the structures of bureaucratic rationalization and consumerist desire. However, capital can not be overcome unless it is replaced, at the level of the subject, with an alternative notion" (109). We suggest that one move in an alternative direction would be the formation of a subject unburdened by innocence and engaged by difference, in the manner discussed by Stuart Hall (1996). Hall calls for rethinking ethnicity in a more diverse and less coercive way, decoupled from its equivalence with nationalism, imperialism, and the state. In short, he refers to an ethnicity that has not been transcendentally stabilized in order to confer an essential guarantee to identity. At the same time, we do not necessarily believe that all identifications with the state are to be shunned, as in the case of national liberation struggles where the collective well-being of the population as a whole takes precedence over individual interests and objectives.

In summary, we must continue to wage new struggles of liberation, creating new class, race, and gendered identities—both global and local—along the way. To this end, critical pedagogy must become a scandal of the political imagination, a set of discursive and material practices designed to transform mass lethargy into political activism against the corporatist and neoliberal practices of the ruling class. As Hall (1997) and others remind us, we must begin to rethink identity more in terms of what we can do for each other (a question of ethics) than in terms of who we are (a question of epistemology). Both issues are important, certainly, but we believe that coalition building in the service of anticapitalist struggle requires us to begin our struggle with an ethical commitment to each other and a political commitment to collectively challenge social relations of production under the current organic crisis of global capitalism. Such a commitment is born not out of a pregiven set of first principles of social justice but rather out of a dialectical and self-reflexive understanding of how our own humanity is implicated in both local and global relations of suffering and capitalist exploitation.

In this chapter, we have stressed a number of new currents for the development of a critical multiculturalism centered on the current reign of the depoliticized global market. In our move toward a radical repoliticization of the global marketplace and a reactivation of the presence of Marx in current history in relation to recent attempts at the deideologization of the multicultural agent, a retreat from active civil society, a lack of civic courage, and an enthrallment in passive, apolitical consumerism, we have challenged the privatization of subjectivity and the role of globalization in the deformation of political agency. We have also sounded a warning against the dethronement of class as a pivotal issue in current debates over multicultural identity and agency.

The question that we would like to pose in order to challenge multicultural education is this: How can the Left protagonize a process of structural change that goes beyond state intervention to achieve internal redistribution and a tacit acceptance of the neoliberal model of free-market integration, not the global economy? While we cannot ignore the important contributions of organized Left parties, we must also recognize and emphasize the importance of grassroots social movements operating outside state structures and organized parties, such as Christian communities, solidarity groups, the Landless Workers of Brazil, and revolutionary groups such as the Mexican Zapatistas (Robinson 1998–1999). How can these new social movements mediate between the state and the masses? Within the transnational space, how can these

struggles contest the hegemony of the transnational elite and their local counterparts? How can a transnationalism from below—from the civil society as
distinct from the political society—challenge the power of the global elite?
We join with our *companeros/as* in Latino America and North America—
workers, women, environmentalists, students, peasants, indigenous groups,
associations of the urban poor, and other sectors of society—to forge a counterhegemonic bloc against global capitalism and the state repression that is directed against those neoliberal structural adjustments. We do so with the hope
that from the rubble of the historical imaginations will emerge a revolutionary multiculturalist pedagogy better able to guide us through the necessary
transformation of the new millennium.

References

Allen, T. W. 1994. *The invention of the white race, volume one: Racial oppression and so-
cial control.* London: Verso.
———. 1997. *The invention of the white race, volume two: The origins of racial oppres-
sion in Anglo-America.* London: Verso.
Anzaldúa, G. 1987. *Borderlands/La frontera: The new mestiza.* San Francisco: Spinsters/
Aunt Lute.
Brown, B. 1997. Global bodies/postnationalities: Charles Johnson's consumer culture.
Representations, no. 58, 24–48.
Cruz, J. 1996. From farce to tragedy: Reflections on the reification of race at century's
end. In *Mapping multiculturalism,* ed. A. F. Gordon and C. Newfield, 19–39. Min-
neapolis: University of Minnesota Press.
Dalla Costa, M. 1996. Capitalism and reproduction. *Capitalism, Nature, Socialism*
7(4): 111–21.
Davies, S., and N. Guppy. 1997. Focus on English speaking democracies: Globalization
and educational reforms in Anglo-American democracies. *Comparative Education
Review* 41(4): 435–59.
Davis, A. Y. 1996. Gender, class, and multiculturalism: Rethinking "race" politics. In
Mapping multiculturalism, ed. A. F. Gordon and C. Newfield, 40–48. Minneapolis:
University of Minnesota Press.
De La Torre, W. 1996. Multiculturalism: A redefinition of citizenship and community.
Urban Education 31(3): 314–45.
D'Souza, D. 1995. *The end of racism: Principles for a multiracial society.* New York: Free
Press.
Flores, L. A., and M. L. McPhail. 1997. From black and white to living color: A dialogic
exposition into the social (re)construction of race, gender, and crime. *Critical Stud-
ies in Mass Communications,* no. 14, 106–22.
Gimenez, M. E. 2004. Conncting Marx and feminism in the era of globalization: A pre-
liminary investigation. *Socialism and Democracy* 18, no. 1 (January–June): 85–105.

Giri, A. K. 1995. The dialectic between globalization and localization: Economic restructuring, women and strategies of cultural reproduction. *Dialectical Anthropology* 20(2): 193–216.

Giroux, H. A. 1994. *Disturbing pleasures: Learning popular culture.* New York: Routledge.

———. 1996. *Fugitive cultures: Race, violence, and youth.* New York: Routledge.

Hall, S. 1996. New ethnicities. In *Stuart Hall: Critical dialogues,* ed. D. Morely and K. Chen, 441–49. London: Routledge.

———. 1997. Old and new identities, old and new ethnicities. In *Culture, globalization and the world-system: Contemporary conditions for the representation of identity,* ed. A. D. King, 41–68. Minneapolis: University of Minnesota Press.

Hamilton, C. 1996. Multiculturalism as political strategy. In *Mapping multiculturalism,* ed. A. F. Gordon and C. Newfield, 167–77. Minneapolis: University of Minnesota Press.

Harris, K. 1994. *Teachers constructing the future.* London: Falmer Press.

Hicks, E. 1991. *Border writing: The multidimensional text.* Minneapolis: University of Minnesota Press.

Igantiev, N. 2004. Whiteness and class struggle. *Historical Materialism* 2(4): 227–35.

James, J. 1996. *Resisting state violence: Radicalism, gender, and race in U.S. culture.* Minneapolis: University of Minnesota Press.

Jusdanis, G. 1996. Culture everywhere: The swell of globalization theory. *Diaspora* 5(1): 141–61.

Kovel, J. 1998. The specter redefined. *Socialism and Democracy* 12(1/2): 105–14.

Lassalle, Y. M., M. and Perez. 1997. "Virtually" Puerto Rican: Dis-locating Puerto Ricanness and its privileged sites of production. *Radical History Review,* no. 68, 54–78.

Limbaugh, R. 1996. Is there intelligent life in our schools? *The Limbaugh Letter* 5(9): 3–5, 15.

———. 1997. What's wrong with American schools? *The Limbaugh Letter* 6(3): 3–4, 15.

Marable, M. 1996. *Beyond black and white.* London: Verso.

Marx, K., and F. Engels. 1995. *The German ideology.* New York: International Publishers.

McCarthy, C. 1993. After the canon: Knowledge and ideological representation in the multicultural discourse on curriculum reform. In *Race and representation in education,* ed. C. McCarthy and W. Crichlow, 289–305. New York: Routledge.

McLaren, P. L. 1993. *Schooling as a ritual performance: Towards a political economy of symbols and gestures.* London: Routledge.

———. 1995. *Critical pedagogy and predatory culture: Oppositional politics in a postmodern era.* London: Routledge.

———. 1997. *Revolutionary multiculturalism: Pedagogies of dissent for the new millennium.* Boulder, Colo.: Westview Press.

McLaren, P., and J. Muñoz. 2000. Contesting Whiteness. In *The politics of multiculturalism and bilingual education: Students and teachers caught in the crossfire,* ed. C. A. Ovando and P. McLaren, 22–49. New York: McGraw-Hill.

Mermain, E. 1997. Being where? Experiencing narratives of ethnographic film. *Visual Anthropology Review* 13(1): 40–51.

Mészáros, I. 1995. *Beyond capital.* New York: Monthly Review Press.

————. 1996. The legacy of Marx. In *A critical sense: Interviews with intellectuals*, ed. P. Osborne, 47–62. London: Routledge.

————. 1998. Globalizing capital. *Monthly Review* 49(2): 27–37.

Mitchell, K. 1993. Multiculturalism, or the united colors of capitalism. *Antipode* 25(4): 263–94.

Moraga, C. 1992. Codex xeri: El momento historica. In *The Chicano codices: Encountering art of the Americas*, 20–22. San Francisco: The Mexican Museum.

Ostendorf, B. 1996. On globalization and fragmentation. *2 Be: A Journal of Ideas* 4(9–10): 40–52.

Phillips, A. 1997. Why worry about multiculturalism? *Dissent* 44(1): 57–63.

Resnick, B. 1997. Confront global capitalism, revision the world: Socialism or Nike? Just do it! *Against the Current* 12(3): 12–15.

Robinson, W. 1998–1999. Latin America and global capitalism. *Race and Class* 40(2–3): 111–31.

Saldívar, J. D. 1997. *Border matters: Remapping American cultural studies*. Berkeley: University of California Press.

San Juan, E., Jr. 1997. Fragments from a Filipino exile's journal. *Amerasia Journal* 23(2): 1–25.

Sandoval, C. 1998. Mestizaje as method: Feminists-of-color challenge the canon. In *Living Chicana theory*, ed. Carla Trujillo, 352–70. Berkeley, Calif.: Third Woman Press.

Schiller, N. G. 1997. The place of race. *Identities: Global Studies in Culture and Power* 3(4): 449–56.

Schlesinger, A. M., Jr. 1993. *The disuniting of America: Reflections on a multicultural society*. London: W. W. Norton.

Scott, J. 1998. Before the White race was invented. *Against the Current* 72: 46–49.

Segal, D. A., and R. Handler. 1995. U.S. multiculturalism and the concept of culture. *Identities: Global Studies in Culture and Power* 1(4): 391–407.

Sleeper, J. 1991. A political paradox. *Democratic Left* 19(4): 5–6.

Winant, H. 1997. Behind blue eyes: Whiteness and contemporary U.S. racial politics. In *Off white: Readings on race, power and society*, ed. M. Fine, L. Weis, L. C. Powell, and L. M. Wong, 40–53. New York: Routledge.

Wood, E. M. 1997. A reply to A. Sivanandan: "Globalization or globaloney"? *Monthly Review* 48(9): 21–32.

5

Globalization, Class, and Multiculturalism: Fragments from a Red Notebook

If this were a dictatorship it'd be a heck of a lot easier.

—George W. Bush

You're Fired!

THE VICTORY OF GLOBAL CAPITALISM over its Cold War adversaries has arrived with Bourbon Street reverie. The bowels of destiny have become unblocked, and history has been set in motion once again. While the challenge of turning the country into one giant theme park to entertain the ruling class has not yet been met in all corners of the globe, the opposition is withering away by the minute. More and more countries are donning what William Greider (2000, 14) has called globalization's "golden straightjacket" of "follow our orders, and we will make you rich (someday)"—forced austerity programs orchestrated by institutions such as the International Monetary Fund that dictate what foreign governments may or may not do and pile-driven assaults on the public assets of poor countries by the World Bank.

Despite all the frenzy and fanfare surrounding the promises of free trade, it remains the case that both advanced and developed countries have been hurt by globalization. Only a few metropolitan centers and select social strata have benefited, and it is no secret who these select occupants are. It's not the case that the poor are next in line to become millionaires. That's not part of the overall scheme. The success of *The Apprentice*, like the success of neoliberal capitalism, has brought with it Donald Trump's repressed double, the unemployed worker who returns to visit the scene of his firing to do some "firing" of his own, only this time through the barrel of an automatic rifle as he guns down his ex-boss and fellow workers. No, the poor are not next in line to enter free-market heaven. Any economic security they once enjoyed has been extirpated by neoliberal capitalism and the mistaken historical verdict that free-trade initiatives assist the economic advancement of developing countries.

In fact, the poor are completely written out of the script; they serve as permanent extras for the background shots for larger millionaire *novelas* of fame for the lucky few and misery and poverty for the unlucky many. We cannot all be soap opera millionaires like Victor Newman who live in the magic realism of our mid-afternoon reveries. But we can become anticapitalist activists. The functional integration among production, trade, global financial markets, and transport and speed technologies that make financial transactions instantaneous has facilitated the redeployment of capital to "least-cost" locations that enable exploitation on the basis of advantages it will bring to those wishing to become part of the "Millionaires-Я-Us Club." Or a lead actor in *The Young and the Restless*.

As global assembly lines increase and as speculative and financial capital strikes across national borders in commando-like assaults ("move in, take the goods, and move out"), the state continues to experience difficulty in managing economic transactions but has not yet detached itself from the infrastructure of corporate imperialism. Transnational corporations and private financial institutions—Gold Card members of the leading worldwide bourgeoisie—have formed what Robinson and Harris (2000) call a "transnational capitalist clan." And while the emergent global capitalist historic bloc is marked by contradictions in terms of how to achieve regulatory order in the current global economy, national capitals and nation-states continue to reproduce themselves. Home markets have not disappeared from the scene since they continue to provide ballast for the imperialist state through ensuring the general conditions for international production and exchange.

Liberal democracies like to pretend that the state is a separate and autonomous sphere of activity because that way they can set up convenient smokescreens against the internal workings of the capitalist production process. They can also prevent the staggering exposure of capitalism's zero-sum game and hinder our understanding of the invidious ways in which the state actually functions to sustain and promote the capitalist system. Not to mention the ways in which the state locates blame within individuals (they are too lazy, ignorant, or unskilled) rather than within their material conditions of existence (i.e., the value form of wealth that is historically specific to capitalism). Within liberal democracies, individuals are conveniently held responsible for their own poverty as blame is shifted away from the capitalist race to the bottom to see who can prosper with the minimum or lowest standards of social and economic justice as well as environmental protection and sustainability. The blame is always shifted away from the means by which surplus value is created through the internal or dialectical relation that exists between labor and capital—that is, away from the way workers are locked into an internal and antagonistic relation to capital in the most alienating and dehumanizing of ways—and away from the fact that exploitation is a constitutive feature of the capitalist production process (Allman 2001).

The globalization of capitalism is not in any way accountable to democratic interest, yet its cheerleaders have hidden its diabolical nature behind the non sequitur claim that the free market promotes democracy. In fact, self-determining governments only get in the way of the goal of transnational corporations, which is "to open all domestic markets, natural resources, built infrastructures, and labor pools of all societies of the world to foreign transnational control without the barrier of self-determining government and people in the way" (McMurtry 1999, 58). The real agenda of transnational corporations is, in other words, to create an antiwelfare capitalism with a human face while drawing attention away from the paradoxical congeniality of capitalism and its repressed underside.

Homo Homini Lupus: The McLaw of Value

Today we can't simply talk about the capitalist law of value, but we rather need to address the "McLaw of value" where a corporation that sells hamburgers has more clout under the North American Free Trade Agreement than many governments of the so-called Third World. Why is it that the World Trade Organization can determine that a corporation such as Time Warner AOL can sue the government of India if it permits an underground market in compact discs by Michael Jackson but remains silent about enforcing human rights and conditions for workers (Collins and Yeskel 2000)? Imperialism has arrived unannounced, this time in a Vegas-style stretch limousine where financial oligarchs and their banker servants and parvenus plot ways to accelerate the concentration of capital and the formation of monopolies, oblivious to the economic refugees languishing on skid row, their shopping carts in tow. But this kind of information will never make the evening news precisely because it draws attention to what McMurtry (1998, 1999) calls the money death sequence of value—the global market's value imperialism.[1]

McMurtry asserts that free-market democracy is a self-certifying term premised on the most odious of lies. Corporations steward us in the direction of market doctrine, a doctrine legitimized by its baptism in the fire of commodity production. He asks, Who are the producers? They are, after all, owners of private capital who purchase the labor of those that produce, including, notes McMurtry (1999), "that of white-collar managerial and technical workers" (174). While some investing owners may also be producers—paying themselves as managers in addition to the remuneration they receive as owners—most corporate "producers" do not actually produce goods. These owners have no roles in the production process and are constituted as fictitious legal entities or "corporate persons." The real producers—the workers—are reduced to faceless "factors of production" employed by the owners of production. There is no freedom for the actual producers within the "free-market economy." This is because the real producers belong to the employer, where they serve as the instruments of the employer's will. What little freedom exists is located at the top levels of management, but even here freedom exists "only so far as it conforms to the ruling command of maximizing profitability for stockholders and owners" (175). McMurtry maintains that obedience to the market god has been perceived as the only path to freedom and fulfillment. He writes,

> Freedom is not simply a slogan, but requires an option to do other than what is prescribed. Few agents of the market system are in truth free, even those at the top. In the end, then, only the "free market" itself is free or self-regulating. As in other fundamentalist creeds, however, obedience to this god is conceived as the acme of personal freedom and self-realization. (178)

The present generation has been sacrificed in advance to the globalization of capital. This poses a major dilemma for teachers and cultural workers. Why try to help young people adapt to a system that is designed to exclude them? As Viviane Forrester (1999) has noted, education under capitalism has caught today's youth in the fabrications and deceits of history, teaching them "about the rudiments of a life already denied to them, an already confiscated life, a life of which they are deprived in advance [and a life no longer viable anyway]" (70). The system does provide roles for our young people, but these are mostly roles as castaways or as pariahs. They are roles as people who have no roles, *los oluidados*, the lost generation, the walking dead. How is it possible to teach today's youth to become part of the very society that rejects them (Giroux 2000a, 2000b)?

The current mind-set of global capitalism can, in fact, be traced to the Trilateral Commission of 1973 (composed of the world's leading corporate chief executive officers, academics, government officials, and so on), who argued that there existed "an excess of democracy" in the Western world and who advocated the legitimacy of hierarchy, coercion, discipline, secrecy, and deception, as well as the noninvolvement of a governable democracy (McMurtry 1999). Mutagenic capitalist values have transmogrified into a social ethos, making it easier for flimflam financial ventures to proliferate, breaking the tenuous accord that has long existed between labor and capital. Adam Smith's notion of the market as a servant of the public good through the shared "wealth of nations" has now achieved the status of a good joke in bad taste. Arching over the blandishments of the value program of the global market is the aerosol figure of George "Dubya" Bush, who is not merely content to have stolen the

election through voter cleansing in his brother Jeb's state of Florida but is determined to realize his potential for manifest delusion and to exercise a stubborn willingness to give away billions of dollars of tax cuts to the wealthiest 1
percent of the population. Bush not only lacks moral intelligence, but he serves
as an understudy for such a lack. He's already upstaged Dan Quayle in the
"wasted mind" department, but it no longer remains to be seen what his boss,
Dick Cheney, has in mind for him. Propped up as a compassionate tough guy
vessel through which Lord Jesus orders the United States into the bloody theater of battle, Bush Jr. is the perfect leader to combat the unwashed barbarians
and to take their country's natural resources from their unworthy hands.

Globalization or Globalony?

How has the globalization of capital fared? The economic performance of industrial countries under globalization in the 1980s and 1990s is much poorer
than during the 1950s and 1960s, when they operated under a more regulated
social-market economy (Singh 2000). Economic growth, as well as growth in
gross domestic product, has been lowered, and productivity has been cut in
half; in addition, unemployment has risen dramatically in countries who are
part of the Organization for Economic Cooperation and Development.

That the United States has fared better on the issue of unemployment than
Western European countries cannot be attributed to the less flexible labor
markets of the latter or on the information technologies revolution. In the
case of Japan and Korea, their periods of fast economic growth, poverty reduction, and raises in the standard of living was under managed trade and
capital controls, not laissez-faire evangelism. When Korea, Malaysia, and Indonesia, for example, liberalized their external capital flows, they suffered economic meltdowns (Singh 2000).

Latin American countries that have liberalized their trading and external
capital regimes have suffered from fallouts and from severe financial crises, including the peso crisis of 1994–1995 in Mexico and the "Samba effect" of 1999
in Brazil. Latin American countries following the Washington consensus have,
since the late 1980s, experienced a long-term growth rate reduction from 6
percent per annum to 3 percent per annum (Singh 2000).

The battle over free trade is not only about profits. It's also about manufacturing ideology. Globalization has been a dismal failure for the vast majority
of the world's capitalist nations. Yet the corporate elite refuse to concede defeat. In fact, they are boldly claiming victory and, furthermore, that history is
on their side. In a sense they are correct. But we have to understand that they
are speaking for themselves. They have been victorious. In fact, they've made
millions. The question remains, At whose expense?

Global capitalism has won the battle over ideology hands down. Global capitalist monocracy has declared itself victorious over socialist and communist ideologies. The latter are being auctioned off at Sotheby's as relics of class struggle from bygone eras to be archived in museums dedicated to democracy's victory over the evil empires spawned by Mr. Marx. For now, capitalism has succeeded in steering the wheels of history to the far Right, to a head-on collision with the reigning neoliberal bloc, where postmodernized signposts on the streets declare the triumph of privatization over socialization, individualism over collectivism, lifestyle identity politics over class politics, cynicism over hope, and barbarism over civilization.

The decaying carcass of communism lies in its red iron casket, only to have grave robbers from the International Monetary Fund stir its bones by removing anything left of monetary value. It wouldn't surprise us if statues of Lenin have been melted down to produce slot machine tokens for Las Vegas gamblers. Fading socialist dreams in the form of Soviet memorabilia can be purchased by credit card on the Internet by graying radicals from 1968 (the *acht und sechziger*).

Capitalism has become our ticket to the gaudy world of tinsel dreams and chloroformed hope, to a subterranean public sphere where *American Psycho* replaces Che Guevara as the icon of the postmodern revolution. Under the beguiling eye of "high-stakes" financial investors, a two-tiered laboring class has been created, with low-skill, low-paid service workers toiling alongside a small segment of highly skilled and well-paid workers. For the millions of people whose lives remain commodified and regulated in the charnel house of "fast-track" capital accumulation and its seductive companion, consumer ideology, the clearly visible contradictions within capitalist social and economic relations of production have become too obvious to be recognized. They have been naturalized as common sense. After all, the buying and selling of human lives as commodities—the creation of what Marx called "wage slaves"—must be guaranteed as a constitutive factor of our democracy, so this condition is carefully disguised as a "voluntary contractual agreement," even though the only alternatives to shaking the sweaty palm of the market's invisible hand are starvation, disease, and death. Liberals and conservatives alike love to heap fulsome praise on the United States as the world's bastion of freedom while ignoring the fact that its grandiloquent dream for saving the world has been a dismal failure and has unleashed a hyper-Leviathan among the aggrieved populations of humanity. For the most part, our public servants (who have personal servants) have chosen to disregard abysmal disparities between effort and reward that accompany real existing capitalism. Marxists know otherwise. Beneath the myth of meritocracy that undergirds the American dream and that locksteps with images of happy consumers in a breathless quest for an earthy paradise lurks the enslaved consciousness of primitive patriotism and the increasing polarization between the rich and the destitute. The only "free" cheese is in the mousetrap. To be free from necessity is a constitutive impossibility within a "democratic" structure of private appropriation and corporate commodification. To be "free" in an advanced capitalist economy means being free to choose between being the exploiter and being the exploited. The backwardness of the economies on the periphery has become a necessary condition for the flourishing of the economies of the center (Kagarlitsky 2000, 58).

Postmodern theorists recognize these contradictions but are largely unable to develop a counterhegemonic politics except by restructuring their observations to the cultural plane and thereby obfuscating the political economy of real existing capitalism. Neil Larsen (2000) warns that

> at best, the culturalist account of globalization results in mere descriptivism—e.g., the work of Garcia Canclini. At worst—e.g., Baudrillard or Bhabha—it results in the kind of pseudo-theory that simply reads off certain of the lateral effects of globalization (e.g., the hybridization of national cultures or the manipulation of global opinion through the mass dissemination of CNN-type "news" simulacra) as the fantasmagorical sites for its subversion or its eternal replication. This is reified thinking taken to the extreme of mistaking the empty shell of a globalized commodity form for the social, human content that it progressively fails to contain. (14)

The social and political antagonisms haunting capitalism today are manifold and can be discerned by utilizing the optic of historical materialist critique. On the one hand, we witness firsthand the vast profusion of material resources able to sustain the livelihood of the 6 billion inhabitants of the earth and provide basic necessities including full employment, housing, and health care. On the other hand, the growing bipolarization and the overaccumulation of capital by the new breed of opulent gangster capitalists from reigning global mafiacracies has reduced the odds of surviving hunger, poverty, malnutrition, famine, and disease for a growing segment of working-class men, women, and children who are now joining the ranks of the urban ghettos and global slum dwellers in their *casas de carton* all over the world. We are talking not only about Calcutta and Rio de Janeiro but also about our own urban communities from New York to Los Angeles.

Instead of celebrating growing economic democracy worldwide, we are facing growing inequality the proportions of which stagger the imagination. As Willie Thompson (1997) notes, "The trend is precisely in the opposite direction, towards intensified polarization, the concentration of misery, suffering, deprivation and hopelessness at the lower end of the scale, mirrored by exorbitant and unceasing accumulation [of capital] at the other pole" (224–25). Whether by increasing the extortion of absolute surplus value through the proliferation of maquiladoras along the U.S.–Mexican *frontera* or increasing relative surplus value extortion through increasing the productivity of labor and reducing the value of labor power, capitalism continues to hold living human labor hostage, fetishizing its own commodity logic and valorization process and recasting the world into its own image. Value—the medium and the outcome of abstract labor—binds individuals to the vertigo of its law of motion. Like Ahab, lifelessly thrashing about on the body of Moby Dick as the White Beast submerges itself into the icy fathoms of eternity, we are carried into the future on the backs of our worst nightmare, in a ghoulish parody of life. Spawned in the social universe of capital, our nightmares chart the course of civilization, illuminated by the dark lamp of history.

According to James Petras (2000), "The boom in the U.S. is fueled in part by an exaggerated speculative bubble that is unsustainable. Stocks are vastly overvalued; savings are negative and the performance of the productive economy has no relation to the paper economy" (16). He further notes that it is clear "that one quarter of the capitalist world cannot prosper when three quarters are in deep crisis—the laws of capitalist accumulation cannot operate in such restricted circumstances" (16).

Teresa Ebert (2001) captures the understanding of globalization that we wish to underscore in this chapter when she describes globalization as the unfolding of capitalism's central contradiction: the separation of the worker from the product of her labor. Ebert is worth quoting at length:

> Globalization . . . is . . . above all, about the structured inequality in the contemporary world, and contesting theories of globalization are really contestations over how to understand and engage this material inequality. . . . Globalization, as Marx and Engels describe it, is a dialectical process. Contrary to its official propaganda, globalization is in no way a remedy for inequality. It reinforces inequality: the fact that it provides jobs for the jobless in no way means that it changes the social relations of production. In fact, globalization is the internationalization of these social relations of production—the internationalization of class structures. (390, 399)

Teresa Ebert has provided a lucid and incisive "materialist" critique of two approaches to globalization—what she calls the globalization-as-transnationalism argument and the political theory of globalization. The former representation of globalization refers to the putative emergence of a new world community based on a shared cosmopolitanism and culture of consumption. This perspective shares a culture and a state orientation. The cultural orientation emphasizes global symbolic exchanges relating to values, preferences, and tastes rather than material inequality and class relations. It is essentially a form of cultural logic. The focus on the state explores the relationship between the local and the global and whether globalization means the reorganization or disappearance of the nation-state. The political theories of globalization generally argue about the sovereign status of the nation-state. They maintain that local legal codes, local currencies, and local habits and customs that enable the rise of capitalism now serve as constraints on capital so that now the new transnational institutions more suitable to the new phase of capitalism are developing.

Ebert's materialist conception of globalization maintains that both cultural and political theories of globalization bury issues of production and labor under questions of consumption of the market. Here, consumption is effectively naturalized as questions of taste, value preference, and sensibilities erase the more fundamental issue of labor and production. Ebert rightly stresses the importance of production and highlights what the politics of globalization is really about: the continuous privatization of the means of production and the creation of expanding markets for capital and the creation of a limitless market of highly skilled and very cheap labor so that capitalists can maintain their competitive rate of profit. In short, this process is all about the internationalization of capitalist relations of exploitation.

Is History Having Fun Yet? Are We Already Tired of the Future?

The fall of the Berlin Wall and the cataclysmic social and political implosions in Russia and Eastern European countries coincides with the premature "end-of-ideology" proclamations and correlative self-canceling pronouncements about the end of history hailed by conservative social theorists such as Francis Fukuyama. In classic red-baiting style, Fukuyama has announced the end of revolutionary movements and the demise of socialism altogether. However, in their mad dash toward capitalist utopia, the growing lumpen-proletariats in Russia and in ex-socialist European countries, drunk on the prospect of get-rich-quick schemes and of reaping enormous windfalls, are stumbling over the balmy corpse of Lenin and learning the lessons of privatization and the empty promises of market socialism the hard way. According to Arrighi, Hopkins, and Wallerstein (2001), "The hold of Milton Friedman on the hearts and minds of his Eastern European and Soviet disciples" is so considerable, and their embrace of the monetarist ideology of the West is so maddeningly strong, that they "have to yet realize that this road is leading them—or at least most of them—not the promised land of North America but to the harsher realities of South America or worse" (43).

Of course, workers in Russia and the former Eastern bloc countries are not the only ones being deceived by capitalism's promises of prosperity. Thousands of workers in Latin American countries whose dictators borrowed from the World Trade Organization—and who stealthily pocketed most of the profits— are suffering through imposed austerity programs in which they have been made to assume repayment of international loans. If the postmodernists want to brag about the disappearance of the U.S. working class and celebrate the new culture of lifestyle consumption, then they need to acknowledge that the so-called disappearing working class is reappearing again in the assembly lines of China, Brazil, Indonesia, and elsewhere, where there exist fewer impediments to U.S. profit making (Žižek 2000).

The world's greatest exponent of class struggle, Karl Marx, still remains under attack (in itself not such a surprising observation). The opponent grabbing the headlines this time is a prominent spokesperson for evolutionary psychology. Maintaining that the Talmud and Tanakh has, over the centuries, ordered Jews to adopt an unconscious eugenics program by insisting that they practice endogamy in order to remain racially pure, Professor Kevin Mac-Donald of California State University, Long Beach, has recently and infamously argued that Jewish emphasis on group cooperation has resulted in Jews having significantly higher IQs than other ethnic groups (Ortega 2000).

Used by publicity-hungry British historian David Irving as an expert witness in a libel lawsuit against Professor Deborah Lipstadt and Penguin Books (a case in which Irving claimed that there were no gas chambers at Auschwitz and, fortunately, a case that he lost), MacDonald not only argued that Judaism is an evolutionary group strategy used to discipline genes as part of a social program of increasing Jewish intelligence beyond other groups and thus ensuring group survival (a strategy that he claims was copied by the Nazis in their philosophy of Aryan superiority developed as a defense against the Jews) but also accused Marxism of being a subversive Jewish-controlled intellectual movement responsible for untold deaths: "In the 20th century many millions of people have been killed in the attempt [by Jews] to establish Marxist societies based on the ideal of complete economic and social leveling, and millions of people have been killed as a result of the failure of Jewish assimilation into European societies" (MacDonald, cited in Ortega 2000, 14).

Here we see both bad science and racist logic taken to the nauseating heights of actually blaming the Holocaust on the Jews themselves and blaming the victims of so-called Marxist regimes on Jewish political theory. Isn't this the same logic that drives today's post-9/11 hatred of Arabs and Muslims by defenders of Western civilization? Aren't Palestinians blamed for fostering hatred as an evolutionary component of their survival? The Cold War may be over, but science has a way of returning, time and time again, to the scene of history's greatest crimes and persecuting its victims all over again.

Technology as Snake Oil

Despite the collapse of any significant opposition movements to neoliberal capitalism, educators have been encouraged to be optimistic as they navigate their way through the first precarious stage of the new millennium. Even though the contradictions of capitalism abound, as the homeless stand shoulder to shoulder with the affluent on the crowded streets of our urban megalopolises, teachers still cling to the Malthusian dream of living in the best of all possible worlds. Such engineered optimism and its accompanying incapacity for dissent has helped capitalism survive for decades through a low-intensity democracy, driven by pitiless bureaucrats who provide just enough equality to keep people from taking to the streets in acts of civil disobedience.

But even this unstated alliance among ruling interests is breaking down, as recent anti–World Trade Organization events in Seattle and Washington, D.C., attest. While Jean-Bertrand Aristide (2000) can note that "history moves in waves—we cannot always live on the crests" (56), the planet remains ill prepared for the impact that the crisis of globalization is currently having on the already poverty-stricken. If the situation already appears out of control, what will happen when we face the Tsunami that will smother vast populations when capital's comet comes crashing from its heavenly heights, smack into the swirling ocean of economic uncertainty?

Teachers are told that they are entering a new postindustrial, high-tech information era that will usher in a gilded age of prosperity for themselves and their students. As James Petras (2000) notes, however, this characterization of current economic conditions is patently false since computer industries represent less than 3 percent of the economy. The electronic superhighway permits financial capital to move with the speed of greased lightning. As capitalism strives to "annihilate . . . space with time" (Marx 1973, 539), it displaces labor in North America while increasing exploitation in Latin America. In this predominantly financial-industrial economy, government leaders in league with privateers and laissez-faire evangelists like to hype the information age–era stuff because in doing so it is easier for them to generate false optimism about the future and to draw attention away from the fact that prosperity is largely confined to speculative-financial and real estate sectors of the capitalist class at a time when retrenchment by the state is draining resources from the poor and redirecting them to already bulging pockets of the rich.

By creating a facade of information-era utopianism through carnival-like hucksterism that accompanies the corporate invasion of our classrooms, calls for educators to be converted into McTeachers, and the growth of a computer technology millenarianism that assures salvation through Internet consciousness, potential criticism can be siphoned away from the fact that we live in a monstrous era. It is an era controlled by monopolistic giants, greedy conglomerates, snake oil privateers, and selective protectionists who support massive state subsidies, the selling off of public enterprises to private monopolies, welfare for the rich, domestic and overseas multibillion-dollar money laundering, arms industry domination of the export sector, and the placing of key state institutions under the influence of financial sectors of civil society—in short, an era populated by capitalist Overworlders who support the creation of a social order in which class warfare runs amok (Petras 2000).

Teachers are also taught that the Internet will "equalize" society by abolishing the borders between the rich and the poor. That is yet another myth. Borders are not transcended but reinscribed. The Internet is supposed to dissolve distance through simultaneity. Yet, as Randy Martin (1999) notes, information and communication technology has created a spatial unevenness "characterized by densities of access and vast exclusions" (10). Such technology reinscribes boundaries—especially when those boundaries occur within those strata with "high regime status" (10). Martin notes importantly that the "info-poor and hidden masses are a spatial effect of technology and not merely those next in the queue to get on-line" (10).

Of course, the marketization, privatization, and neoliberalization of schooling is functionally advantageous to the previously described conditions. Although it has been smuggled in under cover of a revival of the democratic imperative of privatization, schooling has been reduced to a subsector of the economy and continues to provide ballast for existing discourses and practices of class exploitation and white supremacist heteronormative patriarchy (Cole 1998; Hill 1999; Rikowski 1997).

What we are saying certainly is no longer a secret. What is new is the stage-managed resignation that has accompanied the news. When we learn that Latino students are twice as likely as African Americans and three times as likely as whites to drop out of high school or that, in 1997, 25.3 percent of Latinos aged sixteen to twenty-four dropped out of high school compared with 13.4 percent of African Americans and 7.6 percent of whites (McQueen 2000), the information registers but somehow ceases to enrage us. Part of the reason for this is that exploitation through the capitalist marketplace has been so naturalized and the pauperization of the state so dehistoricized and de-politicized that we have learned to accept a certain amount of exploitation and accompanying forms of racism and sexism and homophobia. We feel that it is an inevitable part of living in a developed capitalist democracy.

What we fail to grasp is that capitalism and democracy actually work against each other and that the familiar coupling of the two words is really just a form of linguistic—hence ideological—mystification. We guess that rationale is, If we keep hearing the term "capitalist democracy" frequently enough, we will begin to believe that the two terms are inseparable and unconsciously strip the terms of their association with domination. (This strategy was successful in convincing the public that Iraq was responsible for the attacks of 9/11.)

In fact, the two terms need to be torn apart, not yoked together. Maybe another adjective needs to precede the term "democracy." Maybe "socialist democracy" is a more appropriate coupling for those who wish to make democracy live up to its egalitarian ideals. But since we have been enculturated throughout the Cold War to get a headache even at the mere mention of the word "socialism," it is unlikely we will ever see the topic of "socialist democracy" appear with any mounting regularity in the journals devoted to educational reform, at least not anytime soon.

California is often a precursor to the dominant scenarios of U.S. futurity. It is the state that passes propositions (such as 187, 209, and 227) that routinely are given birth through a marriage of political Monday-morning quarterbacks in the form of rich businessmen such as Ron Unz and manic, mean-spirited, right-wing populists such as Pete Wilson and his ilk, including Arnold Schwarzenegger, bane of all "girlie men" politicians. California's political initiatives often serve as political harbingers for a politics that will eventually spread throughout other states like a runaway contagion, mixing racism, sexism, bourgeois historical amnesia, class arrogance, and homophobia into a political cocktail as wickedly dangerous as any biological weapon invented by the Pentagon.

California is a state that generates a lot of tension around educational reform—a tension that can be traced largely to mind-numbing ethnocentrism, Anglo elitism, and social frameworks of perception and classification that are inextricably connected to the current climate of Latinophobia. This is not hard to understand in an antagonistic geopolitical arena where scapegoating immigrants from Mexico is a common and accepted practice. California is also where the English Only movement is gaining momentum.

Donaldo Macedo (2000) captures the absurdity of the English Only proponents who argue that English is the most effective language for citizens of the United States and that it is the language that will best guarantee a successful future:

> First, if English is the most effective educational language, how can we explain why over 60 million Americans are illiterate or functionally illiterate? Second, if English Only education can guarantee linguistic minorities a better future, as educators like William Bennett promise, why do the majority of Black Americans, whose ancestors have been speaking English for over two hundred years, find themselves still relegated to the ghettos? (16)

In the midst of the widening scenario of immigrant bashing, it is not difficult to make the case that democracy has been discountenanced, its attempts at civic renewal and invigoration of the public sphere rendered detumescent. Two types of reactions predominate. The first is to engage in a half revolution through "reformist" efforts, underwritten by a teleological belief in the evolution of democracy through the free market. The second is to engage in political activism that cuts deeply into the heart of neoliberalism, corporate control of the schooling process, and capitalist relations of exploitation. While the former beggars the praxis of critical struggle, the latter lacks a coherent national and international strategy.

Neoliberalism lingers on with the lethal stubborness of spent uranium in a U.S. military armor-piercing shell. With the exception of a handful of successful antiglobalization campaigns, opposition to neoliberalism has been muted, thanks to the military Keynesianism of the Bush administration and before that, to the polished statecraft of Bill Clinton and his successful cheerleading for an unfettered free market, in the form of a Third Way détente between Keynesian economics and ultracapitalism. Opposition has also been blunted through the efforts and cagey triumphalism of New Right apologists of the free market. The colonial apotheosis of the Bush administration and Pentagon hawks—and the brain-stunting reactionary populism of their political platforms—has met with a lack of any real spirited opposition among the educational Left. But this is due partly to lack of any rival oppositions to global capitalism either nationally or on a world scale. For the foreseeable future, the Left has painted itself into a corner. But it can truck with pessimism for only so long.

Capitalism and the New Racism

The ideology of the new racism no longer operates on biological premises. Rather, it incorporates notions of culture and nation as a justification for white supremacy. The new racism functions as a form of anti-antiracism that opposes "racial privileges" granted to people of color and minorities. And while it explicitly insists that it endorses an inclusionary politics, it implicitly embraces an exclusionary politics nonetheless. For example, it dismisses affirmative action on the basis that it impedes the social and economic mobility of people of color (Ansell 1997).

The New Right's agenda is couched within liberal and progressive discourses that celebrate "difference." However, there is a distinction between right-wing and progressive uses of this term. While a liberal and progressive celebration of differences is aimed at promoting a limited inclusionary politics ("we need to respect the voices of those who are racially and culturally different"), the New Right's celebration of difference ("we are all different, but if we strive to embrace the same conservative political ideology, those differences won't divide us but will reinforce traditional values") is intended to advance an exclusionary politics. The regulating discourse becomes, You *can* be different but on our terms (that is, those set by the white ruling class). If you follow our ground rules, we will celebrate your difference. If you don't, then you can suffer the consequences. Consequently, the New Right's emphasis on "difference" is aimed at harmonizing racial and class privileges in order to evade issues related to property relations by its appeal to an abstract liberal universalism (Ansell 1997).

We take a cautionary step away from crude versions of identity politics—which by and large are situated within essentialist discourses—by arguing that they are incapable of contesting the new racism. While proponents of identity politics align themselves with antiessentialist discourses in their call for "difference," in practice they end up reinforcing existing social relations of exploitation and promoting a politics as exclusionary as the New Right agenda they ostensibly contest. As Linda Gordon (1999) notes,

> Indeed, while calling attention to the need to acknowledge that others have different experiences, "difference" has had a chilling effect on the struggle to recognize connection. At its worst it suggests that communication is impossible, and may thus make actual communicative experience suspect. It may even deter efforts to communicate, which require asking direct questions, risking expressions of ignorance, rejecting the discourse of personal guilt. Just as seriously, difference talk leads us away from specifying the relationships that give rise to gender, racial, class, and many other inequalities and alienations. We need to ask for much, much more than merely respecting difference. (47)

Today the economic and racial privileges of the dominant social classes are couched within conservative and right-wing discourses that claim that poverty and racism(s) are related to the lack of moral and ethical character of individuals rather than the consequence of social and material conditions that individuals and social groups inherit from one generation to the next.

In contrast to the feudal nobility in Europe who conceived their social privileges as natural rights granted to them at birth, today's privileged classes view themselves as possessing the "proper" beliefs, attitudes, and values that only cultivated individuals can acquire through generations of "good breeding." Former Secretary of Education William Bennett believes that our "common culture" is based on moral virtues that all dedicated citizens willing to undertake serious introspection (the kind that can serve as a moral purgative) can acquire regardless of their race, class, and gender background. Bennett (1992) argues,

> Even social scientists now recognize the importance of sound values and moral norms in the upbringing of children. Empirical studies confirm what most people, because of their basic common sense, already know. What determines a young person's behavior in academic, sexual, and social life are his deeply held convictions and beliefs. They determine behavior far more than race, class, and economic background, or ethnicity. (35)

In *The German Ideology*, Marx and Engels (1995) noted that the ruling ideas, values, and beliefs of every epoch represent the ideas, values, and beliefs of the ruling social classes. The particular social and economic interests of the ruling social classes are projected as a representation of the universal interests of all the social classes in society. The call for a "common culture" that is vigorously supported by conservatives such as Bennett [more on Bennett in chapter 9] consists of moral values and beliefs that legitimize individualism and the property rights of the ruling classes. Marx and Engels (1995) emphasized this relationship in no uncertain terms:

> For each new class which puts itself in the place of one ruling before it, is compelled, merely in order to carry through its aim, to represent its interest as the common interest of all members of society, that is, expressed in ideal form: it has to give its ideas the form of universality, and represent them as the only rational, universally valid ones. (66)

Bennett (1992) makes claims to universality similar to those of the ruling classes chastised by Marx and Engels, asserting, "Our common culture is not something manufactured by the upper stratum of society in the elegant salons of Washington, New York, or Cambridge. Rather, it embodies truths that most Americans can recognize and examine for themselves" (34). Here Bennett fails to note that the self-evidentiary character of this "common sense" is due to its ideological embeddedness in ruling class interests. Furthermore, how would Bennett explain his own addition to high-stakes casino gambling?

Unlike the former Soviet Union, Canada, Yugoslavia, and Lebanon—all of which have experienced political, cultural, and economic turmoil—Americans, notes Bennett (1992), are indebted to a "common culture," described as a distinctive national trait that has kept Americans united and indivisible. Bennett views the "common culture" as a social and cultural "immunological system" that protects and preserves Western values and traditions and fosters a commitment to a multicultural and diverse U.S. society. Bennett, of course, acknowledges that *some* multicultural curricula are a necessary component of the public school curriculum. In his opinion, however, a multicultural curriculum should be one that "better reflects the contributions of individuals of different races and backgrounds to the richness of America" (194). Further, Bennett warns against progressives, Left-liberals, and Afrocentrists who seek to politicize the multicultural curriculum and threaten the "common culture" that we all share—or the "civic glue" of our nation—by distorting American history. Finally, Bennett stresses that schools as social institutions have the burden of transmitting traditional common cultural values and beliefs from one generation to the next.

Other conservatives express similar views to Bennett, yet they are often dressed up in different types of argument. In his national best-seller *Cultural Literacy: What Every American Needs to Know* (1988), E. D. Hirsch attempts to link common national culture with civic literacy. Hirsch's program mandates that all students learn 5,000 facts, ideas, and concepts—many reflecting Western and Eurocentric traditional values and beliefs. In contrast to Bennett, who claims that social inequality is the result of the lack of moral character of individuals, Hirsch links social and economic disparities with cultural illiteracy.

According to Hirsch (1988), access to social and economic opportunities for individuals will naturally increase, regardless of an individual's race or class background, only "if one learns the background information and the linguistic convictions that are needed to read, write, and speak effectively" (22). However, in his critique of Hirsch, Bob Peterson (1995) notes that "while he [Hirsch] talks about the 'classless character of cultural literacy' he virtually ignores the history, tradition, and literature of and about the working class and other marginalized groups and their conflicts with dominant society" (78). Hirsch also argues that cultural literacy has reduced class inequality and has eradicated, for the most part, barriers toward equal opportunity. In short, Hirsch (1988) believes that cultural literacy linked with a national culture has had a positive "liberalizing and democratic effect" (91).

Though Hirsch agrees that students should be exposed to multicultural education, he believes that it should be "valuable in itself." In other words, multicultural education is valuable to the extent that it instills tolerance and acceptance of other cultures and traditions and at the same time provides a glowing perspective on Western traditions and cultures. Hirsch firmly believes that multicultural education should not replace national culture, one that is based on traditional Western values and beliefs passed down from one generation to the next. Traditional cultural values are, for Hirsch, fixed, permanent, and tamper-proofed, hermetically sealed from conflicting interpretations. Such a view collides with a critical multicultural perspective which views values as situated within a permanent agon between conflicting positions linked to the division of labor under capitalism.

In *The Closing of the American Mind* (1987), Allan Bloom maintains that the basis for democracy should be located in the natural rights of men and women. Natural rights such as freedom, justice, and the common good are, for Bloom, the most effective means of eliminating differences of class, race, and religion. Bloom supports his arguments by referring to the seventeenth-century political philosopher John Locke, who suggested that natural rights supported the right to private property. According to Locke, property is the fundamental reason why men and women leave their "natural state" and establish a "civil society." A critical multiculturalism challenges the origins of Lockean natural rights that Bloom adamantly defends by raising the following questions: Are these natural rights shared by all Americans? Does Bloom's discourse on natural rights function as a method of masquerading the property rights and social privileges that the dominant social classes have gained at the expense of the exploitation and oppression of minorities, the working class, immigrants, and other marginalized social groups?

Bloom advocates an assimilationist posture regarding U.S. immigrants. For instance, he believes that immigrants should be compelled to accept the new American values, tradition, and culture when they enter the United States. This does not mean that they should necessarily give up the customs, traditions, and beliefs that they had left behind but rather that they subordinate these values and beliefs to "new principles." At the heart of Bloom's argument is a support for a form of ethnocentrism that he believes constitutes the foundation of a "good society."

Other conservatives have produced more sophisticated attacks against multiculturalism. An example is Stanley Fish (1997), who rejects the concept of multiculturalism and criticizes both its liberal and its radical interpretations. Fish describes the liberal perspective as "boutique multiculturalism" and the Left's version as "strong multiculturalism." He explains that boutique multiculturalism recognizes the validity of cultures as long as they do not come into contact with one another, while strong multiculturalism, which is endorsed by the Left, is based on a politics of difference, tolerance, and acceptance.

Fish (1997) rejects multiculturalism as a philosophical concept on the grounds that it consists mainly of demographic statistics and data. Thus, he attempts to divert attention from the relationship among politics, history, and economics by claiming that multiculturalism is merely a philosophical abstraction. According to Fish, definitions of multiculturalism are as various as the cultures that create them. There can therefore never be a common definition of multicultural society, only multiple views. He notes that "no one could possibly be a multiculturalist in any interesting and coherent sense" (384). Fish suggests that the most reasonable approach to the multiplicity of cultures in American society is through "inspired adhoccery," that is, finding alternative temporary solutions to cultural differences.

These examples of attacks on multiculturalism and cultural diversity amount in our view to little more than politically calculated strategies for promoting a uniform American culture linked to the economic and political interests of dominant social groups in society (Kincheloe and Steinberg 1997). This ideology of "Americanization" guarantees the preservation of the power and privilege of the dominant social classes. Giroux (1994) notes that "the deadly paradox in the conservative offensive is constructed around a politics of difference that attempts to depoliticize politics while simultaneously politicizing culture" (58).

In light of the current assault on multicultural education, critical educators need to develop a critical multicultural pedagogy linked to an analysis of the social and economic conditions and lived experiences of marginalized groups in society instead of merely emphasizing the importance of cultural differences and racial inclusion (Sleeter 1996). Darder and Torres (1998) point to the lack of any "substantial critique [within multicultural education] of the social relations and structures of capitalism and the relationship of educational practices to the changing conditions of US political economy. The absence of an analysis of the capitalist wage-labor system and class relations with its structural inequalities of income and power is a serious shortcoming" (83).

The politics of personal responsibility advanced by the New Right, coupled with Christian fundamentalism, encourages educators to search for the sources of pain and suffering in their own manifestation of moral and ethical weakness. Similarly, the New Right's rhetoric of personal responsibility combines the imperatives of neoliberalism with Sunday School ethics and moral certitude, transmuting religion into an instrument for manufacturing consent, marketing hope, and decapitating moral and ethical issues from political and economic ones. In doing so, it hides the sins of the bourgeoisie by camouflaging all signs of their class interest behind a perfumed bouquet of compassion.

The Abolition of Whiteness

Spurred on by a lack of opposition to the race, class, gender, and class exploitation that has been bolstered by neoliberal policies worldwide, multicultural education continues to defang its most emancipatory possibilities by calling for diversity in isolation from an interrogation of its center of sameness known as the hegemony of whiteness. It is this sameness that is the distillate of colonialism and the ether of white lies that spikes the very air we breathe.

Slavoj Žižek (2000) has pointed out that in the Left's call for new multiple political subjectivities (for example, race, class, feminist, and religious), the Left asserts its exact opposite—"an underlying all-pervasive same-ness—a non-antagonistic society in which there is room for all manner of cultural communities, lifestyles, religions, and sexual orientations" (39). Žižek reveals that this sameness relies on an antagonistic split.

We believe that the most determinate split in contemporary capitalist society results from the labor–capital relation sustained by white supremacist capitalist patriarchy. This is why we need to join Noel Ignatiev, David Roediger, and others in calling for the abolition of whiteness. We need to recognize (as we have tried to make clear in our work over the years) that there is no positive value that can be given to the social position known as whiteness. The term cannot be recovered or given a positive spin. White people need to disidentify entirely with the white race. To seek any kind of identity with a white race—or political détente—is ill conceived at best.

As Theodore Allen (1994, 1997) notes, the social function of whiteness is social control, a practice that has colonial origins that can be traced back to the assault on tribal affinities, customs, laws, and institutions of Africans, Native

Americans, and Irish by English/British and Anglo-American colonialism. Such insidious practices of social control reduce all members of oppressed groups to one undifferentiated social status beneath that of any member of the colonizing population. With the rise of the abolitionist movement, racial typologies, classification systems, and criteriologies favoring whiteness and demonizing blackness as the lowest status within humanity's "great chain of being" became widespread in order to justify and legitimize the slavery of Africans and ensure the contribution of lifetime chattel bond servitude.

White racial identity found its way into Euro-American consciousness at the end of seventeenth century during a period when the southern plantocracy recognized that African slaves were a more profitable venture than indentured servants who were from primarily impoverished European backgrounds. Thus, by the beginning of the 1700s, half the labor force consisted of slave labor.

While there existed 2 million slave owners in the South by 1860, 75 percent of slaves belonged to 8,000 plantation owners (representing 7 percent of the total slave owners). Moreover, the economic power of the small yet powerful planter class enabled them to wield political power over 5 million Europeans who did not own slaves.

In order to fracture intraclass consciousness between European indentured servants and African slaves, the plantocracy offered the indentured servants a place in the corporate infrastructure of the plantocracy where they were given the role of policing the behavior of the Africans. This also included the right to citizenship and a "white" identity. The theologian Thandeka (1999) identifies this as a form of "white classism." Offering white identity to indentured Europeans allowed them to identify "racially" with the plantation owners. In addition, it manufactured a class illusion by having poor whites identify with the class interests of plantation owners without enjoying any of their economic privileges. Eventually, white racism allowed poor whites to blame Africans for their economic hardships while harmonizing the class conflict between plantation owners and poor whites. While the African slaves were fully aware that they were victims of white racism, poor Europeans failed to recognize that they were the victims of white classism.

By granting racial/corporate membership to the European bond laborer who had the responsibility of preventing rebellion against the dominant center, the corporate state that emerged out of the plantocracy was able to survive and flourish. Poor white laborers were offered membership in the corporate plantocracy in order to control the subalterned nonwhite labor force. Whites were thus given a double role: as workers and as white people. White laborers were given membership at the center of the corporate plantation structure while still serving as a marginalized labor force. By using whiteness as a means of guaranteeing allegiance, the plantocracy secured its hegemony through white solidarity and the integration of labor relations (wage labor, prison labor, and so on) into the white confraternal society, or what Martinot (2000) calls the "overarching white social machine" (50). Whiteness or white solidarity became an "administrative apparatus" of the slave/class economy that served as a "matrix of social cohesion" that located whites "in a structural relation to each other" (52).

Whiteness became such a powerful social position that class struggle often fell short of actually challenging the basis of the corporate structure because such a structure was synonymous with profitability and allegiance. The white working class—in order to become a class in itself and for itself—had, tragically, to exist in collaboration with white capital. White corporate society functioned as the ruling class with respect to the nonwhite people that it exploited. Martinot (2000) further points out that because white workers in the United States have a different relation to black workers (since the former belong to the corporate state) and because the primary relation between white workers and capital is not mainly across the means of production but through a social administrative hierarchy whose purpose is to administer those "Others" who exist outside the corporate state, the idea of working-class struggle aimed at the overthrow of class society "has never made sense to the white working class in the United States" (56) whose resistance to class exploitation rarely attempted to undermine profitability or contested its legitimacy. This helps explain why, in Martinot's words, "Marxism has never extended itself beyond trade union consciousness because it was never able to fathom the structure of white solidarity by which the white working-class was constructed" (56). African Americans today are sometimes granted the status of recognition of black worker but only as "adjuncts to white hegemony" or as "white-by-association" (56).

The initial objective of white racism was not to construct racial boundaries so much as to maintain class relations. Racism was instrumental in protecting Virginia's class structure by ensuring that poor whites and blacks would not recognize their common class interests. In short, racism was an instrument for maintaining and reproducing the plantocracy's property relations. Of course, what transpired throughout the brutal history of European and U.S. imperialism and colonialism was that African Americans became literally denounced and relegated to the bottom tier of a social hierarchy that functioned like a caste system with African Americans being positioned as "untouchables." The brutal torture and murder of African slaves and the history of racism against African Americans up to the present day constitutes one of the world's most shameful legacies. Another of the world's most egregious historical legacies involves the genocidal practices of Europeans and Euro-Americans in the massacre of North America's indigenous peoples. A major driving force in these acts of genocide was conquest and profit.While eliminating capitalism will not bring about the end of racism, it is certainly a necessary step in that direction.

Today "whiteness" has become naturalized as part of our "commonsense" reality. Whiteness is not a unified, homogeneous culture but a social position. As Ignatiev (1998b) comments,

> There is nothing positive about white identity. As James Baldwin said, "As long as you think you're white, there's no hope for you." Whiteness is not a culture. There is Irish culture and Italian culture and American culture; there is youth culture and drug culture and queer culture. There is no such thing as white culture. Shakespeare was *not* white; he was English. Mozart was not white; he was Austrian. Whiteness has nothing to do with culture and everything to do with social position. Without the privileges attached to it, there would be no white race, and fair skin would have the same significance as big feet. (199)

Ignatiev (1998a) warns that the abolition of whiteness is a necessary act in the struggle for freedom. He deserves to be quoted in extens:

> The white race is a club, in which people are normally enrolled at birth, without their consent. Most members go through life following the rules and accepting the benefits of membership without thinking about the costs. Many times, they are not conscious of its existence—until it is challenged, when they rally militantly to its defense. Immigrants to the United States, coming to the club later in life, are often more conscious than natives of the white race as a social rather than a natural formation. The club works like any exclusive club, in that membership does not require that all members be active participants, merely that they defer to the prejudices of others. . . . The United States, like every capitalist society, is composed of masters and slaves. The problem is that many of the slaves think they are part of the master class because they partake of the privileges of white skin. The abolitionists' aim is not racial harmony but the abolition of the white race, as part of the mobilization of our side for class war. There are many poor whites in the United States. In fact, the majority of the poor are white. Whiteness does not exempt them from exploitation, it reconciles them to it. It holds down more whites than blacks, because it makes them feel part of a system that exploits and degrades them. For those people, whiteness does not bring freedom and dignity. It is a substitute for freedom and dignity. It is for those who have nothing else. Its abolition is in the interests of all those who want to be free, "whites" no less than others.

Ignatiev (1998b) writes that identification with white privilege reconnects whites to relations of exploitation. The answer to this plight, notes Ignatiev, is for whites to cease to exist as whites. Whites "must commit suicide as whites to come alive as workers or youth or women or artists or whatever other identity will let them stop being the miserable, petulant, subordinated creatures they now are and become freely associated, developing human beings" (200). He goes on to say,

The task at hand is not to convince more whites to oppose "racism"; there are already enough "antiracists" to do the job. The task is to make it impossible for anyone to be white. What would white people have to do to accomplish this? They would have to break the laws of whiteness so flagrantly as to destroy the myth of white unanimity. They would have to respond to every manifestation of white supremacy as if it were directed against them. (202)

Although the ideology of whiteness needs to be vigorously critiqued, this task only partially fulfills the requirements for anticapitalist and antiracist struggles. What is needed further is an acute recognition of how the ideology of whiteness contributes to the reproduction of class divisions—particularly divisions between working-class Anglo-Americans and ethnic minorities—in order to reinforce existing property relations.

Along with efforts to abolish the white race (not white people; there is, of course, a distinct difference), we must support efforts to abolish capital. While it may be true that the globalization of capital brings in its wake the trappings of democracy, it is important not to mistake these seductive trappings for the real thing. As Perry Anderson (1992) notes,

Democracy is indeed now more widespread than ever before. But it is also thinner—as if the more universally available it becomes, the less active meaning it retains. The United States itself is the paradigmatic example: a society in which less than half of the citizens vote, 90 percent of congressmen are re-elected, and the price of office is cash by the millions. (356)

At this point we would like to mention that we don't want those who advocate the abolition of whiteness or who engage in criticism of white social, cultural, and political practices to be acknowledged as part of a "white movement." We don't want to see academic departments dedicated to white studies, nor do we wish the burgeoning literature on whiteness to serve as yet another vehicle used by white scholars to dominate the academic scene. At the same time, we believe that scholarship that focuses on the intricacies of white hegemony is exceedingly important, provided that such studies also are part of a larger antiracist and anticapitalist project dedicated to the abolition of the white race. If white educators wish to transform themselves into agents of social justice (and we would encourage them to do so), then we suggest that they accomplish this as Polish, Irish, Canadian, English, or French, and so on and not by identifying themselves with the vile historical fiction known as the white race.

Radical educators are becoming fed up with white lies. They see through them. They are beginning to attach a language to them and are starting to theorize the issues more completely and more deeply. Are decorous shifts toward decentralization, rigorous academic standards, multiculturalism, teacher accountability, and parental choice supposed to fool anyone? Have recent attempts to camouflage the deep assumptions of terms such as "accountability" so frequently bruited about by neoliberal pundits these days effectively blinded teachers to the protofascist elements of the New Right gospellers and free-market evangelists? Are teachers fooled by such aerosol terms as "empowerment" that are shouted as much in the boardrooms of corporations as they are in teacher education programs? Teachers are no fools, and they are not to be fooled with. While we might inhabit a period of political defeat at the ballot box, we find ourselves on the cusp of a moral victory as teachers begin to exercise their voices of dissent (Kincheloe and Steinberg 1997).

Mainstream Multiculturalism: Liberals Who Champion Différence

By focusing on the margins rather than the hegemonic center of the Anglosphere, mainstream multiculturalists have airbrushed the most vexing dilemmas in the liberal humanist call for diversity and have left uncontested the ever-present discourses of liberal democracy and the workability of capital—discourses that naturalize events so that their outcome no longer seems open to debate. By championing the values of a well-tempered democracy, liberal multiculturalists have also left unchallenged the social relations of production.

Latent in the spectrality that has been disclosed by the discursive and representational practices of mainstream multiculturalism is the continuing advance of white supremacist logic and social practices. Ghosted into the ideas of mainstream multiculturalists is a promiscuous fascination with difference and epistemological exoticisms and the return of the erstwhile eclipsed Other. Mainstream multiculturalism remains permeated by the capitalist mode of production through structures of class, race, gender, and sexual domination.

Beyond the Mainstream: Marxist Multiculturalism

On a somewhat more familiar ground—that of Los Angeles—we are facing a "new work order" in one of the most brutal epicenters of global capitalism. The 1990s was a tumultuous and crisis-ridden decade for one of the most segregated cities in the United States, a city ravaged by growing social and economic inequality. The brutal Rodney King beating in 1991 and the subsequent civil unrest in the spring of 1992 attest to an accelerating oppression of minority groups in the face of widespread racism, sexism, and economic exploitation: the anti-immigrant backlash of Proposition 187 aimed primarily at undocumented immigrant workers, the reactionary Proposition 227 supported by Euro-American nativists who consider multiculturalism to be a threat to their political power and economic privileges, and finally the covert CIA involvement in the trafficking and distribution of narcotics in working-class urban communities of South Central Los Angeles. These events only confirm what has been previously feared: the ever-increasing dismantling and destruction of urban working-class communities and increasing social economic inequality.

The civil unrest in 1992—one of the most violent and destructive events in twentieth-century urban U.S. history—was the result of the growing class polarization between the working class and the ruling class. Social and economic antagonisms between wealthy and the poor communities in Los Angeles continue to increase at an alarming rate. A growing number of reports suggest that "the distribution of earnings was more unequal in Los Angeles than the national average in 1987: Proportionately, Los Angeles has both more low-wage and more high-wage workers than the rest of the United States" (Western Center on Law and Poverty 1991, 38). It is clear that Los Angeles characterizes a necropolis mirroring the contradictions inherent within capitalism's social, economic, and political disorder.

The metropolitan Los Angeles area, with an area nearly the size of Ireland and a GNP bigger than India's, "is the fastest growing metropolis in the world of advanced industrial nations" (Davis 1990, 6). The intensification of class division, the exponential growth of social and economic disparities, the weary resignation of the poor to their continued economic strife, the seemingly insurmountable gap between attainable aspiration and perceived reality among many minority constituencies, and a process of renegacy surrounding the expansion of civil rights for minority populations have transformed Los Angeles into the new Third World mecca among Western industrial cities. Waldinger and Bozorgmehr (1996) note that Los Angeles has "the largest pool of cheap unskilled immigrant labor of any advanced capitalist city" (34). At the same time, Klein (1990) warns us that "Greater Los Angeles is about to become the new Pacific Byzantium, with only a minority of whites, and a population exceeding Greater New York" (31). Bearing in mind the central antagonisms inherent within capitalist social relations, Los Angeles can be said to embody "most of the contradictions of late twentieth century capitalism, with its extremes of wealth and poverty . . . [and] with deteriorating inner city ghettos beset by gangs, drugs, and crime; high salaried, skilled professionals and technicians and unskilled, low waged service and sweatshop workers" (Chinchilla, Hamilton, and Loucky 1993, 51).

In California, the regulation of the flow of cheap labor from south of the border is being conducted over "a bridge of high-tech probes and scopes, laser beams and long range lenses" (Wilgoren 1998, A5). The Clinton administration waged a war on illegal immigrants with a new state-of-the-art "electronic wall" (Wilgoren 1998). Advanced computer and intelligence systems once used during the Cold War have been reissued to the Immigration and Naturalization Service. This surveillance equipment includes remote video surveillance sites, thermal infrared images, long-range infrared systems, fiber-optic bore scopes, maxibeam, night-vision goggles, and intelligent computer-aided detection. The goal is to increase the number of border patrol agents from 3,965 (in 1993) to nearly 8,000 in the next few years. The initial cost of building this controversial electronic surveillance wall is estimated at $300 million (Wilgoren 1998).

It is difficult to miss the concentration of poverty, especially in the Pico-Union/Westlake neighborhood directly abutting downtown, as well as in South Central Los Angeles, where the 1992 uprising took place and the port-adjacent areas of Long Beach. Employment in high-tech durable manufacturing has declined dramatically (especially aerospace), while there have been some modest gains in nondurable manufacturing (printing, food processing, and apparel). Los Angeles remains the largest manufacturing center in the United States. Even within high-wage industries (such as motion pictures), there exists a dramatic bifurcation of income. Most of the areas of working-poor employment are in manufacturing and retail, and most of the working poor fill laborer and service positions (Los Angeles Alliance for a New Economy 2000). The regional economies of Los Angeles and those throughout the United States and other countries need to be understood from the perspective of the global marketplace and correspondingly from the vantage point of Marx's labor theory of value.

Corporate-driven education has been contemporary society's great swindle of fulfillment. Much of the work of educational research has been dedicated to giving a rational account of teaching and learning, and finding ways of reconciling "what could be" with "what is," that is, with rationalizing the educational enterprise "in itself" with existing property relations and state rule. Schooling is very much an abstract form of estrangement that has real, concrete effects on the lives of working people. The worst of these effects are correspondingly disproportionate for individuals who are classified as "people of color" and are female. While it is clear that there exists in the United States a distinguished left liberal and neo-Marxist educational tradition of challenging neoconservative policy, practice, and pedagogy and admirable efforts at understanding schooling from the perspective of race, class, and gender relations, the connections with Marxist revolutionary theory and socialist praxis is tenuous at best. Hence, we remain in dire need of a Marxist critique of corporate schooling. The centerpiece of such a critique would be focused on the labor theory of value.

Maintaining that we live in the social universe of capital whose primary substance is value, Glenn Rikowski (2000) notes several important things about how such value operates. Claiming that it is the "matter and anti-matter of Marx's social universe"—a manifestation of "social energy" that is permanently being transformed and created—he argues that it constitutes itself as capital in the form of surplus value. As such, value cannot be self-generating. It cannot create itself, nor can it magically transform into capital on its own accord. It must be fueled by the living furnace of labor. It is labor that powers its transformations—and its transmogrifications. It is labor, the ultimate alchemist, that fires the engines of value, transforming it first into capital on the basis of surplus value and then into the myriad forms of capital springing from surplus value. Rikowksi grounds his analysis in the observations made by Marx (1973) in the *Grundrisse*:

> Labour is the living, form-giving fire; it is the transitoriness of things, their temporality, as their formation by living time. (361)

But Rikowski does not end his observations here. He further notes, following Marx, that while value depends on our labor, labor, in turn, depends on labor power, which is our capacity to labor; the energy, skills, knowledge, and physical and personal qualities that we, as laborers, possess. It is labor power that constitutes the central actor around which the entire drama of capital unfolds. Labor power ceases to have only virtual or potential existence when it is transformed into labor. In the labor process, labor power (potential, capacity to labor) is transformed into something very concrete—labor. It achieves its actuality by the active will of the laborer once it has been sold to the capitalist for a definite period of time and for a price. The price of labor power is measured in labor hours and minutes and is embodied in whatever workers require to sustain them and keep them fit for working (that is, a living wage). Wages are determined by the (fluctuating) price that labor power fetches as a commodity in the marketplace. Understanding this process has important implications for education since labor power not only includes the mechanical or functional "skills" and knowledge it takes to get the job done but also incorporates the attitudes and personality traits essential for effective performance within the labor process. It depends on what is included within what Rikowski refers to as "mental capacities." So that when employers assess labor power, they are referring to "mental capacities" that include work attitudes, social attitudes, and personality traits—aspects of our "personalities." Rikowski's focus on labor power has profound implications for the way in which knowledge is produced both within and outside of school settings. Education and training are heavily implicated in the social production of labor power. Insofar as Marxism is a theory of society, it attempts, notes Rikowski, to theoretically and practically dissolve the value form of labor, classes, and all other forms of oppression.

Marxist multiculturalists recognize the political primacy of making structural changes in the larger social system while fighting the ability of capital to reabsorb reform efforts within its own commodity logic. Consequently, many Marxist multiculturalists see the need for a direct-action politics centered on anti-imperalism, antiracism, and a politics of difference. This is decidedly not a politics of piecemeal increments. It is a revolutionary praxis for the present that we refer to as "revolutionary multiculturalism." For those who imperiously dismiss Marx as an irrelevant figure to the debate over the future of multicultural society or who are determined to believe that his vision of communism was similar to those gloomy gray photos of robotized factory workers in the plants of the former Soviet Union, they should try reading Marx. Marx believed that it was possible to create a society based on social relations that would not only help to meet one another's needs but also foster a desire to do so. Furthermore, Marx believed that we can fully realize our individual potential as human beings only through meeting the needs of others, and therefore the greater the diversity of our society, the more fulfilling the society would be for all. Marx believed that diversity increases our potential to enrich the quality of our lives. (Through September 1999, BBC News Online ran a cyber poll to discover "the thinker of the millennium." Thousands of people worldwide participated, and Karl Marx was ranked number one, followed by Albert Einstein.)

Revolutionary multiculturalism emphasizes the collective experiences of marginalized people in the context of their political activism and social mobilization. We distinguish revolutionary multiculturalism from the dominant ideologies of multiculturalism, which seek to legitimize the social order through racial harmony, and a national identity based on the "Americanization" of marginalized cultures. As a framework for developing a pedagogical praxis, revolutionary multiculturalism opens up social and political spaces for the oppressed to challenge on their own terms and in their own ways the various forms of class, race, and gender oppression that are produced and reproduced by dominant social relations.

We believe that by using their lived experiences, histories, and narratives as tools for social struggle (McLaren 1995), subaltern groups can interpret and reconstruct their oppressive social conditions into meaningful social and political action (McLaren 1995, 1997). Revolutionary multicultural pedagogy encourages marginalized groups and communities to forge political alliances and in so doing to eradicate cultural homogeneity by interpreting and (re)constructing their own history (McLaren 1995). As part of a concerted effort of anticapitalist struggle, revolutionary multiculturalism seeks to establish social and economic equality in contrast to the conservative and liberal ideology of "equal opportunity" that masks the existing unequal distribution of power and wealth at the heart of capitalist society.

It is important to note here that revolutionary multiculturalism does not privilege class oppression over race, gender, or sexual oppression but it does not see them as coprimary. Rather, it sees the exploitation of human labor within capitalist societies as representing the constitutive condition that set into motion the antagonisms of racism and sexism. In other words, class exploitation in capitalist society provides the condition of possibility for racism and sexism. We believe that by linking antiracist, antisexist, and antihomophobic struggles to local and internationalist anticapitalist struggle, such struggles will be better equipped to succeed in the long run. We are not arguing that race, gender, or sexual oppression be reduced to economic issues, nor do we wish to marginalize or displace the important work that continues to be done in antiracist and feminist scholarship. To suggest that revolutionary pedagogy is an alternative to work being done in cultural studies is to fall into the "divide and rule" traps of bourgeois capitalist scholarship, which fears the establishment of worldwide efforts at alliance-building against capital relations of exploitation.

We acknowledge that we live in a heterogeneous society that is comprised of conflicting and contradictory social formations and the diversity of social and cultural life. Yet we also acknowledge that such diversity is a contested one. The question we raise is, Diversity for whom? We do not subscribe to a politics in which specific and disparate social movements are cobbled into a form of artificial, mechanical unification or totality. There has to be some establishment of priorities, a leadership of some kind, although we don't envision returning to the Bolshevik model here.

Neither do we support front organizations of specialized movements; rather, we foresee a model in which various groups independently address issues and create new discourses and forms of mobilization. This would take place within an overall form of intergroup and interethnic solidarity. But this would not be a mechanical coalition of diverse groups brought together as a broad-based historical bloc, with each group's goal representing an equal strategic priority. We follow Boris Kagarlitsky (2000) in advocating for a "hierarchy of strategic priorities but at the same time a real equality of people in the movement" (71). He articulates the struggle as follows:

We must realize our ecological project; we must affirm women's rights and minorities' rights through and in the process of anti-capitalist struggle, not as a substitution or alternative to it. Finally, this does not mean that other movements, not addressing the central issues of the system, must necessarily be seen as enemies or rivals of socialists. These movements are just as legitimate. Everyone has the same rights. It means simply that no one must expect the socialist left to drop its own culture, tradition and, last but not least, its identity for the sake of "democratic equivalence." (71–72)

We must move beyond the liberal socialism of those who espouse radical democracy in order to embrace a unified struggle in which a collective political consciousness is not only possible but also necessary. Such a consciousness would involve, after Marx, understanding not only how capital produces social relations but also how capital itself is produced. We don't need to scrap universalism, as the postmodernists would advocate, but rather to assiduously struggle for what Kagarlitsky (2000, 75) refers to as an "open universalism" based on a dialogue of cultures. After all, universals are not static; they are rooted (routed) in movement. They are nomadically grounded in living, breathing subjects of history who toil and who labor under conditions not of their own making.

We must continue to attack the restricted Western bourgeois character of Enlightenment universalism, but to attack universalism itself is not only foolish but also politically dangerous. Bruce Robbins (1999) is correct when he asserts that all universal standards are in some way provisional. In other words, they deal with "provisional agreements arrived at by particular agents" (74). He goes on to maintain that universal standards "are provided in a situation of unequal power, and they are applied in a situation of unequal power" (74). There is no such thing as a clean universalism that is not tainted by power and interest of some sort. Robbins concludes, "All universalisms are dirty. And it is only dirty universalism that will help us against the powers and agents of still dirtier ones" (75).

Although we support the Enlightenment's project of universalism, we also recognize its limitations. This is in sharp contrast to those postmodern educators who frequently associate Enlightenment universalism with Eurocentrism's emphasis on objectivity and rationality. While we resist efforts to police the expression of non-European viewpoints, we find the politics of postmodern pluralism—that is, providing voice to those marginalized social groups who have been denied political participation—to be problematic. The belief that an increased diversity of marginalized voices will automatically ensure that marginalized social groups will gain social, political, and economic demands and interests is politically naive. We argue that the struggle for diversity must be accompanied by a revolutionary socialist politics.

Kenan Malik (1996) asserts convincingly that postmodernism's refutation of universalism is, for the most part, similar to the crude nineteenth-century racial theories that rejected universal categories and instead emphasized relativism. Malik further adds that "in its hostility to universalism and in its embrace of the particular and the relative, poststructuralism embodies the same romantic notions of human difference as are contained in racial theory" (4). Malik asserts, "While difference can arise from equality, equality can never arise from difference" (4).

We believe that it is important to reject a politics where the Left is implicated in the "divide and rule" tactics of the ruling elite. A. Sivanandan describes how such a politics plays out in Britain:

> Government funding of self-help groups undermined the self-reliance, the self-created social and economic base, of [groups]. . . . Multiculturalism deflected the political concerns of the black community into the cultural concerns of different communities, the struggle against racism into the struggle for culture. (cited in Kagarlitsky 2000, 84)

At the current historical juncture, when the workers' movement has been demoralized, supporters of postmodern radicalism have, in effect, strengthened the bourgeoisie. Kagarlitsky (2000) writes,

> The supporters of identity politics make an assiduous pretence of not knowing a simple, obvious fact: that the quantity of resources and activists at the disposal of the left is extremely limited. This means that in conditions when neoliberalism threatens the very bases of people's normal human existence, these resources and strengths should not be dispersed over a range of "different, but equal struggles," but should be concentrated as far as possible on the main lines of resistance. Neo-liberal politicians know this, and do not squander their energies on trifles. They turned their fire against supporters of identity politics only after dealing with the labor movement, and they concern themselves with identity politics only to the extent to which it hinders them in carrying out specific tasks. (96)

Toward a Revolutionary Multicultural Pedagogy

In our view, a critical pedagogy is clearly a necessary yet insufficient condition for revolutionary praxis. Critical pedagogy, in other words, must do more than unweave at night what each day is stitched together by the commodity logic of capital; it must build a new vision of society freed from capital's law of value. A critical pedagogy, in order to advance revolutionary praxis, must be able to endorse the cultural struggles of workers and coordinate such struggle as part of a broader "cross-border" social movement unionism aimed at organizing and supporting the working classes and marginalized cultural workers in their efforts to build new international anticapitalist struggles along the road to socialism.

Recognizing that global capitalism has ushered in a period marked by accelerating class polarization along with the upward redistribution of wealth, Edna Bonacich and Richard Appelbaum (2000) propose a strategic deployment of workers' centers as a way of building political movements that would directly address the rights of workers. Such workers' centers would be instrumental in providing basic social services and assisting workers in a number of crucial ways. For instance, they could help workers fight for higher wages and back pay in addition to providing legal assistance on issues related to immigration.

In our opinion, political education plays a crucial role in raising workers' revolutionary consciousness and promoting an in-depth understanding of political economy, particularly with respect to the existing antagonisms between capital and labor. Workers' self-education can bring into critical relief the contradictions between democracy and capitalism. In the larger social arena, political education can help workers recognize how imperialism is linked with the rhetoric of "humanitarian aid." Finally, workers' centers can assist in organizing workers to participate in political struggles so crucial to demonstrating the power of the working class to resist the rule of capital.

A revolutionary multicultural pedagogy recognizes the necessity of a worker-centered pedagogy that is empowering, democratic, and participatory and that is also able to address the material conditions of the workers. Thus, the revolutionary multicultural pedagogy we are advocating here is one that stresses worker participation and worker self-organization on the basis of collective economic and political interests. As a consequence, a central practice of a revolutionary multicultural pedagogy is an examination of how identities of workers are lived conjuncturally, particularly in terms of class, race, and gender relations.

The corporate-sponsored multiculturalism that we witness today in school classrooms maintains class and racial divisions by articulating a liberal version of equality that is grounded in equal recognition of cultural practices. While this is a good thing as far as it goes, it overlooks the exploitation of wage labor by focusing for the most part on cultural practices, which mainstream multiculturalists frequently divorce from the social relations of production. In this instance, the social identities of marginalized minorities become articulated around consumption practices rather that production or labor practices. In the same manner, identity politics effectively detaches cultural practices from labor practices.

Multicultural capitalism acknowledges social groups primarily as consumers in the global market. We ignore at our peril capitalism's ability to accommodate differences by linking them to its own global market operations that encompass flexible methods of production and the personification of services and goods for diverse ethnic, cultural, and linguistic minorities. Capitalism gives recognition to ethnic and racial minorities who possess capital, while minorities without sufficient disposable income are systematically marginalized (LaFeber 1999).

We believe that a precondition for a "globalized borderless capital" is "cross-border cooperation" of ethnic, cultural, and linguistic communities of people (LaFeber 1999). But such cooperation is double edged. While border crossing facilitates capitalist flows, it also consolidates the advantage of the capitalist class. Thus, it is imperative that border pedagogy moves beyond the celebration of hybridized identities and pluralism and encompasses an analysis of political economy and class exploitation. That is, border pedagogy should engage in a critique of the existing contradictions between capital and labor, the exploitation of labor, and profiteerism. It is a pedagogical struggle that addresses the importance of unity and difference not only as a sense of political mobilization but also as a practice of cultural authenticity that neither fetishizes tradition nor forecloses its allegiance to traditional knowledges (Grande 2000). It is a revolutionary project that seeks alliances with diverse groups while respecting and learning from competing moral visions and a reimagination of the political space surrounding identity (Grande 2000).

Equal representation does not necessarily guarantee social and economic equality under capitalism. Thus, a revolutionary multicultural pedagogy must refocus on the issue of redistribution of wealth by recognizing that equality must be struggled for within the social relations of production—particularly property relations (McLaren and Farahmandpur 1999a, 1999b, 2000). A revolutionary multiculturalism undresses capitalism as a pernicious system and exposes regimes of exploitation hitherto silenced or undeclared. It attempts to reveal how relations of exploitation are insinuated into the warp and woof of "embodied" everyday life. As Morris-Suzuki (2000) notes, "The contemporary world of global capital is not a universe where the non-material has conquered or subordinated the material: it is one where matter and symbol increasingly interpenetrate. We must therefore find ways of looking at political agency which unite the material and symbolic dimensions of life rather than counterposing them" (70). A revolutionary multiculturalism seeks to map the fault lines of agency, where discourses and social relations converge in the activities of everyday life.

We need nothing short of a social revolution. This mandates not only the transformation of our social and economic conditions but also the transformation of our relationship to the "Other." This also means abolishing the contradictions or the internal relation between capital and labor as well as the value form of wealth that is historically specific to capitalism (Allman 2001). This is necessary in order to break the self-replicating cycle of poverty brought about by money exchange. Here we recognize that many readers might find our platform to be naive, impractical, or hopelessly utopian. We wish to remind these readers that such a turn to socialism in no way diminishes the importance of industrial, postindustrial, or technological development, which we believe must continue. However, in our socialist vision, individuals would contribute labor according to ability, and the material means of life would be distributed according to need. Ideally, a redistributive socialism would be followed by the managed obsolescence of the money exchange.

A revolutionary multicultural pedagogy links the social identities of marginalized and oppressed groups—particularly the working class, indigenous groups, and marginalized populations—with their reproduction within capitalist relations of production. It also examines how the reproduction of social, ethnic, racial, and sexual identities, as particular social and cultural constructs as well as shared histories of struggle, are linked with the reproduction of the social division of labor. It therefore moves beyond the often fragmented and atomized entrapments of identity politics, which frequently polarizes differences instead of uniting them around the common economic and political interests of marginalized social groups.

We have witnessed the development of crude forms of identity politics where "critical pedagogy" is discussed—often derisively—as an approach reserved for white activists only because it is focused mainly on issues of social class. This position does a disservice to scholars and activists of color who historically have been at the forefront of struggles against class oppression. Furthermore, it artificially truncates the scope and depth of critical pedagogy, which—at least in the revolutionary tradition that we are advocating here—is strongly antiracist, antisexist, and antihomophobic. To pit, for example, critical race theory (for scholars of color) against critical pedagogy (for white scholars) is to set up a false opposition. It does grave injustice to both educators of color and white educators who critically appropriate from the best of both traditions of scholarship and activism. Such an rendition of identity politics is more concerned with who is more "authentically" Asian, Latino/a, African American, Canadian, Irish, and so on than with understanding the relationship among class oppression, sexism, and racism or with building active working-class coalitions against multiple forms of exploitation. We are arguing not against cultural authenticity but rather against practices that reduce authenticity to the laws of genetics or cultural purity. We view authenticity in the context of a shared history of struggle and survival. By underscoring the importance of "diversity" without interrogating how capitalist social relations set limits to what passes as diversity and what forms of diversity will be "accepted," these crude forms of identity politics also mask the important connections among the capitalist law of value, the exploitation of human labor, and gender- and race-specific forms of exploitation. The unwitting outcome of such an identity politics is a strengthening of the rule of capital. This works to the detriment of all working-class groups. Linda Gordon (1999) notes,

> Diversity talk tends to proscribe respect and recognition as the solution to racism or other ill treatment. It highlights individual attitudes and behaviors. So if working-class or Latina or disabled or lesbian women felt uncomfortable, ignored, or insulted in white-dominated feminist discourse, the fault can seem to lie with speakers or organizers who failed to acknowledge diversity. The solution was personal re-education rather than structural social change. Many white women's groups, for example, tried to compensate for their lack of sufficient diversity with guilt-inducing individual self-examination. Many feminist organizations, including academic women's-studies programs, developed antiracist programs that encouraged whites to confess their innermost racist thoughts and feelings—but rarely to study, say, the impact of economic globalization on racial formations. (46)

It bears repeating that our aim here is not to ignore the cultural and ethnic identities of marginalized social groups, to relegate antiracist struggles to a distant sideshow, or to elevate the centrality of capitalist exploitation over racialized social practices but rather to argue that one of the most insidious aspects of capitalism is precisely that its relations of exploitation hurt people of color in particularly invidious—and disproportionately disabling—ways. We wish to bring into deeper focus than one often finds in critical race theory or multicultural education the relationships that obtain among race, gender, ethnic, and class identities with the purpose of articulating a political framework that moves toward transnational ethnic alliances. Our central aim is the abolition of the rule of capital and the forms of exploitation and violence that flourish under capital's watch.

Faced with the uncertainty of the present, some look to religion to save us from ourselves. It has been said that religion is for those who fear hell; but it could also be said that educational activism is for those of us who have already been there. The educational activists of today are those who are not afraid to recognize the type of social evil that we see all around us and to name it as such. And they are committed to fighting the racist, sexist, and corporate evil that still envelopes us.

Perhaps Jesus was a dark-skinned Egyptian, and Mary Magdalene was from Somalia and possibly even a priestess and the bride of Christ (literally). If such claims and conjectures were one day proven to be true (this is highly doubtful), could that help put an end to racism and sexism, at least among white Christians? Certainly it would help. But it wouldn't diminish the material conditions that enable structural racism and sexism to flourish within capitalist societies. To that end, revolutionary multicultural pedagogy continues on its path. We can't end racism by abolishing capitalism alone. We need a dual-pronged approach of attacking racist mythologies as well as dismantling the value form of labor which invites such mythologies to flourish and sometimes develop a life of their own.

Notes

1. It has become impermissible to promote any criticism of capital's internally determining law of maximizing, by any vehicle available, the ratio of its owners' money-demand increases to money-demand inputs. The corporate media select only for those messages that do not contradict the money-sequence organization of social bodies. The regulating code of this growth sequence has resulted in the enslavement and genocide of entire societies. Anything that gets in the way of this decoupled or delinked growth is life depredated and gets eaten up.

2. It is interesting to observe that in countries where "traditional" workers' movements are stronger, the position of women also improved quite dramatically in the 1980s and 1990s (Kagarlitsky 2000).

References

Allen, T. 1994. *The invention of the white race, volume one: Racial oppression and social control*. London: Verso.

———. 1997. *The invention of the white race, volume two: The origins of racial oppression in Anglo-America*. London: Verso.

Allman, P. 2001. *Critical education against global capital: Karl Marx and revolutionary critical education*. Westport, Conn.: Bergin and Garvey.

Anderson, P. 1992. *A zone of engagement*. London: Verso.

Ansell, A. E. 1997. *New Right, new racism: Race and reaction in the United States and Britain*. New York: New York University Press.

Aristide, J. B. 2000. *Eyes of the heart: Seeking a path for the poor in the age of globalization*. Monroe, Maine: Common Courage Press.

Arrighi, G., T. K. Hopkins, and I. Wallerstein. 2001. 1989: The continuation of 1968. In *After the fall: 1989 and the future of freedom*, ed. G. Katsiaficas, 35–51. New York: Routledge.

Bennett, W. J. 1992. *The de-valuing of America: The fight for our culture and our children*. New York: Simon & Schuster.

Bloom, A. 1987. *The closing of the American mind*. New York: Simon & Schuster.

Bonacich, E., and R. P. Appelbaum. 2000. *Behind the label: Inequality in the Los Angeles apparel industry*. Berkeley: University of California Press.

Chinchilla, N., N. Hamilton, and J. Loucky. 1993. Central Americans in Los Angeles: An immigrant community in transition. In *The Barrios: Latinos and the underclass debate*, ed. J. Moore and R. Pinderhughes, 51–78. New York: Russell Sage Foundation.

Cole, M. 1998. Globalization, modernisation, and competitiveness: A critique of the Labor project in education. *International Studies in the Sociology of Education* 8(3): 315–32.

Collins, C., and F. Yeskel. 2000. *Economic apartheid in America: A primer on economic inequality and security.* New York: New Press.

Darder, A., and R. Torres. 1998. From race to racism: The politics of "race" language in "postmodern education." In *The promise of multiculturalism: Education and autonomy in the 21st century,* ed. G. Katsiaficas and T. Kiros, 82–88. New York: Routledge.

Davis, M. 1990. *City of quartz: Excavating the future in Los Angeles.* New York: Vintage.

Ebert, T. 2001. Globalization, internationalism, and the class politics of cynical reason. *Nature, Society, and Thought* 12(4): 389–410.

Fish, S. 1997. Boutique multiculturalism, or, why liberals are incapable of thinking about hate speech. *Critical Inquiry* 23(2): 378–95.

Forrester, V. 1999. *The economic horror.* Malden, Mass.: Blackwell Publishers.

Giroux, H. A. 1994. *Disturbing pleasures: Learning popular culture.* New York: Routledge.

———. 2000a. *Impure acts: The practical politics of cultural studies.* New York: Routledge.

———. 2000b. *Stealing innocence: Youth, corporate power, and the politics of culture.* New York: St. Martin's Press.

Gordon, L. 1999. The trouble with difference. *Dissent* 46(2): 41–47.

Grande, S. M. A. 2000. American Indian identity and power: At the crossroads of Indigena and Mestizaje. *Harvard Educational Review* 70(4): 467–98.

Greider, W. 2000. Time to rein in global finance. *The Nation* 270(16): 13–20.

Hill, D. 1999. *New Labor and education: Policy, ideology, and the Third Way.* A HillCole Pamphlet. London: Tufnell Press.

Hirsch, E. D. 1988. *Cultural literacy: What every American needs to know.* New York: Vintage Books.

Ignatiev, N. 1998a. Abolitionism and "white studies." *Race Traitor.* www.postfun.com/racetraitor/features/whitestudies.html (accessed May 15, 2001).

———. 1998b. The new abolitionists. *Transition,* no. 73, 199–203.

Kagarlitsky, B. 2000. *The return of radicalism: Reshaping the left institutions.* Translated by Renfrey Clark. London: Pluto Press.

Kincheloe, J. L., and S. R. Steinberg. 1997. *Changing multiculturalisms.* Milton Keynes, U.K.: Open University Press.

Klein, N. M. 1990. The sunshine strategy: Buying and selling the fantasy of Los Angeles. In *20th century Los Angeles: Power, promotion, and social conflict,* ed. N. M. Klein and M. J. Schiesl, 1–38. Claremont, Calif.: Regina Books.

LaFeber, W. 1999. *Michael Jordan and the new global capitalism.* New York: W. W. Norton.

Larsen, N. 2000. Dialectics and "globalization": The problem of how (not) to think about a new internationalism. *Working Papers in Cultural Studies,* no. 22, 6–16. Pullman: Washington State University, Department of Comparative American Cultures.

Los Angeles Alliance for a New Economy. 2000. *The other Los Angeles: The working poor in the city of the 21st century.* Los Angeles: Los Angeles Alliance for a New Economy.

Macedo, D. 2000. The colonialism of the English only movement. *Educational Researcher* 29(3): 15–24.

Malik, K. 1996. Universalism and difference: Race and the postmodernists. *Race & Class* 37(3): 1–16.

Martin, R. 1999. Globalization? The dependencies of a question. *Social Text* 17(3): 1–14.

Martinot, S. 2000. The racialized construction of class in the United States. *Social Justice* 27(1): 43–60.

Marx, K. 1973 [1858]. *Grundrisse: Foundations of the critique of political economy*. Harmondsworth: Penguin.

———. 1993. *Grundrisse*. London: Penguin.

Marx, K., and F. Engels. 1995. *The German ideology*. New York: International Publishers.

McLaren, P. 1995. *Critical pedagogy and predatory culture: Oppositional politics in a postmodern era*. London: Routledge.

———. 1997. *Revolutionary multiculturalism: Pedagogies of dissent for the new millennium*. Boulder, Colo.: Westview Press.

———. 2000. *Che Guevara, Paulo Freire, and the pedagogy of revolution*. Lanham, Md.: Rowman & Littlefield.

McLaren, P., and R. Farahmandpur. 1999a. Critical multiculturalism and globalization: Some implications for a politics of resistance. *Journal of Curriculum Theorizing* 15(3): 27–46.

———. 1999b. Critical pedagogy, postmodernism, and the retreat from class: Towards a contraband pedagogy. *Theoria*, no. 93, 83–115.

———. 2000. Reconsidering Marx in post-Marxist times: A requiem for postmodernism? *Educational Researcher* 29(3): 25–33.

McMurtry, J. 1998. *Unequal freedoms: The global market as an ethical system*. West Hartford, Conn.: Kumarian Press.

———. 1999. *The cancer stage of capitalism*. London: Pluto Press.

McQueen, A. 2000. Dropout rate of Latino students rises. *Daily Bruin News*, March 16, 8, 14.

Morris-Suzuki, T. 2000. For and against NGOs. *New Left Review*, no. 2 (2nd ser.), 63–84.

Ortega, T. 2000. In the hot seat. *New Times Los Angeles*. www.newtimesla.com/issues/2000-05-25/faultlines.html (accessed May 25, 2000).

Peterson, B. 1995. What should children learn? A teacher looks at E. D. Hirsch. In *Rethinking schools: An agenda for change*, ed. D. Levin, R. Lowe, B. Peterson, and R. Tenorio, 74–88. New York: New Press.

Petras, J. 2000. The Third Way: Myth and reality. *Monthly Review* 51(10): 19–35.

Rikowski, G. 1997. Scorched earth: Prelude in rebuilding Marxist educational theory. *British Journal of Sociology of Education* 17(4): 415–51.

———. 2000. Messing with the explosive commodity: School improvement, educational research and labour-power in the era of global capitalism. Paper prepared for the symposium "If We Aren't Pursuing Improvement, What Are We Doing?" British Education Research Association Conference, session 3.4, Cardiff University, Wales, September 7.

Robbins, B. 1999. *Feeling global: Inter-nationalism in distress*. New York: New York University Press.

Robinson, W., and J. Harris. 2000. Towards a global ruling class? Globalization and the transnational capitalist class. *Science & Society* 64(1): 11–54.

Singh, A. 2000. Free trade and the "starving child" defense: A forum. *The Nation* 270(16): 24–26.

Sleeter, C. E. 1996. *Multicultural education as social activism.* Albany: State University of New York Press.

Thandeka. 1999. *Learning to be white: Money, race, and God in America.* New York: Continuum.

Thompson, W. 1997. *The Left in history: Revolution and reform in twentieth-century politics.* London: Pluto Press.

Waldinger, R., and M. Bozorgmehr, ed. 1996. The making of a multicultural metropolis. In *Ethnic Los Angeles,* 3–37. New York: Russell Sage Foundation.

Western Center on Law and Poverty. 1991. *Taking it to the bank: Race, poverty, and credit in Los Angeles.* Los Angeles: Western Center on Law and Poverty.

Wilgoren, J. 1998. Electronic wall going up along the border. *Los Angeles Times,* March 17, A5.

Žižek, S. 2000. Why we all love to hate Haider. *New Left Review,* no. 2 (2nd ser.), 37–46.

6

Teaching against Globalization
and the New Imperialism:
Toward a Revolutionary Pedagogy

No teacher giving instruction in any school, or on any property belonging to any agencies included in the public school system, shall advocate or teach communism with the intent to indoctrinate or to inculcate in the mind of any pupil a preference for communism. In prohibiting the advocacy or teaching of communism with the intent of indoctrinating or inculcating a preference in the mind of any pupil for such doctrine, the Legislature does not intend to prevent the teaching of the facts about communism. Rather, the Legislature intends to prevent the advocacy of, or inculcation and indoctrination into, communism as is hereinafter defined, for the purpose of undermining patriotism for, and the belief in, the government of the United States and of this state. For the purposes of this section, communism is a political theory that the presently existing form of government of the United States or of this state should be changed, by force, violence, or other unconstitutional means, to a totalitarian dictatorship which is based on the principles of communism as expounded by Marx, Lenin, and Stalin.

—California Education Code, section 51530

THE PURPOSE OF THIS CHAPTER—which is in clear violation of the California Education Code, Section 51530—is to discuss teacher education reform in the United States from the context of critical pedagogy in general and a theory of imperialism and class struggle that is indebted to the Marxist–Leninist tradition. Many of the current discussions of globalization and, for that matter, critical pedagogy have themselves become conceptually impoverished and politically domesticated (McLaren 1998b, 2000; McLaren and Farahmandpur 2000).

Hence, we have taken pains to offer for public consumption some counterpropaganda to the pronouncements of the corporate mullahs, aggravating the debate over critical pedagogy before it can accommodate to their supernal demand. We have secured our analysis within a Marxist problematic that takes seriously the imperative of steering critical pedagogy firmly toward anticapitalist struggle (see McLaren 2000; McLaren and Farahmandpur 2000). We contend that within critical pedagogy, the issue of class has been egregiously overlooked. Critical pedagogy has, of late, drifted dangerously toward the cultural terrain of identity politics in which class is reduced to an effect rather than understood as a cause and in which a hierarchy of oppression is (usually unwittingly) constituted as a controlling paradigm that frequently leaves the exploitative power of capitalist social relations largely unaddressed. Understanding exploitation as embodied in forms of racist and patriarchal social practices should constitute a central focus of critical pedagogy. On this point we have no quarrel. However, this objective should not be achieved at the grievous expense of understanding how political economy and class struggle operate as the motor force of history and society (Parenti 1997). With this assertion, we identify the political architecture necessary to contest the enfeeblement and domestication of critical pedagogy and to develop what we call a revolutionary working-class pedagogy.

Facing Global Capitalism

As we anticipate the savage ferocity of the new imperialism, exemplified by the boy emperor in Washington and his lean and hungry cabal of Straussian nobility, we bear witness to the unabated mercilessness of global capitalism and the impassable fissure between capital and labor. Today, millions of workers are being exploited by a relatively small yet cunningly powerful global ruling class driven by an unslakable desire for accumulation of profit. Little opposition exists as capitalism runs amok, unhampered and undisturbed by the tectonic upheaval that is occurring in the geopolitical landscape—one that has recently witnessed the collapse of the Soviet Union and the regimes of the Eastern bloc.

Because of the fast-paced and frenetic changes taking place around us in the wired realms of global technologies and free-trade initiatives, we are hard pressed to chart out our daily struggles against oppression and exploitation instituted by a growing breed of techno-crazed global robber barons. As we attempt to flee a culture of endless acquisition, we find ourselves at the mercy of an even more terrifying corporate culture shaping our subjectivities. According to Hayat Imam (1997), "Today . . . 'creation of wealth' has become the fundamental value at the center of global society and analyses of economics are devoid of issues of morality, human needs, and social conscience" (13). Mutagenic social relations that permit such molten greed to flourish have produced severance packages for corporate bosses that shamelessly exceed the combined salaries of an army of factory workers. Yet there is no authority by which greed can be brought to trial. But when greed is identified as exploitation, that changes the terms of the debate by shifting the concepts from the realm of individualistic psychology to that of historical materialism.

Immovably entrenched social, political, and economic disparities and antagonisms compel us as educators and cultural workers to create alternatives to the logic of capitalist accumulation. Yet the creation of alternatives to the logic of capital is a formidable—and what many of our more cynical brothers and sisters in education would deem today an insurmountable—challenge. We are struggling and suffering (some much more than we are) through a time when there exists a dictatorship of the marketplace in a capitalist system whose inequalities are becoming more evident than ever before. This is especially true at this current moment, when the Republican theft of a presidency is followed by a continued commitment to Disneyland capitalism: the free marketeers meet the Mouseketeers.

The Politics of Neoliberalism

Neoliberal free-market economics—the purpose of which is to avoid stasis and keep businesses in healthy flux—functions as a type of binding arbitration, legitimizing a host of questionable practices and outcomes: deregulation, unrestricted access to consumer markets, downsizing, outsourcing, flexible arrangements of labor, intensification of competition among transnational corporations, increasing centralization of economic and political power, and, finally, widening class polarization. Neoliberalism is currently embarking on ways of "reimagining" democracy through the importation of the market discourse of parasitic financial oligarchies into increasingly domesticated democratic practices and through the valorization of capital and the unrestrained economic power of private property (Teeple 1995).

The triumph of neoliberalism represents at once the incalculably expanded scope of the culture of consumption and the implosion of social relations into a universal signifier—namely, capital—that Marx metaphorically referred to as the "universal pimp." Marx likened money to a "visible god" that in the generalized commodity form

> spreads this illusory perception throughout society, dissolving all previous identities and distinctions, and remolding human consciousness in its own image. In the fully developed form of capital, money achieves an active, self-regulating power through which it shapes the lives of concrete individuals. (Hawkes 1996, 101–2)

For those who believe that uninterrupted accumulation and increasing international concentration of capital is a good thing, that the shift from an international economy to a world economy is a sign of progress, that capital's vampiric thirst for new surplus valve is healthy, that the feedback mechanisms of the unfettered "free" market are fair, that only democracy will spring forth from its spontaneous order, and that the common good will magically advance from its networked complexity, there is reason to be wildly optimistic about the future. Imagine the possibilities for privatizing public spaces and spreading neoliberal domination over vast exotic populations hitherto unconquered! But for educators who reject the idea that the social system under capitalism is a self-organizing totality and who view the globalization of capital as an irredeemable assault on democracy, the future appears perilous indeed. We refuse to elevate the victimization of the working class to a regulatory ideal of democracy and decline to treat the economy as a thing or endow it with self-evident democratic agency. After Marx, we view the economy as a social relation and not a self-sustaining natural entity. Capitalism is not powered by a transcendental metaphysic but is a social relation overburdened by its constituent requirement for exploitation, accumulation, endless growth, and class conflict. It remains predicated on the extraction of surplus value from workers (value produced by workers beyond that which the capitalist must pay out in wages so that the workers can reproduce their labor power).

Unlike its well-known predecessors—slavery and feudalism—capitalism is predicated on the overaccumulation of capital and the superexploitation of rank-and-file wage laborers. The irreversible contradictions inherent within capitalist social and economic relations—those between capital and labor—are taking us further away from democratic accountability and steering us closer to what Rosa Luxemburg (1919) referred to as an age of "barbarism." Peery (1997) makes the point that in comparison to the political economy that sustained slavery or feudalism, the social and economic contradictions in the present-day capitalist mode of production are much more virulent and unremitting. This is because the production, distribution, and consumption of commodities are in constant contradiction with labor power and prevents the logic of capital from validating any logic other than its own. Many social and political theorists have studied the phenomenon of globalization extensively and have pronounced it a discomfiting inevitability for some but a powerful, life-enhancing economic tonic for many. Yet, in our opinion, globalization represents an ideological facade that camouflages the manifold operations of imperialism. In fact, the concept of globalization has effectively replaced the term "imperialism" in the lexicon of the privileged class for the purpose of exaggerating the global character of capitalism—as an all-encompassing and indefatigable power that apparently no nation-state has the means to resist or oppose. Furthermore, it deceitfully suggests that capitalism is no longer dependent on the nation-state. This position occludes the fact that a large portion of production in Western European countries takes place within national boundaries. Moreover, the globalization thesis maintains that whereas state power can be used in the interests of the large multinational corporations, it cannot be employed in the interest of the working class.

To call globalization a form of imperialism might seem a rhetorical exaggeration. But we believe that this identification is necessary because the term "globalization" is calculated by bourgeois critics to render any radical politicization of it extreme. The ideology of this move is invisibly to enframe the concept of globalization within a culturalist logic that reduces it to mean a standardization of commodities (that is, the same designer clothes appearing in shopping plazas throughout the world). By contrast, we see the process as inextricably tied to the politics of neoliberalism, in which violence asserts itself as stability through a recomposition of the capital–labor relationship. Such a recomposition entails the subordination of social reproduction to the reproduction of capital (Dinerstein 1999), the deregulation of the labor market, the globalization of liquid capital, the outsourcing of production to cheap labor markets, and the transfer of local capital intended for social services into finance capital for global investment.

The new imperialism to which we refer is a combination of old-style military and financial practices as well as recent attempts by developed nations to impose the law of the market on the whole of humanity itself. Having obscured the distinction between the sacred and the profane, the global aristocracy's new world order has set out to expand the free market in the interest of quick profits, to increase global production, to raise the level of exports in the manufacturing sector, and to intensify competition among transnational corporations. It has also benefited from part-time and contingent work, reduced the pool of full-time employment, and accelerated immigration from Third World and developing countries to industrial nations (Bonacich and Appelbaum 2000). In addition to our description of globalization as imperialism, we might add the following: imperialist military intervention primarily disguised as humanitarian aid, the submission of international institutions such as the United Nations to the social and economic demands of imperialist conquest, and the instigation of ethnic and nationalistic conflicts to weaken nations refusing to submit to the rule of the market (Azad 2000).

Contrary to popular opinion, wealth depletion among developing nations is not rescued by capital from advanced capitalist countries. This is because transnational corporations drain the local capital from poor countries rather than bring in new capital. Because their savings are often low, banks in developing countries would rather lend to their own subsidiary corporations (who send their profits back to advanced nations) than to struggling local businesses in developing nations. Faced with low prices for exports, high tariffs on processed goods, and a lack of capital and rising prices, local businesses are locked into entrenched impoverishment because of structural adjustment measures to balance the budget. Such measures are financed through cuts in spending for human development (Imam 1997). The World Trade Organization does not permit poor countries to prioritize fighting poverty over increasing exports or choosing a development path that will advance the interests of the countries' own populations. By 1996, the resulting concentration of wealth had "the income of the world's richest individuals . . . equal to the income of 52 percent of humanity" (Imam 1997, 13).

The Privatization and Commercialization of Public Education

Examining education policies within the context of economic globalization and neoliberalism raises a number of critical questions that include the following: What are some of the effects of globalization on public schools and public education? To what extent is the content of teaching and curriculum under the perilous influence of the shifting social, economic, and political relations within global capitalism? Spring (1998) identifies a key paradox that frames education and economic policies pursued in the United States and other advanced capital societies. First, education under globalization is viewed as a vehicle that assists the growing market economy. For many developing countries, an educated and skilled workforce ostensibly would mean higher levels of productivity and economic development. Second, education is viewed as a tool in solving problems associated with economic globalization, such as unemployment and poverty. If, however, the market economy (by means of the capitalist law of value) is itself the cause of social and economic inequality, then it would appear a contradiction in terms to argue that the goal of education should be to assist in the expansion of the market economy (Spring 1998). Economic globalization not only has failed to provide political stability and social and economic equality for many nations around the world but has also led to deepening social and economic polarization. Willie Thompson (1997) notes,

> Marx's insights into the nature of capital's reproduction and accumulation have never been bettered or displaced: his prevision of its future was extraordinarily percipient and impressively fulfilled. He was never a better prophet than when he insisted that capitalism was hastening towards its unavoidable destruction, that its internal forces carried it in a certain identifiable direction, which (contra Keynes) cannot be reversed or evaded. What capital produces above all is its own gravediggers. Marx meant the working class, and he was mistaken. What looks

more likely to be capitalism's executioner is capitalism itself—the problem is that everything else is practically certain to be entombed with it. (224)

As the logic of capital accumulation is shifting toward knowledge-based economies and as new forms of computer technology and biotechnology are being integrated into today's high-tech economy, information itself is fast becoming a high-priced new commodity. Transnational corporations are laboring vigorously to privatize the socially produced knowledge associated with the educational system. Decreased government funding of public education has forced an unholy partnership with private corporations who are seeking to create "high-tech knowledge industries" (Witheford 1997). Transnational corporations are sponsoring research centers in universities across the United States by donating millions of dollars for the research, development, and production of for-profit technologies. This has resulted in the "high-tech colonization of education," transforming public universities into corporate-operated "techopolises" that have little interest in coexistence with the poor (Witheford 1997).

Under the command of the market economy, not even universities, colleges, and vocational schools are immune from the economic policies favoring capital accumulation. Niemark (1999) reports that the increasing social policies that support for-profit universities have made higher education an extension of the market economy. She writes that social policies that support privatization have moved in the direction of

> establishing for-profit degree-granting institutions (such as the University of Phoenix); outsourcing curriculum, instruction, counseling, operations, and administration (in such areas as bookstores, food services, libraries, computer operations, plant maintenance, security, printing, and payroll); signing campus-corporate research and development partnership and licensing agreements; and selling exclusive on-campus marketing rights to companies that sell products as varied as soft drinks, fast food, computers, and credit and telephone calling cards. The campus is becoming virtually indistinguishable from the marketplace, and both universities and their faculties are becoming entrepreneurs. (24)

The restructuring of higher education can clearly be seen as reinforcing class inequality and exposing public higher education to social and economic policies governed by the laws of the market economy (that is, commodification, proletarianization, and capital accumulation). It also visibly functions as an impediment to the education and active participation of citizens in a democratic decision-making process dedicated to coexistence (Niemark 1999).

The shift toward the privatization and corporatization of public education is best exemplified by the corporate raider Michael Milken, the Wall Street wizard and junk bond king of the mid-1980s who lured investors into high-risk investment schemes. Milken has returned to the business world, this time by focusing on the lucrative $800 billion education market, and has decided to create for-profit education enterprises with the help of his powerful—yet comparatively obscure—$500 million company known as Knowledge Universe. Milken has invested heavily in several companies producing educational materials. Knowledge Universe owns companies such as Children's Discovery Centers, Bookman Testing Services, Pyramid Imaging Inc., Nobel Education Dynamics, and Leapfrog, which produces educational tools used at learning centers of the Riordan Foundation (Vrana 1998). In a recent interview with the *Los Angeles Times*, Milken calculated that if the net worth of the United States is placed at $120 trillion, roughly $75 trillion consists of human capital. This means that every American is worth $400,000 to $500,000 (Vrana 1998). In short, Milken has discovered that the knowledge business is a profitable commodity.

Recent attempts by corporations to influence policy and curriculum decisions in urban schools abound. According to Kalle Lasn (1999),

> Corporate advertising (or is it the commercial media?) is the largest psychological project ever undertaken by the human race. Yet for all of that, its impact on us remains unknown and largely ignored. When I think of the media's influence over years, over decades, I think of those brainwashing experiments conducted by Dr. Ewen Cameron in a Montreal psychiatric hospital in the 1950s. The idea of the CIA-sponsored "depatterning" experiment was to outfit conscious, unconscious or semiconscious subjects with headphones, and flood their brain with thousands of repetitive "driving" messages that would alter their behavior over time. Sound familiar? Advertising aims to do the same thing. Dr. Cameron's guinea pigs emerged from the Montreal trials with serious psychological damage. It was a great scandal. But no one is saying boo about the ongoing experiment of mass media advertising. In fact, new guinea pigs voluntarily come on board every day. (19)

It is not unusual these days to see school buses in certain states covered with advertisements for Burger King and Wendy's fast-food chain restaurants. It has become fashionable for elementary school children to carry books wrapped in free book covers plastered with ads for Kellogg's Pop Tarts and FOX television personalities. School districts have gleefully granted Coca-Cola and Pepsi exclusive contracts to sell their products in schools. In health education classes, students are taught nutrition by the Hershey Corporation in a scheme that includes a discussion of the important place of chocolate in a balanced diet. A classroom business course teaches students to value work by exploring how McDonald's restaurants are operated and what skills are needed to become a successful McDonald's manager and provides instructions on how to apply for a job at McDonald's. Ecological and environmental education now involves students learning ecology from a "Life of an Ant" poster sponsored by Skittles candy and an environmental curriculum video produced by Shell Oil that concentrates on the virtues of the external combustion engine. Finally, a new company called Zap Me! lures schools into accepting thousands of dollars worth of computer equipment, including a satellite dish, fifteen top-level personal computers, a furnished computer lab, and high-speed Internet access in return for a constant display of on-screen advertisements in the lower left-hand corner of the screen (see Fischman and McLaren 2000). Lasn (1999) writes,

> Your kids watch Pepsi and Snickers ads in the classroom (The school has made the devil's bargain of accepting free audiovisual equipment in exchange for airing these ads on "Channel One"). . . . Administrators in a Texas school district announce plans to boost revenues by selling ad space on the roofs of the district's seventeen schools—arresting the attention of the fifty-eight million commercial jet passengers who fly into Dallas each year. Kids tattoo their calves with swooshes. Other kids, at raves, begin wearing actual bar codes that other kids can scan, revealing messages such as "I'd like to sleep with you." . . . A few years ago, marketers began installing ad boards in men's washrooms on college campuses, at eye level above the urinals. From their perspective, it was a brilliant coup: Where else is a guy going to look? But when I first heard this was being done, I was incensed. One of the last private acts was being co-opted. (19–21)

A math book published by McGraw-Hill is spiked with references to Nike, Gatorade, Disney, McDonald's, Nabisco, Mattel Barbie dolls, Sony PlayStations, Cocoa Frosted Flakes, Spalding basketballs, and Topps baseball cards (Collins and Yeskel 2000, 78). John Borowski (1999), a public school teacher, noted in the *New York Times,*

> At least 234 corporations are now flooding the public schools with films, textbooks and computer software under the guise of "instructional material." A lesson in self-esteem sponsored by Revlon includes an investigation of "good and bad hair days." In a history lesson, Tootsie Rolls are touted as a part of soldiers' diets during World War II. Exxon provides a video on the Valdez spill playing down its ecological impact. And Chevron, in a lesson for use in civics science classes, reminds students that they will soon be able to vote and make "important decisions" about global warming, which the company then rebuts as incomplete science. (A23)

Another example of corporatism in schools is Channel One, a commercially produced news station that now operates in many American schools. As part of a contractual agreement, teachers agree to broadcast Channel One programs in class for ten minutes a day in return for a satellite dish, videocassette recorders, and as many television sets as they want. A study of its effects revealed that the students were no better informed than their contemporaries but that the advertisements broadcast on the channel had a significant effect on their consumer tastes (Aitkenhead, cited in Cole 1998, 327).

While students, teachers, staff, and local and community activists have admirably resisted the corporate pillage of public education, such resistance has been muted by zero-tolerance policies and the posting of "free speech zones" in university and college campuses as well as in public school settings. In some cases, this has led to the suspension of students who have vociferously protested against the corporate takeover of public schools. Consider the incident in May 2001 involving fifteen-year-old Tristan Kading, who objected to a McDonald's representative carrying out mock job interviews with students in the school's cafeteria. Kading blasted McDonald's for the corporation's unethical practices and cover-up involving its preparation of its french fries (while McDonald's had claimed that its french fries were prepared in vegetable oil, it also had failed to disclose that it added beef extract in the process, a fact that infuriated many vegetarians). But standing up against the Goliath fast-food conglomerate came at a high cost for Kading, who found himself in the principal's office and threatened with suspension unless he agreed to write an apology to the McDonald's representative and broadcast it over the school's PA system. Under extreme pressure and in fear of further humiliation, Kading complied. But after the incident, Kading decided to contact a local newspaper that reported the incident. After much ensuing publicity, the school district was forced to rethink its partnership with the McDonald's job fair at the school.

Corporations have set foot in the lucrative and profitable market of "branding" adolescence consciousness—literally. In England, the marketing agency Cunning Stunts has developed an innovative approach to advertising commercial brand products. The company has found that students' foreheads can be made into a profitable venture. The advertising agency is hiring students who are willing to wear a corporate logo on their heads for a minimum of three hours a day for £88.20 a week. As John Cassy (2003) of *The Guardian* reports, "The brand or product message will be attached by a vegetable dye transfer and the students will be paid to leave the logos untouched."

Consider a national organization called Field Trip Factory. As part of its "Be a Smart Shopper" program, the company organizes field trips for students who live in the Boston metropolitan area. Students visit local chain stores, such as Sports Authority. And for their homework assignment, students are encouraged to check their local newspaper for Roche Bros. and Sudbury Farms coupons and make a "shopping list."

What is evident from these examples is that corporations are not preparing students for critical citizenship but rather preparing them to play their roles as consumer–citizens. Whereas the former encourages students to question, conceptualize, analyze, theorize, and critically reflect on their experiences, the latter lures students into an uncritical and blind acceptance of market values and practices designed to reinforce and maintain capitalist social relations of production. As Charles Sullivan (2003) remarks,

> Of course it is not in the self-interest of capitalism to educate people who can see capitalism for what it is, to think critically about it, and perhaps even do something to change it. Corporate education exists to promote programming consumers and providing an obedient work force to an unfair slave wage system, not to provide society with a well informed and politically active citizenry. In fact these are the things that pose the greatest threat to America's corporate oligarchy.

To penetrate deeper into the profitable market of the younger generation of students, the food conglomerate Nabisco has dedicated a website to its popular brand of Oreo cookies. The website offers students math, English, art, and science lessons based on its brand of Oreo cookies. Students can improve their math and measurement skills by investigating the number of Oreo cookies it takes to make one foot. To improve their English skills, students can write a story describing the best method to eat an Oreo cookie. The website encourages students to enhance their survey skills by documenting the Oreo cookie-eating habits of their classmates and by asking questions such as, Do you eat out the middle first? Do you dunk your Oreo in the milk?

Students can further study the "Oreo fact sheet," which includes statistics such as that the St. Louis Arch (630 feet) is 15,120 Oreo cookies high, the Golden Gate Bridge (4,200 feet) is 28,800 Oreo cookies in length, and that 345 billion Oreo cookies have been consumed. For an art project, students can create "Oreo booklets" using black construction paper for the booklet's cover (representing the cookie) and white paper stapled inside the cover (representing the white cream filling). Afterward, students can write a journal entry describing their "Oreo experience." Finally, students can test their science skills by analyzing the nutritional content of Oreo cookies and measure the number of calories of each Oreo cookie.

With an estimated revenue of $4.4 billion in 2002 and a workforce of 33,000 full-time permanent employees and 224,000 full-time seasonal or temporary employees in ninety countries, the conglomerate Dole Food Company offers math, science, environmental awareness, and language arts lesson plans on its website to students, teachers, and parents. Dole also offers a "toolkit" titled "Nutritional Adventures," which is based on its "5-a-day" nutrition program. The manifest purpose of the program is to encourage children to eat fruits and vegetables. While this is not a bad thing, the latent goal here is for students to identify healthy eating habits with the brand product name of Dole.

Faced with growing budget deficits and dwindling resources, many public schools have been forced to sign "pouring contracts" worth millions of dollars with soda companies. These contracts allow soda companies to place their vending machines in cafeterias and in other strategic locations throughout schools that would be visible to students. For example, in 1997, Coca-Cola signed a ten-year contract worth $11 million with the Colorado Springs, Colorado, school district, and Dr. Pepper signed a ten-year, $4 million contract with Dallas's Grapevine High School. As part of the deal, Coca-Cola is permitted to place the company's logo on the roofs of the school's buildings. Not to be outperformed by its competitors, Pepsi has been negotiating a lucrative twelve-year, $50 million deal with Hillsborough County Schools in St. Petersburg, Florida. But soda conglomerates are not alone in the corporatization and commercialization of public schools. As Brian Bakst (2003) reports,

> Two South Carolina districts recently hired a marketing company to locate advertisers for auditoriums and lunch rooms. Last summer, paint-maker Rust-Oleum put $100,000 toward a Chicago-area high school's new football stadium, earning it naming rights and plaques. In 2001, the ShopRite supermarket chain agreed to pay $100,000 over 20 years to get its name on an elementary school gym in Brooklawn, N.J.

Finally, in Minnesota, General Mills gambled on an ethically questionable advertising ploy that involved paying local schoolteachers $250 in exchange for plastering their cars with Reese's Puffs cereal logo. As part of the agreement, teachers were required to park their cars close to school buses in order to capture the attention of unsuspecting schoolchildren. However, the scheme soon backfired as teachers and parents voiced their opposition to the tactics devised by General Mills.

Another effective corporate tactic is to promote school contests. A notable example is Oakdale Elementary School in Frederick County, Maryland, which participated in Oscar Mayer's "School House Jam" contest and won $10,000 for performing the "best interpretation" of Oscar Mayer's famous wiener song. The conglomerate Nestlé Company, famous for its chocolate, awarded $10,000 to the school that came up with the most creative art project using the company's brand candy, SweeTarts. This year, a whopping 5,200 schools participated in the SweeTart contest. As Caroline Mayer (2003) reports, the art projects in the contest included a "SweeTart mosaic of Leonardo da Vinci's Mona Lisa and a life-size, three-dimensional car called the Sweetmobile that was covered in thousands of pieces of the pastel candy.

The grand prize went to a Boston school for its staircase mural, with replicas of famous paintings by Monet, Van Gogh and Dali, each incorporating the candy in some way."

Even tissue paper companies are taking advantage of the budget crisis in public schools to market their brand products. Angel Soft toilet paper company has created the "Angel in Action" program, which awards $10,000 to the school that develops the best community service program. A recent recipient was Baltimore Stadium School's youth-run youth center. Finally, there is Dunkin' Donuts, which sponsors a "Homework Stars" commercial contest. The company awards $6,000 to the school that creates the best one-minute commercial emphasizing the importance of homework. Dunkin' Donuts also awards students with an "eight-page activity guide" and provides Dunkin' Donuts coupons to students who complete their homework on a consistent basis.

The corporate assault on public schools does not end with the display of brand products in school hallways and corporate-sponsored curricula in the classrooms. A small yet growing trend is the development of work-site schools—a collaborative effort between the private business sector and public school districts. The partnership calls for the private sector to finance and construct classroom space and building facilities and for school districts to provide teachers, textbooks, and instructional materials. These schools (which at the moment number approximately forty-five throughout the United States) target "at-risk" students or children of company employees. A case in point is the Mall Academy, a joint venture between the Seattle School District and the Simon Youth Foundation. Housed in Northgate Shopping Mall, the Mall Academy offers four concentrated areas of study for students between the ages of sixteen and twenty-one. These include Middle College, Applied Health Occupation, Career Ladders, and Marketing on the Mall. The idea behind the school-in-the-mall concept is to provide students with "hands-on" experiences in the retail industry, which students can gain at Northgate Mall. Of course, one of the controversies surrounding the school-in-the-mall concept is that it provides private business access to a pool of cheap labor. In addition, it helps cut back on costs associated with the training and education of labor (Lockery 2003).

Henry Giroux (2001) warns that with the advent of neoliberalism, public schools are no longer seen as a public asset but rather as a private good. Advocates of neoliberalism, he says, are "aggressively waging a war against the very possibility of creating non-commodified public spheres and forums that provide the conditions for critical education" (30). Here neoliberalism is conceptualized "as both a set of economic policies and an impoverished notion of citizenship . . . [that] represents not just a series of market-driven programs but also a coherent set of cultural, political, and educational practices" (30). Giroux is worth quoting further:

> Neoliberalism works not only to produce a depoliticized consumer culture, it also limits the possibilities for *any* noncommodified social domains where young and old alike can experience dissent and difference as part of a multicultural democracy, locate metaphors of hope, respond to those who carry on the legacies of moral witnessing, and imagine relationships outside of the dictates of the market and the authoritarian rule of penal control. Educators and others need to rethink what it means to not only challenge a system that turns its children into a generation of suspects, but also how it might be possible to radically transform a social order marked by zero tolerance policies that reinforce modes of authoritarian control and social amnesia in a vast and related number of powerful institutional spheres. This suggests the need for both a collective struggle for public space and a public dialogue about how to imagine reappropriating a notion of politics that contributes to the development of authentic democracy while simultaneously articulating a new discourse, set of theoretical tools, and social possibilities for reviving civic education as a basis for political agency and social transformation. (58)

On the one hand, schools do contribute to the ideals of democratic organizations (in terms of providing access to relevant knowledge and equal opportunities). On the other hand, schools operate at the same time in sustaining and reinforcing the logic of capitalism by functioning as a reproductive force that offers different and unequal kinds of knowledge and rewards based on class, gender, and race (McLaren 1997). Here we see inequality as having to do with how society regulates the distribution of different types of capital. Perrucci and Wysong (1999) describe these as consumption capital (having to do with wages or salary), investment capital (having to do with a surplus of consumption capital that you can invest and on which you can earn interest), skills capital (having to do with specialized knowledge that people accumulate through their work experience, training, or education), and social capital (having to do with the network of social ties that people have to family, friends, and acquaintances as well as the collectively owned economic and cultural capital of a group). Educators have long made the case that schools traffic in cultural capital (values, attitudes, dress, mannerisms, personal style, and so on) (McLaren 1997), but they have rarely linked the production of cultural capital to the international division of labor brought about by uneven development.

Race, Class, or Gender? Beyond the Either–Or Impasse

Read against the continuing globalization of capital, the concept of class remains a taboo subject within the guarded precincts of academic discourses.

Seldom do politicians, intellectuals, or the media openly discuss class inequality in a language that situates it within the larger problematic of global capitalism and relations of exploitation and oppression linked to imperialism. To understand how educational inequalities are reproduced within schools, it is crucial not to leave class in the shade and to analyze the concept of class and class relations in a contextually nuanced way. Michael Parenti (1994) underscores the importance of class relations when he argues,

> Class realities permeate our society, determining much about our lifestyles and life chances, our capacity to make serviceable things happen, our access to power. How the dynamics and crises of capitalism are handled, and how the state is organized, are core questions for political struggle. They also are inescapably class questions. There are class interests involved in how the law is written and enforced, how political leaders pursue issues, how science and social science are studied and funded, how work is done, how a university is ruled, how the news is reported, how mass culture is created and manipulated, how careers are advanced or retarded, how the environment is treated, how racism and sexism are activated and reinforced, and how social reality itself is defined. (64)

The concept of class expresses the relationship that social groups have to the means of production; it refers to those who own the factories, machinery, media, hotels, hospitals, and so on and those who must sell their labor in exchange for wages (Parenti 1994). Wages that workers receive in the form of money are equivalent to only part of the value they create by their labor. Wealth so construed constitutes accumulated surplus or the unpaid wages of the workers.

Postmodernists—whose work now composes the fountainhead of radical educational critique—frequently overlook the centrality of class warfare as the overarching mechanism that inscribes individuals and groups in the reproduction of social relations of exploitation under capitalism. Although admittedly an individual's subjectivity or identity cannot be reduced to class interests, nevertheless social oppression and economic exploitation are much more than tangentially linked to class background and the social relations of production. In fact, forms of racial and gender oppression can best be understood against the background of class analysis. Marxists maintain that the eradication of poverty, racism, sexism, and patriarchal exploitation requires an understanding of class struggle. There are two reasons for identifying the working class as the central agent of social transformation. First, the working class continues to possess the ability to halt production lines. Second, a revolutionary working-class politics seeks to abolish all forms of social oppression. Postmodernists, on the other hand, seek to create a radical democracy through new social movements that

concentrate on ending particular or local forms of oppression. In the words of
Dana L. Cloud (1994),

> While a person's subjectivity is not a simple matter of class determination, his or
> her oppression and exploitation are directly connected to his/her economic sta-
> tus and position in the relations of production. Marxists believe there is more to
> liberation than the articulation of alternative subjectivities; an end to poverty,
> hunger, exploitation and abuse are more central, and require a notion of class
> position, agency and interests. From this perspective there are two good reasons
> for privileging working-class struggles. First, the working class has the power to
> stop production and bring the profit-making system down. Second, the working
> class, the group of men and women of all races and sexual orientations whose
> labour produces profits for the few, has an objective . . . interest in overthrowing
> capitalism, whereas some members of many cross-class, non-socialist groups or-
> ganized around other antagonisms (women's rights, environmental issues) have
> vested interests in maintaining the profit system. (242)

According to E. San Juan Jr. (1992), identity politics frequently and tragically leads to a privatization of political issues that "recuperates an autonomous will, and indigenous Otherness" (107) and in doing so voids resistance of its historical density. What identity politics fails to address is the fact
that diversity and difference are allowed to proliferate and flourish provided
that they remain within the prevailing forms of capitalist social arrangements,
including hierarchical property arrangements. San Juan argues that there is a
"blind spot which identity politics cannot apprehend" (107). He refers here to
the fact that

> the contingencies of a hegemonic struggle can generate a variety of subject po-
> sitions which are neither fixed nor shifting but capable of being articulated in
> various directions according to the play of political forces and the conjunctural
> alignment of multi-layered determinants. (107)

Along with San Juan, we worry about the engineered collusion between an
identity politics that stresses autonomous lived experience and a neoliberalism that encourages the erasure of the public sphere and the ascendancy of a
capitalist triumphalism that synchronizes so-called autonomous agency to
the hierarchical imperatives of advanced capitalism. What also disturbs us
are the denunciations by some radical educators that anticapitalist struggles
can operate only as a foolish rhetorical device and what is needed is an equal
distribution of economic resources. Although we favor economic equality, we
find that the anti-Marxist sentiments among some radical educators constitutes an egregious capitulation to the value form of labor (often under the
banner of a positive populism) and the iron law of motions of capital accu-

mulation. It is a position innocent of insight into contemporary social relations of production.

What Boris Kagarlitsky (2000) calls a "strategic hierarchy of goals" grounded in the overthrow of the social hierarchy of capitalist society is a measure that we take seriously. We acknowledge that political struggle for race, class, gender, and sexual equality is a tightly interwoven struggle. But we understand class politics as the engine of our struggle for proletarian hegemony. As Robert McChesney (1996) asserts,

> Radicals are opposed to all forms of oppression and it is ludicrous to debate which of sexism, racism, "classism," or homophobia is most terrible, as if we were in some zero-sum game. Socialists have traditionally emphasized class—and continue to do so today—because the engine of a capitalist society is profit maximization and class struggle. Moreover, it is only through class politics that human liberation can truly be reached. (4–5)

In acknowledging this, we do not follow postmodernists in calling for an equivalence among various struggles. Rather, we call for a strategic integration of different yet equally important struggles. Recognizing that the legacy of racism and sexism is far from over (in fact, in many ways it is intensifying), we offer possible ways in which race and gender antagonisms can be addressed and overcome within the larger project of class struggle. As Adolph Reed Jr. (2000) maintains, "Recent debates that juxtapose identity politics or cultural politics to class politics are miscast. Cultural politics and identity politics are class politics" (xxii). The ways in which the contradiction between capital and labor is lived at the level of everyday life are almost certainly racialized and gendered. The modalities in which class exploitation are lived have specific consequences related to race, sexuality, age, and religion, and these must be placed at center stage in the struggle against oppression. We want to make clear that we are not subordinating race, ethnic, and gender struggles to class struggle. We simply are saying that without overcoming capitalist relations of production, other struggles will have little chance of succeeding. Yet to make such an assertion is to identify a structured silence within many postmodernized versions of critical pedagogy: the disappearance of class struggle.

Overcoming racism and sexism are not sidebar issues but are central to the revolutionary multiculturalism endorsed here. We do not intend to use class relations as a conceptual or political shield for racism or sexism or to make the jejune claim that a focus on racial inequality undermines working-class efforts at organizing against the transnational capitalist oligopolies. Nor do we agree with some of our well-meaning white colleagues that an emphasis on class struggle takes away from the efforts of educators of color in their struggle against racism. This criticism fails to acknowledge that many educators of color have been at the forefront of the class struggle. Although strategically our dependent variable remains that of class, independent variables such as gender, race, religion, sexuality, and political ideology are not seen as cursory sites of antagonisms—they factor in our analysis in very central and distinctive ways.

Class: The Outmoded or Forgotten Antagonism

We believe not that class struggle is outmoded but rather that it constitutes one of the crucial missing dimensions of contemporary educational criticism (McLaren 1998b). We are rejecting neo-Weberian concept of class based on consumption-based patterns, status, and occupational hierarchies that tell us little about the relationship between social classes. Along with British Marxist educators Dave Hill and Mike Cole, we reject technicist reductions of class into "fractions" or segments that hide or disguise common interests such as common consciousness among these groups comprising the working class in opposition to the exploiting capitalist class (Hill and Cole 2001).

We feel it is important for the educational researcher to recognize both the political and the pedagogical import of the dilemma put forward by Ellen Meiksins Wood (1994): "Once you replace the concept of capitalism with an undifferentiated plurality of social identities and special oppressions, socialism as the antithesis to capitalism loses all meaning" (29). Here the critical educational researcher challenges the relativism of the gender–race–class grid of reflexive positionality by recognizing that class antagonism or struggle is not simply one in a series of social antagonisms but rather constitutes the part of this series that sustains the horizon of the series itself. In other words, class struggle is the specific antagonism that assigns rank to and modifies the particularities of the other antagonisms in the series (Žižek 1999).

Despite recent attacks on critical pedagogy as universalist and totalizing (see Lather 2001), the critical educational researcher refuses to evacuate reference to historical structures of totality and universality by recognizing that class struggle itself enables the proliferation of new political subjectivities. Both conservative and liberal bourgeois anti-Marxists refuse to see how class struggle structures in advance the very terrain of political antagonisms. Such a failure of recognition has led them to annex the enterprise of progressive educational criticism to the discourse of liberal democracy (albeit cloaked in fashionable transgressive attire). Postmodern theorists recognize these contradictions hidden in the arid soil of advanced capitalist democracies but are largely unable to develop an anticapitalist political agenda except by restricting their observations to cultural formations and thereby obfuscating the political economy of real existing capitalism.

On the other hand, we are confronted by the protestations and denunciations of some Derridean poststructuralists who reject Marxism, *tout court*, as hopelessly outdated. Patti Lather's (2001) plaintive cry of "Ten Years Later, Yet Again" (which is intended to raise the issue of why Marxists pedagogues still work within supposedly received and exhausted masculinist categories after poststructuralists had, ten years earlier, shown them how to be less self-assured and to adopt a less transparent analysis under the advance guard of "teletechnic dislocation, rhizomatic spreading and acceleration, and new experiences of frontier and identity") is the latest example. We maintain that such condemnations amount to little more than intellectual scrap metal and should be read against another cry in the face of the barbarianized academy: "One Hundred and Fifty Years after the Communist Manifesto: Ruling Class Pedagogues Cloaked as Avant-Gardist Defending the Capitalist Class, Yet Again." Bourgeois educationalists from today's battered and beleaguered Left who write under the sign of anti-Marxist chic have largely abandoned the struggles of the world's poor, uncoupling history from the fight for liberation. Michael Parenti (2001) writes:

> Most Left intellectuals in the United States are busy fighting the ghost of Stalin, dwelling on the tabloid reports of the "horrors" of communism, doing fearless battle against imaginary hordes of "doctrinaire" Marxists at home and abroad, or in some other way flashing their anti-communist credentials and shoring up their credibility. So busy in these pursuits are they that they seem relatively unconcerned about the real dangers we face, about how the rights and life chances of millions of people throughout the world have been seriously damaged. (158)

Patti Lather (2001), in particular, not only demonstrates an understanding of human agency as untethered to social relations of production but also unwittingly advocates a move toward centrist politics that etherealizes class struggle into questions of antiessentializing epistemology and evacuates historicity under the guise of a fashionable anti-Marxism. Her position, popular in the postmodern academy, represents what San Juan (1999) calls "the new conformism." His comment is apposite here:

> Anyone caught "totalizing" or rehearsing "grand metanarratives" of the Eurocentric variety can be flunked, denied tenure, ostracized. But the new conformism that claims to be more radical than anything proves, on closer examination, to be just an application of the old paradigm of close New Critical

reading—a more sophisticated encoding/decoding exercise—to shopping malls, television and film, museums, rituals high and low, and the practices of everyday life. The hermeneutics of Lyotard, Baudrillard, de Certeau, Clifford, etc. is now in vogue. The "linguistic turn" in the seventies, together with the uncritical appropriation of Althusser and other poststructuralist doxa, may be responsible for the return of formalism and metaphysics in new guises. Could this have been anticipated if the Williams road of the "long revolution" were followed? (118)

According to Slavoj Žižek (2001b), class struggle "is not the last horizon of meaning, the last signified of all social phenomena, but the formal generative matrix of the different ideological horizons of understanding" (16–17). In Žižek's terms, class struggle sets the ground for the empty place of universality, enabling it to be filled variously with contents of different sorts (ecology, feminism, antiracism). He notes, important for our purposes, that "the economy is at one and the same time the genus and one of its own species" (2001a, 193).

Toward a Revolutionary Working-Class Pedagogy

One centerpiece of a revolutionary working-class pedagogy is engaging in ideology critique in light of understanding the unseen grammar of commodity logic that serves as the regulatory lexicon of everyday life. Such a pedagogy involves struggle over the production of meaning, a struggle that would enable marginalized social groups to name, identify, and take initial steps to transform the sources of their oppression and exploitation (McLaren 1998a). It would also encourage them to analyze the myriad ways in which asymmetrical relations of power are both ideologically congealed in and concealed by the dominant discourses of equality, difference, and freedom (Giroux and McLaren 1986). Although students are admittedly more than unconscious bearers of social structures, we are cognizant of the power of objective social structures to engineer complicity among both students and teachers in relations of exploitation and oppression. Consequently, a revolutionary working-class pedagogy stresses the importance of acquiring a critical literacy—where literacy is defined as a practice of reflecting, analyzing, and making critical judgments in relation to social, economic, and political issues (see Lankshear and McLaren 1993; see also Giroux, Lankshear, McLaren, and Peters 1996). Furthermore, it invites subordinate groups to represent through classroom interaction and dialogue their lived reality in relation to objective social structures that shape their lives. This is done to solidify their beliefs, values, and experiences and also to challenge their everyday beliefs when they are discovered to be hegemonically advantageous (in the sense that they constitute dispositions that lead to concrete social practices or a complicity with certain social arrangements) to the reproduction of capitalist relations of exploitation (Giroux et al. 1996). In addition, this approach challenges students and workers to analyze the various meanings that underlie commonsensical concepts by drawing on everyday understandings that reflect their own social experiences. Teachers as revolutionary intellectuals contest the manufactured meaning of democracy by calling on students, workers, and intellectuals to critically examine socially constructed concepts such as freedom and democracy, which have been manufactured by neoliberal ideologues in the service of transnational capitalism (Fischman and McLaren 2000; McLaren and Fischman 1998). Students are invited to analyze the stories and narratives that animate their lives by setting them against a normative backdrop of heterosexist and Eurocentric assumptions (McLaren 1998a; Ovando and McLaren 2000; Sleeter and McLaren 1995).

Mainstream pedagogy assiduously disregards as crucial a knowledge of how asymmetrical relations of power become embedded in race, gender, and class antagonisms that are reinforced through the dominant social and ideological apparatuses of the state. In contrast, a revolutionary working-class pedagogy sets as its goal the transformation of existing social and economic relations by encouraging marginalized social groups both to critique and to transform capitalist social relations of production. Here the classroom is conceived as a political arena for legitimizing the lived experiences of the oppressed social classes without assuming that such experiences are transparent or absent of racism or sexism (Freire 1970, 1998; Giroux 1988; McLaren 1995, 1997).

Attributes of a Revolutionary Working-Class Pedagogy

A working-class pedagogy entails struggles over meaning, representation, and identity in relation to a moral and ethical commitment to social justice (Cole 1998; Cole and Hill 1995; Cole, Hill, and Rikowski 1997). Knoblauch and Brannon (1993) argue that citizenship within a capitalist democracy

> includes an allegiance to passive consumerism, rather than active engagement in the construction of social life, and a long-standing hostility to practices of critical inquiry, certainly including liberatory pedagogy but also, historically, the challenges of labor unions, feminists, gays, environmental activists, and anyone else posing a conceivable threat to economic interests and managerial hierarchies that the media help to maintain. (31)

This is in marked contrast to a revolutionary working-class pedagogy that underscores the active participation of students and workers in their own self-education as active citizens linked to the struggle for self-realization and coexistence—a process by which workers gain control over both their intellectual and their physical labor. This also entails promoting among students and workers—especially in countries where subsistence or state coercion dominate everyday life—alternative networks of popular organizing that include revolutionary social movements (McLaren and Farahmandpur 2000).

A revolutionary working-class pedagogy aims at transforming the consciousness of being in alienation by developing a critical consciousness. We should stress that alienation is not rooted in the world of Hegelian abstractions but rather is embedded within the social and material relations of production. This raises questions as to whether an alienated consciousness is an inert totality and if it can be transcended. According to Mészáros (1989), alienated activity produces not only an alienated consciousness but also a consciousness of being in alienation. Therefore, it is advisable to create those pedagogical conditions that, for the working class, facilitate the development of a critical consciousness to overcome economic alienation and transform the existing social conditions of production through mass political action. Such action must be capable of creating egalitarian structures that are able to achieve—at an increasing level and in an ever-expanding scope—the institutionalization of popular democracy. Of course, this means aggregating diverse constituencies that might be distrustful of one another. We want to be clear that pedagogically we are not arguing for the teacher to serve as the mediator between imputed and factual consciousness, as someone who compels the student to activate or actualize revolutionary consciousness, who imports socialist insight from her rucksack in the Sierra Maestra to student *foco* groups in the United States. This position is tantamount to an externally imposed dictatorship of the teacher that relies on the false opposition of ideal type and factual actualization. Rather, our approach is Freirean in that it argues that revolutionary consciousness is a political act of knowing, an active intervention against the barriers that prevent the students from achieving their role as agents of history.

It is critical to remember that as revolutionary educators, we need to identify alternative subject positions that we might assume or counternarratives and countermemories that we might make available to our students to contest existing regimes of representation and social practice. But we cannot be content to remain here. We need to identify the historical determinations of domination and oppression as part of the struggle to develop concrete practices of counterrepresentation. The search for external causes of domination and exploitation should not be forgotten in the fashionable rush on the part of some postmodern educators to encounter and explain différence in subjective terms. Emphasizing freedom as the realization of humanity's purpose, by which labor as a social means fulfills its human needs, is an important characteristic of the revolutionary working-class pedagogy that we are envisioning. It engages teachers as reflexive practitioners in their daily lives. To become a critically reflective practitioner requires the ability to engage in complex analyses of social class accompanied by trenchant investigations of other forms of oppression as they are linked to capitalist exploitation—relations linked to race, gender, and sexual orientation. In short, it requires a comprehensive form of political agency that moves beyond the particular struggles of select groups (McLaren and Farahmandpur 2000).

A revolutionary working-class pedagogy does not adventitiously discard the term "working class" for the more politically acceptable term "disadvantaged"— the latter being an exceedingly popular term in Left-liberal stratification models that stress *structural location* over *social relation*. Stratification models that view class as a structural location factor out power and exploitation between social classes, whereas viewing class as a social relation links class situations to antagonisms and conditions of struggle in which people are distributed into a division of labor by relations of production (Hatcher 2000). Here, we agree with Richard Hatcher (2000), who argues that

> Class does not have an equivalent conceptual status to "race" and gender. This is also true with respect to disability and sexuality. It is not a question of creating a "hierarchy of oppressions" but of recognizing that class is constitutive of capitalist society in a way that "race," gender, sexuality and disability are not. Furthermore, race is not purely an economic category which leaves other areas of social life to other social identities alone. Capitalism is an overarching totalizing system which is constituted by class but which shapes all social oppressions. While it is indifferent to the identities of those it exploits, it also systematically co-opts and structures extra-economic oppressions. (186–87)

Hatcher (2000) explores class differences in the relations between the student and knowledge, a relation that is rooted in the social division of labor. Here, social origin structures educational outcomes but does not determine them. Working-class knowledge is "practical" and context specific and can be distinguished from the "abstract" knowledge of more affluent students who have a greater opportunity to acquire high-status knowledge. Drawing on the work of Bob Connell and Bernard Charlot, Hacker explains that typical of low-achieving students is their relationship to the learning situation. In addition, working-class students tend to see learning in terms of completing tasks rather than as the process of entering into a different universe of knowledge and don't conceptualize the link between schoolwork and their future in the way that most middle-class students do, for instance, as something intrinsically rewarding in itself as well as extrinsically helpful in getting a good job in the future. The key is for working-class students to have a meaningful relation to knowledge.

The question that teachers need to ask is the following: In what ways can working-class students use school knowledge in order to, in Hatcher's (2000) words, "organize understandings and actions in order to further his or her own meanings and purposes"(190)? Crucially important is the reconstruction of the curriculum so that the alienating aspects of modes of transmitting knowledge can be eliminated. An important aim is not simply "equality of outcome," that is, helping to provide the context for working-class students to embrace the skills and knowledge for success within the existing system but also enabling students to acquire the necessary skills and competences for collective struggle against the system. One way to facilitate this process is through inquiry-oriented activities that involve a real-world application of knowledge (Hatcher 2000). These ideas have been detailed in McLaren's (1998a) own public school teaching experiences documented in his *Life in Schools*. Of course, the overarching goal of revolutionary critical pedagogy is to conscript collective agency among localities to "transnation agency" through the creation of a transnational, antiracist, anti-imperialist, gender-balanced social movement dedicated to creating political options outside of capitalism's law of value.

A revolutionary working-class pedagogy seeks to transgress the boundaries that set high culture apart from popular culture and that privilege the former over the latter. Empowering the working class and marginalized social groups in society means giving them an opportunity to interrogate theoretically (in the sense articulated by both Marx and Lenin) forms of both high culture and popular culture so that they can analyze, articulate, express, and construct meaning from multiple positionalities located in their lived experiences dealing with racism, sexism, and class exploitation. In addition, disenfranchised groups need to control the means of production of their symbolic economies, not to mention their material existence. Because a revolutionary working-class pedagogy also recognizes that the language and the discourses practiced within the classroom setting as well as in the workplace are ideologically tainted with the values, beliefs, and interests of the privileged social classes so as to conceal asymmetrical relations of power, an important step involves the encouragement of critical dialogues among teachers, students, and workers. The central purpose of such dialogues would be to raise class consciousness and help students and workers recognize how

their subjectivities and social identities are configured in ways that are structurally advantageous to the status quo. This requires that students are able to
see themselves in relation to their role as the potential gravediggers of capitalism and to be provided with an opportunity to develop class consciousness. This does not mean that class consciousness excludes other aspects of
identity. As Reed (2000) points out,

> The claim that being a worker is not the most crucial identity for members of
> marginalized groups is debatable. To say the least. But even if that claim were true,
> what it means simply is that people see themselves in many ways simultaneously.
> We all have our own sets of experiences fashioned by our social position, our fam-
> ily upbringing, our local political culture, and our voluntary associations. Each of
> these goes into the mix, modifying, cross-cutting, even at times overriding iden-
> tities based on race or ethnicity, gender, or sexual orientation. . . . The fact of the
> existence of a capitalist economic order doesn't automatically tell us how people
> interpret their positions within it. Class consciousness, no less than other identi-
> ties, is contingent, the product of political debate and struggle. (137)

It is imperative in our view that the struggles of teachers in schools are
linked to the struggles of other workers. A revolutionary working-class pedagogy of labor stresses that the empowerment of workers (that is, teachers,
postal workers, factory workers) can be successfully achieved through organizing labor unions that are committed to anticapitalist struggle and a
proletarian praxis. Yet we must also emphasize that the political and economic empowerment of workers will depend on their active participation
and self-education. Here we oppose the tradition of "workerism" that is
often anti-intellectual and looks on theory with suspicion and often contempt. Instead, we applaud the recent struggles of intellectuals such as
Pierre Bourdieu of France to coordinate the efforts of numerous European
social movements through his organization, Raisons d'Agir. The ability of
teachers and prospective teachers to interpret contemporary social relations
of production as a set of interconnected social and material practices helps
them understand that success in a capitalist society is not the result of individual capacities but rather is constrained and enabled by asymmetrical relations of power linked to race, class, gender, and sexual economies of privilege. We believe that workers committed to social justice have the
opportunity to become liberatory intellectuals (what Antonio Gramsci
[1971] referred to as "organic" intellectuals) who possess the capacity to
make meaningful choices and decisions in their lives (McLaren, Fischman,
Serra, and Antelo 1998). Thus, teachers who are central to the process of
raising students' political consciousness must themselves become theoreti-
cians of their own teaching practices. Accordingly, our task as organic and

committed intellectuals is to create the conditions for the development of a revolutionary consciousness among the working class in general and teachers and students in particular.

In developing a framework for forging solidarity and collective action among workers and students, we find the three conditions that Weinbaum (1998) proposes to be particularly instructive. First, the central role of critical educators must be directed at facilitating dialogues among workers and students concerning everyday labor practices at the workplace and teaching practices within schools. Second, teachers and workers must be presented with opportunities for transforming those relationships that link their individual interests and issues at the local and community level to broader social and economic relations at a global level. And finally, Weinbaum stresses the active political role that critical educators in labor unions and schools must play both in their communities and in progressive organizations.

We believe that a revolutionary working-class pedagogy that aims at consciousness raising, political activism, and social empowerment can be a critical tool for self-determination and also for transforming existing social conditions. Yet we feel it is necessary to stress that working-class pedagogy can be effective only to the degree that marginalized social groups are able to organize into oppositional social and political movements against global capitalism and remain committed to a metanarrative of social justice both inside and outside the classroom. This stipulates that a stress on difference not undercut the possibility of political solidarity. As Reed (2000) notes,

> Insofar as identity politics insists on recognizing difference as the central truth of political life, it undercuts establishing a broad base as a goal of organizing. Its reflex is to define ever more distinct voices and to approach collective action from an attitude more like suspicion than solidarity. (xxii)

Conclusion: Teachers as Activists

Capitalism cannot remain a sustainable social and economic system under the guidance of neoliberal free-market economics without periodic wars and financial crises. Following Marx, we believe that the exploitation powered by capitalist social relations can be overcome only by the redistribution of wealth through class struggle and, finally, by the abolition of private property and capital itself.

A revolutionary working-class pedagogy seeks to reclaim revolutionary ideas from the frozen stasis of their exile, an exile that occured after what John Leonard (2000) calls "the 1989 collapse of the non-profit police states of Eastern Europe" (14). Rebuilding revolutionary ideas and practices can be achieved, in part, by forming coalitions among gay and lesbian organizations, ethnic minority groups, indigenous movements, and labor constituencies of various stripes. Here we are not advancing the revolutionary adventurist rhetoric that Lenin warned against; rather, we are criticizing uncommitted intellectuals in academic circles who constrain rather than enable the advancement of a revolutionary praxis. Such intellectuals too often succumb to a paralysis of the political will.

Struggles against social and economic injustice can effectively be organized and articulated among various anti-imperialist groups when they coalesce around mutual and shared interests. Revolutionary movements can succeed on a global basis only when differences over ideological interests and political goals can be resolved or at least temporarily put aside. This is not an argument for a unification of several political parties under the leadership of one party (for example, the Rainbow Coalition); rather, we are insisting that a successful revolutionary praxis must occur as the culmination of historical processes in which various social movements with different interests develop an understanding of each others' often conflicting experiences as the victims of societal oppression.

A revolutionary or "remilitantized" critical pedagogy requires moving anticapitalist struggles in the direction of a new transnationalism that extends beyond the nation-state. Organizing teachers as part of a larger compendium of social movements struggling toward a set of common objective goals (such as the abolition of economic exploitation, sexism, and racism) is necessary for the development of an effective revolutionary politics—one that can demonstrably create the necessary conditions for disenfranchised social groups to empower themselves (McLaren 1998b; McLaren and Farahmandpur 1999a, 1999b, 2000). This is not a romantic call to don a *bleu de travail* and rush the corporate barricades erected by procapitalist ideologues but to understand how the forces of globalization and neoliberalism are not forces in their own right but are connected to a wider system of exploitation that is as old as capitalism itself. We do not seek to answer the question of whether a new capitalist class has been created by the globalization of capital but rather acknowledge the competitive struggles among various capitalists in the context of the tension between labor and capital and the link between horizontal intercapitalist relations and vertical class relations and class conflict (Allman 2001). The connective tissue that holds the various social movements in place should not be a commitment to a diffuse counterhegemonic struggle but a dedication to the achievement of proletarian hegemony.

We use the term "proletarian," which may seem antiquated, to identify all those whose labor is exploited for its surplus value in the interests of profit. While admittedly there has been a global restructuring of the class composition of wage labor, we are using the term in its broadest sense. There is a danger here that the drive toward socialism advocated by some Marxists will be restricted mainly to an ethical socialism, socialist republicanism, or market socialism.

Revolutionary critical pedagogy seeks to create a context in which freedom from the enslaving subordination of the individual to the crisis-prone nature of capital accumulation replaces the arid realm of necessity, where the satisfaction of social need replaces the entrapment within the division of labor, where the development of the creative capacities of the individual replaces the laws of capital and landed property, and where worker self-rule and the free development of individuals replaces the current entrapment in the Byzantine maze of capitalist bureaucracy and the bureaucratization and atomization and alienation of social life. As Marx and Engels wrote in the *Manifesto*, the goal of socialist society is expressed as "an association, in which the free development of each is the condition for the free development of all."

Teacher educators as part of a broader revolutionary anticapitalist movement based on the development of a new transnationalist class politics (in the form of a historical bloc rather than a political party) must be attentive to the diverse social and political interests as well as the needs of different constituencies in the struggle. Furthermore, Marxist revolutionary theory must be flexible enough to reinvent itself in the context of current social, economic, and political restructuring under the economic policies of neoliberalism. As Marx noted, theory becomes a material force when it grips the masses. Good theory not only attempts to understand the complex events that mark the current historical juncture and develops in step with new conflicts and challenges but also attempts to transform existing social relations. Revolutionary educators do not have endure the Golgotha of revolutionary praxis, as in the historical example of Che Guevara, in order to effect mindful social transformation. Marxist theory is set forth here not as a universal truth but as a weapon of interpretation. No theory can fully anticipate or account for the consequences of its application, but theory remains a living aperture through which specific histories are made visible and intelligible. In this sense, Marxist theory provides the oppressed with the theoretical knowledge for analyzing and challenging capitalist production. It is here that Marxist theory can be used to advance proletarian hegemony through the work of organic and transformative intellectuals (see Giroux 1988) engaged in revolutionary socialist praxis aimed at the transformation of the bourgeois state. We don't believe that we are destined to live our lives forever in the whisky-soaked and blood-drenched Hobbesian universe of *The Gangs of New York*. Nor in the fear-infested hovels of a national security state overseen by John Ashcroft, a religious fanatic who fears calico cats and likens himself to the Christian messiah, where the specters of hirsute and turbaned terrorists are used to terrify a population into giving up constitutional protections. Nor in the sanctuary of the Oval Office, where a boy emperor who likes to wear the tight-fitting and gonad-enhancing flight suits of the "top guns" and who claims to be taking orders directly from God enacts a foreign policy that threatens the world with a permanent state of terrorism.

The "battle in Seattle" (as well as other anti–World Trade Organization demonstrations in Quebec City and throughout Europe) can teach educators important lessons (Rikowski 2001). There are times when anticapitalist struggles require an organized revolutionary class that has, in the course of its protracted political activities, gained a significant measure of class consciousness and recognizes itself not only as a class in itself but also as a class for itself. At other moments, anticapitalist struggles take the form of what Jim Hightower (cited in Marshall 2000) refers to as "spontaneous and unauthorized outbreaks of democracy," as in the case of the anti–World Trade Organization protests in Seattle. There are moments, too, when class struggle can consist of isolated individual or collective acts of resistance against corporate colonization and commodification of the life world. A case in point is the French farmer José Bova, who protested against genetically modified food by driving his tractor into a McDonald's restaurant under construction in the south of France. All these efforts have their importance. The main point we wish to emphasize here is that it is crucial to struggle against all attempts to decenter political struggle so that the social basis of exploitation is dissolved beyond class politics. In this regard, the concept of globalization needs to be reformulated so that historical subjects or actors are given the basis to challenge the hegemony of international capital in the defense of justice, solidarity, and working-class struggle for socialism. Those who are prevented from creating history—or, worse, who choose to remain passive in its wake—are forced to recycle the past, combing the shoreline for dreams washed up in bottles of Pepsi and Coca-Cola as the river of time, which waits for no none, rushes by in a vast swirl of regret. We must not allow our individual acts of resistance to lead to reformism or economism or to derail the proletarian and popular movements from its focus on anticapitalist struggle.

Finally, we want to emphasize that although social transformation is achieved, in part, by structures put in place by historical necessity, to move beyond these structures requires the exercise of considerable political agency. It is by means of exercising this agency through collective struggle that the limits of social transformation set by existing historical structures can be laid bare and eventually transcended. We are referring to agency as a form of both intellectual labor and concrete social practice—in short, a critical praxis. This requires, in the words of David McNally (1993), "treating human beings as 'both authors and actors of their own drama'" (153) and situating their actions in the context of the development of their productive forces.

References

Allman, P. 2001. *Critical education against global capitalism.* Wesport, Conn.: Bergen and Garvey.

Azad, B. 2000. *Heroic struggle!—bitter defeat: Factors contributing to the dismantling of the socialist state in the USSR.* New York: International.

Bakst, B. 2003. What's in a name? Some school districts say money. *Duluth News Tribune,* May 12. www.duluthsuperior.com/mld/duluthsuperior/news/5841147.htm (accessed May 15, 2003).

Bonacich, E., and R. P. Appelbaum. 2000. *Behind the label: Inequality in the Los Angeles apparel industry.* Berkeley: University of California Press.

Borowski, J. 1999. Schools with a slant. *New York Times,* August 21, A23.

Cassy, J. 2003. Students cash in on "human billboards" plan. *The Guardian.* www.guardian .co.uk/Print/0,3858,4600434,00.htm (accessed June 15, 2003).

Cloud, D. L. 1994. "Socialism of the mind": The new age of post-Marxism. In *After postmodernism: Reconstructing ideology critique,* ed. H. W. Somins and M. Billig, 222–51. London: Sage.

Cole, M. 1998. Globalization, modernisation and competitiveness: A critique of the New Labour Project in Education. *International Studies in Sociology of Education* no. 8: 315–32.

Cole, M., and D. Hill. 1995. Games of despair and rhetorics of resistance: Postmodernism, education and reaction. *British Journal of Sociology of Education* 16(2): 165–82.

Cole, M., D. Hill, and G. Rikowski. 1997. Between postmodernism and nowhere: The predicament of the postmodernist. *British Journal of Educational Studies* 45(2): 187–200.

Collins, C., and F. Yeskel. 2000. *Economic apartheid in America: A primer on economic inequality and security.* New York: New Press.

Dinerstein, A. 1999. The violence of stability: Argentina in the 1990s. In *Global humanization: Studies in the manufacture of labor,* ed. M. Neary, 47–76. London: Mansell.

Fischman, G., and P. McLaren. 2000. Schooling for democracy: Towards a critical utopianism. *Contemporary Society* 29(1): 168–79.

Freire, P. 1970. *Pedagogy of the oppressed.* New York: Continuum.

———. 1998. *Pedagogy of freedom: Ethics, democracy, and civic courage.* Lanham, Md.: Rowman & Littlefield.

Giroux, H. A. 1988. *Teachers as intellectuals: Toward a critical pedagogy of learning.* New York: Bergin and Garvey.

————. 2001. Zero tolerance: Creating a generation of suspects. *Tikkun* 16(2): 29–32, 58–59.

Giroux, H. A., C. Lankshear, P. McLaren, and M. Peters, eds. 1996. *Counternarratives: Cultural studies and critical pedagogies in postmodern spaces.* New York: Routledge.

Giroux, H. A., and P. McLaren. 1986. Teacher education and the politics of engagement: The case for democratic schooling. *Harvard Educational Review* 56(3): 213–38.

Gramsci, A. 1971. *Selections from the prison notebooks.* Edited and translated by Q. Hoare and G. Nowell-Smith. London: Lawrence and Wishart.

Hatcher, R. 2000. Social class and school: relationships to knowledge. In *Schooling and equality: Fact, concept and policy,* ed. D. Hill and M. Cole, 182–99. London: Kogan Page.

Hawkes, D. 1996. *Ideology.* London: Routledge.

Hill, D., and M. Cole. 2001. Social class. In *Schooling and equality: Fact, concept and policy,* ed. D. Hill and M. Cole, 137–59. London: Kogan Page.

Imam, H. 1997. Global subjects: How did we get here? *Women in Action* 3: 12–15.

Kagarlitsky, B. 2000. *The return of radicalism: Reshaping the left institutions.* Translated by R. Clarke. London: Pluto Press.

Knoblauch, C. H., and L. Brannon. 1993. *Critical literacy and the idea of literacy.* Portsmouth, N.H.: Boynton and Cook.

Lankshear, C., and P. McLaren, eds. 1993. *Critical literacy: Politics, praxis, and the postmodern.* New York: State University of New York Press.

Larsen, N. 2000. Dialectics and "globalization": The problem of how (not) to think about a new internationalism. *Working Papers in Cultural Studies,* 22. Pullman: Department of Comparative American Cultures, Washington State University, 6–16.

Lasn, K. 1999. *Culture jam: The uncooling of America.* New York: Eagle Brook.

Lather, P. 2001. Ten years later, yet again: Critical pedagogy and its complicities. In *Feminist engagements: Reading, resisting, and revisioning male theorists in education and cultural studies,* ed. K. Weiler, 183–95. New York: Routledge.

Leonard, J. 2000. How a caged bird learns to sing: Or, my life at the *New York Times,* CBS and other pillars of the media establishment. *The Nation* 270(25): 11–19.

Lockery, T. 2003. Shopping for answers at the Mall Academy, *The Seattle Press.* www.seattlepress.com/article-9433.html (accessed July 2, 2003).

Luxemburg, R. 1919. *The crisis in German social democracy: The Junius pamphlet.* New York: Socialist Publication Society.

Marshall, S. 2000. Rattling the global corporate suites. *Political Affairs* 79(1): 6–12.

Mayer, C. 2003. It's a jingle out there in school classrooms. *Seattle Times,* June 16. www.seattletimes.com (accessed June 20, 2003).

McChesney, R. 1996. Is there any hope for cultural studies? *Monthly Review* 47(10): 1–18.

McLaren, P. 1995. *Critical pedagogy and predatory culture: Oppositional politics in a postmodern era.* London: Routledge.

————. 1997. *Revolutionary multiculturalism: Pedagogies of dissent for the new millennium.* Boulder, Colo.: Westview Press.

————. 1998a. *Life in schools: An introduction to critical pedagogy in the foundations of education.* 3rd ed. New York: Longman.

———. 1998b. Revolutionary pedagogy in post-revolutionary times: Rethinking the political economy of critical education. *Educational Theory* 48(4): 431–62.

———. 2000. *Che Guevara, Paulo Freire, and the pedagogy of revolution.* Boulder, Colo.: Rowan & Littlefield.

McLaren, P., and R. Farahmandpur. 1999a. Critical multiculturalism and globalization: Some implications for a politics of resistance. *Journal of Curriculum Theorizing* 15(3): 27–46.

———. 1999b. Critical pedagogy, postmodernism, and the retreat from class: Towards a contraband pedagogy. *Theoria* 93: 83–115.

———. 2000. Reconsidering Marx in post-Marxist times: A requiem for postmodernism? *Educational Researcher* 29(3): 25–33.

McLaren, P., and G. Fischman. 1998. Reclaiming hope: Teacher education and social justice in the age of globalization. *Teacher Education Quarterly* 25(4): 125–33.

McLaren, P., G. Fischman, S. Serra, and E. Antelo. 1998. The specters of Gramsci: Revolutionary praxis and the committed intellectual. *Journal of Thought* 33(3): 9–42.

McNally, D. 1993. *Against the market: Political economy, market socialism and the Marxist critique.* London: Verso.

Mészáros, I. 1989. *Marx's theory of alienation.* London: Merlin.

Niemark, M. K. 1999. If it's so important, why won't they pay for it? Public higher education at the turn of the century. *Monthly Review* 51(5): 20–31.

Ovando, C. J., and P. McLaren, eds. 2000. *The politics of multiculturalism: Students and teachers caught in the cross fire.* Boston: McGraw-Hill.

Parenti, M. 1994. *Land of idols: Political mythology in America.* New York: St. Martin's Press.

———. 1997. *Blackshirts and reds: Rational fascism and the overthrow of communism.* San Francisco: City Lights Books.

———. 2001. Rollback: Aftermath of the overthrow of communism. In *After the fall: 1989 and the future of freedom,* ed. G. Katsiaficas, 153–58. New York: Routledge.

Peery, N. 1997. The birth of a modern proletariat. In *Cutting edge: Technology, information, capitalism and social revolution,* ed. J. Davis, T. Hirschl, and M. Stack, 297–302. London: Verso.

Perrucci, R., and E. Wysong. 1999. *The new class society.* Boulder, Colo.: Rowman & Littlefield.

Reed, A., Jr. 2000. *Class notes: Posing as politics and other thoughts on the American scene.* New York: New Press.

Rikowski, G. 2001. *The battle of Seattle.* London: Tufnell Press.

San Juan, E., Jr. 1992. *Racial formations/critical transformations: Articulations of power in ethnic and racial studies in the United States.* Atlantic Highlands, N.J.: Humanities Press.

———. 1999. Raymond Williams and the idea of cultural revolution. *College Literature* 26(2): 118–36.

Sleeter, C., and P. McLaren, eds. 1995. *Multicultural education, critical pedagogy, and the politics of difference.* New York: State University of New York Press.

Spring, J. 1998. *Education and the rise of the global economy.* Mahwah, N.J.: Lawrence Erlbaum Associates.

Sullivan, C. 2003. Programming the work force: The failure of mass education. *Counterpunch*. http://counterpunch.org/sullivan02252003.html (accessed July 1, 2003).

Teeple, G. 1995. *Globalization and the decline of social reform*. Toronto: Garmond Press.

Thompson, W. 1997. *The left in history: Revolution and reform in twentieth-century politics*. London: Pluto Press.

Vrana, D. 1998. Education's pied piper with a dark past. *Los Angeles Times*, September 7, A1.

Weinbaum, E. S. 1998. Education without paper: Teaching workers to build a labor movement. *Radical History Review* 72: 68–77.

Witheford, N. 1997. Cycles of circuits and struggles in high-technology capitalism. In *Cutting edge: Technology, information, capitalism and social revolution*, ed. J. Davis, T. Hirschil, and M. Stack, 195–242. London: Verso.

Wood, E. M. 1994. Identity crisis. *In These Times*, June 13, 28–29.

Žižek, S. 1999. *The ticklish subject: The absent center of political ontology*. London: Verso.

———. 2001a. *Did somebody say totalitarianism? Five interventions in the (mis)use of a notion*. London: Verso.

———. 2001b. *Repeating Lenin*. Unpublished manuscript.

7

Educational Policy and the Socialist Imagination: Revolutionary Citizenship as a Pedagogy of Resistance

When I was coming up, it was a dangerous world, and you know exactly who they are . . . it was us versus them, and it was clear who them was. Today we are not so sure who the they are, but we know they're there.

—George W. Bush (Quoted in Ehrenreich 2000b, 20–21)

When I give food to the poor, they call me a saint. . . . And when I ask why they have no food, they call me a communist.

—Brazilian Bishop Helder Cámara (Quoted in Galeano 2000, 311)

A S WE INDULGE IN CONSUMER ORGIES celebrating the unending promise of
1,000 years more of uninterrupted shopping at Planet Mall, we pretend that the social and economic horrors that we have come to associate with Western capitalist democracies have been a temporary spike in global capitalism's blood pressure. We want to believe that in history's long march toward civilization, capitalist exploitation will amount to little more than faint footprints left on the side of the road by Marx's reserve army of labor. But history has proven a worthy opponent in its stubborn refusal to come to an end or to succumb to our best rationalizations. Capitalism's grim legacy of the poverty of the many thriving amid the wealth of the few is more than just a flicker in the cabinet of lost nineteenth-century memories. It is still the main show in town. In fact, it has enjoyed a record-breaking run ever since the feudal lords were kicked off their estates. But how long can capitalism's vaudeville antics and slapstick financial maneuvering keep us laughing when the ruling class is

ensured that it will have the last laugh? As long, it seems, as the march of progress remains obscured by the myths woven into its telling.

Capitalism has become so intensified that it represses our ability to acknowledge the process of repression itself. It naturalizes repression so completely that the current economic horror has come to be seen as part of the everyday woof and warp of things that we have blithely come to name "the daily grind." Consequently, even progressive educators who are vigorously engaged in the debate over global capitalism and theories that oppose one another within it frequently fail to address the fateful implications of capitalism's confiscation of freedom and kidnapping of hope. Yet capitalism constitutes more than transforming the globe into a version of Minneapolis' Mall of America or a *paradis artificiel* designed after *The Truman Show*; it is a living horror, a total social universe for those who must endure the full force of economic injustice and the excruciating currents of hopelessness and despair. And the global expanse of capitalism that we have been witnessing over the past few decades has been nothing less than exploitation on stilts. As Alex Callinicos (2000) remarked, "Most of us live in the shadow of the blackmail of capital" (129).

Hypnotized by the silken seductiveness of lingerie capitalism— superexploitation trussed in attire from Frederick's of Hollywood—we are beckoned into a patriarchal mansion of consumer pleasures where fulfillment is untiringly supplanted by the promise of something better. The universe is for sale, and if you can dress it up in a leather corset, so much the better. The serpent ouroboros is now chasing investment portfolios instead of its own tail. While capitalism seeks its global advantage, millions of the world's toilers remain captive of the testosterone-fueled dreams of wealth and power as they are forced to mortgage their lives in their futile quest for what has now surely become a tired oxymoron: capitalist democracy. And although U.S. citizens are not indifferent to the salacious thirst of the privileged social classes for power and wealth, they simply find it difficult to imagine a capitalist world where this would not be the case. Callinicos (2000) noted (paraphrasing G. A. Cohen) that the ruling class, predicting "that they will produce less, making the poor suffer, unless they continue to be specially rewarded [is like] a kidnapper who predicts that the child he has taken will suffer unless his or her parents come up with the ransom money" (128).

As the tumultuous history of twentieth-century class struggle is capriciously flung aside to make room for capitalism's victory celebration, littering all paths to the future with hollow triumphs and ticker-tape fantasies, we stand as helpless onlookers before one of the most flagrantly vulgar and decadent epochs experienced by Western civilization. Such a statement may seem the flashy product of an overworked Hollywood screenwriter laboring over a low-budget pilot about Pokémon at Armageddon or of John Ashcroft dream where he replaces

St. Paul with himself in the pantheon of the Christian aristocracy, but we are deadly serious. The neoliberal formation of the 1980s, whose spinal cord was capital accumulation at the expense of workers' financial mobility, defeated organized labor and left it seriously paralyzed. The neoliberal offensive—a pugilistic capitalism sporting brass knuckles—has increased its hold over the past decade as the majority of the U.S. voting public appears content to follow political leaders who refuse to stand up to the corporate oligopolies. The richest one-tenth of households in the United States own 83 percent of the country's financial assets, whereas the poorest four-fifths own only 8 percent. The Center for the Study of Popular Economics noted, "If a Ford Escort represents the average financial wealth of an African-American household, you would need a stretch limousine 300 yards long to show the average for a white household" (Heintz and Folbre 2000, 17). Citing John Roemer, Callinicos (2000) similarly noted that

> to achieve "deep" equality of opportunity with respect to education in the United States, with the objective of ensuring that children in whatever circumstances who expend the same effort will have the same adult earning capacity, would require spending $900 on every white student and $2900 on every black student. (88)

We don't need to worry about such expenditures if Bush's No Child Left Behind Act achieves its goal of making it officially possible to label all public education a failure. After all, how can a public school system survive when 95 percent of all students in grades 3 through 8 are required to be tested every year in math and reading and at least once in high school, given that a school could be labeled a failing school if any subgroup of students (black students, special education students, bilingual students) fails to meet its mandated target in one test or even at one grade level? How is it feasible to have all students proficient by the year 2014, as Bush's plan stipulates (see Miner 2004)? In a broader sense, consider this long list of startling observations: the cost of providing basic education and health care, as well as adequate food and safe water for the entire population of the earth, is estimated to be $40 billion (less than the net worth of Bill Gates); the combined wealth of the three richest people in the world exceeds the combined gross domestic products (GDPs) of the forty-eight poorest countries; the combined wealth of the thirty-two richest people exceeds the total GDP of South Asia; and the combined wealth of the 225 richest people is roughly equal to the annual income of the poorest 47 percent of the world's population of more than 2.2 billion people (Heintz and Folbre 2000, 19).

Governed by a lethal symbiosis of neoliberalism and globalization, the new social and economic global order has met with catastrophic consequences: the Mexican peso devaluation crisis of 1995, the Asian financial crisis of 1997, the Russian financial meltdown of 1998, the Brazilian "Samba effect" of 1999, and the fierce acceleration of Third World debt, among others (Kagarlitsky 1999).

What has become increasingly clear is that multinational corporations now operate as oligopolies and function as supernational entities. Not only do these oligopolies consolidate and concentrate capital on a global scale, but they also exercise worldwide political influence within the governmental offices of nation-states through lobbying, campaign donations, and unholy business partnerships (Boggs 2000). The uncomfortable truth of U.S. global hegemony is that it has been secured historically by the ability of the United States to reorganize the world system in its own economic, political, and military dimensions. Samir Amin (2000) summarized American global strategy as follows:

> To neutralize and subjugate the other partners in the triad (Europe and Japan), while minimizing their ability to act outside the orbit of the United States; to establish military control over NATO [North Atlantic Treaty Organization] while "Latin-Americanizing" the fragments of the former Soviet world; to exert uncontested influence in the Middle East and Central Asia, especially over their petroleum resources; to dismantle China, ensure the subordination of the other great nations (India and Brazil), and prevent the constitution of regional blocks potentially capable of negotiating the terms of globalization; and to marginalize the regions of the South that represent no strategic interest. (15)

The global military advantage enjoyed by the United States (largely through its control of NATO) is unprecedented and guarantees the superiority of the triad (the United States, Europe, and Japan) over the planet and ensures the formation of a unipolar globalization:

> The strategy employed by the triad, under U.S. direction, takes as its aim the construction of a unipolar world organized along two complementary principles: the unilateral dictatorship of dominant TNC [transnational corporation] capital and the unfurling of a U.S. military empire, to which all nations must be compelled to submit. No other project may be tolerated within this perspective, not even the European project of subaltern NATO allies and especially not a project entailing some degrees of autonomy, like China's, which must be broken by force if necessary. (Amin 2000, 16)

The post–World War II period has witnessed with dismaying regularity an obscene concentration and centralization of social, political, and economic power in the hands of a relatively small number of oligopolies. One of the recent shifts in capitalist production has been the transference of fiercely competitive capital from Western countries to cheaper markets, giving rise to the phenomenon known as the "globalization of capital." Globalization is not a new stage of capitalist development but has intensified some of the most essential features of imperialism. The term "globalization" has several definitions and has been associated frequently with social, economic, and political shifts in late twentieth-century capitalism. Perhaps a more fitting

and close-to-the-bone term to describe contemporary capitalism is "gob-
bleization": the hostile takeovers, megamergers, and aggressive acquisitions
of small corporations by larger, more financially powerful and politically
connected corporations. Reports confirm that by 1997, fifty-one of the
world's one hundred largest economies were corporations, and the leading
five hundred transnational corporations held a monopoly over 42 percent of
the wealth generated worldwide (Lasn 1999).

   Capitalist "Overworlders" have coined the term "globalization" to refer to
the expansion of capitalist social relations throughout the globe. However,
when viewed against the backdrop of today's tumultuous political events, such
a term can be read only as a genteel appellation used by the capitalist class as
a means of diverting attention from what is, in effect, an imperialist assault on
human dignity throughout the world and a value orientation within which
freedom can be found only in the unmolested core of capital. Lee Dlugin
(1999) unhesitatingly characterized the relationship between globalization
and imperialism as follows:

> Globalization is a qualitative development of monopoly capitalism on a world
> scale. It is based on the free flow of capital. The "free market" is the imperialist
> code word for the free unimpeded flow of capital of the biggest monopolies seek-
> ing maximum profits, for their freedom to plunder the natural resources of whole
> nations and capture the biggest share of the world's production and markets. The
> process develops so that monopoly capital takes over whole industries around the
> world, agriculture production, transportation, finance operations and other eco-
> nomic spheres. It wipes out all forms of economic competition and it uses both
> legal and extra-legal measures to achieve its goals, including the use of military
> force. Through the IMF [International Monetary Fund] and the World Bank, it
> compels privatization of government services and nationalized industries. From
> this vantage point it is able to dominate and usurp these industries. (20)

Contemporary scholars have iterated the protean potential surrounding the
concept of globalization and in the process have inflated its coinage but at the
same time devalued its explanatory capacity. In his analysis of the recent social and economic shifts in late capitalist economies, István Mészáros (1999)
proposed the use of the terms "total social capital" and "totality of labor" instead of "globalization" as conceptual tools in explaining and analyzing contemporary capitalism and its deformation and reterritorialization of human
activity. Mészáros wisely cautioned against the excessive association of "globalization of capital" with its homogenizing tendencies. Capital, as Mészáros
noted, cannot be conceived of as a "homogeneous entity" because it consists
of a "multiplicity of divisions and antagonisms" corresponding to a multiplicity of capitals competing with one another at both the intranational and the
international level. In a similar fashion, imperialism (linked to capital) is non-

synchronous and works in contextually and geopolitically specific ways. In fact, globalization is so overwhelmingly triumphant today that it no longer relies on the hierarchical forms of domination associated with industrial capitalist formations, dissolving patriarchal and other fixed forms of domination and replacing them with fluid, hybrid identities, resulting in the unleashing of forces of contradiction and the exposition of capital's crushing machineries of exploitation. Here, forms of subjectivities, even the so-called resistant subjectivities of postmodernism, are able to resignify their own logic to fit the overall frame of capital's voracious logic (Hardt and Negri 2000). Finally, and contrary to the views of many social and political theorists, globalization as a social and economic phenomenon cannot be considered to exist apart from its incestuous relationship with the nation-state (McLaren and Farahmandpur 1999b). In other words, the globalization of capital operates within and cooperates with mechanisms associated with the formation of the nation-state (Wood 1995). In our view, the popular notion that the state is weakening as a result of the global deregulation of markets signals an erroneous conclusion on the part of social and political theorists. Without the protection of the state, capital becomes a contradiction in terms because existing asymmetrical property relations are protected by various branches of the state apparatus (for example, law enforcement and the judiciary system). We also note that the state serves the ruling classes but is not an instrument of the ruling classes in that it is directly controlled by them. Although the state plays little or no role in appropriating a surplus, it protects the private property of capitalists who do not need access to the state to extract surplus value from proletariats separated from their means of production and subsistence (R. Brenner, personal communication, October 30, 2000). The model for global capital's new moral framework is that of the "'network-extender,' light and mobile, tolerant of difference and ambivalence, realistic about people's desires, informal and friendly" (Budgen 2000, 153). Of course, such a model of connectionist capitalism and entrepreneurial leadership really amounts to little more than giving a "face-lift" to the practice of exploitation and, in doing so, "a new form of the extortion of surplus value" (Budgen 2000, 155). It is a form of bleeding the workers, hiding the source of the wound, and facilitating the hemorrhage through treating its victims as disposable pariahs whose lives are not worth confiscating.

Truth Decay in the Government of Misery

Today, it is impossible to deny the fact that transnational corporations have successfully conquered the world's economies. This victory has been achieved through a unified strategy that philosopher John McMurtry has claimed was applied across the cold war divide itself. McMurtry (2000) described this as a strategy "to defund all social sectors which provide life-serving, non-profit goods into crisis or bankruptcy so that they are forced into private corporate control" (1). Consider the situation in Tijuana's Colonia Chilpancingo, a neighborhood of more than 1,000 families that sits beneath a large industrial park at Otay Mesa. These families live amid the lead waste and corroding batteries of a lead smelter and car battery recycler that closed down in 1994. The waste has contaminated the water that supplies the neighborhood through an open arroyo that passes through the grounds of a local kindergarten. What chance do the inhabitants have of getting help from the Commission for Environmental Cooperation, which was created through NAFTA? After all, labor rights and environmental rights guarantees are unenforceable. Of course, as Ben Ehrenreich (2000a) noted, NAFTA gives corporations recourse to challenge any interference with their abilities to extract surplus labor from workers.

How do transnational corporations avoid paying their way in the very society on whose infrastructures, resources, and markets they depend for their material transactions? They manage to thrive because the global market has been reengineered to permit them to sell at high prices anywhere while producing at the lowest cost anywhere else and evading domestic tax contributions, First World wages and benefits, and compliance with environmental and labor regulations. Transnational corporations operate under the banner of democracy and in the guise of freedom to sell back to home markets through free-trade agreements and corporate–government partnerships. As a result, defunding education achieves the following corporate goals: it lowers corporate costs through depriving social sectors such as school districts of their revenue bases, and it makes schools more dependent on corporate funding (McMurtry 2000). Privatized public debts are kept intentionally high by calls for more tax cuts. Consider the words of a Citibank (Rockefeller) official: "Nobody's debts are going to be paid. The issue is the borrower remaining creditworthy and able to carry the debt, but not repay it" (quoted in McMurtry 2000, 3). McMurtry added, "Government borrowers 'remain creditworthy' for banks and bond-merchants by reducing obligations to non-profit programs" (3).

The "big lie" of our time, noted McMurtry (2000), is that blame for the lack of government funding for education (and the social sector in general) is the increased debts on public sector life goods. That is, the blame is placed on supposed "out-of-control social spending." This amounts to an obscene distortion, an unvarnished deception. In Canada, for instance, less than 6 percent of the increased government deficit was due to increased social spending, whereas 50 percent was due to increased interest charges, and 44 percent was due to tax cuts for corporations and individuals in high-income tax brackets, according to a Statistics Canada report that was, it is worth noting, engaged by the federal finance ministry and the corporate mass media (McMurtry 2000). What rarely gets reported is that the nonprofit sector, which funds social services, is perceived as an untapped market worth trillions of dollars. Big business is salivating. With the assistance of the government, big business is now appropriating social sector funding to help generate corporate profits for the rich. Increased public debt is in effect a corporate–government strategy that ensures that public sector revenues are ripe for corporate appropriation. And, it is all occurring under the banner of freedom. Education is now a for-profit industry. An "academic gold rush" is in full swing, and the inexorably proliferating corporate–government partnerships are reaping vast benefits through their restructuring of public and higher education for permanent market use

> with the unstated terminus ad quem of this process the reproduction of all present and future students as consumers and employees whose desires for commodities and willingness to compete for corporate functions are imprinted reliably into their neuronal processes from the moment they enter school to their graduation. (McMurtry 2000, 6)

We now live in the perfumed world of performance budgets linked to capital's inbred ideology of self-maximization and monetary incentives. McMurtry (2000) argued that interest-based education is the ruling principle of the corporate market. Rather than requiring educators to address problems independent of their monetary payoffs, the regulating principle of thought of the corporate management model is the maximization of the private funds of the corporation and "selecting against any knowledge or advance of knowledge which does not fulfill or which conflicts with this goal" (McMurtry 2000, 7). McMurtry's illustration is telling:

> Consider a teacher presenting or a student studying the material of any subject who followed the rules of producing and selling a product for profit in the global market-place. The anti-educational principles of thought and action would be: Do not address any problem which does not promise opportunity for profit. Reject contra-indicative evidence to profitable results. Reduce the cost of work input to your product to the minimum possible. Always represent it as unique and without flaw. Treat the customers as always right. In short, the ruling goals of the corporate market subverts knowledge and inquiry itself, closes out critical debate, and blocks any disinterested pursuit of truth by its very nature. (7)

The corporate management model of education demands private patent and copyright control of every piece of knowledge and information that a corporation can accumulate, and "the maximum price people are willing to pay is imposed on every service which can be identified, with no educational or other life service to anyone if it is not money-profitable" (McMurtry 2000, 7). We urge readers to ponder the next illustration proffered by McMurtry (2000):

> Consider a school or university which priced its knowledge transactions, required its agents to do no more than required by commercial contract with student buyers, and sought to privatize more and more of the school's and library's information for its own monetary profit. There could hardly be a more anti-educational regime. Yet all of these requirements are intrinsic to the logic of the market model. Even if the price system is set aside, dissemination in the market is by conditioning and soliciting appetites, as opposed to disseminating what can be substantiated by evidence and reason. (7–8)

Independent literacy and problem-solving capabilities are jettisoned in the corporate management model in favor of linking individual capability to monetary demand, which establishes all market value. Global market competition becomes the grounds for all skills and competencies. Consider another of McMurtry's (2000) examples:

> If a student or a teacher followed the canonical rules of the global free market and voluntarily exchanged for any price that he or she could get the goods of course essays, tests and assignments, he or she as a student would be expelled as a cheat, and as a teacher would be dismissed for the grossest moral turpitude. If an educational system as a whole were to develop more and more people with such dependencies on others' work, this regime would undermine education at its foundation. (8)

In the corporate management model, problems of evidence or reason are not open to scrutiny or critical discussion. What gets communicated to students is dictated in a top-down chain of command that "rules out any questions which do not comply with these orders, and repudiates any who transgress this chain of command as unemployable" (McMurtry 2000, 8). McMurtry (2000) noted,

> If principals, teachers, or professors followed this managerial method of top-down command as their model of communication, and decided what was to be thought, said and done with the exclusion of critical dialogue or question on behalf of seeking truth, they would be supplanting education with coercive indoctrination and would be shown unfit to remain in a place of learning. (8)

Corporate Philanthropy

The Center for a New American Dream (2000) reported that since 1980, advertising expenditures in the United States have doubled from nearly $106 billion to $200 billion in 1998. More than $2 billion alone is spent annually on advertising that specifically targets children, twenty times more than a decade ago. Channel One, the brainchild of Chris Whittle, has a captive audience that is nearly fifty times larger than the number of teenagers who watch MTV. The average child of today is exposed to between 20,000 and 40,000 commercials each year. From age six to eighteen, children view nearly 16,000 hours of television programming and are exposed to 4,000 hours of radio and music programming. Children also spend more time viewing television and commercial programs than they spend in school. Nearly one of four children under the age of six has a television set in his or her bedroom. Jean Kilbourne (1999) wrote,

> The average American is exposed to at least three thousand ads every day and will spend three years of his or her life watching television commercials. Advertising makes up about 70 percent of our newspapers and 40 percent of our mail. (58–59)

In 1996, corporate philanthropy funneled nearly $1.3 billion into the education marketplace, constituting 20 percent of the $6.3 billion in total corporate handouts. According to Corporate Watch (2000), the education industry consists of (1) public schools sponsored by corporations, such as American Express, Celebration School, and the American Bankers Insurance Group; (2) corporate charter schools or educational maintenance organizations, such as the Edison Project, Advantage Schools Inc., and Educational Alternatives Inc.; (3) marketing and investment companies in the school business, such as Lehman Brothers, EduVentures, and Kid Connection; (4) corporations offering sponsored educational materials, such as Lifetime Learning Systems, Enterprise for Education, the Mazer Corporation, Media Options, Inc., and Youth Marketing International; (5) in-school advertising firms, such as Scholastic Inc., Adopt-a-School, and Cover Concepts Marketing Service, Inc.; (6) lunch programs funded by Pizza Hut, Subway, Arby's, and the American School Food Service Association; and (7) conservative and right-wing think tanks that influence educational policies, such as the Heritage Foundation, the Educational Excellence Network (which is part of the Hudson Institute, overseen by Chester Finn and Diane Ravitch), and the Landmark Legal Foundation.

In public schools across the country, textbook covers are splashed with corporate logos, and specially designed corporate-sponsored curricula are provided to schools willing to accept free "lessons in a box" in exchange for financial assistance from private corporations. Many poorly funded public school districts are signing contracts that give corporations advertising rights on public school property. For example, the American Passage Media Corporation has installed billboards in high school locker rooms, where their commercial message reaches nearly 3 million students. These "Gymboards" advertise a variety of commercial products, including Tampax tampons. Pizza Hut offers a reading program titled "Book It," whereby in exchange for a specified period of reading in the classroom, students receive free Pizza Hut coupons. American Express finances "Academies of Travel & Tourism" in four public high schools located in New York City that prepare students for jobs in the tourist industry. Students also learn about world geography and foreign cultures. Lifetime Learning Systems provides free textbook covers that expose 16 million students to advertising and commercials that are largely paid for by corporations such as Nike, McDonald's, and Hershey. The Center for Commercial-Free Public Education (2000) asserted that public schools are signing contracts that permit corporate sponsors such as Burger King and Coca-Cola to place their advertisements on school buses. In New York City, the board of education signed a nine-year, $53 million contract that allows advertisements to be placed on the district's school buses.

Supported by a complex infrastructure, the global empire of McDonald's (which consists of 25,000 restaurants in more than one hundred countries) is aggressively pursuing its ultimate goal of the "McDomination" of the fast-food industry. McDonald's has a state-of-the-art university, Hamburger University, located in Oak Brook, Illinois (there are also branches in the United Kingdom, Germany, Japan, and Australia), where it trains its future managers. In a concerted effort to increase consumer loyalty, McDonald's provides public schools with free educational materials. At Pembroke Lakes Elementary School in Broward County, Florida, students are introduced to the world of work by learning how a McDonald's restaurant is operated and managed, how to complete an employment application, and how to interview for a job at McDonald's. Students are also required to learn about the "nutritional" values of the high-fat, high-cholesterol, low-protein foods served at McDonald's. By providing free educational materials and resources to schools, McDonald's is able to achieve two important goals. First, it expands its market share and influences public school curricula. Second, McDonald's secures the foundation for recruiting future employees from a vast pool of the working class and students of color in urban schools, thus making the transition from school to low-paid work more efficient (see the work of Joe Kincheloe, 2002). While the United States appears to be pulling out of its worst jobless recovery of the post–World War II era, the news jobs that are being created are mainly in restaurants and building services, and many are temporary positions. So it seems like some students will be well prepared.

Although there has been vociferous public protest against the corporate takeover of education, corporations have not remained silent and have aggressively fought back against student, teacher, and parent activism. In public schools, colleges, and universities across the country, students have been penalized for resisting corporate colonization. In 1998, Mike Cameron, a senior at Greenbrier High School in Evans, Georgia, was suspended for wearing a Pepsi T-shirt on the day the school was participating in Coca-Cola's "school-sponsored Coke day," a national competition with other schools to win $10,000 (Klein 1999). Jennifer Beatty, a college student who attended Morain Valley Community College in Palos Hills, Illinois, protested against the growing corporate influence over and commercialization of colleges and universities by chaining herself to the metal mesh curtains of the McDonald's Student Center. Beatty was later arrested and expelled from the college (Lasn 2000).

In recent years, the profit-driven corporate coup d'état has shifted toward a "corporate-sponsored curriculum" supported in part by AT&T, McDonald's, Nike, Coca-Cola, PepsiCo, the Campbell Soup Company, and other corporations that are eagerly seeking new consumer markets. Corporate propaganda has been successful partly because of its ability to associate corporate interests with environmental and health issues. For example, Nike provides teachers with "sneaker-making kits" that teach students how Nike shoes are assembled; the lesson also focuses on how Nike is protecting the environment.

The Center for Commercial-Free Public Education (2000) reported that in a concerted effort to restore its much-tainted image after the *Valdez* oil spill in Alaska, Exxon provides free educational videos to classroom teachers. Exxon portrays itself as an environmentally friendly corporation by showing how it is helping to protect the wildlife in Alaska. Hershey teaches the nutritional values of its chocolate candies to students and suggests how chocolate can constitute an integral part of a balanced daily diet. Finally, the Campbell Soup Company provides teachers with free science lesson plans that attempt to prove that its Prego spaghetti sauce is thicker than the Ragu brand made by a competitor, Lipton.

Today, the impress of capital is found in the subjectivities of the young and old alike. Children spend $35 billion of their own money annually while influencing their parents to spend another $300 billion. In consumer culture, brand awareness and consumer loyalty are the key ingredients for the successful "cradle-to-grave" marketing strategies of corporations. To lure potential consumers, corporations devise slick advertisement campaigns that frequently involve giving away merchandise and prizes. In short, the commercialization of public schools through campaigns such as Pepsi Stuff, Marlboro Gear, Camel Cash, McDonald's Happy Meals, and the Budweiser frogs attests to the disturbing, growing trend of the privatization of the public life and the increasing transfer of capital from the public to the private sphere.[1]

Education and the Resurgence of the Right

Prompted by the rise of conservative politics and their impact on school curricula (Apple 1993, 1996; Brosio 1998; Spring 1997, 1998) and the recent blitzkrieg led by the pundits of globalization and their neoliberal counterparts whose economic policies[2] have aimed at creating flexible labor markets, deregulation, downsizing,[3] and outsourcing[4] (Lauder and Brown, 1997; McLaren and Farahmandpur 1999a, 1999b, 2000), critical educators have grown increasingly active in decrying a free-market economy that reduces politics to the tortuous logic of privatization[5] and to brazenly unapologetic attempts to tie Friedmanian and Hayekian neoliberal economic principles to the production of school curricula (Apple 1996; Brosio 1998; McLaren and Farahmandpur 2000; Spring 1997, 1998; Tyack and Cuban 1995). Some have engaged in a spirited counteroffensive to current economic policies aimed at widespread support for standardized tests, mandated textbooks, school-based management, a shared school mission, and the deskilling of teachers' labor (Apple 1989; Berliner and Biddle 1995).

Although in no way offering a Marxist alternative, Michael Apple (1996) nevertheless has identified social policies favoring privatization, centralization, vocationalization, and the differentiation of school curricula as the "conservative restoration." He distinguished between neoliberal and neoconservative politics by correctly pointing out that the former support economic policies that seek to weaken the role of the state, whereas the latter articulate a morality and an ethics that support a strong state. Apple regarded these contradictory social and economic policies as part of what he has called "conservative modernization." In short, the combination of privatization and a relatively strong state has increasingly removed access to education from the public domain.

Educational policies under the influence of neoliberalism aim at controlling school curricula through national standards (Spring 1998). These standards are geared toward increasing student knowledge by creating a "common curriculum." In the new economic order, students are increasingly urged to acquire basic skills in their journey from school to work and as a part of their "lifelong learning." Many educational policymakers who seek to employ education as a tool for advancing neoliberal economics believe that the barrier between education and work should be removed without a trace (Banfield 2000). In their opinion, lifelong learning is synonymous with lifelong accreditation.

In 1983, the report *A Nation at Risk* famously announced that public schools were to blame for the declining global competitiveness of the United States. Influenced by the report, socioeconomic policies under a burgeoning neoliberalism established control of school curricula by introducing national standards. A common curriculum was believed to be the most effective way of raising overall educational standards (Spring 1998) and linking educational achievement to increasing the economic competitiveness of the United States

(Berliner and Biddle 1995). Although traditional Republicans viewed economic performance as indissolubly connected to the quality of schools, neoconservatives and their procorporate allies asserted that low academic standards were unequivocally responsible for the poor academic performance of both students and teachers. By the 1980s, the goal of educational performance became synonymous with excellence, and a strong emphasis was placed on increasing the number of school days, providing rigorous academic courses along with back-to-basics teaching methods, and placing increased emphasis and importance on teacher evaluation and accountability and standardized tests (Tyack and Cuban 1995).

During the Reagan administration, educational policies plunged teachers and students headlong into the abyss of greed. Education's relation to capital was far from an innocent dalliance. Policies were underwritten by a confluence of free-market ideology, conservative Christian ideology, and nationalist sentiments (Spring 1997). In 1989, the Goals 2000 initiative proposed by President Bush targeted the development of national academic standards and national achievement tests. By 1995, the call for national standards made by the Clinton administration proposed a history curriculum that aimed at concealing issues related to U.S. imperialism, exploitation, and political power (Spring 1997). A cabal of conservatives (including Chester Finn, Diane Ravitch, and Dick Cheney) launched a national curriculum campaign that unreservedly supported U.S. foreign policy and unswervingly put education on the path of for-profit schooling.

The far Right, supported by organizations such as the Heritage Foundation, continues to be represented by powerful conservative political figures such as William Bennett and Newt Gingrich, who blame the government for the declining social and economic status of the United States in the global economy. The goal of these pundits and their corporate allies is to decentralize education and privatize public schools. The Religious Right has accused the government of promoting homosexuality, secular humanism, and scientific creationism; banning school prayer; and downplaying the importance of family values. Neoconservatives supported by the American Enterprise Institute have largely positioned themselves as political centrists who in their frenetic drive for academic excellence advocate a strong role for the federal government and support for private schools. Many of these conservative groups call for a return to the heterosexist patriarchy and stillborn democracy of *Leave It to Beaver* and *Lassie*, pop culture's Elysian fields as dreamt by Norman Rockwell on melatonin. We are living Nickelodeon reruns of the American Dream, only in reverse.

Mainstream policy pundits manifestly view a national curriculum and strong educational standards as part of the modernization of the curriculum.

However, an important latent function of such a curriculum is to impose efficient methods of production through the exploitation of labor power. Efforts
to build a national curriculum and national standards that emphasize accountability, performance, ranking, and the differential placement of students
into educational tracks (Oakes 1985) is also part of a larger agenda of steering
public schools toward a free-market model that advocates giving a wide range
of "choices" to parents (choices that will ultimately decimate the public sphere,
morphing education into the structural unconscious of the billionaire boys'
club of Bill Gates, Warren Edward Buffet, Paul Gardner, and Steve Ballmer).

Teachers' Work and the Value Form of Labor

We believe that it is important to engage the issue of educational reform from
the perspective of Marx's value theory of labor. Marx's value theory of labor
does not attempt to reduce labor to an economic category alone but is illus-
trative of how labor as a value form constitutes our very social universe, one
that has been underwritten by the logic of capital. Value is not some hollow
formality, neutral precinct, or barren hinterland empty of power and politics
but the very matter and antimatter of Marx's social universe (Rikowski 2000).
It is important to keep in mind that the production of value is not the same
as the production of wealth.

The production of value is historically specific and emerges whenever labor
assumes its dual character. This is most clearly explicated in Marx's discussion
of the contradictory nature of the commodity form and the expansive capacity
of the commodity known as labor power. To Marx, the commodity was highly
unstable and nonidentical. Its concrete particularity (use value) is subsumed by
its existence as value in motion (see Rikowski 2000) or by what we have come
to know as "capital" (value is always in motion because of the increase in capital's productivity that is required to maintain expansion). The issue here is not
simply that workers are exploited for their surplus value but that all forms of
human sociability are constituted by the logic of capitalist work. Labor, therefore, cannot be seen as the negation of capital or the antithesis of capital but as
the human form through and against which capitalist work exists (Rikowski
2000). Capitalist relations of production become hegemonic precisely when the
process of the production of abstraction conquers the concrete processes of
production, resulting in the expansion of the logic of capitalist work.

Class struggle has now been displaced to the realm of the totality of human
relations, as abstract social structures such as labor now exist as the transub-
stantiation of human life as capital (Neary 2000). So, when we look at the
issue of educational reform, it is important to address the issue of teachers'

work within capitalist society as a form of alienated labor, that is, as the specific production of the value form of labor. This becomes clearer when we begin to understand that one of the fundamental functions of schooling is to traffic in labor power, in the engineering and enhancement of the capacity to labor so that such labor power can be harnessed in the interests of capital. Rikowski's premise is provocative yet compelling and perhaps deceptively simple. Education is involved in the direct production of the one commodity that generates the entire social universe of capital in all its dynamic and multiform existence: labor power. Within the social universe of capital, individuals sell their capacity to labor—their labor power—for a wage. Because they are included in this social universe on a differential and unequal basis, people can get paid above or below the value of their labor power. Because labor power is implicated in human will or agency and because it is impossible for capital to exist without it, education can be redesigned within a social justice agenda that will reclaim labor power for socialist alternatives to human capital formation.

Helen Raduntz (1999) has made a convincing argument that teachers' work, implicated in the trafficking of labor power, is fraught with contradictions and is situated on both sides of the labor–capital divide. More specifically, teachers' work is located both on the side of capital and on the side of wage labor. It is also an important process of mediation in the class struggle between capital and wage labor, especially as both sides attempt to maximize their margins of surplus value.

Raduntz argued that the major source of contraction in teachers' work arises from the social relations of production. Teachers' work is a productive activity, both structurally and developmentally, and it is constitutive of the reproduction of capitalist social relations. Yet teachers' work is integral to class struggle. This is because education is fundamental in the process of human development, but such a process becomes dehumanizing when it attempts to regulate education to coincide with and support the interests of capital. Raduntz called for informed human development by teachers into this process of dehumanization. The struggle entails understanding that teachers' work is productive both for capital and for wage labor. It is productive for capital in that teachers' work constitutes value transferred to wage laborers' labor power in the acquisition of knowledge and skills; the value of teachers' work is also embedded as a component of the capital earned from surplus value as well as the wage paid to workers. In producing the use value of labor power for capital, teachers' work is productive for capital. But teachers' work is also productive for workers because it adds to the value of workers' labor power and their ability to attract a wage that will enable them to sustain a livelihood. What is needed is an approach to educational reform that can help teachers understand their relationships to both capital and labor and thus challenge education's embodiment in the value form of labor via corporatization and privatization and push toward reclaiming labor power for the fulfillment of human needs. Then it may be possible to develop a model of education outside the current neoliberal agenda that can enable educators and their students to navigate and survive and eventually flourish outside the social universe of capital. This requires exploiting the tensions between the "statist" project of labor-power (human capital) enhancement and the neoliberal businessification of schools underwritten by a view of education as a site for capital accumulation and profit making (Rikowski 2000). Of course, to offer an alternative to capitalist social relations is a daunting struggle and one that has untiringly exercised socialists for generations. Once such struggles occupied the efforts of labor unions, but especially since the demise of the Soviet Union and the Eastern bloc countries, unions have been all too happy to coexist with the value form of labor under capitalism.

The New Teacher Unionism

The growing trend in comanagement efforts taking place between teacher unions and school districts could be called the "new teacher unionism." At the core of the new comanagement plan is "peer reviewing," in which experienced or veteran teachers mentor new teachers and teachers who exhibit teaching performance below the standards set forth by their schools or school districts (Jordan 1999). As many critics have pointed out, however, peer reviewing can work to reinforce deprofessionalization and the disempowerment of teachers, partly because the new teacher unionism aligns the teaching profession closely, and often urgently, with the demands of the global market economy. Nowhere in the new unionism is there a sustained acknowledgment of the theft of teachers' labor power by the state. Teachers are now required to respond to economic demands for the increased efficiency, productivity, and flexibility of the labor market. Thus, the new teacher unionism not only undermines and weakens the function of more traditional teacher unions but also forces teachers to hire and fire other teachers. The new teacher unionism gives ballast to the exploitative, privileging hierarchies of corporate capitalism by further integrating the role of schools into the forces of production and the social relations of capital accumulation.

The panoptic glance of the new neoliberal economic and political order provides the warrant and guarantee for schools to forcibly maintain educational efficiency by incorporating standardized testing, social promotion, and get-tough policies that place the overriding responsibility for the academic achievement of students on schools, teachers, parents, and students themselves instead of addressing sufficiently the role of social and economic relations in the production and unequal distribution of selected forms of knowledge. An unstated contradiction is that school and state bureaucracies are seeking to improve student performance and teaching practices without additional funding for or investment in public schools (Allen 1999; Leonardo 2000). Schooling is becoming increasingly addicted to capital's need for the downsizing, outsourcing, and restructuring of the labor force to gain a competitive edge in the global economy. Eugene Plawiuk (1999) suggested that globalization driven by neoliberal economic policies seeks to "recreate public education in the corporate image, to create market driven schools" (20). Here, the capitalist marketplace and democracy function metonymically so that teachers read them off against each other. They "stand in" for each other and have been "homologized" to mean essentially the same thing.

Critical educators must examine how workers' empowerment can be connected to their daily experiences at work and also to their relationships with the forces and relations of production and the "cartelization" of the knowledge industry. Resisting new capitalist production can be achieved by refusing to remain politically passive and by becoming morally and politically active social agents. Gee, Hull, and Lankshear (1997) offered the following strategies in the struggle against the current formation of what they called "fast-capitalist texts." First, critical educators must recognize how the identities of workers are socially and historically grounded. Second, the co-optation of critical ideas and concepts such as "empowerment," "liberation," and "collaboration" by the doyens of the new capitalism compels critical educators to focus on the moral and political aims of teaching. To critique the discourses of fast-capitalist texts in both the workplace and the schools, the development of a critical language becomes fundamentally important. Thus, according to Gee et al.,

Fast capitalists do not . . . want to promote critical reflection in the sense of questioning systems as wholes and in their political relations to other systems. On the contrary, they are keen to pre-empt this, as we have seen in the case of self-directed learning. (99)

With recent criticisms launched against the failures of public education, conservative and right-wing alliances have increasingly supported the privatization of education through charter schools, school choice, and voucher plans. They support the privatization of public schools because they contend that the private sector can manage schools with much more efficiency and productivity than the public sector. There is, of course, a motivated oversight about the private sector being driven by profit and an engineered silence surrounding the absence of long-term studies indicating that the private sector has produced better schools.

Not only must the struggle waged by teachers on behalf of improved public schools and better working conditions be linked with the labor movements, community activists, progressive organizations, schools of education, and parent and student organizations, but it also must be placed within the broader social and economic relations, specifically those linked to the struggle between capital and labor (Kincheloe 1993, 1998; McLaren 2000; McLaren and Farahmandpur 1999a, 1999b, 2000).

Our position takes a cautious step away from the simple assertion that coalitional politics that advance "labor reform" is the favored union strategy because such an unreflective position tacitly endorses existing arrangements produced by the law of the motion of capital, the forces of production, and the social relations of production. In other words, this position willfully ignores the complex means whereby the schooling process itself is implicated in the historical development of knowledge as a form of private ownership of the intellectual labor of the many for the profit of the few. Through its implication in the historical development of knowledge, labor reform fatefully naturalizes, institutionalizes, legitimizes, and makes hegemonic commonsense understandings of the relationship between schooling and capitalism that serves to refunction and reproduce neoliberal educational ideology.

According to the contemporary wave of procapitalist educational reformers, the only way that schools can "outmuscle" corporations that regularly "outsource" to the Third World or offshore labor pools is to transform whatever in education still remains public into a for-profit activity through the mechanics of privatization (Cole, Hill, and Rikowski 1997; Cole, Hill, Rikowski, and McLaren 2000). If education can continue to be recast within a "user-pays" optic, then it will be free to fulfill its capitalist destiny by smashing all remaining barriers to the downsizing of education into a consumerist, corporate bunker, or so the neoliberal argument goes. We are warned that if workers in advanced capitalist countries continue to require union protection, contribute to inefficient work practices, and demand industry protection, economic regulation, a living wage, and competitive prices, then economic disaster will surely strike.

Educational critics such as Smyth and Shacklock (1998) are aware that the real disaster here for the neoliberals is the falling profit margin of the capitalist class, which desires only to accumulate as much capital as possible in the shortest amount of time. Smyth and Shacklock maintained that globalization has not brought about a fundamental repositioning and reconfiguring of the work of teaching. Although teaching has always served as a technology of discipline through regulating modes of social control (for example, time and spatial management), it has now manacled itself with new forms of ideological capture through the proliferation of new technologies linked to cyborg visions of a world marketplace. In addition to the old external apparatus of teacher appraisal as a mechanism of social control that gives ballast to the reigning imperatives of capitalist accumulation, we are now confronted by an evolving species of ideational hegemonies created through the administration of the new professionalism, school development planning, marketized forms of management, performance- and outcome-based indicators, competencies, skills formation, and the like. Recent moves to transform education into a for-profit, low-trust activity through marketization, the establishment of central inspectorates, and so forth fall squarely within the ideological imperative of the World Bank's recommendation to developing countries: their curricula and syllabuses should be securely tied to performance standards and measures of outcome (Cole et al. 2000).

Within the expanded horizon of enterprise culture, under the flagship of economic rationalization, and as part of the prime directive of reconstructing teaching as economic work, Smyth and Shacklock (1998) asked what kind of competencies are invoked for inclusion in the lexicon of the "preferred teacher" (preferred, that is, by the established guardians of the public interest and their corporate comprador counterparts) and required for remaking the global citizen friendly to commerce and hospitable to the directives of the corporate bottom line. Although Smyth and Shacklock clearly revealed that such competencies are designed to mobilize consent for the status quo, they also illustrated how these competencies are being coated in deception through claims that such competencies are disinterested, scientific, and professional. Under the cover of policy hysteria surrounding the future of the global economy and the role that schooling must play in such a future, an "evaluative mode of an economically rational state" has been carefully cobbled out of the detritus of democracy's failed mission. This functions as a "silk glove" form of accountability (tied to technical and nominally "objective" forms of observation and appraisal), requiring individual teachers to implement systemic policy initiatives as a fundamental part of their work, a requirement that allows for a greater external monitoring of the "effectiveness" of teacher work. In the final analysis, educational critics such as Smyth and Shacklock have revealed how competencies that are prefixed and externally circumscribed and administered serve to limit what counts as skilled work in classrooms, undermine indigenous ways of talking about the world in general, and create a hidden blueprint for excluding teachers' active theorization of and experimentation with pedagogical practices. We want to raise an issue of *litem lite resolvere*. Educational policies grounded in the ideology of economic rationalism engineers a view of democratic schooling as premised on the harmonization of differences among ethnic groups and social classes, thereby mistaking the phenomenon needing explanation for the explanation itself. Racism in a capitalist state is a symptom of the exploitation of human labor, not the cause of social affliction. Hence, teachers are deflected from examining the interrelationship among race, class, and gender oppression within the context of global capitalist relations.

Toward a Revolutionary Citizenship

Part of the pedagogical project for creating a new revolutionary politics is what we refer to as the praxis of revolutionary citizenship. Such a praxis can be won in the classrooms, in the workplace, in class struggle for ownership of the means of production, and in those volatile and contested spaces of the public sphere where people struggle to redefine the meaning of democratic social life. Because it is a sociopolitical form of praxis, it ventures beyond abstractions and platitudes and refuses to linger inactively in the ambit of the apologists. Citizenship, as it is constructed within capitalist democracy, can be described as "a sociopolitical form that isolates individuals from social problems that have their roots in the individualization of goods and their sellers . . . [and] negates real social life by creating a political abstraction that obfuscates the major contradictions of society" (Costilla 2000, 94). By contrast, revolutionary citizenship heeds unflinchingly the intrepid role of the activist and condemns those who would pusillanimously evade the moral issues surrounding neoliberalism's scandalously unbalanced assault on and treatment of the world's poor and aggrieved communities.

The project of revolutionary citizenship works directly against the politics of neoliberalism and seeks to build alliances between unionized workers and political leadership in the interest of increased socialist democracy. Revolutionary citizens work toward a new type of democratic governance and a redistribution of economic and political power that results in an oppositional form of globalization that, according to Costilla (2000), "is not subordinated to capital but humane in its economy, political system, mass media, culture, and citizenship" (87).

We argue that the revolutionary citizenship praxis as a form of creative collective action should be centered on the devalorization of capital as a process of dealienation. That is, the revolutionary citizenship praxis should recognize, following Dinerstein (1997), the contradictory mode of existence of labor; that is, it should grasp that action is a form of alienation and dealienation. Because society fundamentally involves the objectification of subjectivity, revolutionary citizenship becomes the constitution of subjectivity within the class struggle itself and the tension produced between the acceptance and negation of capitalist relationships (Dinerstein 1997). In obtaining some necessary political justice for our project, we follow Sam Gindin and Leo Panitch (2000) in arguing for a rethinking and reformulation of socialist utopian goals that exceed what capital and the state will accommodate. Rehabilitating a distinctly concrete Marxist utopianism, Gindin and Panitch addressed an "educated desire" as distinct from a "conservative desire." The former type of desire is described by the notion that "I want to change the world" and the latter by the notion that "I want to change my own place in the world" (Gindin and Panitch 2000, 41). Gindin and Panitch argued that socialist morality

> educates desire toward the goal of realizing our potential to be full human beings and extending that principle to all members of society. Socialist analysis discovers, in the dynamics of capitalist society, the repressed possibility of that new world and the agency that, in the process of "doing-other," can change both itself (including its dreams) and society, thereby "becoming-other." (41)

The utopian Marxism and reenchantment of socialist agency that is articulated in the project of revolutionary citizenship refuses to obliterate liberal democracy's traumatic origin in the production systems of imperialism and capitalist exploitation. It is underwritten by a socialist hope nurtured by particular social capacities that represents the crucial link between the ideal and the possibility of constructing a class collective in which workers "develop the social capacity to dream, to understand, to participate, and to act politically" (Gindin and Panitch 2000, 41). Socialist dreaming is not about the liberation of the individual from the social but is about a collective dreaming through the social in the service of ensuring that workers are able to create a new world on their own terms and in their own voice without seeking permission to narrate their own futures. It enables workers to see the past as (to borrow a phrase from Lukács) "the prehistory of the present." It also enables a vision of the future that interweaves with the objective movement of history itself. The race-based uprisings that took place in Los Angeles and that, more recently, occurred in Cincinnati have revealed to us that the melting pot has turned into a meltdown. The ravages of capital—including institutionalized forms of racist violence against African Americans and Latina/os—have singled out all of the working class as its victim, but the cruelest forms of violence and exploitation have been reserved for people of color. Surely, it is among the people of color where the leadership will arise to lead the assault against capitalism and its racist formations and practices.

The most important social capacity is that of acting politically as a class; this serves as the coordinating mechanism for other capacities and attempts to make them less sporadic and more cumulative, especially with respect to the role of workers' organizations. Ideals that help steer such a collective vision include overcoming alienation, attenuating the division of labor, transforming consumption, creating alternative ways of living, socializing markets, planning ecologically, internationalizing equality, communicating democratically, and abolishing private property. As Gindin and Panitch (2000) pointed out, capitalism is "the wrong dream" (50).

Capital agitates out of its productive forces a narrow range of social capacities and human activities. The narrowing of human capacities under global capitalism is due to the fact that they are constitutive of the logic of the corporate regime itself. The underlying structure of the corporate regime is by its very nature life-denying and psychopathic. As McMurtry (2000) asserted,

> The underlying general fact of our condition is that the transnational corporate regime is a profoundly incompetent regime in virtually every capability of life understanding and development. This is because it is based on an engineering paradigm which is in principle life-blind. *Its system has only mastered the methods of machine-manufacture and money-sequencing cost-inputs into greater money outputs, with the through-puts of all of human and environmental life blinkered out as having any value except as mechanized means of these money-sequences.* This structure of understanding civil and planetary life-organization is, from a wider standpoint, insane. As a system-decider for ruling the life-world, it is psychopathic, its paradigm and practice do not and cannot recognize life or educational values—including its vaunted electronic delivery circuits which do not and cannot tell the difference between true and false. (9; italics in orginal)

Furthermore, problems that do not offer corporate profits as a result of their solutions are no longer defined as problems. The corporate funding of education is about assisting education in solving profitable problems. McMurtry (2000) noted,

> The fact that corporately directed science and medicine devotes little or no research funds to resurgent malaria, dengue fever or river blindness (whose many millions of victims lack market demand to pay for cures), while it invests billions of dollars into researching and marketing dubious and often lethal drugs to treat non-diseases of consumers in rich markets, demonstrates this agenda's principle of selection of problems to address. There is no reason to suppose that market corporations would behave differently with education on unprofitable problems than in their investment in researching them. . . . This commercialized research has led to insider trading by faculty members, and attack on dissemination of research findings, including a University of South Florida filing of criminal charges against an M.A. student whose continued research on a patented project was alleged as "stealing university property," a charge which resulted in the student's sentence to a state chain gang. (15)

Thus, we argue that capitalism instrumentalizes and fetishizes human capacities by truncating and depotentiating what McMurtry (1998) called the "civil commons," defined as "society's organized and community-funded capacity of universally accessible resources to provide for the life preservation and growth of society's members and their environmental life-host" (24). The civil commons provides the essential backdrop for revolutionary citizenship and socialist dreaming; it provides a space for individuals to participate in social activities that do not follow the logic of the market's exchange value. The civil commons further encompasses such areas as language, education, literacy, and cultural heritage as well as organizations and opportunities traditionally associated with the public sphere. These include but are not limited to public health and education, water and power, the postal service, public access to the media, libraries, and parks (McMurtry 1998).

The civil commons constitutes assurances that basic human rights such as free health care, education, and employment will be central to the lifeblood of the community. The value system of the civil commons exists in contraposition to the value system of the free market, even though the free market perceives its value system to be identical with that of the civil commons. In reality, the market serves a minority ruling class whose interests are antagonistic to the interests of the rest of society (see also Giroux 1983, 1992). The civil commons in the United States is afflicted by what the Children's Defense Fund (2000) termed "affluenza": "the poverty of having too much that is worth too little" (xviii). According to its recent report, millions of American children of all ethnicities in every part of the country

> are given every material thing they desire—cell phones, cars, every latest trendy fashion, CD and electronic gadgets, and live in big houses in well-to-do neighborhoods. But too many are not given enough parental and community attention, limit setting, and moral guidance. (xiii–xiv)

The narrowing of human capacities and capitalism's attack on the civil commons must be transcended by breaking the power of capital and by setting free the human possibilities fostered by democratic community, social collectivity, and political solidarity. Thus, a pedagogy of revolutionary citizenship must stipulate as its primary focus the exposure of the lie of progress that is folded into the promise of neoliberalism. This entails a recognition and overcoming of the multifarious dimensions of deceit that shape the neoliberal utopian agenda. But a critique of neoliberalism must be accompanied by a broader social revolution of the type described by Marx (Allman 1999; Neary and Rikowski 2000).

Revolutionary citizenship as a form of proletarian solidarity refutes the claims made by the supporters of the free market that, under a socialist system, individual rights are sacrificed for community rights. Although the community guarantees individuals rights to universal health care, education, and employment, the value system of the market is unable to meet the social needs of all community members. Consequently, the value system of the civil commons and the market are not identical because the market is fundamentally rooted in producing profit before meeting the social and economic needs of community members (McMurtry 1998). We do not hold out as much promise as does McMurtry that capitalist exploitation can be challenged successfully at the level of civil society. Hence, we remain disappointed in those who advocate for a "radical democracy" but fail to explain how workers are to gain the means of capitalist production without a direct assault on the power of the state through oppositional parties and an emphasis on international proletarian hegemony.

We do not advocate legislating for knowledge from a vanguard position from above that hinders its translation into popular action from below. Rather, we support appeals to and conceptions of the knowing, experiencing, and acting subject that claim a descent from Marx and Engels but remain flexibly attuned to the contextual specificity of the present—a position that in our view remains consistent with the Marxist problematic. We draw a conspicuous distinction between critical revolutionary praxis as a real possibility in the advancement of a socialist alternative and the mechanistic and reductionist forms of Marxist theories that consider socialism and communism as historical inevitabilities. Daniel Singer (1999) wisely remarked, "Socialism may be a historical possibility or even necessary to eliminate the evils of capitalism, but this does not mean that it will inevitably take its place" (272). Although we recognize that we live in different social, historical, and geopolitical contexts than the nineteenth-century world of which Marx wrote, we nevertheless affirm his central claims. For example, we recognize the central role of the working class in the struggle for socialism and the ongoing battle against imperialism worldwide.

Following the demise of socialism in Russia and Eastern Europe, the working class has been relegated to the footnotes of history. The declassing of the working class led by ex-Marxists, post-Marxists, and anti-Marxists who have retreated into the rutted streets of academic ghettos to sell at inflated prices cultural studies, deconstructionism, postmodernism, poststructuralism, and various theories of globalization that are often openly hostile to Marxism only prolongs the deferment of revolutionary praxis (Allman 1999; Cole and Hill 1995; Hill 1999; McLaren and Farahmandpur 2000; Rikowski 2000). We are equally as critical of leftist progressives who advocate strategic alliances with the Right and who push for alternatives without sufficiently challenging the capitalist frames of reference and social practices that they claim to hold in disdain. Even those radical academics sympathetic to issues on the Left often become trapped in the self-referential mystification of their own bourgeois criteria as they attempt to push the boundaries of social critique through the luminous portals of the ivory tower. Michael Burawoy (2000) remarked,

> One has to wonder to what extent the radicals are giving expression to their own conditions of existence. Is it an accident that high-flying academics, hotel-circuiting consultants, conference-hopping professionals, and netscaping virtuosos should develop concepts of the network society, should imagine a manichean world of placeless power and powerless places, should expound on time-space compression or aesthetic cognitive maps? It is perhaps fitting that Giddens should traverse the world from capital to capital as he delivers his Reith lectures, ruminating on risk in Hong Kong, tradition in Delhi, family in Washington, and democracy in London. Their theories of globalization are theories of privileged men, who appear in a privileged airspace above the world they theorize. Their absence from their own accounts aspires to objectivity, but it cannot hide the unspoken, unreflected, stratospheric situatedness of their knowledges. How much of their theorizing is the projection of insulated journeys, unspoken genealogies, self-referential worlds? (340)

It may be as difficult for a high-priced ruling class academic to grasp—let alone transform—the exigencies and map the fault lines of working-class struggle as it is for a camel to pass through the eye of a needle or for a rich man or woman to enter the kingdom of heaven (or for Venezuela's president, Hugo Chavez, to spend a night at the Bush's ranch in Crawford, Texas). What is needed is what Paulo Freire (1970, 1998) referred to as a willingness to commit class suicide and a commitment to resist the rule of capital in all dimensions of social life.

Transforming revolutionary praxis into a real socialist alternative necessitates developing a political imaginary that embraces an acute awareness of the social ills induced by capitalism and is capable of producing a political ideology that can unify the oppressed classes into a revolutionary class willing to challenge the relations of capitalist exploitation with the intention of eventually transforming them. Finally, developing a political imaginary means treating "capitalism not as an eternity, but as a historical phase with a distant beginning and a possible proximate end" (Singer 1999, 257).

How do we move beyond nervously twiddling our thumbs while waiting for the next stage of history and merely thumbing our noses at capitalism? After all, unlike some educational leftists and pseudo-leftists, we do not believe that anticapitalist struggle is naive or merely a rhetorical argument. Nor do we believe for an instant that revolutionary pedagogy is a form of "romantic possibilitarianism." Are moderate, reformist ideologies enough? Do we simply carry out the ideology of reform and development? Do we revamp the traditional model of Western parliamentary democracy so that it can be mechanically applied to the peripheral Third World countries of Asia, Latin

America, Eastern Europe, and the Middle East? Is there a way to avoid the dangers of both authoritarianism and parliamentarianism?

Boris Kagarlitsky (2000) argued that there is indeed an alternative that is based on creating neither larger nor smaller states but fundamentally different kinds of states that are neither liberal nor bourgeois but place the public sector as an active player in the economy. The public sector is placed in the hands of the workers and their parties such that self-management within state structures will bring about democratic forms of representation. As Kagarlitsky noted, we must change the very nature of our approach to development. We note here by example the efforts of the Workers Party in Brazil to institute participatory budgets and to reinvest in the infrastructures of cities (although at the same time we register our disappointment with Lula).

A revolutionary citizenship must move beyond the centralizing trends of the old statist industrial economy while recognizing the potential role of the state in providing accelerated development in Third World countries. Accumulation and investment policy must be subordinated to the needs of the people. This presupposes a broader notion of the national organization of production. Capitalists began this process; socialists must finish it. Every decision made on behalf of growth must guarantee the rights of the individual. One precondition for this is the social ownership by the workers of the technological base of society. This means struggling for a democratic compatibility between socioeconomic and political structures. We cannot afford to think in phases or that a democratic revolution will naturally precede a socialist one. Socialist institutions must drive development, and this includes the schools. As Arthur MacWean (1999) opined,

> in a democratic development strategy, it is not enough to expand the schooling system as a means to promote equality; it is also necessary to equalize the educational system itself and eliminate the connection between family income and the quality of education that people receive. (186)

Contemporary approaches to critical pedagogy have bled much of the political praxis capabilities out of it, rendering critical pedagogy ideologically and conceptually anemic and politically detumescent; in fact, many progressive educators claiming to endorse critical pedagogy have made sure that the questions posed in this chapter are not part of the larger educational agenda. Short-term advances in educational reform have become impaled on the long-term intractability of capitalist relations of exploitation. Critical pedagogy must do more than paint a happy face on capitalist social relations (Allen 1999; Leonardo 2000; McLaren 2000).

The postmodern Left in education has argued for transgressive forms of resignification of the symbolic order in the ideological struggle for hegemony. More specifically, it has attempted a radical transformation of the universal structuring principle of the existing symbolic order. Yet in doing so, it has failed to sufficiently problematize the social universe of capital. Slavoj Žižek (2000) remarked how post-Marxists such as Judith Butler and Ernest Laclau have in their respective critiques of so-called essentialist Marxism neglected to contest the rule of capital. As Žižek noted,

> Today's Real which sets a limit to resignification is capital: the smooth function-ing of Capital is that which remains the same, that which "always returns to its place," in the unconstrained struggle for hegemony. Is this not demonstrated by the fact that Butler, as well as Laclau, in their criticism of the old "essentialist" Marxism, none the less silently accept a set of premises: they never question the fundamentals of the capitalist market economy and the liberal-democratic po-litical regime; they never envisage the possibility of a completely different eco-nomico-political regime. In this way, they fully participate in the abandonment of these questions by the "postmodern" Left: all the changes they propose are changes within this economico-political regime. (223)

We are not interested only in palliative damage control measures within the social universe of capital production and exchange mechanisms. We are inter-ested in the total revolution of which Marx speaks. Here we want to underscore the importance of autonomous movements such as the Zapatistas. Our Marx-ian solidarity is powered not by attempts to conscript revolutionary praxis into conformity with a monolithic, Eurocentric weltanschauung premised on En-lightenment rationality but by a commitment to multiple forms of organiza-tion, human sociality, and solidarity. Such a commitment sets itself against the social, economic, and spiritual forms of wreckage brought about by those im-perialist forces unchained by the globalization of capital and global neoliberal-ism (Grande 2000, Richardson and Villenas 2000).

Revolutionary pedagogy examines the conjoined spaces of the pedagogical field to interrogate it in all its capillary detail. In doing so, revolutionary ped-agogy imposes on the educator a new set of obligations, the most important being that of creating revolutionary agency and citizenship. In excavating the planes of practical action that define the space of the pedagogical and the po-litical, as well as their intersection, revolutionary educators recognize that the struggle for educational reform stipulates anticapitalist struggle in both local and global contexts. In doing so, they encourage strategies of conflict and crit-icism to halt the pretenses of any single conception of the pedagogical.

We cannot afford to be lured by the manufactured daydreams or the halcyon nights of contemporary commodity culture where social agents are reduced to gleeful spectators celebrating the *comédie noire* of capitalism. Democracy can-not be pandered to the demands of a dangerously unrestricted capitalism. In the words of Boris Kagarlitsky (1999), "Democracy [under capitalism] . . . is a façade, mere window-dressing" (144). Contrary to the opinion of many post-modern savants and post-Marxist illuminati, we believe that Marx's chiliastic analyses of capitalism will continue to be vital well into the twenty-first century and beyond. The potential of Marxist theory for reinvigorating our understanding of and political resistance to the commodification and corporatization of schooling is only beginning to be fully recognized. As Michael Parenti (1997) so pertinently argued,

> Marx's major work was capital, a study not of "existing socialism," which actually did not exist in his day, but of capitalism—a subject that remains terribly relevant to our lives. It would make more sense to declare Marxism obsolete if and when capitalism is abolished, rather than socialism. I wish to argue not merely that Marx is still relevant but that he is more relevant today than he was in the nineteenth century, that the forces of capitalist motion and development are operating with greater scope than when he first studied them. (122)

We believe that the time has come for critical educators to answer the following questions or face the consequences: Do we merely fight the excesses of capitalism, or do we work toward overthrowing them? Do we fight against the shrinkage of basic industry and its outsourcing, or do we struggle for workers' rights internationally? Do we participate in the task of increasing shopping opportunities for the rich, or should our efforts be directed at bringing the globalization of capital to an end? Is our task as critical educators to address the inner contradictions within capital–labor relations, or do we in a concrete and even perhaps militant fashion enter the struggle between workers and capitalists? Do we struggle for a redistribution of resources, as most radical educational critics encourage, or do we also develop a socialist future that will serve an unlimitedly developing humankind? Is our goal to manage the crisis of capital or bring down the capitalist system? Will the prime function of critical educators be to articulate and manage conflicts or deepen the development of social struggles? As Samir Amin (2000) aptly put it,

> The central question, therefore, is how conflicts and social struggles (it is important to differentiate between the two) will be articulated. Which will triumph? Will social struggles be subordinated, framed by conflicts, and therefore mastered by the dominant powers, even made instruments to the benefit of those powers? Or will social struggles surmount their autonomy and force the major powers to respond to their urgent demands? (17)

Do we put our faith in the possibility that abstract labor might negate itself and recompose the relation between capital and labor or between the wage laborers and the bourgeoisie, or do we begin the necessary task of creating a mass revolutionary organization that is aligned with the everyday struggles of the working class and is capable of striking at the heart of the capitalist system? Do we trawl hesitatingly between the Scylla of neoliberalism and the Charybdis of a Third Way politics, or do we move full throttle into the untested waters of mass internationalist movements? Do we retreat into the academic salons of the post-Marxist theorists, or do we rent the vaults of capital with defiant cries from the picket lines with strategies of refusal won on the playing fields of a resurgent Marxist theory? Here we direct our efforts at Rosemary Hennessy's (2001) brilliant work on the renarrating of identities from the standpoint of the collectivity of those whose surplus human needs capitalism has refused to meet. Hennessy emphasizes the historical and material conditions of the possibility of identity formation that does not renounce racial, gender, or sexual identities in favor of a class identity but approaches these identities as features of social reality and lived experience that demands a comprehensive historical and materialist explanation. Especially after the "battle in Seattle," we should be emboldened to accelerate our struggles and recover confidence in our potential capacities and powers. As Alex Callinicos (2000) noted, "To demand equality is to propose revolution" (128). He further warned, "The greatest obstacle to change is not, however, the revolt it would evoke from the privileged, but the belief that it is impossible" (128). Our search must be directed toward new forms of sociality that do not run parallel to the social universe of capital but that are linked to a praxis-driven revolutionary politics dedicated to transforming capitalist social relations of production. Michael Löwy (2000) averred when he wrote,

> What alternative exists to the totalitarian grip of "really existing" world capitalism? The old pseudo-internationalism of the Stalinist Comintern, of the followers of various "Socialist fatherlands," is dead and buried. A new internationalist alternative of the oppressed and exploited is badly needed. . . . It is from the fusion between the international socialist, democratic and anti-imperialist tradition of the labor movement (still much alive among revolutionaries of various tendencies, radical trade unionists, critical communists, left-socialists, etc.) and the new universalist culture of social movements like ecology, feminism, anti-racism and third world solidarity that the new internationalism of tomorrow will rise. This tendency may be a minority now, but it is nevertheless the seed of a different future and the ultimate guarantee against barbarism. (12)

We can no longer afford to remain indifferent to the horrors and savageries committed by capitalism's self-destructive mechanisms, which are steering civilization into a collision course with barbarism. Our deafening silence offers despair a victory and foreshortens the hope necessary for overcoming cynicism in our efforts to create a democratic and egalitarian socialist society. As the gravediggers of capitalism, we must keep our shovels poised to keep digging. History does not end at the doorstep of capitalism, nor is it scripted by the ruling classes. The course of history can be altered by collective struggle. The future remains in the hands of those whose revolutionary activities are directed at creating it. That includes, first and foremost, the workers in whose service we dedicate ourselves. We have been handed the red thread that will lead us out of the labyrinth of capital. What we need now is the courage to clutch it and to steel ourselves for the long and winding road to victory. That road will not be easy to tread because we must do more than simply retrace our steps only to find ourselves back in the streets of statist Communism and reformist social democracy. The new path we need to forge must move beyond nationalization of industry and the state control of the economy. Clearly, struggling for a noncapitalist future will require tremendous creativity and insight and much can be learned from what is already internal to the mass movements for liberation afoot today.

Notes

1. In a discussion of marketization and educational change, Kari Dehli (1996) argued that the concept of marketization must be made more problematic and must be conceptually differentiated. Dehli identified four forms of marketization: privatization, commercialization, commodification, and residualization. Dehli wrote, "Privatisation refers to the movement of programs, resources and staff from the public to the private sector, including corporations, families or 'voluntary' organisations, as well as the movement of previously 'private' services and programs—such as parent 'volunteers,' social services, and corporate partnerships—into publicly funded schools; commercialisation incorporates exchange-based relations to shape the internal organisation of educational institutions, relations between schools, and relations between schools and their publics; commodification suggests the ascendancy of packaged and quantifiable forms of knowledge and assessment, such as outcome-based curricula, performance indicators and skills testing techniques; while residualisation attends to the structural consequences of individualised choice in public services. These concepts are helpful in sorting through the often confusing and disorienting features and processes of marketisation. They make it possible to tease out the distinctive features of specific practices, and to compare the shape, content and effects of different processes and reactions to them" (365).

2. Business governed by the laws of supply and demand, not restrained by government interference, regulation, or subsidy. According to this point of view, capitalism as an economic system is most efficient and productive when there is regulation or interference by the government.

3. Downsizing refers to reducing the total number of employees at a company through terminations, retirements, or spin-offs.

4. Outsourcing refers to work done for a company by workers other than the company's full-time employees. A majority of these workers are from Third World nations and are hired by companies contracted by multinational corporations.

5. Privatization refers to the transfer of the management of public schools to private or for-profit educational organizations. Privatization emphasizes typical business-oriented concepts such as customer satisfaction and managerial autonomy in running schools.

References

Allen, R. L. 1999. The socio-spatial making and marking of "us": Toward a critical postmodern spatial theory of difference and community. *Social Identities* 5(3): 249–77.

Allman, P. 1999. *Revolutionary social transformation: Democratic hopes, political possibilities and critical education.* Westport, Conn.: Bergin and Garvey.

Amin, S. 2000. The political economy of the twentieth century. *Monthly Review* 52(2): 1–17.

Apple, M. W. 1989. *Teachers and texts: A political economy of class and gender relation in education.* New York: Routledge.

———. 1993. *Official knowledge: Democratic education in a conservative age.* New York: Routledge.

———. 1996. *Cultural politics and education.* New York: Teachers College Press.

Banfield, G. 2000. Schooling and the spirit of enterprise: Producing the power top labor. *Education and Social Justice* 2(3): 23–28.

Berliner, D. C., and B. J. Biddle. 1995. *The manufactured crises: Myths, fraud, and the attack on America's public schools.* Reading, Mass.: Addison-Wesley.

Boggs, C. 2000. *The end of politics: Corporate power and the decline of the public sphere.* New York: Guilford.

Brosio, R. A. 1998. End of the millennium: Capitalism's dynamism, civic crises, and corresponding consequences for education. In *Critical social issues in American education: Transformation in a postmodern world,* 2nd ed., ed. H. S. Shapiro and D. E. Purpel, 27–44. Mahwah, N.J.: Lawrence Erlbaum Associates.

Budgen, S. 2000. A new "spirit of capitalism." *New Left Review* 1: 149–56.

Burawoy, M. 2000. Grounding globalization. In *Global ethnography: Forces, connections, and imaginations in a postmodern world,* ed. M. Burawoy, J. A. Blum, S. George, Z. Gille, T. Gowan, L. Haney, M. Klawiter, S. H. Lopez, S. Riain, and M. Thayer, 337–50. Berkeley: University of California Press.

Callinicos, A. 2000. *Equality.* Cambridge: Polity Press.

Center for Commercial-Free Public Education. 2000. Commercialism in the schools. www.commercialfree.org/commercialism.html (accessed February 21, 2000).

Center for a New American Dream. 2000. Kids and commercialism. www.newdream .org/campaign/kids/facts.html (accessed February 22, 2000).

Children's Defense Fund. 2000. *The state of America's children.* Boston: Beacon Press.

Cole, M., and D. Hill. 1995. Games of despair and rhetorics of resistance: Postmodernism, education and reaction. *British Journal of Sociology of Education* 16(2): 165–82.

Cole, M., D. Hill, and G. Rikowski. 1997. Between postmodernism and nowhere: The predicament of the postmodernist. *British Journal of Educational Studies* 45(2): 187–200.

Cole, M., D. Hill, G. Rikowski, and P. McLaren. 2000. *Red chalk: On schooling, capitalism and politics.* London: Tufnell Press.

Corporate Watch. 2000. The education industry fact sheet. www.corpwatch.org/trac/feature/education/industry/fact.html (accessed February 21, 2001).

Costilla, L. F. O. 2000. The reconstitution of power and democracy in the age of capital globalization. *Latin American Perspectives* 27(1): 82–104.

Dehli, K. 1996. Between "market" and "state?" Engendered education in the 1990s. *Discourse: Studies in Cultural Politics of Education* 17(3): 363–76.

Dinerstein, A. 1997. Marxism and subjectivity: Searching for the marvelous (prelude to a Marxist notion of action). *Common Sense* 22: 83–96.

Dlugin, L. 1999. Globalization. *Political Affairs* 78(11): 20–22.

Ehrenreich, B. 2000a. Global stench. *LA Weekly,* October 26–29, 19–20.

———. 2000b. Terrible waste. *LA Weekly,* June 2–8, 20–21.

Freire, P. 1970. *Pedagogy of the oppressed.* New York: Continuum.

———. 1998. *Pedagogy of freedom: Ethics, democracy, and civic courage.* Lanham, Md.: Rowman & Littlefield.

Galeano, E. 2000. *Upside down: A primer for the looking-class world.* Translated by M. Fried. New York: Metropolitan Books.

Gee, J. P., G. Hull, and C. Lankshear. 1997. *The new work order: Behind the language of the new capitalism.* Boulder, Colo.: Westview Press.

Gindin, S., and L. Panitch. 2000. Rethinking socialist imagination: Utopian vision and working-class capacities. *Monthly Review* 51(10): 36–51.

Giroux, H. 1983. *Theory and resistance in education: A pedagogy for the opposition.* South Hadley, Mass.: Bergin and Garvey.

———. 1992. *Border crossings.* New York: Routledge.

Grande, S. M. A. 2000. American Indian identity and power: At the crossroads of Indigena and Mestizaje. *Harvard Educational Review* 70(4): 467–98.

Hardt, M., and A. Negri. 2000. *Empire.* Cambridge, Mass.: Harvard University Press.

Heintz, J., and N. Folbre. 2000. *The ultimate field guide to the U.S. economy: A compact and irreverent guide to economic life in America.* New York: New Press.

Hennessy, R. 2001. Building social movement out of unmet needs: Class consciousness, the permanent plantón, and love. Keynote address at the conference "Almost Always Deceived: Revolutionary Praxis and Reinventions of Need," University of Florida, Gainesville, March 31.

Hill, D. 1999. *New Labour and education: Policy, ideology and the Third Way.* London: Tufnell Press.

Jordan, J. 1999. Peer review and the new teacher unionism: Mutual support or policing? *Against the Current* 14(4): 13–16.

Kagarlitsky, B. 1999. *New realism new barbarism: Socialist theory in the era of globalization.* Translated by R. Clark. London: Pluto Press.

———. 2000. *The return of radicalism: Reshaping the left institutions.* Translated by R. Clark. London: Pluto Press.

Kilbourne, J. 1999. *Deadly persuasion: Why women and girls must fight the addictive power of advertising.* New York: Free Press.

Kincheloe, J. 1993. *Towards a critical politics of teacher thinking: Mapping the postmodern.* Westport, Conn.: Bergin and Garvey.

———. 1998. *How do we tell the workers? The socioeconomic foundations of work and vocational education.* Boulder, Colo.: Westview Press.

———. 2002. *The sign of the burger: McDonald's and the culture of power.* Philadelphia: Temple University Press.

Klein, N. 1999. *No logo: Taking aim at the brand bullies.* New York: Picador.

Lasn, K. 1999. *Culture jam: The uncooling of America.* New York: Eagle.

———. 2000. USA TM. *Adbusters* 28: 52–55.

Lauder, H., and P. Brown. 1997. Education, globalization, and economic development. In *Education: Culture, economy, society,* ed. A. H. Hasley, H. Lauder, P. Brown, and A. S. Wells, 172–92. Oxford: Oxford University Press.

Leonardo, Z. 2000. Betwixt and between: An introduction to the politics of identity. In *Charting new terrains of Chicana(o)/Latina(o) education,* ed. C. Tejada, C. Martinez, and Z. Leonardo, 107–29. Creskill, N.J.: Hampton Press.

Löwy, M. 2000. Nationalism and the new world order. Working Papers Series in Cultural Studies, Ethnicity, and Race Relations. Pullman: Washington State University, Department of Comparative American Cultures.

MacWean, A. 1999. *Neoliberalism or democracy? Economic strategy, markets, and alternatives for the 21st century.* London: Zed Books.

McLaren, P. 2000. *Che Guevara, Paulo Freire, and the pedagogy of revolution.* Lanham, Md.: Rowman & Littlefield.

McLaren, P., and R. Farahmandpur. 1999a. Critical multiculturalism and globalization: Some implications for a politics of resistance. *Journal of Curriculum Theorizing* 15(3): 27–46.

———. 1999b. Critical pedagogy, postmodernism, and the retreat from class: Toward a contraband pedagogy. *Theoria: A Journal of Social and Political Theory* 93: 83–115.

———. 2000. Reconsidering Marx in post-Marxist times: A requiem for postmodernism? *Educational Researcher* 29(3): 25–33.

McMurtry, J. 1998. *Unequal freedoms: The global market as an ethical system.* West Hartford, Conn.: Kumarian.

———. 2000. Seeing through the corporate agenda: Education, life-value and the global economy. Paper presented at the annual meeting of the Queen's University Faculty of Education Colloquium, Kingston, Ontario, March.

Mészáros, I. 1999. Marxism, the capital system, and social revolution: An interview with István Mészáros. *Science and Society* 63(3): 338–61.

Miner, B. 2004. Educate all children. *In These Times* 28(18/19): 30–31.

Neary, M. 2000. Travels in Moishe Postone's social universe: A contribution to a critique of political cosmology. Unpublished manuscript.

Neary, M., and G. Rikowski. 2000. The speed of life: The significance of Karl Marx's concept of socially necessary labour-time. Paper presented at the annual conference of the British Sociological Association, York, United Kingdom, April.

Oakes, J. 1985. *Keeping track: How schools structure inequality.* New Haven, Conn.: Yale University Press.

Parenti, M. 1997. *Blackshirts and Reds: Rational fascism and the overthrow of communism.* San Francisco: City Lights.

Plawiuk, E. 1999. Assaulting public education in Canada: Privatization plague spreads. *Against the Current* 14(4): 18–20.

Raduntz, H. 1999. A Marxian critique of teachers' work in an era of capitalist globalization. Paper presented at the annual conference of the Australian Association for Research in Education and the New Zealand Association for Research in Education, Melbourne, Australia, November–December.

Richardson, T., and S. Villenas. 2000. "Other" encounters: Dances with whiteness in multicultural education. *Educational Theory* 50(2): 255–74.

Rikowski, G. 2000. Messing with the explosive commodity: School improvement, educational research and labor-power in the era of global capitalism. Paper presented at the annual conference of the British Educational Research Association, Cardiff, United Kingdom, September.

Singer, D. 1999. *Whose millennium? Theirs or ours?* New York: Monthly Review Press.

Smyth, G., and G. Shacklock. 1998. *Re-Making teaching: Ideology, policy and practice.* London: Routledge.

Spring, J. 1997. *Political agendas for education: From the Christian coalition to the Green Party.* Mahwah, N.J.: Lawrence Erlbaum Associates.

———. 1998. *Education and the rise of the global economy.* Mahwah, N.J.: Lawrence Erlbaum Associates.

Tyack, D., and L. Cuban. 1995. *Tinkering toward utopia: A century of public education reform.* Cambridge, Mass.: Harvard University Press.

Wood, E. M. 1995. *Democracy against capitalism: Renewing historical materialism.* Cambridge: Cambridge University Press.

Žižek, S. 2000. Holding the place. In *Contingency, hegemony, universality: Contemporary dialogues on the left,* ed. J. Butler, E. Laclau, and S. Žižek, 308–29. London: Verso.

8

Teaching in and against the Empire: Critical Pedagogy as Revolutionary Praxis

With Gregory Martin and Nathalia Jaramillo

> When fascism comes to America, it will come in the name of democracy.
>
> —Huey Long

Globalization, Terrorism, and the Crisis of Democracy

WE LIVE IN URGENT TIMES. The unconscionable duplicity of the Bush regime and its permanent war on terrorism has plunged the nation into a furious firestorm where the nature and purpose of democracy is being redefined. Our self and social formation as citizens has become a permanent battleground—the agon for the winning of our consent to the new dictates and mandates emanating from the White House. The Bush gang has launched an all-out battle for the final liberation of the ruling class from any remaining constraints to their goal of full-spectrum political dominance of the globe.

All across the country, critical educators are fighting on dozens of fronts, searching in both form and content for a coherent pedagogical expression that captures their opposition to what they perceive as momentous developments: the pandemic of economic globalization, U.S. geopolitical imperialism and the rabid manner in which the Bush administration—crazed with power—is defining and responding to the current war on terrorism, the linking of patriotism to an unquestioning and unthinking adherence to the Bush administration's antiterrorist agenda, the neoliberal mandates of the Western capitalist countries and the international dictatorship of transnational corporations, and the ideological agenda embedded in the Bush administration's approach to educational change. Clearly, all these fronts are interrelated and important. We do not have the space to discuss in depth all these fronts or the issues to which they refer. While we will mention some of these fronts in our discussion, our focus will be on expanding the concept so that it addresses both the urgency and the scope of the current crisis of capitalism in relation to the crisis of educational reform and takes as its central aim the struggle against capitalism and imperialism.

The current crisis of global capitalism and the juggernaut of privatization has spread exponentially and mutated more rapidly than the SARS virus, outmaneuvering the hastily developed defenses erected by workers whose wages and benefits continue to be decimated in the face of the rule of finance and speculative capital and the Enronization of corporate life (see McLaren and Farahmandpur 2001a, 2001b, 2001c, 2002). One recent example is the move by the Bush administration to privatize half the federal civil service jobs and transform one of the few remaining precincts of financial social protection into a spot labor market, virtually abolishing the jobs, retirement security, and health benefits of 850,000 blue- and white-collar workers who will be replaced by low-paid crews in a "race-to-the-bottom" budget gimmick. This crisis not only affects the civil service and private industry but now engulfs public schools, universities, and colleges across the nation. For example, the past decade witnessed a rising tide of part-time and "perma-temp" faculty and instructors who teach full time at institutions of higher education but are nevertheless denied health care and pension benefits offered to tenure-track faculty. Leslie Berger (2002) of the *New York Times* reports that 43 percent of professors and instructors who are now teaching at institutions of higher education are part-time employees. In fact, between 1993 and 1998, this has been a growing trend in universities, colleges, and junior colleges, which have been forced to cut back on spending on educational programs and services while raising tuition fees. Berger also writes that within the same five-year span, universities and colleges have reduced their full-time faculty by 22 percent and have instead hired part-time and temporary instructors. A case in point is New York University, where 2,700 of the 6,000 faculty members are part-time instructors. What is clear is that downsizing, outsourcing, and "flexible" methods of labor practices on production lines in factories have now trickled down to encompass universities and colleges across the United States.

Conversely, universities and colleges are demanding that professors be more productive scholars. Faculty members are expected to publish more articles, books, and essays; attend conferences and seminars; and obtain research funds by submitting grants to various public and private foundations. These demands are taking place at a time when there are fewer funds available to support faculty scholarship. In the absence of funds, a large number of state universities have been forced to place a freeze on faculty travel expenses for the purpose of attending conferences. Heated debates have also taken place over who merits tenure. Many universities are now openly favoring faculty who produce knowledge over those who teach knowledge, creating a division of labor and hierarchy among professors. Faced with increasing exploitation of their intellectual labor by capital, New York University's adjunct professors and instructors have responded by organizing themselves. One strategy they have employed has been to unite with the United Auto Workers. Contrast this scenario with the Pentagon's new "peacetime budget" of $399.1 billion—$379.9 billion for the Defense Department and $19.3 billion for the nuclear weapons functions of the Department of Energy—designed to keep the United States on a permanent war footing in its battle against "evildoers" throughout the world (Burns 2003; Hellman 2003).

And what about the unraveling and threadbare conditions of public schools today? Recent estimates put the amount of money sorely needed to fix the infrastructure of public schools in America at $100 billion. But ever since the publication of Kozol's classic book *Savage Inequalities* (1991), which famously exposed the unequal conditions in American public schools, there has yet to be any major improvements made to the infrastructure of public schools, in particular those in urban communities. In California, more than 47,000 uncertified teachers are teaching in its public schools, and within the next ten years there will be a demand for 300,000 new teachers. Maryland is also experiencing similar problems. Nearly 6 percent of its teaching force lack full certification. In Baltimore, that statistic is even far more grim: over one-third of the school district's teachers do not hold full teaching credentials. The probability that students will end up in classes with uncertified teachers is much higher for working-class and minority students. As a result of this growing trend, in 1998 a record 47 percent of all entering freshmen to the California State University system were required to take remedial English, and 54 percent enrolled in remedial math classes. In Chicago, it has been documented that public school classrooms are filled with as many as fifty-four students. At Winton Place Elementary in Ohio, teachers spend anywhere from $500 to $1,500 of their own money every academic year to purchase classroom supplies and material such as scissors and glue (Fattah 2002).

For some time now, we have been calling attention to the devastating impact of neoliberal social and economic policies on public schools and public education (McLaren and Farahmandpur, 1999, 2001a, 2001b, 2001c; McLaren and Jaramillo 2002). Self-proclaimed as the "education president," George W.

Bush signed into law the No Child Left Behind (NCLB) Act of 2001, lauded as the major education reform package of the millennium. If we examine this act in light of political history, however, NCLB represents a decades-old neoliberal relay race launched in the Reagan era with Bush currently bearing the flaming torch. Clearly, NCLB is the embodiment of contradictions and tensions within evolving neoliberal models of education. Whereas one of the basic premises of neoliberal market forces is "small government," educators and community members across the country are experiencing a relentless assault on their autonomy when it comes to participating in purported democratic decision-making processes. Federally engineered testing and accountability systems, instructional program mandates, and the forced militarization of our public high schools point toward highly regulated and controlled governing systems.

At the end of the year, every public school child in grades 3 to 8 will experience standardized testing that was developed with an estimated price tag of $2.7 billion to $7 billion (as cited in Metcalf 2002). Based on these test scores, schools with 40 percent or greater populations of poor students will face a litany of punitive measures if and when they do not demonstrate "adequate yearly progress"—a quantifiable year-to-year increment in the percentage of students reaching an arbitrarily established testing "proficient" benchmark. Touted as the way to hold schools and districts accountable for the perpetual "underachievement" (achievement measured solely by invalid and unreliable aptitude tests) of the poor and students of color, sanctions in the form of alternative governance and supplemental services have widened the doors to corporate and faith-based sponsorship of school programs with federal tax dollars. The most severe consequences will undoubtedly impact communities with the greatest concentration of poverty—children dealt with the most egregious schooling conditions while confronting health care and living conditions that run parallel to Third World levels of poverty. On the backs of the progressively stooped and strained poor, for-profit education entities will continue to witness exponential profit margins while children succumb to the dumbing down of instruction through technocratic exercises intended to alter test score percentages.

With respect to instructional program mandates, the Bush administration has seized the moment to establish a $1 billion grant funding "scientifically valid" reading programs. To solve the "scientifically valid" dilemma, an assembled panel of experts largely reminiscent of Bush's literacy copatriots in Texas will evaluate and approve each state's reading programs throughout the country. Up to this point, the Bush administration has supported the findings of a previously assembled National Reading Panel to define what is considered to be "scientifically valid," a euphemism for phonics-based reading programs

(Metcalf 2002). Regardless of where educators stand in the literacy debate, what cannot remain undisputed is the proliferation of corporate reading programs that support highly regimented, rote, and prescriptive reading instruction endorsed by the Bush administration as "scientifically valid." California—to cite one example—will follow suit by funding only those schools adopting Houghton Mifflin and McGraw-Hill reading programs (California Department of Education 2003).

Finally, one of the remaining staple items of the Bush administration's NCLB is the forced militarization of public high schools. Local jurisdictions with previously passed regulations against military recruitment on high school campuses face no alternative than to open their doors to a proliferation of recruitment efforts unless they would rather sacrifice funding to cover operational costs. With tight budgets and "supplemental services" on the chopping block for upcoming fiscal years, high school counselors originally hired to support college-going seniors either will change positions or pay a visit to the unemployment office. With weekly in-class recruitment presentations and no other seemingly viable options made available to our youth, the U.S. government may very well refuel its military ranks—a military that is necessary for ongoing imperialist operations around the globe.

The imposition of testing and accountability regimes that depend upon failing schools, the corporate and faith-based sponsorship of public education, the instructional mandates serving corporate interests rather than those of students, and the forced militarization of public high schools demonstrate that education no longer exists as we once knew it. No Child Left Behind is correct in at least one regard: no child will be left behind the neoliberal autocracy of the U.S. government unless critical educators, students, and families halt the aggression. As William Tabb (2001) notes, "Destroying the quality of public-sector education is necessary for the full marketization of education," and this is exactly what we are experiencing through NCLB strongholds. We would add only that in addition to a full-fledged "marketization" of education, our most marginalized student populations will in the future have to endure increased militarization. After all, imperial capital needs its capitalist fedayeen: the U.S. military.

Antiterrorism as American Imperialism

In public discussions of educational reform today, it is almost impossible not to see such reforms in light of the Bush administration's permanent war against terrorism. William Bennett, former drug czar and secretary of education under Reagan and Bush *padre* as well as candidate for president in the 2000 Republican primaries, has become one of Bush's most outspoken public defenders and has assumed the mantle of "philosopher king" of the Republican Party. He is a founding member of the right-wing think tank Project for the New American Century and its so-called peace through strength policy along with the Neocons Gone Wild fraternity of Pearle, Wolfowitz, Bolton, and Cheney, who not only have the president's ear on matters of foreign policy but also have harmonized his will to power to their own political machinations. Chairman of the National Endowment for the Humanities and author of the bestseller *The Book of Virtues* (1993), Bennett recently published *Why We Fight: Moral Clarity and the War on Terrorism* (2002). Bennett's book rewrites bald imperialism as a democratic obligation to free the world from evildoers. Bennett's adolescent narcissism, along with his unwavering support for the U.S. war machine and its politics of preemptive or "preventive" strikes, is as politically ill conceived as it is ethically misguided. Bennett's toxic screed dressed up in the philosophical diapers of Plato echoes those of many conservative and libertarian media pundits, especially the testosterone posse of FOX News. We see little redeeming virtue in giving carpet bombing philosophical warrant and the killing of innocent civilians by U.S. soldiers moral respectability.

The doyen of Republican virtues and character education, Bennett has always been given over to partisan invective in the form of exercising his moral outrage against everything from "homosexual unions" to drugs and violence in America's schools. We find it tragically hypocritical that one of Bill Clinton's most unrelenting critics during the Monica Lewinsky scandal could support an act of "preventive" war that not only defied international law and, in fact, was perhaps the most unwanted war in world history but also was one of the most "transparent" wars of all time (except in the United States) in that it had the word "oil" written all over it. We also find such hypocrisy to be standard fare with the nation's leading spokesperson on virtue, especially in light of recent revelations that he has lost more than $8 million over the past decade in gambling casinos where he has operated as a high roller with limos at his disposal and tens of thousands of dollars in complimentary hotel rooms (Alter and Green 2003; Helmore 2003; Kinsley 2003). His organization, Empower America, speaks out vehemently against "pathological gamblers" at the same time as Bennett collects $50,000 a speech in order to cover his gambling habit (Green 2003). We cannot think of a more appropriate example of Republican virtue.

All in all, we consider Bennett's line of reasoning to be complete baloney. One does not need to be awakened to the scary truth that as events in Iraq have unfolded since September 11, the objectives of the imperialists in Washington relate only secondarily and diminishingly to the events of the September 11 attacks. As the ruling class of the United States spews forth a new torrent of reactionary violence, repression, terror, and death, what is emerging is not "security" or "world peace" but new imperialist centers of rivalry as evidenced by the two-day summit between Russia, France, and Germany in Russia on April 11–12, 2003. In declaring an open-ended war with the sovereign right to wage war on anybody, for any reason, at any time, by any means—including nuclear weapons—the objective of the U.S. warlords is to bludgeon into place the hegemony of the United States throughout the world. As this selective process of "reconstruction" and "nation building" takes place abroad, the favorite excuse trotted out by the bourgeoisie is that the situation here in the "homeland" is different following the tragic events of September 11. Yet this claim is not borne out by the facts. September 11 has not stopped police brutality by racist cops, the building of more jails than schools, attacks on affirmative action, Bible Belt bigotry against gays, or the flawed and barbaric system of capital punishment. In fact, domestic oppression has increased with the passage of the Patriot Act (which disproportionately affects immigrants and people of color) and the slashing of essential services, even as Bush and Co. rush to spend billions of dollars on a racist war machine. What matters here is that the United States, as the richest nation on earth, has the capacity to fund a world-class education and health system to which everybody has access, but we simply do not have a government prepared to make this a social priority.

So we should not pretend in the aftermath of September 11 that "everything has changed" when the state is continuing to obstruct the dispensing of social and economic "justice" at home even as it wages multiple and enduring wars of "justice" and "liberation" abroad. In other words, what this whole juggernaut of privatization and imperialist war reveals is not only a whole set of howling contradictions but also the actual nature of the entire imperialist system. The plain fact is that the state, which stands "*above* society," is committed to the rule of the capitalist class and that imperialist wars are fought to advance only the interests of the ruling class (Lenin 1965, 9). Thus, while we need to develop local or national struggles in their own right and according to their own dynamic, we should also be prepared to connect them to the new context in which they are dialectically unfolding.

Unfortunately, creating the pedagogical conditions for students to critically examine and intervene in the world around them will not be an easy task given the recent wave of attacks on people who dare to question U.S. capitalism and foreign policy (Giroux 2002). Right now, a cabal of right-wingers, media pundits, and government officials are witch-hunting teachers in both K–12 and higher education who express opinions critical of U.S. policy. We repudiate this kind of craven, primitive, flag-saluting "patriotism," which is

aimed at getting the broad masses of people to submit to policies that are reducing their civil liberties, including the right to free speech. Yet even school
administrators are punishing "defiant" students and working in cahoots with
the cops to discipline high school students who participate in antiwar protests.
For example, after walking out of class in solidarity with the Books Not
Bombs protests that took place across the country on March 5, 2003, high
school students in California not only had some of their "privileges" revoked
by the principal at Arroyo High School (including the right to walk in the
graduation ceremony) but also were met by police officers at rally sites who
ticketed students (for example, Fillmore High School), rounded them up, and
brought them back to school in a school bus (Pierre 2003; Poblete 2003; Students United Against War 2003). Courageously, students at Foothill Tech, a
high school in the city of Ventura, organized a teach-in to protest the march
toward war in Iraq and the domestic consequences of the war on terrorism as
well as the hostility of the school's administration, which threatened anyone
who walked out with severe disciplinary action (Poblete 2003). Still, such bla-
tant examples of intolerance and repression are not at odds with bourgeois
"democracy." In fact, it expresses in perfect clarity the historical role and
meaning of the capitalist state (including its organs of mass indoctrination
such as schools), which is to keep class antagonisms in check by quashing political dissent (Lenin 1965).

Political dissent is often a virtue championed in university and public
school classrooms but not always practiced. After September 11, both students
and professors have to think twice before voicing opinions about the current
Washington regime. Often in such circumstances, teachers who affirm principles of justice or encourage students to actively engage "controversial" policies
as well as the historical, ideological, and political contexts in which they are
taking place are putting themselves at risk (Giroux 2002). To take just one personal example, Larry Elder, a popular libertarian right-wing talk show host on
KABC Radio in Los Angeles (who reflects many of the sentiments expressed
by Bennett), has targeted an article written by Farahmandpur and McLaren
(2001) titled "Critical Literacy for Global Citizenship" in the *Center X Forum*,
a newsletter published by the Graduate School of Education and Information
Studies, University of California, Los Angeles. Elder clearly is unsympathetic
to criticisms of economic globalization, especially when they are exercised by
two Marxist educators critical of the Bush regime. In response to the critique
of the growing social, political, and economic inequality under capitalism
provided by Farahmandpur and McLaren, Elder cites a letter that he received
from a disgruntled sixteen-year-old student who complains that universities
and colleges across the United States have now been overtaken by leftist professors and teachers:

My problem and endless rage enters when comments are made by my extreme-liberal teachers, and my response is literally cut off. These teachers constantly avoid allowing me to contradict their senseless preaching. I know I have to learn to accept this, because liberal bias in high school is only a fraction of the liberal in college. However, it is becoming extremely tougher to deal with, when more and more of my peers are thinking that socialism and communism are the "fairest" answer. This ignorance is mind-boggling, because these kids, teachers, etc. have never lived under socialism and communism. I have constantly offered to buy them a one way ticket to Cuba, but shockingly they refuse. . . . These people are hypocrites, and their answer to my arguments are never backed-up and are completely childish. The shadow of logic, reason and common sense is frightening to these teachers. Look no further, this is the problem with public school system. (Alec Mouhibian, cited in Elder 2002, 97–98)

We are not sure when Elder last visited UCLA (or any other university or college for that matter), but the claim that leftist professors and teachers have taken over universities is clearly misguided. In fact, to proclaim this charge publicly has been a longstanding right-wing strategy from the days of Joe McCarthy in order to create a climate of fear surrounding the continuing threat of communist subversion on U.S. soil. If Elder's claim is in fact true, then we should ask why corporations and foundations continue to fund universities that are allegedly stacked with leftist professors. On the contrary, corporations and private foundations have enjoyed a longstanding relationship with public universities and colleges (Parenti 1993).

Despite the right-wing libertarian propaganda vomited up by Larry Elder and others of his ilk that depict public universities and colleges as a hotbed of leftists and communists, a recent article by David Gibbs (2001) in the *Los Angeles Times* raises a number of disquieting questions regarding the role and influence of the Central Intelligence Agency (CIA) in the academy. Gibbs informs us that CIA–university partnerships are not new. It has been known for some time now that Ivy League universities such as Yale have collaborated with the CIA in the past. Since the late 1940s and the early 1950s, universities have served as recruitment centers for future CIA operatives as well as drop-off points for the distribution and circulation of CIA propaganda. In 1991, Congress passed the National Security Education Act, which offers a trust fund worth $150 million whose oversight authority is the Defense Intelligence College. The fund offers undergraduate scholarships and graduate fellowships to promising U.S. citizens who are encouraged to pursue scholarly activities and research both in the United States and abroad. The program also offers grants to participating universities seeking to develop and enhance their foreign language and area studies programs (MacMichael 2002). Funded by the CIA, universities and colleges that show interest can take advantage of the CIA officer-in-residence program. Under this program, CIA officers are hired as faculty members in history, political science, and economics departments where they teach courses and provide seminars on various pressing topics. The purpose of this program is for career CIA officers-turned-academics to share the experience, knowledge, and skills that they have gained in the course of their history in the CIA with college students (MacMichael 2002).

Citing a 1996 article in the academic journal *Lingua Franca*, Gibbs (2001) notes that prominent social scientists such as Columbia's Robert Jarvis, former president-elect of the American Political Science Association, and Harvard professor Joseph S. Nye have openly admitted to working for the CIA. If this is true, then there is good reason to believe that the pursuit of scholarly research by social scientists in universities is often politically motivated in the direction of American imperialism. As Gibbs (2001) remarks,

> The CIA is not an ordinary government agency; it is an espionage agency and the practices of espionage—which include secrecy, propaganda and deception—are diametrically opposed to those of scholarship. Scholarship is supposed to favor objective analysis and open discussion. The close relationship between intelligence agencies and scholars thus poses a conflict of interest. After all, the CIA has been a key part to many of the international conflicts that academics must study. If political scientists are working for the CIA, how can they function as objective and disinterested scholars? (M2)

Gibbs's criticism of the CIA as an impediment to the generation of objective knowledge is woefully naive since the very call for objective knowledge carries an ideological weight of its own. The issue for critical educators is not that knowledge should be objective and depoliticized but that the ideological characteristics of all knowledge production need to be analyzed and openly debated.

What we find disturbing as critical educators is the inability of critics of the Bush administration to get their dissenting voices into organs of the popular media. And it is certainly not the result of a lack of trying. On the one hand, in distinguished publications on the left, such as *Monthly Review*, we can find documentation by the Research Unit for Political Economy (2003), which, for instance, reveals that the United States "was the sole country to vote against the 1986 Security Council statement condemning Iraq's use of mustard gas on Iranian troops—an atrocity in which it now emerges the United States was directly implicated" (30); that "the U.S. administration provided 'crop-spraying' helicopters (to be used for chemical attacks in 1988), let Dow Chemicals ship its chemicals for use on humans, seconded its air force officers to work with their Iraq counterparts (from 1986), and approved technological exports to Iraq's missile procurement agency to extend the missiles' range (1988)" (30); "that during the Iran-Iraq war *the United*

States used the latter to make biological weapons" (30); that Saddam Hussein's attacks on the Kurds in 1988 had the full support of the United States; and that the destruction of Iraq's civilian infrastructure in 1991 and the continuing UN sanctions over eleven years amounts, in the opinion of three UN humanitarian coordinators in Iraq from 1997 to 2000, to deliberate "genocide" (43). On the other hand, the corporate media are clearly preventing these facts from being released to the public, and when teachers make them available to their students, they run the risk of being labeled traitors at worst and unpatriotic at best. Sheldon Wolin (2003) has aptly characterized U.S. government at this time as "inverted totalitarianism" (13). He notes that while conditions in the United States are decidedly different than in the former Nazi regime, many of the objectives are the same. Wolin warns,

> Thus the elements are in place: a weak legislative body, a legal system that is both compliant and repressive, a party system in which one party, whether in opposition or in the majority, is bent upon reconstituting the existing system so as to permanently favor a ruling class of the wealthy, the well-connected and the corporate, while leaving the poorer citizens with a sense of helplessness and political despair, and, at the same time, keeping the middle classes dangling between fear of unemployment and expectations of fantastic rewards once the new economy recovers. That scheme is abetted by a sycophantic and increasingly concentrated media; by the integration of universities with their corporate benefactors; by a propaganda machine institutionalized in well-funded think tanks and conservative foundations; by the increasingly closer cooperation between local police and national law enforcement agencies aimed at identifying terrorists, suspicious aliens and domestic dissidents. (14–15)

More than ever, we need to take seriously the reality of U.S. imperialism, both informal (as in free trade) and formal (as in the case of colonial annexations of territory), which, we argue after Lenin, is linked to the evolution of capitalist development in all its complexity (military/political/economic) and has now arrived at its monopoly stage (Foster 2003). As an inherent agent of capitalism, the so-called new imperialism most closely associated with the United States is connected to the increased competition for control over global territories (raw materials and resources) between imperialist rivals such as the United States, Britain, and France; the coming of age of "new mammoth" corporations that seek competitive advantage through their own home-based nation-states; and the development of an entire world system of colonization that creates uneven development and economic dependencies (Foster 2003; Lenin 1939). Thus, despite the ridiculous claims of "globalization" theorists such as Anthony Giddens (1999), the world capitalist system is not becoming homogeneous—far from it. Instead, what is taking place today, as Lenin (1939) put it, is "the financial strangulation of the overwhelming majority of the world by a handful of 'advanced' countries" (10–11).

Radical Teacher Education Reform

In a series of articles and books, British educationalist Dave Hill (1999, 2001, 2002b, in press) has analyzed neoliberal capitalism's challenge to teacher agency and autonomy. Hill does not pull punches and specifically warns against the current trend toward markets in education and the resulting role of schools as a "disciplinary force of the capitalist class through the corporate managerialization of teacher education" (in press, 3). He forcefully warns that the success of the globalization, businessification, and militarization of social life has scarcely been contested in advanced capitalist nations. This has resulted in a considerable restructuring of teacher education, leading to a detheorization of teacher education research, a "quietist and overwhelmingly conservative set of 'standards' for student teachers," a teacher training approach that emphasizes technical and managerial skills rather than examining "the 'whys and the why nots' and the contexts of curriculum, pedagogy, educational purposes and structures and the effects these have on reproducing capitalist economy, society and politics" (3).

Hill importantly defines a radical Left project within teacher education for retheorizing egalitarian education as a whole, followed by a set of principles and proposals for the teacher education curriculum. His overarching radical Left principles include but do not exhaust the following: vastly increasing equality of outcome, comprehensive provision as distinct from private or selective provision of schooling, democratic community control over education, and the use of local or regional constituencies and the national state to build an egalitarian, antidiscriminatory society rather than to reproduce an inegalitarian meritocratic focus on equal opportunities that often leads to increasingly unequal outcomes. His radical Left perspective is expressed through a lengthy series of proposals for teacher education programs that include the need for macro- and microtheory regarding teaching and learning that explicitly reveals the sociopolitical and economic contexts of schooling and education and that takes into account a theoretical grasp of the interrelationship among children, schooling, and society as well as alternative views and methods of classroom organization, schooling, and their economic and political relationship to the larger social totality; a rejection of labeling, underexpectation, stereotyping, and prejudice expressed by teachers and peers; a context for enabling the formation of critical, reflective teachers who are able to decode media distortion in Ministry of Education reports, bias, and propaganda on falling standards in schools and institutions of teacher education; the development of effective classroom-skilled teachers who understand the relationship between theory and practice; and the formation of cadres of teachers who possess critical reflection in addition to situational and technical reflection and who can answer the following questions: Whose interests are being served? Who wins? Who loses? Who has to deny identity in order to join the winners, if this is at all possible? and Who is likely to have to continue accepting a subordinate and exploited position in society (by virtue of their membership in oppressed groups)?

The characteristics of the curriculum developed by Hill are voluminous but worth listing in full. They include the development of reflective skills in pupil/student learning, teaching, and classroom management; a commitment to developing an ethical/moral dimension of critical reflection as well as making connections between economic and social justice; utilizing data on racism, sexism, social class inequality, homophobia, and discrimination on the basis of disability and special needs; the pursuit of educational practices beyond white, Anglo-Saxon, middle-class, and heterosexual educational norms and requiring teachers to explore the subjugated knowledges of women, minority groups, and indigenous groups; developing a holistic and social class-based approach to economic and social justice in the curriculum; requiring student teachers to explore the class-based nature of exploitation within the capitalist economic system and its educational, legal, and other apparatuses; ensuring that student teachers acquire skills in dealing with classroom incidences of racism, homophobia, sexism, and classism; creating open forums on social justice for students and faculty; enabling student teachers to develop the skills to critically examine the ideological nature of teachers' work; promoting a concurrent rather than consecutive development of critical reflection on the part of student teachers; and finally supporting a substantially predetermined rather than primarily negotiated curriculum—a move that is necessary for the acquisition of a broad span of critical theoretical insights. At the same time, Hill argues for the model of the teacher as a transformative intellectual who does not tell students what to think but who learns to think dialectically and who develops a critical consciousness aimed at social transformation.

Hill's suggestions speak to the role of teacher educators as social agents who pursue a "democratic, anti-authoritarian, socially responsible and socially and economically just society" (in press, 16). The cardinal ingredient in Hill's proposal—and the one that makes his work so radically different from his North American counterparts—is his insistence that teacher educators should be advocating education as part of a larger agenda of anticapitalist social transformation toward a socialist alternative (see also Cole 1998).

Desanitizing Critical Pedagogy

As schools become increasingly financed by corporations that function as service industries for transnational capitalism and as bourgeois educational professionalism continues to guide educational policy and practice, educators in the United States face a challenging educational reality. While liberal educators are calling for the need for capital controls, controls in foreign exchange, a return to the old forms of financial regulation that kept investment and commercial banking separate, tougher lending on stock speculation, rules for fair play, the stimulation of growth and wages, labor rights enforcement for nations borrowing from the United States, and the removal of financial aid from banking and capital until they concede to the centrality of the wage problem and insist on labor rights, very few of them are calling for the abolition of capital itself. It is this quiet acquiescence that distinguishes revolutionary critical pedagogy from progressive education. The former wishes to challenge capital as a social relation and replace it with a socialist alternative. The latter considers the capitalist marketplace as the only viable arena in which education can take place.

In the United States, critical pedagogy regrettably has limited itself to an essentially liberal progressive educational agenda that encourages teachers to create "communities of learners" in classrooms; to bridge the gap between student culture and the culture of the school; to engage in cross-cultural understandings; to integrate multicultural content and teaching across the curriculum; to develop techniques for reducing racial prejudice and conflict resolution strategies; to challenge Eurocentric teaching and learning as well as the "ideological formations" of European immigration history by which many white teachers judge African American, Latino/a, and Asian students; to challenge the meritocratic foundation of public policy that purportedly is politically neutral and racially color blind; to create teacher-generated narratives as a way of analyzing teaching from a "transformative" perspective; to improve academic achievement in culturally diverse schools; to affirm and utilize multiple perspectives and ways of teaching and learning; and to dereify the curriculum and to expose "metanarratives of exclusion." Lest we appear overly dismissive of these achievements, we enthusiastically wish to affirm that these attempts are welcomed as far as they go but that they do not go nearly far enough. In the face of such a contemporary intensification of global capitalist relations and permanent structural crisis, we need to develop a critical pedagogy capable of engaging all of social life and not simply life inside school classrooms. We need, in other words, to challenge capitalist social relations while acknowledging global capital's structurally determined inability to share power with the oppressed; its constitutive embeddedness in racist, sexist, and homophobic relations; its functional relationship to xenophobic nationalism; and its tendency toward empire. It means acknowledging the educational Left's dependency on the very object of its negation: capital. It means struggling to develop a lateral, polycentric concept of anticapitalist alliances-in-diversity in order to slow down capitalism's metabolic movement—with the eventual aim of shutting it down completely. It means developing and advancing an educational philosophy that is designed to resist the "capitalization" of subjectivity, a pedagogy that we have called (after the British Marxist educator Paula Allman [2001]) revolutionary critical pedagogy.

The key to resistance, in our view, is to develop a critical pedagogy that will not only enable the multiracial, gendered working class to discover how the use value of their labor power is being exploited by capital but also how working-class initiative, creativity, and power can destroy this type of determination and force a recomposition of class relations by directly confronting capital in all of its hydra-headed dimensions. Efforts can be made to break down capital's control of the creation of new labor power and to resist the endless subordination of life to work in the social factory of everyday life (Cleaver 2000; see also Rikowski 2001).

Revolutionary Critical Pedagogy

Admitting that there exists no official vulgate of critical pedagogy and that there are as many instantiations of critical pedagogy as there are theorists and practitioners, we nevertheless hold to the claim that its most political characteristics have been defanged and sterilized; crucial elements have been expurgated such that it redounds most heavily to the advantage of the liberal capitalist state and its bourgeois cadre of educational reformers. What precisely has been coarsened has been those elements dealing with critical pedagogy's critique of political economy, those aspects of it that challenge the social relations of production and class society (McLaren 2000, 2003; McLaren and Farahmandpur 2000, 2001a, 2002). While there has been a concerted attempt to redress material inequality, it needs to be acknowledged that, as admirable as this has been, such a move has always been undertaken within the precinct of capitalism itself. That is, even within the work of many leading exponents of critical pedagogy, there is rarely a challenge to the capitalist state, a push, if you will, to transform it into a socialist one. The viruliferous attacks on leftist academics as "enemies of civilization" or as "critical demagogues" (see Rochester 2003) by quislings and admirers of the current Bush administration clearly have not helped strengthen the political resolve of critical educators in potentially taking an anticapitalist position.

We need to think about the extent of this dilemma: If the most anticapitalist strands of critical pedagogy offer the strongest challenge to the existing status quo offered by U.S. progressive educationalists, then why does critical pedagogy not constitute a more vibrant and robust presence in schools of education, most particularly in teacher education programs? If leading education journals are reluctant to publish articles by those exponents of critical pedagogy who directly challenge the existence of capitalist social relations, then what does this tell us about the hegemony of the educational establishment as well as the state of the educational Left? When teacher education programs with decidedly social justice agendas do deal with the critical educational tradition, even when they studiously prepare their teachers within the context of antiracist and antisexist frameworks, they almost invariably exclude unvarnished critiques of the capitalist state by Marxist educational scholars. While we remain depressingly exercised by this dilemma, we cannot within the space of this chapter sufficiently explore more than a few of its ramifications.

Drawing on our own experiences as products of teacher educational institutions as well as practitioner/scholars within them, we wish to begin by identifying the central dilemma that we have perceived with respect to critical pedagogy: its bowdlerization, vulgarization, and domestication. Frankly, should we find this dilemma all that surprising in professional schools of education within the academy given that so many of them are, after all, decidedly centrist institutions? Many (but of course not all) educators who work in the field of teacher education are sometimes given over to blaming teachers for the so-called decline in student achievement, and within such institutions control over teachers exists in the form of teacher competency tests, certification, and exams. Too often excluded from consideration is the notion that education can be a vehicle for social transformation, as a way of addressing larger social contradictions and antagonisms. There is a certain sense, then, in which current domesticated incarnations of critical pedagogy validate education as something that must be sensitive to the needs of the poor and exploited classes in such a way that actually precludes the possibility that those needs can be met. Resolving the challenges facing capitalist democracy can only be made more difficult when you are not even permitted to restate them in terms of class struggle. We are not saying that critical educators are silkily deft at obfuscation or deception. In most instances, critical educators are themselves aware of the contractions that undercut their objectives but feel powerless to operate in ways that can transcend them. We are simply arguing that, despite the best intentions of critical educators, critical pedagogy can indeed serve to rehabilitate the very class hierarchies that it was originally set up to challenge if not roundly to depose. Indeed, much of critical pedagogy has already been subsumed into procapitalist common sense, co-opted through a professional patronage to the state. In fact, it may serve unwittingly to defend the bourgeois state by legitimating a commitment to diversity without sufficiently affirming diversity through the necessary development of explicitly antiracist, antisexist, and anti-imperialist curriculum. Deflecting questions about how class and racial formations are linked to current social relations of production and the interpellating strategies of the ideological state apparatus, critical pedagogy, in its currently watered-down and depotentiated forms, actually serves to delimit the debate over liberal capitalist democracy rather than expand it (McLaren and Farahmandpur 2000). This is not a call for a formulaic Marxism that is box trained and fed on a diet of dogma and doxa and deformations of Marx's dialectical theory but an approach that centers educational reform within the reigning political antagonism of our age: the contradiction between labor and capital.

Critical pedagogy programs, often built around Dewey's monistic idealism, where social change is predicated on moral reconstruction, ignore in the main the historical materialist conditions that lead to social transformation through class struggle (McLaren and Farahmandpur 2002). Such conditions begin with the question of the changing needs of civil society and the development of the productive forces and relations of exchange. While teachers and students may not consider the mode of production of society—commandeered by the capitalist elite—to be the primary engine driving the development of human consciousness as fully as do many Marxists, at least this position should be presented for consideration. Teachers need to ask, What is the relationship between the ruling "material" force of society and the ruling "intellectual" or "ideological" force? To what extent are the dominant ideas about and ideals associated with capitalism merely or mainly the ideal expressions of the dominant material relationships within late capitalist society? To what extent do teacher education programs regulate both the production and the distribution of the prevailing ideas about capitalist society? (see Farahmandpur 2002; McLaren 2000).

Critical pedagogy is, of course, all about revolutionary ideas. Just as we need to explore the way in which dominant ideas about capitalism are linked to their conditions of production within the context of the dominant social class, we need to connect the revolutionary ideas of critical pedagogy to the existence of a revolutionary class of educators. These educators are preoccupied with questions such as, What are the contradictions between prevailing notions of capitalist democracy and the manner in which democracy is lived in the streets by social agents with competing class interests and who exist within vastly different social conditions? We have found that in our own classrooms, teachers from working-class backgrounds (often students of color) are the most favorably disposed to an undiluted critical pedagogy.

Our work in critical pedagogy constitutes in one sense the performative register for class struggle. While it sets as its goal the decolonization of subjectivity, it also emphasizes the development of critical social agency while at the same time targeting the material basis of capitalist social relations. Critical educators seek to realize in their classrooms important social values and to believe in their possibilities—consequently, we argue that they need to go outside the protected precincts of their classrooms and analyze and explore the workings of capital there. Critical revolutionary pedagogy sets as its goal the reclamation of public life under the relentless corporatization, privatization, and businessification of the lifeworld (which includes the corporate–academic complex). It seeks to make the division of labor coincident with the free vocation of each individual and the association of free producers. At first blush this may seem a paradisiacal notion in that it posits a radically eschatological and incomparably "other" endpoint for society as we know it. Yet this is not a blueprint but a contingent utopian vision that offers direction not only in unpicking the apparatus of bourgeois illusion but also in diversifying the theoretical itinerary of the critical educator so that new questions can be generated along with new perspectives in which to raise them. Here the emphasis is not only on denouncing the manifest injustices of neoliberal capitalism and serving as a counterforce to neoliberal ideological hegemony but also on establishing the conditions for new social arrangements that transcend the false opposition between the market and the state.

In contrast to postmodern education, revolutionary critical pedagogy emphasizes the material dimensions of its own constitutive possibility and recognizes knowledge as implicated within the social relations of production (that is, the relations between labor and capital). We are using the term "materialism" here not in its postmodernist sense as a resistance to conceptuality, a refusal of the closure of meaning, or whatever "excess" cannot be subsumed within the symbol or cannot be absorbed by tropes but rather in the context of material social relations, a structure of class conflict, and an effect of the social division of labor (Ebert 2002). Historical changes in the forces of production have reached the point where the fundamental needs of people can be met—but the existing social relations of production prevent this because the logic of access to "need" is "profit" based on the value of people's labor for capital. Consequently, critical revolutionary pedagogy argues that without a class analysis, critical pedagogy is impeded from effecting praxiological changes (changes in social relations).

We need to learn not only how to educate but also how to be educated in terms of ripening class antagonisms. Teachers disqualify themselves from historical struggle when they fail to locate their own formation as educators within the degenerative process of contemporary capitalist society and the enduring and intractable class-driven social arrangements, to wit, within the agonistic arena of class struggle.

As the science of the inherent contradictions of capitalism, Marxism enables capitalism to be uncovered in all its protean, complex materiality. It is in a singular position to uncover the ontological dimension of capitalism by beginning with the real, messy world of everyday social life. Marxism helps critique suprahistorical theory that has severed its connections to the material work of social struggle. Marxism is grounded in the contextual specificity of the global universe of capital in which we find ourselves today, where we are witnessing the internationalization of antagonism between exploiters and producers; where globalization is presided over by a ruling class of individuals with proprietary rights over the means of production; where power, wealth, and income are not allocated fairly; where the capitalist class increasingly extracts unpaid labor time from the direct producers, the workers, and peasants; and where neoliberalism is disarticulating the social base of the Left, depotentiating it by dividing the classes against each other.

John Holloway (2002) has made some interesting points with respect to Marxism. First, it is not a theory of society, but a theory against society; Marxism is not in the business of providing a better social science but is concerned mainly with a critique of the bourgeois social sciences (that is, a critique of political economy) and with locating the fault lines or weak points of the rule of capital. He notes—rightly in our view—that Marxism is a theory not of capitalist oppression but of the contradictions of that oppression, so that Marxism is able to articulate the contradictory positions in which individuals and groups are engaged. It is also able to locate the contradictions within the oppressive social relations that are created by capitalist representatives and their organizations. Marxism begins with the premise that everyday social life within capitalist society is contradiction ridden, and Marxism highlights these contradictions and explores their origins and effects in order to free us from the oppressions of everyday social relations. In doing so it provides us with a philosophy of praxis and a deep resolve in our participation in anticapitalist struggles. Holloway's Marxist trajectory asserts that any social form of life, social relation, or institution is simultaneously both in and against forms of capitalist power. It explores the various social formations that make up the unity of capitalist society, with particular attention given to those social forms suppressed in such a society. In this sense, labor has the power of being independent of capital, but only within noncapitalist societies. Marxists ask, what are the origins and effects of living within the contradictions of capitalist society, and what are their implications for struggling against capital? Marxism provides an understanding of the concrete, empirical conditions of class struggle by elucidating capitalist social relations within which class struggle can obtain and unfold. The contradictions within capitalism provide a space for critique and transformation of the social relations that create the contradictions.

In these current times of deep divisions between the classes, when the acerbity and virulence of the antagonisms between them has grown more intense, especially in recent years, we cannot afford to demote class struggle to the category of "socioeconomic status," which drains the concept of class struggle of its history within capitalist society and turns it into a synonym for a "natural state" in a necessarily imperfect society underlain by principles of meritocracy. True, calling for the abolition of capitalism in the United States is not realistic in the short term given the current outlook and psychology of the working class. Only deluded sectarians could possibly imagine that the road ahead is straight and narrow. But at the very least, such calls can expose the injustices of capitalism and help galvanize the fresh forces of young people, the underemployed, and the growing ranks of the unemployed who are increasingly being cast into the pit of pauperism.

Reform or Transformation? Beyond the Either–Or Impasse

We want to make it clear that educational reforms are important, but we believe that such reforms should be allied to a constant advancement of socialist democracy. The idea of reform and revolutionary transformation has often been erroneously contraposed in critical pedagogy. We do not crudely juxtapose these terms as much as we "mediate" them—pushing reform further and further to the edges of bourgeois social and economic relations. We do not consider reform efforts incompatible with the larger anticapitalist struggle. We believe that reform and transformation have to be approached dialectically, and here critical pedagogy can become an artifact of mediation: working toward reform while at the same time exercising a praxis that has as its larger goal the advancement of socialism and the creation of a society free of class divisions. While each development within critical pedagogy will bear the stamp of its own particularity, we believe that it can formulate principles of solidarity with new networks and organs of popular participation, including social movements that advocate antiracist, antisexist, and antihomophobic practices while at the same time deepening its anticapitalist agenda.

Of course, the problem goes well beyond the crony capitalism of corporate insiders and the chief executive officers of Enron or WorldCom. Like the ACEs (armored combat earthmovers) that the U.S. army employed in the last Gulf War to sever the arms, legs, and heads of Iraqi soldiers protruding from the sand after being buried alive by bulldozers attached to tanks, capitalism today tries to sanitize its crimes so that the body count seems lower and less dramatic to American citizens, many of whom get their political education from the likes of CNN, FOX News, or their local newspapers. The victims of capitalism are rendered faceless and soulless by transforming them into unemployment statistics or by demonizing the poor in media reports of urban violence and crime. Our prosaic odyssey through the charnel house of global capitalism is not the result of mistakes made by the higher echelon of the corporate world or by desperate measures taken by the powerless and poor but is a priori defined by the antagonism between capital and labor. Our position, which we have already rehearsed in previous chapters, is that capital grounds all social mediation as a form of value and that the substance of labor itself must be interrogated because doing so brings us closer to understanding the nature of capital's social universe out of which our subjectivities and our daily social practices and *Lebenswelt* are created. Because the logic of capitalist work has invaded all forms of human sociability, society can be considered a totality of different types of labor.

We stress that it is urgently necessary for educators to examine the particular forms that labor takes within capitalism. In other words, value needs to be approached as a social relation, not as some kind of accounting device to measure rates of exploitation or domination. As a result, educators should not take value as simply a "given" category but should render it an *object of critique* and examine it as an abstract social structure. We need to remember here that the production of value is not the same as the production of wealth. The production of value is historically specific and emerges whenever labor assumes its dual character.

This is most clearly explicated in Marx's discussion of the contradictory nature of the commodity form and the expansive capacity of the commodity known as labor power. In this sense, labor power becomes the supreme commodity, the source of all value (see also Rikowski 2002). Forgive us for being so repetitive on this issue. For Marx, the commodity is highly unstable and nonidentical. Its concrete particularity (use value) is subsumed by its existence as value in motion or by what we have come to know as "capital" (value is always in motion because of the increase in capital's productivity that is required to maintain expansion). Abstract universal labor linked to a certain organization of society, under capitalism, is the type of labor that creates value. The dual aspect of labor within the commodity (use value and exchange value) enables one single commodity—money—to act as the value measure of the commodity. Money becomes the representative of labor in its abstract form. Thus, the commodity must be considered not a thing but a social relationship.

Capitalist production in this sense involves the extraction from living labor of all the unpaid hours of labor that amounts to surplus value or profit. If this is the case—and we have tried in this book to make an argument that we must recognize that capitalism is not something that can be fixed or humanized because its very "value form" is premised on the exploitation of human labor—we are, in a way, tied to the mast like Ulysses as the sirens of consumption beckon us to a fool's paradise. Yet even in progressive circles, scholars on the parochial Anglo-American Left have dismissed Marxist educators calling for a socialist democracy as extremists or juvenile leftists.

Consequently, critical revolutionary educators need to pose to their progressive liberal counterparts questions that include the following: Can liberal reformers—even World Bank dissenters such as Jeff Sachs, George Soros, and former senior vice president and chief economist of the World Bank and Nobel Prize recipient Joseph Stiglitz (2002)—rebuild and redirect the capitalist financial system in the interests of the poor and powerless? Can they prevent the rationality of financial capital—which is more interested in short-term profits than investing in fixed capital and long-term technological progress—from prevailing over what is rational from the standpoint of society as a whole? Can they prevent the suffering of workers due to the dismantling of protectionist trade barriers? Can they stop privatization from resulting in oligopolies and monopolies? Can they adequately safeguard against the human tragedies that follow economic downsizing? Can they prevent the chaos that results from massive capital inflows and outflows? Can they stop the International Monetary Fund (IMF) from bailing out international investors and granting elites the opportunity to protect their financial assets by massive capital flight while placing the burden of repaying loans, in the words of Tony Smith (2002), "on the very group that benefited least from them, working men and women"? Do they have the power to prevent the gangster capitalists of Russia, for instance, from buying up most of the privatized assets and natural resources of the country? Can they stop the multilateral agencies from advancing the particular interests of the United States? Can they prevent new nation state-driven racisms that follow in the wake of the new U.S. phallomilitary warrior nationalism currently providing ideological ballast for its practices of primitive accumulation via cluster bombing Iraq? Can they transcend the creation of plutocratic political subjectivities from above in order to combat the uneven development of epidemics such as AIDS and SARS in the equal opportunity inevitability of death? Can they reverse the damage to the poor as a result of financial market liberalization accompanied by high interest rates? Can they reverse the systematic tendencies to crises of overcapacity or overaccumulation or the structural mechanisms generating uneven development? Can they prevent speculative bubbles from expanding and bursting? Can the balance of power in capital–wage labor relations shift in favor of labor? Can the fundamental dynamic of capitalist property relations be challenged?

Questions such as these cut to the roots of the capitalist system. From the perspective of our analysis, honest answers to these questions will lead to a resounding "no." Liberal capitalist reformers in the main fail to comprehend "that money is the alien form of appearance of abstract labor," and they refuse to challenge the money fetish as the master trope of capitalist social relations (Smith 2002).

Of course, liberal reform efforts to make global capitalism more "humane" are welcomed—such as debt relief and a more balanced trade agenda, adequate laws enforcing competition, the creation of adequate safety nets and job creation programs, state expenditures to stimulate the economy, appropriate regulatory structures for trade liberalization, making loans available to countries to buy insurance against fluctuations in the international capital markets, cutting back on the bailout packages by the IMF, government oversight committees to ensure that monopoly powers are not abused, and restrictions on speculative real estate lending—but it still remains the case that in the last instance they cannot prevent financial disaster from being visited on developing countries or the poor in general because these problems are inherent in the system of property and productive relations that constitute the very blood and gristle of the capitalist system (Smith 2002).

The key point here is that liberal capitalist democracy sustains the alibi that the corrupt behavior of corporate bosses is an aberration and not the "spectral double" of law-abiding business leaders; it sustains the myth that the "real" American corporate leader is a churchgoing philanthropist who wants to contribute to making the United States a better place for working men and women. Liberal democracy occludes the fact that violence (of corporate leaders, police, and criminals) is a symptom of liberal democracy's failure to respond to the suffering of others (Žižek 2002).

If we see liberal democracy as a totality, then we can recognize it as a dialectical unity of itself and its other. The notion that we live in a meritocracy is the form of appearance of its very opposite: the absence of equality in a society divided by race and class. Liberal democracy, as a master signifier of "America," constitutes an imaginary supplement or, in Lacanian terms, a "big Other" that acts on behalf of all citizens, an excess that serves ideologically to justify all acts in its name on the basis that it is ultimately for the common good of humanity. This "supplement" enables U.S. citizens to endure America's unbearable contradictions, such as its lack of medical insurance for the poor; its growing homeless population; its corporate scandals; its institutionalized forms of racism; its torture training center at the School of the Americas at Fort Benning, Georgia; its past support of a long list of fascist dictatorships in Guatemala, El Salvador, Iran, Indonesia, and Chile; its past funding and training of the Contra terrorists; its invasions of Panama and Grenada; and its recent role in the coup attempt in Venezuela, its successful coup in Haiti, not to mention its massive financial and military aid to the ruthless Colombian military regime. To call up these horrors has attracted the condemnation of conservative "patriots" who feel that this is tantamount to anti-Americanism. Far from justifying the terrorist attacks against the United States on September 11, 2001, it is meant to signal how we should be in solidarity with all victims of terror. As Slavoj Žižek (2002) writes,

We do not yet know all the consequences this event will have for the economy, ideology, politics, warfare, but one thing is certain: The USA—which, hitherto, perceived itself as an island exempt from this kind of violence, witnessing this kind of thing only from the safe distance of the TV screen—is now directly involved. So the alternative is: will the Americans decide to fortify their sphere further, or will they risk stepping out of it? Either America will persist in—even strengthen—the deeply *immoral* attitude of "Why should this happen to us? Things like this just don't happen *here!*," leading to more aggressivity towards the threatening Outside—in short: to a paranoid acting-out. Or America will finally risk stepping through the fantasmatic screen separating it from the Outside World, accepting its arrival in the Real world, making the long overdue move from "A thing like this shouldn't happen *here!*" to "A thing like this shouldn't happen *anywhere!*" That is the true lesson of the attacks: the only way to ensure that it will not happen *here* again is to prevent it happening *anywhere else.* In short, America should learn humbly to accept its own vulnerability as part of this world, enacting the punishment of those responsible as a sad duty, not as an exhilarating retaliation. (243–44)

If we refuse to endorse the "blatantly ideological position of American innocence under attack by Third World Evil" (Žižek 2002, 244), we must be careful that we do not fall into the trap of blaming the victim. To do this, we can follow Žižek's advice and adopt the category of totality and refuse to support both Arab terrorism and U.S. innocence simultaneously, which draws us up against the limit of moral reasoning: "From the moral standpoint, the victims are innocent, the act was an abominable crime; however, this very innocence is not innocent—to adopt such an 'innocent' position in today's global capitalist universe is in itself a false abstraction" (244).

Critical Pedagogy and Antiwar Efforts

The following characterization of the United States by John Bellamy Foster may be unsettling to some, but far-fetched it certainly is not to anyone acquainted with U.S. Cold War history over the past half century: "By any objective standard, the United States is the most destructive nation on earth. It has killed and terrorized more populations around the globe than any other nation since the Second World War" (8). It is precisely this question that critical educators need to engage, as morally repellent as it may be to some. As U.S. tanks roll over the dead and dying in Baghdad and other Iraqi cities, we assert that one of the principle contradictions today is between the criminal ruling class of U.S. imperialism along with its international coalition of big (Britain) and little imperialists (Australia) on the one side and the exploited and oppressed peoples and nations around the world on the other. Regardless of the recent so-called shock-and-awe "victory" of Bush and his quislings in Iraq, we argue that the working out of this contradiction constitutes one of the major forms of motion that will determine human history and geography in the decades and perhaps centuries ahead.

Admittedly, the sobering truth is that following the mass slaughter in Iraq, a cloud of pessimism will no doubt engulf the Arab world (do not forget that the Gaza Strip is already littered with bodies and ruins) as well as hope-deprived workers in oppressed nations around the world. That is the bad news. The good news is that we are already beginning to see the moral and political limits of the "old-fashioned" use of imperialist power by the United States in its bloody territorial struggles. Even before the invasion of Iraq, a massive antiwar movement developed internationally both in the neocolonies as well as in the home citadels of imperialism such as the United States and Britain. While the outcome of the antiwar movement is much too difficult to determine in advance, it is clear that in distributing an Old Testament form of moral retribution and imperialist aggression in defiance of international law, Bush has shocked and enraged a broad array of social forces, including a whole new generation of youth who are now bristling with militancy and taking the first steps to becoming politically active. Although some of the more politically conscious and active youth already had a profound loathing of U.S. imperialism and its cruelties (such as the antisweatshop movement), many more young people, including students, are now for the first time looking not only for an explanation of what has taken place but also for a program to fight for and a strategy to win (Martin 2002). They are asking, "What can we do to stop the United States?"

This is a question of special importance to those of us living in the "homeland" of U.S. imperialism, especially given its long history of violent expansionism, gunboat diplomacy, and racist oppression.

Our starting point is that socialism is not a discredited dream. It is a current that runs through periods such as the menacing present and is animated by and in struggle against all forms of oppression and exploitation (Anderson 1995). While the antiwar movement will undoubtedly have to overcome certain internal problems to grow much larger and to curb future wars in Syria, Iran, or Venezuela, what we are seeing today is the emergence of a completely new quality of social consciousness that could provide the concrete basis for an internationalist political movement (Bloom 2003). What matters here is that against the backdrop of U.S. imperialism, the only way students are ever going to win "peace" or the right to a decent education or job is through the linking of their struggles with all the victims of the vicious ruling class, including workers, whose blood, sweat, and toil is the living fuel that makes the economy run (Bloom 2003; Rikowski 2002).

In creating the conditions for social change, then, the best pedagogy recognizes the limits of traditional "pragmatist" and reformist pedagogical practice by prioritizing the need to question the deeper problems, particularly the violent contradictions (such as the gap between racism and the American Dream) under which students are forced to live. This means confronting the anti-intellectual thuggery that pervades teacher education programs, particularly the kind that "rejects 'theory' (the knowledge of totality)" (Zavarzadeh and Morton 1994, 3). Acknowledging that capitalist education acts as a drag on the development of "critical" or "class" consciousness by presenting a lifeless world empty of contradictions, we argue for a theory of the "big picture," which enables people to translate their daily free-floating frustrations with the "system" into a set of other ideas, beliefs, and feelings that provide the basis not only for coherence and explanation but also for action (Zavarzadeh and Morton 1994, 3).

The challenge over the past several decades has been to humanize the classroom environment and to create pedagogical spaces for linking education to the praxiological dimensions of social justice initiatives, and to that end we have been enduring indebted to critical pedagogy. Approaching social transformation through the optic of revolutionary critical pedagogy ratchets up the struggle ahead. Revolutionary critical pedagogy dilates the aperture that critical pedagogy has struggled to provide teachers and students over the past several decades by further opening up the pedagogical encounter to its embeddedness in globalized social relations of exploitation and also to the revolutionary potential of a transnational, gender-balanced, multiracial, anti-imperialist struggle. A revolutionary critical pedagogy poses the following questions for consideration by teachers, students, and other cultural workers: How can we liberate the use value of human beings from their subordination to exchange value? How can we convert what is least functional about ourselves as far as the abstract utilitarian logic of capitalist society is concerned—our self-realizing, sensuous, species-being—into our major instrument of self-definition? How can we make what we represent to capital as replaceable commodities subordinate to who we have also become as critical social agents of history? How can we make critical self-reflexivity a demarcating principle of who we are and critical global citizenship the substance of what we want to become? How can we make the cultivation of a politics of hope and possibility a radical end in itself? How can we decommodify our subjectivities? How can we materialize our self-activity as a revolutionary force and struggle for the self-determination of free and equal citizens in a just system of appropriation and distribution of social wealth? How can we make and remake our own nature within historically specific conventions of capitalist society such that we can make this self-activity a revolutionary force to dismantle capitalism itself and create the conditions for the development of our full human potential? How can we confront our "producers" (that is, social relations of production, the corporate media, cultural formations, and institutional structures) as an independent power?

Critical revolutionary pedagogy is designed to break the pathology of dependency between the oppressor and the oppressed that occurs when such questions are ignored. It attempts to create conditions so that the oppressed reflect upon how and why they are situated in the larger social totality and devise strategies to liberate themselves. Critical revolutionary pedagogy also invites the oppressors to examine their desire to oppress and to liberate themselves from that desire. In this way critical revolutionary pedagogy is more than a residual pastime; it is, in fact, a living critique that constitutes the foundation for a way of life. It is a pedagogy that ruptures the presumptions and practices of the U.S. empire, a pedagogy directed at the underside of progress on behalf of those who live on the periphery of hope.

Note

Gregory Martin is a lecturer in education at Griffith University, Australia, and Nathalia Jaramillo is a doctoral student in the Graduate School of Education and Information Studies, University of California, Los Angeles.

References

Allman, P. 2001. *Critical education against capitalism: Karl Marx and revolutionary critical education.* Westport, Conn.: Bergin and Garvey.

Alter, J., and J. Green. 2003. The man of virtues has a vice. *Newsweek.* www.msnbc.com/news/908430.asp?0cv=KA01 (accessed September 15, 2003).

Anderson, K. 1995. *Lenin, Hegel, and Western Marxism: A Critical Study.* Champaign: University of Illinois Press.

Bennett, W. J. 1993. *The book of virtues: A treasury of great moral stories.* New York: Simon and Schuster.

———. 2002. *Why we fight: Moral clarity and the war on terrorism.* New York: Doubleday.

Berger, L. 2002. The rise of the perma-temp. *New York Times.* August 4. www.nytimes.com/2002/08/04/edlife/04BERGERT.html (accessed August 4, 2002).

Bloom, S. 2003. The kind of antiwar movement that we need. *Atlanta Solidarity.* www.atlantasolidarity.org/cgi/article.pl?file=movement_we_need.html (accessed April 1, 2003).

Burns, R. 2003. Defense budget doesn't cover terror war. www.presentdanger.org/commentary/2003/0303pentbudget_body.html (accessed April 3, 2003).

California Department of Education, 2003. Subchapter 22. Reading First Program §11990. www.cde.ca.gov (accessed April 10, 2003).

Cleaver, H. 2000. *Reading capital politically.* Leeds: AK Press.

Cole, M. 1998. Globalization, modernisation and competitiveness: A critique of the New Labour Project in Education. *International Studies in Sociology of Education* 8(3): 315–32.

Ebert, T. 2002. University, class, and citizenship. Unpublished manuscript.

Elder, L. 2002. *Showdown.* New York: St. Martin's Press.

Farahmandpur, R. 2002. Class, hegemony, and ideology: A critique of neo-Marxist approaches to educational reform. Doctoral diss., University of California, Los Angeles.

Farahmandpur, R., and P. McLaren. 2001. Critical literacy for global citizenship. *Center X Forum* 1(2): 1, 9–10.

Fattah, C. 2002. Unequal education in America: A look at stories from around the country. www.house.gov/fattah/education/ed_sbruneq.htm (accessed January 15, 2003).

Foster, J. B. 2003. Imperial America and war. *Monthly Review* 55(1): 1–10.

Gibbs, D. N. 2001. The CIA: Academics and spies: The silence that roars. *Los Angeles Times,* January 28, Opinion section, M2.

Giddens, A. 1999. *Runaway world: How globalization is reshaping our lives.* New York: Routledge.

Giroux, H. 2002. Democracy, freedom, and justice after September 11th: Rethinking the role of educators and the politics of schooling. *TCRecord.org.*www.tcrecord.org/Content.asp?ContentID=10871 (accessed January 12, 2003).

Green, J. 2003. The bookie of virtue. *Washington Monthly.* www.washingtonmonthly.com/features/2003/0306.green.html (accessed July 1, 2003).

Hellman, C. 2003. Pentagon budget: More of the same. *Much, much, more.* www.presentdanger.org/commentary/2003/0303pentbudget_body.html (accessed February 1, 2003).

Helmore, E. 2003. Moral voice of US gambles on his credibility. *The Observer.* www.observer.co.uk/international/story/0,6903,949010,00html (accessed March 15, 2003)

——. 1999. *New Labour and education: Policy, ideology and the Third Way.* London: Tuffnell Press.

——. 2001. State theory and the neo-liberal reconstruction of schooling and teacher education: A structuralist neo-Marxist critique of postmodernist, quasi-postmodernist, and culturalist neo-Marxist theory. *British Journal of Sociology of Education* 22(1): 137–57.

Hill, D. 1999. *New Labor and Education: Policy, Ideology and the Third Way.* London: Tufnell Press.

——. 2001. State theory and the neo-liberal reconstruction of schooling and teacher education: A structuralist neo-Marxist critique of postmodernist, quasi-postmodernist, and culturalist neo-Marxist theory. *The British Journal of Sociology of Education* 22(1): 137–57.

———. 2002a. Global capital, neo-liberalism, and education policy: The growth of educational inequality. *The Taiwan Journal of Sociology of Education* 2(1): 234–68.

———. 2002b. Global capital, neo-liberalism, and the growth of educational inequality. *The School Field: International Journal of Theory and Research in Education* 13 (1/2): 81–107.

———. In press. Critical education for economic and social justice. *Education and Social Justice.*

Holloway, J. 2002. Twelve theses on changing the world without taking power. *The Commoner,* no. 4. www.commoner.org.uk/04holloway2.pdf (accessed may 15, 2003).

Kinsley, M. 2003. Bill Bennett's bad bet, *Slate.* http://slate.msn.com/id/2082526 (accessed May 4, 2003).

Kozol, J. 1991. *Savage inequalities.* New York: Crown Publishers.

Lenin, V. I. 1939. *Imperialism: The highest stage of capitalism.* New York: International Publishers.

———. 1965. *The state and revolution.* Peking: Foreign Languages Press.

MacMichael, D. 2002. CIA and RIT fundamentally incompatible: "Intelligence and higher education." *Covert Action Quarterly,* no. 73, 13–17, 47.

Martin, G. 2002. What is to be done? Toward a revolutionary praxis. *Journal of Critical Inquiry into Curriculum and Instruction* 3(3): 42–45.

McLaren, P. 2000. *Che Guevara, Paulo Freire, and the pedagogy of revolution.* Lanham, Md.: Rowman & Littlefield.

———. 2003. The lesson of war. www.socialistfuture.org.uk/msf/YourSay.htm#war (accessed January 10, 2003).

McLaren, P., and R. Farahmandpur. 1999. Critical pedagogy, postmodernism, and the retreat from class: Towards a contraband pedagogy. *Theoria* 93: 83–115.

———. 2000. Reconsidering Marx in post-Marxist times: A requiem for postmodernism? *Educational Researcher* 29(3): 25–33.

———. 2001a. Class, cultism, and multiculturalism: A notebook on forging a revolutionary multiculturalism. *Multicultural Education* 8(3): 2–14.

———. 2001b. Educational policy and the socialist imagination: Revolutionary citizenship as a pedagogy of resistance. *Educational Policy* 15(3): 343–78.

———. 2001c. Teaching against globalization and the new imperialism: Toward a revolutionary pedagogy. *Journal of Teacher Education* 52(2): 136–50.

———. 2002. Breaking signifying chains: A Marxist position on postmodernism. In *Marxism against postmodernism in educational theory,* ed. D. Hill, P. McLaren, M. Cole, and G. Rikowski, 35–66. Lanham, Md.: Lexington Books.

McLaren, P., and N. Jaramillo. 2002. Critical pedagogy as organizational praxis: Challenging the demise of civil society in a time of permanent war. *Educational Foundations* 16(4): 5–32.

Metcalf, S. 2002. Reading between the lines. *The Nation,* January 28. www.thenation.com/docprint.mhtml?i=20020128&s=metcalf (accessed January 15, 2003).

Parenti, M. 1993. *Land of idols: Political Mythology in America.* New York: St. Martins Press.

Parenti, M. 2003. To kill Iraq: The reasons why. www.michaelparenti.org/IRAQ George2.htm (accessed January 20, 2003).

Pierre, R. E. 2003. Students across U.S. mount antiwar protests. *Washington Post*, March 6, A16.

Pobelte, J. 2003. Ventura county students walkout and demonstrate against war. http://la.indymedia.org/news/2003/03/33585.php (accessed January 12, 2003).

Research Unit for Political Economy. 2003. Behind the war on Iraq. *Monthly Review* 55(1): 20–49.

Rikowski, G. 2001. *The battle in Seattle: Its significance for education.* London: Tufnell Press.

———. 2002. Fuel for the living fire: Labour-power! In *The Labour Debate*, ed. A. Dinerstein and M. Neary, 179–202. Burlington, Vt.: Ashgate Publishing.

Rochester, M. J. 2003. Critical demagogues: The writings of Henry Giroux and Peter McLaren. *Education Next* 3 (Fall). As retrieved from www.educationnext.org/2004/77.html

Smith, T. 2002. An assessment of Joseph Stiglitz's *Globalization and Its Discontents.* Department seminar, Department of Philosophy, Iowa State University, October 29. Teach-in sponsored by Alliance for Global Justice, Ames, October 16, 2002. www.public.iastate.edu/~tonys/Stiglitz.html (accessed January 20, 2003).

Stiglitz, J. 2002. The roaring nineties. *The Atlantic Monthly*, October. www.theatlantic.com/issues/2002/10/stiglitz.htm (accessed January 21, 2003).

Students United Against War. 2003. Ventura County students united against war. www.nionventura.org/Ventura_County_Students_United_Against_War.htm (accessed January 30, 2003).

Tabb, W. 2001. Globalization and education as a commodity. www.psc-cuny.org/jcglobalization.htm (accessed January 3, 2003).

Wolin, S. 2003. Inverted totalitarianism. *The Nation* 276(19): 13–15.

Zavarzadeh, M., and D. Morton. 1994. *Theory as resistance: Politics and culture after (post)structuralism.* New York: Guilford Press.

Žižek, S. 2002. *Revolution at the gates: Selected writings of Lenin from 1917.* New York: Verso.

9

Critical Revolutionary Pedagogy at Ground Zero: Renewing the Educational Left after September 11

Marx's legacy is no mere heirloom, but a live body of ideas and perspectives that is in need of concretization. Every moment of Marx's development, as well as the totality of his works, spells out the need for "revolution in permanence." This is the absolute challenge to our age.

—Raya Dunayevskaya 2004, 195

THIS FINAL CHAPTER ADDRESSES THE IMPORTANCE of teachers developing their abilities to engage students in discussions on terrorism and creating pedagogical spaces inside their classrooms in which students can express their concerns about the September 11 tragedy, the "permanent" war on terrorism, and their fears and acute anxieties about the possibility of future attacks. One productive, but in the climate of hyperpatriotism—despairingly infrequent—means of approaching this task is to discuss, debate, analyze, and reflect on the social and historical construction of such concepts as terrorism and patriotism. We believe that in most school settings such concepts are not only ideologically constructed to serve the interests of the dominant class but also intended to represent a narrow vision of the complex social world in which we live. Teachers can help students develop a "language of critique" to guide them in investigating how such concepts are "selectively" employed by the ruling class to represent and reproduce existing relations of power among dominant and subordinate groups in society. For example, teachers can help students understand how contemporary right-wing forces have taken advantage of the September 11 tragedy by making patriotism synonymous with the ideology of Americanism and how terrorism is portrayed to represent violence by Arabs against westerners and not vice versa.

We believe that educators have a moral and ethical obligation to provide a forum in which students can question and critique the right wing's efforts to rally people around its domestic and foreign U.S. policy initiatives. This demands scrutinizing efforts by the media punditocracy and the right-wing elements to make patriotism synonymous with capitalism, free-market democracy, and consumerism. In this context, critical media literacy can play an important role in deepening students' understanding of the tragic events surrounding the September 11 attacks by providing them with the necessary pedagogical tools to decode and interpret images, sound bites, and texts produced by the mainstream media. To unmask the contradictions between patriotism and consumerism, between patriotism and democracy, and between patriotism and Americanism requires students to have access to a *language of critique*. In writing this chapter, we hope to contribute toward the development of this language by illuminating what we believe to be some of the more essential connections between corporatism and militarism that are the focus of this book. We also hope to offer pedagogical strategies, a *language of possibility*, that critically minded educators might use to preempt any sense of helplessness that might be engendered through the exploration of such themes.

Whose Terror?

Understanding the causes of terrorism constitutes the first steps that students and teachers can undertake toward its eradication. Chalmers Johnson's (2000) model of "blowback" (a term first used by the Central Intelligence Agency [CIA] but adopted by some leftists to refer to actions that result from unintended consequences of U.S. policies kept secret from the American public) offers a lucid framework for analyzing the attacks of September 11. Johnson argues what the mainstream media reports as the malign acts of "terrorists" or "drug lords" or "rogue states" or "illegal arms merchants" often turn out to be "blowback" from earlier covert U.S. operations (see Kellner 2001). Blowback related to U.S. foreign policy occurred when the United States trained and funded terrorist groups and assisted economically and militarily authoritarian regimes in Asia, Latin America, and the Middle East.

The events of September 11 can be seen as a textbook example of "blowback" since Osama bin Laden and the radical Islamic forces associated with the al Qaeda network were supported, funded, trained, and armed by several U.S. administrations and by the CIA. The CIA's catastrophic failure was not only its inability to coordinate its intelligence in analyzing the impending attacks and taking the appropriate action to prevent them but also to have actively contributed to producing those very groups who were implicated in the terrorist attacks on the United States on September 11 (see Kellner 2001). Cockburn and St. Clair's *Whiteout: the CIA, Drugs, and the Press* reveals just how assidu-ously the CIA assisted the opium lords who took over Afghanistan and helped usher the Taliban into power, eventually helping in the financing of bin Laden's al Qaeda network. Eventually these U.S. clients turned against their sponsors.

The United States imposes severe economic sanctions on Muslim countries that commit human rights abuses and that accumulate weapons of mass de-struction. At the same time, the United States ignores Muslim victims of human rights abuses in Palestine, Bosnia, Kosovo, Kashmir, and Chechnya. Through vast weapons sales, the United States props up its economy. Yet it in-sists on economic sanctions to prevent weapons development in Libya, Sudan, Iran, and Iraq. And, as Steve Niva (2001) points out, "The U.S. pro-Israel pol-icy unfairly puts higher demands on Palestinians to renounce violence than on Israelis to halt new settlements and adhere to U.N. resolutions calling for an Israeli withdrawal from Palestinian lands" (3). The United States regularly gives tacit approval to Israel's extrajudicial killings of Palestinian leaders who allegedly are involved in terrorist activities. These government-sanctioned as-sassinations, usually by missiles fired from Israeli helicopters, often kill scores of innocent bystanders, including children. Recently, President Bush shocked the world by effectively dismissing as unrealistic the right of return of Pales-tinians who were forced to leave their lands during the creation of the Israeli state, thereby setting back the Middle East peace process by a half century.

More broadly speaking, we believe that the events of September 11 should be examined in the context of the crisis of world capitalism. Here we are not so much referring to corporate executives—"the Ebola viruses of capital-ism"—as we are to the globalization of the productive forces under free-trade liberalization. We follow a number of the central assertions of William Robin-son (2001), namely, that in recent decades the capitalist production process it-self has become increasingly transnationalized. We have moved from a world economy to a new epoch known as the global economy. Whereas formerly the world economy was composed of the development of national economies and national circuits of accumulation that were linked to each other through com-modity trade and capital flows (in an integrated international market while nation-states mediated the boundaries between differently articulated modes of production), today national production systems are reorganized and func-tionally integrated into global circuits, creating a single and increasingly un-differentiated field for world capitalism. We are talking about the transna-tionalization of the production of goods and services (globalization) and not just the extension of trade and financial flows across national borders (inter-nationalization). The new global financial system disperses profits worldwide as the world becomes unified into a single mode of production and single global system, bringing about the organic integration of different countries and regions into a global economy.

The consequences of the restructuring of the world-productive apparatus are staggering. We agree with Robinson (2001) that technological changes are the result of class struggle—in this case, the restraints on accumulation imposed by popular classes worldwide. Global class formation is occurring, with supranational integration of national classes accompanying the transnational integration of national productive structures. This has accelerated the division of the world into a global bourgeoisie (the hegemonic global class fraction) and a global proletariat. That is, dominant groups fuse into a class or class fraction within transnational space. There exists an emergent capitalist historic bloc sustained by a transnational capitalist class and represented by a transnational bourgeoisie. The United States is playing a leadership role on behalf of the emerging transnational elite; that is, the United States is taking the lead in developing policies and strategies on behalf of the global capitalist agenda of the transnational elite. It follows from this that revolutionary social struggle must become transnationalized as power from below in order to counter transnationalized capitalist power from above.

Today the marketplace is really a continuation of the core ideology of Reaganism, what Manning Marable (2001a) describes as free markets, unregulated corporations, an aggressive militarization abroad, and the suppression of civil liberties and civil rights at home. In an acutely troubling sense, the United States is now closer to the Reagan ideal of the national security state "where the legitimate functions of government were narrowly restricted to matters of national defense, public safety, and providing tax subsidies to the wealthy" (2001a, 4). It is the flourishing of Reagan's "military Keynesianism"—"the deficit spending of hundreds of billions of dollar on military hardware and speculative weapons schemes such as 'Star Wars'" (2001b, 4). In contrast to what is currently being said in the mainstream press about Reagan, as the country continues to mourn his recent death, the so-called "Reagan revolution" ushered in one of the bloodiest eras in the history of the Western Hemisphere. Reagan's Contra war resulted in the United States being the only country in the world to have been condemned by the World Court for "unlawful use of force," in effect, for international terrorism, as it helped the Salvadorian military butcher between 50,000 and 70,000 of its people. The United States achieved similar results in Guatemala, in this case helping the military exterminate 200,000 of its indigenous peoples. The Reagan legacy was a legacy of horror for all but the rich, whom Reagan helped profit immeasurably during his tenure in office.

It is also clear that today world capitalism is trying to reestablish itself in transnationalized formations since its current forms are virtually unsustainable. In other words, the transnational capitalist elites are seizing opportunities to use military force to protect their markets and create new ones. In fact, a more dangerous threat than individual acts of terror today are the multifarious contradictions internal to the system of world capitalism. Throughout its history, U.S. capitalism has tried to survive in times of crisis by eliminating production and jobs, forcing those in work to accept worse conditions of labor, and seizing opportunities that might arise in which the public would support military action to protect what the United States defines as its vital interests. Developed and underdeveloped population groups occupying contradictory and unstable locations in an increasingly transnational environment, coupled with cultural and religious antagonisms among the capitalist actors, create conditions of desperation and anger among the fractions of the oppressed. We say this not to give credibility to terrorism as a response to such anger but to seek to understand and prevent the conditions in which terrorism is ignited. Marable warns, "The question, 'Why Do They Hate Us?,' can only be answered from the vantage point of the Third World's widespread poverty, hunger and economic exploitation" (2001a, 1).

Given this daunting global challenge, it is important that educators ask the following: Is there a viable socialist alternative to capitalism? What would a world without wage labor be like? Without living labor being subsumed by dead labor? Would a world without the extraction of surplus value and the imperialist exploitation that accompanies it be a safer and more just world, a world less likely to be infested with the conditions that breed terrorism?

Unmasking Neoliberal Globalization

Contrary to the myths that have been circulated by the corporate-owned media, globalization does not, in any sense of the word, bring about the conditions for political harmony or economic stability. Nor does it furnish mutual economic growth for those nations, particularly Third World countries, that are forced to participate in the global economy under the leadership of the United States. The big scandal of our time, write Petras and Veltmeyer (2001), is that globalization fabricates the ideology that all countries benefit equally from the internationalization of trade. Yet globalization is not by any stretch of the imagination, what we have been repeatedly told by corporate pundits: an "irreversible" and unstoppable process that arose from certain social and historical conditions. In fact, we contend that globalization is a process orchestrated by advocates of neoliberal social and economic policies. Yet we do not have to resign to the inevitability of neoliberal globalization.

It is worth noting that under the banner of globalization, corporate overworlders claim that the internationalization of capital is the solution to the declining rate of profit. For the cheerleaders of the free market, which include Milton Friedman, globalization is the cure to the accumulation crisis of capital.

However, we unequivocally dismiss the claims that globalization represents, by and large, a qualitative leap in capitalist production. In our view, globalization represents a number of fundamental developments in capitalist economic crisis that include, among other things, the following:

- A short-term solution to the long-term declining productivity
- The intensification of competition among the leading imperialist nations, most notably, the United States, Japan, and Germany (the largest Western industrial economies that have shifted part of their production to Third World countries)
- The internationalization of investment and speculative capital
- The international division of labor created by the integration of new technologies in an effort to raise productivity
- The employment of new methods of flexible production largely derived from post-Fordist regimes of accumulation
- The surging attacks on the working class and the poor by the Right on behalf of the ruling classes

In our opinion, the concept of globalization serves to detract attention from the broader objectives of U.S. imperialism: to establish political domination, to facilitate economic exploitation, and to loot the natural resources of Third World nations. In other words, the concept of globalization serves as a smokescreen to conceal the main objectives of U.S. imperialism's quest for global hegemony. As such, we believe that the concept of imperialism better reflects U.S. foreign policy objectives.

Finally, we should also mention that one of the objectives of neoliberal social and economic policies is liberating capital from any regulations that may be imposed on it by government agencies. Part of the neoliberal social and economic policies is carried out through *privatization*—the "e-baying" of state-owned enterprises, industries, and publicly owned goods and services to the private sector, which is carried out largely under the banner of "efficiency" and "productivity," two buzzwords that are employed to mask corporate theft of social resources. Furthermore, *deregulation* acts as a "buffer zone" to ward off any formidable threats against corporate profits despite the growing unemployment and environmental damage that it has caused, not to mention reducing public expenditures on social services that include public education, health services, and child care, to cite a few examples. In the end, what it all comes down to is that the objective of the Right is to abolish the concept of "public good" and to replace it with the ideology of "personal responsibility" of George Bush's "compassionate conservatism."

The New Niche Market: Global Slavery

Capitalism is more than a sobering lesson for historians; it provides the ideal showcase for the tragedy of the human species. It includes not only men and women who are forced to work in hazardous working conditions, for barely endurable hours, and for much less than a living wage but also children who labor perilously inside factories and sweatshops manufacturing numerous consumer goods (such as Nike shoes) that are shipped to consumer markets located in advanced capitalist countries. Capitalism does not screen its victims—anyone is fair game. It "sizes up" everyone. Anyone is ripe for exploitation. It should therefore surprise no one that capitalism is happily at war with children. Worldwide, nearly 250 million children are presently working (some estimate that it is as high as 400 million). Nearly 90 million of the 179 million children in India work. Children in the southern region of India work sixteen hours a day, six days a week, for a meager $1.30-a-week salary. In Bangladesh, the number of working children is 6.1 million. In Thailand, there are nearly 13,000 child prostitutes (some estimate the figure to be closer to 800,000). In Nairobi, 30,000 children live on the streets. In Colombia, 28 percent of Bogota's prostitutes are young girls between the ages of ten and fourteen. In the United States, nearly 290,000 children are illegally employed in various industries; this includes 59,600 children who are under the age of fourteen (Kameras 1998). For the profiteers of capital, the children's war is a famously lucrative one.

Slavery is far from dead. Approximately 27 million people worldwide are paid no wages, and their lives are completely controlled by others through violence. According to Kevin Bales (2000), "slavery itself keeps changing and growing" (36). Slavery has largely disappeared as "the legal ownership of one person by another," but it remains inescapably true that slavery is a growing industry worldwide, from the brothels of Thailand to the charcoal mines of Brazil to women in the West who have been kidnapped from Eastern Europe. According to Bales,

> At US $2,000 the young woman in a Thai brothel is one of the world's more costly slaves. People, especially children, can be enslaved today for little as US $45. The 11-year-old boy I met in India six weeks ago had been placed in bondage by his parents in exchange for about US $35. He now works 14 hours a day, seven days a week making *beedi* cigarettes. This lad is held in "debt bondage," one of the most common variations on the theme of slavery. Debt bondage is slavery with a twist. Instead of being property, the slave is collateral. The boy and all his work belong to the slaveholder as long as the debt is unpaid, but not a penny is applied to the debt. Until his parents find the money, this boy is a cigarette-rolling machine, fed just enough to keep him at his task. People may be enslaved in the name of religion,

like the *Devdasi* of India or the *trokosi* of West Africa. They may be enslaved by their own government, like the hundreds of thousands of people identified by the International Labour Organisation in Burma. Whoever enslaves them, and through whatever trickery, false contract, debt or kidnap method, the reality for the slave is much the same. (38)

The reason why slavery escapes our notice is because Western jobs are not threatened and multinationals are not undercut by slave-based enterprises. In fact, citizens of 74 percent of countries with a high international debt load are regularly trafficked into slavery. For countries with a low international debt load, the figure is 29 percent. In 50 percent of countries with a high international debt load, slavery is a regular feature the economy, compared with just 12 percent of countries with a low international debt load (Bales 2000). A recently leaked CIA report notes that as many as 50,000 women and children are forced to work as slave laborers in the United States each year. They are lured from Asia, Africa, Latin America, and Eastern Europe and serve largely as prostitutes, domestic servants, or bonded workers. In 1995, seventy-two Thai workers were found imprisoned in a Los Angeles sweatshop. They were forced to work twenty-two hours a day for sixty-two cents an hour (Grey 2000).

Those who naively believe that slavery has disappeared in the United States may be surprised to learn that in many prisons across the United States, slavery has been upgraded to "bonded labor." A number of corporations, including JCPenney, IBM, Toys Я Us, TWA, and Victoria's Secret have shamelessly profited from prison labor. And what about the close to 50,000 women and children who are forced into prostitution, domestic servitude, and sweatshop labor each year?

The deteriorating working and living conditions for laborers in Third World countries is comparable—and in many respects exceeds—the horrid working and living conditions of the English working class as described by Friedrich Engels in his book *The Conditions of the Working Class in England* ([1847] 1987). In Sri Lanka, many workers must work fourteen hours a day; in Indonesia and the Philippines, they work twelve-hour day shifts; and in the southern regions of China, sixteen-hour workdays are the norm. Working conditions for many women in the United States is not much better than in developing countries. In Little Saigon, located in Orange County, California, the average minimum wage for undocumented immigrants working in illegal sweatshops has been reported to be one dollar an hour (Parks 1997). Inside sweatshops and factories around the world, young women are placed under incessant surveillance and subjected to humiliating working conditions by plant managers in order to ensure the efficient operation of production lines. For instance, young women are frequently given amphetamines to prolong working hours, and their menstrual cycles are placed under continual supervision to prevent pregnancy, a condition that is detrimental to business because it slows down production lines (Parks 1997). In the maquiladoras, women's biological reproduction is regulated and synchronized to the pulse of new methods of lean and flexible production in order to maximize profitability and minimize labor costs. Young women are forced to provide evidence that they are menstruating each month by participating in "monthly sanitary-pad checks" (Klein 1999). As part of the contingent labor force, women are employed on twenty-eight-day contracts that coincide with their menstrual cycle. Those who are found pregnant are automatically fired and summarily released from the factory premises.

In 1998, Nike Corporation, with its global army of 500,000 contingent semiskilled workers in Third World countries, managed to amass a record revenue of $6.4 billion with the "assistance" of environmental laws promoting deregulation and nonunionized cheap labor. In poor underdeveloped countries such as Haiti, hourly wages are reported to be twelve cents an hour, while in Honduras, workers' hourly wages are thirty-one cents an hour. The cost of manufacturing a pair of Nike shoes—whose retail cost is $120—is estimated to be seventy to eighty cents in the dank sweatshops of Indonesia.

The recent assaults on welfare programs, bilingual education, multicultural education, and affirmative action boldly illustrate the incompatibility of capitalism with democracy. Mark Dery (1999) paints an eerie picture of contemporary capitalism at the end of twentieth century:

> Communism may have been consigned to the desktop recycle bin of history, as free-market cheerleaders never tire of reminding us, and Marx may be an ironic icon of nineties retro chic, but the old bearded devil may have the last laugh: As we round the bend to the millennium, class war and the percolating rage of the "workers of the world" are emerging as the lightning-rod social issues of the coming century. Growing income inequality, accompanied by the hemorrhaging of U.S. manufacturing jobs because of automation or their relocation in the low-wage, nonunion "developing world," is sowing dragon's teeth. The disappearance of even unskilled factory work at time when economic growth is insufficient to absorb dislocated workers is dire enough; that it is happening at a moment when traditional safety values no longer function—owing to the wasting away of the labor movement, the conservative dismantling of social services in favor of "market solutions" to social ills, and the ongoing buyout of representative government by corporate power—has created fertile soil for the apocalyptic politics of the disaffected. (262–63)

Contrary to popular mythology, money is not the source of capitalism's wealth; rather, its source is the sweat and blood of exploited workers and toilers on behalf of the valorization process of capital. It is the savage manipulation of their labor power that creates revenue for the money moguls of the advanced capitalist West. Daniel Singer (1999) writes, "The obscene equivalence between the wealth of the world's top few hundred billionaires and the income of nearly three billion wretched of the earth illustrates this point" (216).

As we speak, there are an estimated 5 billion men, women, and children who are forced to subsist on $2 a day. Meanwhile, the 200 largest corporations in the world who have a combined 28 percent monopoly over global economic activities, merely employ 0.25 percent of the global workforce. To put things into perspective, the combined wealth of the eighty-four richest individuals in the world exceeds the gross domestic product of China, which has a population of 1.3 billion.

The staggering and loathsome disparities between the rich and the poor can no longer adventitiously or capriciously be cast aside by politicians and pundits as a necessary evil of capitalist democracy. The contradictions inherent within capitalist social relations of production are transparent for those who are brave enough to face the truth about the current crisis of global capitalism. To cite one example, between 1997 and 1999, the average wealth of the rich who were lucky enough to be listed on the Forbes 400 increased by $940 million. In sharp contrast, in the past twelve years, the net worth of the bottom 40 percent of the households in the United States declined by a dramatic 80 percent. Or take the example of the chief executive officer of Disney, Michael Eisner, whose annual salary in 1998 was estimated to be $575.6 million. Compare that to the average annual salary of Disney employees, which stands at $25,070. We must question why, for example, the hourly wage of a worker in Guatemala is thirty-seven cents an hour while Phil Knight, the chief executive officer of Nike, has amassed a fortune of $5.8 billion.

The contradictions of capital in general and the imperfections of the market in the advanced capitalist countries of the West in particular are especially evident throughout the United States. Today, nearly 700,000 people are homeless on any given night in the United States. Annually, 2 million experience homelessness. Tragically, one out of every four homeless persons is an innocent child. In the majority of large metropolitan cities across the United States, homelessness is considered a crime. A number of innovative methods have been implemented to make homeless people invisible. In Chicago, for example, homeless people are arrested and prosecuted daily. These are the casualties of unceremonious economic excommunication. Before he became reinvented as the purebred embodiment of New York City itself, Rudolph Giuliani initiated a "quality-of-life" campaign in New York City that involved nightly sweeps and crackdowns on homeless people to ensure that they did not transgress the boundaries dividing the wealthy neighborhoods from the poor neighborhoods.

By a sheer suicidal will to obliterate the past, modern-day capitalists of the Enron school of ethics have unburdened history of its complexity and temporality and purified it of the stench of its victims. We can firebomb democracy and pulverize its logic into the Stone Age sensibility of "survival of the fittest" as long as we don't show the corpses that are filling our city morgues. Capitalist accumulation can be experienced as the glow of an eternal "now," forever self-fellating and pleasure-giving, never reneging on its promise of eternal happiness. If there is any justice folded into the transcendent order of things, it is this: when Bush's chief Bubba, "Kenny Boy" Lay, is invited to drink at Plato's River of Forgetfulness, he'll be persuaded by the prophet of Necessity to return to the Republic in his most unvarnished incarnation: a hog squealing at the trough, waiting to be served up as Sunday dinner for all those "whose pension funds were pumped dry to provide the hog wallow with loot" (Cockburn 2002, 8).

The United States is by far the most powerful capitalist country in the world. Consider the list of 497 billionaires (down from 551 before 2001 as a result of global recession) in the world; 216 of billionaires are Americans, followed by Germany with thirty-five and Japan with twenty-five, respectively. The combined wealth of these 497 billionaires equals the incomes of the most impoverished half of the human population. Yet in the wealthiest nation on earth, the United States, one out of every six children lives in poverty. According to a published report by the progressive think tank, the Economic Policy Institute, one in four Americans was making poverty-level wages in 2000, and while major health care providers such as Johns Hopkins Hospital in Baltimore are developing special health coverage programs that offer "platinum service" to the rich (complimentary massage and sauna time with physical exams in state-of-the-art testing labs), nearly 40 million Americans lack health insurance.

The United States has declared the September 11 attacks to be an act of war. While these acts were indeed brutally warlike and a loathsome and despicable crime against humanity, clearly they did not constitute an act of war—an armed attack by one state against another—but rather acts of terrorism (which surely makes them no less hideous). Having failed to get authorization for the use of military force from the UN Security Council, Bush Jr. and his administration tried to get a formal declaration of war from Congress but instead were given a war powers resolution authorization (only one member of Congress, Barbara Lee, an African American representative from Oakland, demonstrated the courage to vote against it as a matter of principle). The Bush administration then convinced the North Atlantic Treaty Organization (NATO) to invoke article 5 of the NATO pact in an attempt to get some type of multilateral justification for U.S. military action. After failing on two attempts to get Security Council approval for military action, the U.S. ambassador to the United Nations, John Negroponte, sent a letter to the Security Council asserting article 51 of the UN Charter, claiming that the United States reserves its right to use force against any state that it wishes as part of its fight against international terrorism (Negro-ponte was former U.S. ambassador in Honduras during the Contra war and oversaw the funding of Battalion 316 that all but wiped out the democratic opposition; his confirmation was rammed through the day after the attacks).

The New Citizenship

President Bush now has his war mandate and is operating with a blank check for arming the military machine to its depleted uranium teeth. He is prepared to unleash Shock and Awe against any individual or state that he alleges was involved in the attacks on September 11 or else sheltered, harbored, or assisted individuals in those attacks (see Boyle 2001). President Bush has made it unequivocally clear: those who are not with him are against him.

Such an attitude communicates an ominous message to America's youth regarding the roles and responsibilities of democratic citizenship. The Bush administration has stooped to the most deplorable levels of political opportunism by using the unforgiving and unforgivable attacks of September 11 as a pretext for ushering in new realm of citizenship that irreparably fractures the once inseparable connection between democracy and justice. Reason has been sacrificed at the altar of unreflective action. Hatred of the Other that had been gestating for decades since the Reagan era has now been unleashed with the Bush/Cheney junta's furious assault on terrorism and all things turbaned, with the terrorists substituting for our former enemies: the Red Menace from the Georgian steppes. Now we must search for a new pair of tender geopolitical testicles to which we can attach the electrodes of democracy and freedom and the lessons of our great leaders. Members of the ruling class have been the frontline defenders of the war on terrorism and are all too willing to sacrifice civil rights if it will protect their position in the global division of labor. The already complicated equilibrium of our cities has gone into frenzied fibrillations at the prospect of death and destruction suddenly reigning down on our innocents. The ever-imminent but undefined hope that the world is getting better has been forever silenced by September 11. The reflective impoverishment of the American public—raised for generations on junk media Kmart realism, trailer park fiction, and Diet-Pepsi minimalism—has proven advantageous to President Bush, whose popularity as the Christian crusader whom God instructed to remove Saddam from power remains steady among evangelicals and Christian Zionists. Bush's mental glacier is in no danger of being shrunk by global warming. It continues to float the most hawkish ideas since Ronald Reagan past a largely unsuspecting public convinced that only Bush has the mettle to wipe the planet clean of Muhammad's holy militia.

In this latest Bush era, it has become dangerous to think, to ask too many questions, or to look beyond the face value of whatever commentary is served up to us by our politicians, our military, and our so-called intelligence agencies and those who have disingenuously become their Beverly Hills lapdogs: the media. Among most media commentators, dialectical thought has been lamentably undervalued and shamefully underpracticed. It is a world where it is safer to engage in rehearsed reactions to what we encounter on our television screens. It is safer to react in ways that newscaster/entertainers big on acrimonious scapegoating and short on analysis define for us as patriotic: applaud all actions by governmental authorities (especially those of the president) as if they were sacerdotal or morally apodictic. During the invasion of Afghanistan, CNN declared it "perverse" to focus on civilian suffering, exercising a racist arithmetic that deems civilian casualties in the United States to be superior to those in Afghanistan (and now Iraq). And it is clear that FOX television is little more than the *Pravda* of the Bush administration protecting George Bush Jr. from public scrutiny and steadfastly supporting his "enemy-of-the-month club."

Former secretary of education and candidate for president in the 2000 Republican primaries, William Bennett, has become one of Bush's most outspoken public defenders and has assumed the mantle of "philosopher king" of the Republican Party (despite recent revelations that he bets millions of dollars at the gambling casinos in Las Vegas and loses more in a single night than it would take to feed an entire inner-city community for a month). Bennett, who obviously benefited from Henry Kissinger's advice that anyone who wishes to become a recognized "expert" must learn to articulate the consensus of the powerful, has recently published *Why We Fight: Moral Clarity and the War on Terrorism* (2002). An angry and indomitable cheerleader for the American war machine, whose public pronouncements shift easily from sciolism to pedantry, Bennett continues to serve as a despotic mouthpiece and polemical hack for the most self-righteous and morally apodictic wing of the Republican far Right, mixing religious triumphalism (in Bennett's case, Catholic) with an overwhelming sense of his own importance and an absolute exclusion of any possibility of doubt or disillusionment on the issue of U.S. moral superiority in the world. Philosophically bankrupt, morally indignant, intellectually suspect, unburdened by an excess of imagination, and stamped with the temptation of careerism, *Why We Fight* is a half-baked criticism of the peace movement and what Bennett believes to be its benighted and morally dysfunctional leaders whom he blames for the failure of the United States to defeat the North Vietnamese and for aiding the enemies of civilization through their ongoing criticism of President Bush's permanent war on terrorism. Determined to give revenge by carpet bombing a moral justification and "payback" a philosophical warrant—not to mention the imprimatur of the Republican elite—Bennett's book rewrites bald imperialism as a democratic obligation to free the world from evildoers. Bennett's unwavering support for the

U.S. war machine and its politics of preemptive strikes is as blinkered as it is pernicious. His unforgiving absolutism and elitist adulation for Plato's *Republic* betray a contempt for dialectical reasoning and a blind allegiance to conservative
dogma. For Bennett, merely raising the question of why the terrorist attacks of
September 11 happened is an act of moral turpitude and a betrayal of the homeland. Bennett fails to connect the history of global capitalism to the history of
U.S. foreign policy and avoids any discussion of the contradiction between its
supposed leadership in the fight for democracy with its support for Latin American dictators, its training of death squad leaders in the (recently re-funded)
School of the Americas (now called WHISC: Western Hemisphere Institute for
Security Cooperation), its clandestine overthrow of democratically elected socialist governments, its buttressing of anticommunist warlords in Southeast Asia,
its slavish dedication to moneyed interests, and its willingness to punish all those
who resist the encroachment of global corporatism.

In an era when videos like *Bumfights* are produced in the United States and
shown worldwide through the Internet—the video shows homeless people
being paid to fight each other and to abuse themselves and to submit to being
abused by the show's hosts—is it any wonder that U.S. troops would be sus-
ceptible to torturing Iraqi prisoners? Especially after the Abu Ghraib photos
were released, the savagery of U.S. imperialism has been stigmatized publicly
and unstintingly. The routine stripping and beating of Iraqi prisoners in Abu
Ghraib and other U.S. torture centers in Iraq, Afghanistan, and Guantanamo
Bay are referred to as "unconventional methods" used by deranged reservists
while in fact they represent just a brief glimpse of abuse that is systematic and
sanctioned by the military. Not only does the Iraqi prison scandal reflect how
nearly 2.1 million inmates are systematically abused in U.S. prisons today—
where there exists an incarceration rate five to ten times greater than any other
so-called democratic state—it also serves as a shocking metaphor for how U.S.
imperialism treats people of color worldwide. Some of the images harken back
to the U.S. South during the decade when African Americans were tortured
and lynched and then photographed with leering white mobs that included
women and children. What is not being reported in the United States at the
time of this writing is the treatment of prisoners at Al-Amariyah, the Baghdad
prison where Iraq's new primer minister, Iyad Allawi, is alleged to have exe-
cuted six suspected insurgents. The Red Cross reports that at this prison detainees are subjected to the same torture used in the days of Saddam Hussein.

Today talk radio sadists such as Rush Limbaugh and Michael Savage gleefully
cheer the torture and execution of Iraqi detainees and exhort the millions of their
listeners to do the same, with Savage calling for dynamite to be placed in the prisoners' orifices and for Arab prisoners to be dropped out of airplanes (a favorite
technique of the Chilean military during the time of Pinochet) and for surpass-
ing the genocidal tactics of smallpox-infected blankets presented to the Cherokee

Indians by the U.S. Army during the "taming" of the West. While Bennett is hardly in the same hate-filled league as these talk radio American icons, he nevertheless appears to show their abysmal and willful ignorance of U.S. history.

The Militarization of Public Schools after September 11

Recent measures taken by a number of school officials targeting students and teachers who openly opposed the Bush administration's prowar foreign policies has undermined the long-standing perception that public schools are democratic institutions where students can freely express and exchange differing social, political, and religious viewpoints with each other (as well as with their teachers) without fear of being punished or reprimanded. One well-known example is that of Bretton Barber, a sixteen-year-old from Dearborn High School in Dearborn, Michigan, who expressed his disagreement with the war in Afghanistan. Barber was sent home for wearing a T-shirt that had a picture of president Bush with the words "International Terrorist" printed on it. School officials gave Barber an ultimatum: turn the shirt inside out, take it off, or return home. Instead of complying with what he felt to be an infringement on his freedom of speech, Barber decided to go home. Another case involves David Dial, a seventeen-year-old from Legacy High School in Denver who was suspended for one day from school after he decided to organize an international walkout on March 5, 2003, in opposition to the war against Iraq by posting fliers on the school walls instead of the community information table.

Then there is the case of Sara Doyle and her two brothers in Louisville, Kentucky. Doyle, a seventh-grade student, decided to remain seated along with her two brothers during the school's daily Pledge of Allegiance as a symbolic gesture to protest the war against Iraq. As punishment for her conduct, Sarah's teacher forced her to recite the Pledge of Allegiance in front of the class not once but twice. In Portland, Maine, after families of military personnel filed complaints to their local schools about the antiwar views of some teachers, school officials took immediate action by chastising teachers who had publicly expressed antiwar sentiments. Raising moral and ethical questions about the motives of the Bush administration's decision to go to war with Iraq has become increasingly dangerous for teachers. Teachers and school personnel who voiced their dissent against the war were scolded and berated by Republican Senator Susan Collins, who lashed out against opponents of the war by commenting that "any suggestion that their parents are doing something wrong is extremely unfortunate and could have a harmful effect, particularly on young children" (Canfield 2003). In Putaluma High School in Sonoma County, California, close to fifty high school students who participated in an antiwar walkout in November 2002 were suspended from school. It took the efforts of community activists and parents, who banded together and protested against the callous punishment, to finally force the school administration to back down and agree to remove the word "suspension" from the permanent record of the students who participated in the walkout.

Finally, there is Bill Nevins, a humanities teacher at Rio Rancho High School in Albuquerque, New Mexico. When the school administration found out that a poetry student in the Slam Team/Write Club that Nevins coached had recited anti-Bush poems over the school's closed-circuit TV system, he was summarily suspended from his teaching post. In New Mexico, two teachers were suspended after they declined to take down their antiwar posters from the classroom walls. In Richmond, Virginia, the superintendent of Henrico County Schools instructed principals to use "discretion" in discussing the war. In Chicago, Allan Alson, the superintendent of Evanston High School District 202, issued a memorandum explaining why he was enforcing a policy that prohibited teachers from wearing "no war" and "peace" buttons in their classrooms. The administration justified its policy by claiming that discussions centered on the war may cause "disruption" to the "educational process" and that teachers may inadvertently offer students a one-sided view of the conflict. But some parents questioned the district's double standard in which school administrators showcased their jingoistic patriotism by wearing flag pins.

These examples and others raise a number of important questions for teachers and teacher educators. For example, by what measures and means can teachers, parents, students, and community activists challenge and prevent the businessification of public schools? In what ways can parents protect their children from the dictatorship of the markets? In what pedagogical strategies and political actions can ordinary citizens participate in order to redraw and to widen the public sphere? The answer to these questions and others may be found in the emerging social movements at the grassroots level. One recent example is the grassroots movement led by Brita Butler-Wall, who successfully mobilized community leaders, parents, teachers, and students to prevent the superintendent of the school district from selling advertising space on high school walls. Since then, the organization has expanded with over 2,000 members and forty organizational supporters, including churches, state political parties, unions, and the National PTA (Applebaum 2003).

The No Child Left Behind Act, signed into law on January 8, 2002, requires public schools to hand over student contact lists to military recruiters. Not only does the military siphon off needed funds from the public schools, it also puts our youth into battle to fight its imperialist wars. According to a flyer from the National Youth and Militarism Program of the American Friends Service Committee, ever since Congress lifted the cap on how many public schools across the United States could have JROTC programs, the Department of Defense has been taking advantage of the lack of affordable housing, college financial aid, and jobs and has been recruiting relentlessly, especially in Puerto Rico, where there is a 40 percent unemployment rate. On the island, the recruiters are able to garner more than four times the number of recruits than anywhere on the mainland. More than 50 percent of JROTC programs are delivered in working-class communities, predominantly populated by youth of color. The ASVAB (American Services Vocational Aptitude Battery) test (administered free by the Pentagon) is administered in over 14,000 schools throughout the United States, and while it is meant to serve as a placement tool for the U.S. military, it is often used in inner-city school districts as an inexpensive way to assess students. What military recruiters don't tell students is that very few job skills are transferable from military to civilian life (unless, of course, you want to be a prison guard), and youth of color are often given low-level jobs, passed over for promotion, and sent to the front lines in battle. Students need to be made aware that they have the legal right to request that their names not be given to military re-cruiters, but they need to officially notify the school board. The goal should be to provide military-free zones in our schools.

A Primer for a Post–September 11 Critical Pedagogy

We believe that the study of terrorism can be and should be integrated as part of a broader multidisciplinary curriculum in classrooms. Bob Kumamoto (1993) has offered a number of helpful strategies that teachers can use as part of their curriculum to help students explore terrorism in a systematic fashion. Kumamoto's approach involves the study of history, economics, political science, geography, anthropology, social psychology, and sociology. Teachers can begin this project by dividing their students into several groups. Each group concentrates on one of the factors or one of the majors areas related to terrorism. For example, one group of students can examine how oil from the Middle East and the U.S. arms sales to Israel contributes to the ongoing conflicts and tensions in that region of the world. From a sociological standpoint, students can study how the harsh and brutal living conditions endured by Palestinians in refugee camps contribute to terrorism. In addition, students can investigate geographical complexities of the Middle East region that have ignited disputes and quarrels over the Holy Land and the occupied territories. In the political arena, students can find connections between the rise of Palestinian and Arab nationalism and U.S. economic and political interests in that region. Students can also examine Islamic fundamentalism through its historical opposition to Marxism and its embrace of capitalist social relations of production. From a historical perspective, students can explore the root causes of both Palestinian terrorism and Israeli state-sponsored terrorism in an effort to discover alternatives to both. Finally, by drawing upon the literature in social psychology, students can investigate the various motivating factors that cause individuals and groups to engage in terrorism and violence against innocent men, women, and children.

After their initial investigation, each group can report back to the class and share their findings. Teachers can then guide students to make connections between their findings and social and historical processes that have shaped that region of the world. For instance, teachers can assist students in making connections between acts of terrorism and practices such as colonization and imperialism. Second, students can explore the relationship between new media technologies and how acts of terrorism are reported to the public in specific geopolitical contexts. Third, students can examine how new "weapons of mass destruction" (biological, chemical, and nuclear), which may fall in the hands of terrorist organizations, can pose new threats to world peace and global stability. Other areas and topics that students can connect their findings to include state-sponsored terrorism, narcoterrorism, and ecoterrorism (Kumamoto 1993). For example, students can explore which states actively promote terrorism to protect their social, economic, and political interests.

Contextualizing the September 11 terrorist attacks mandates that we also question U.S. foreign policy along with its vital political and economic interests in the Middle East region, not to mention its support for the Israeli state. We believe that U.S. foreign policy has generated deep-seated bitterness and resentment among Arabs and that, in some instances, it has been a motivating factor in the rise of Palestinian extremism (Kumamoto 1993). This is not to suggest that criticism be deflected from the anti-Semitism, sexism, and homophobia exhibited by some Islamic fundamentalist groups (or by Christian fundamentalists for that matter). Students of history can also see whether they can find connections between their findings and the causes for the long-standing tradition of "Yankeephobia" in Latin American and South American countries. Further, students would do well to investigate how unjust labor practices of multinational corporations in Third World countries make U.S. citizens easy targets of anti-American sentiments. Finally, we want to remind students and teachers that the purpose of such activities is not to find a justification or a rationale for terrorism and violence but to understand what motivates individuals and groups to resort to political terrorism.

Finally, we should remind teachers that exercising democratic rights demands that they engage their students in meaningful dialogue and discussion over social, economic, and political issues that affect their lives. As such, we want to differentiate between *formal* citizenship and *substantive* citizenship (Petras and Veltmeyer 2001). Whereas formal citizenship is linked to the legal dimensions of citizenship under capitalist democracy in which political rights are disjoined and severed from economic rights, substantive citizenship is intimately connected to the "capacity of individuals to exercise those powers in actual debate, and in the resolution of political issues" (Petras and Veltmeyer 2001, 151). We believe that it is important for teachers to broaden and strengthen pedagogical spaces whereby students can exercise "substantive citizenship." Within the parameters of these social and political pedagogical spaces, teachers, students, and workers can undertake the task of self-empowerment by directly participating in the decision-making processes over issues that have an immediate impact on their daily lives at both the local and the community level. These include but are certainly not limited to engaging in discussions and debates over issues such as housing, taxation, education, health services, and social programs.

Toward a Critical Revolutionary Pedagogy

Critical educators across the country must continue to oppose what we are now seeing throughout the United States: a senseless xenophobic statism, militarism, the erosion of civil liberties, and a quest for permanent military interventions overseas within the fracture zones of geopolitical instability that have followed in the wake of the attacks, all of which can have only unsalutary consequences for world peace. This is particularly crucial, especially in light of the history of U.S. imperialism and in light of one of Said's (2001) trenchant observations that "bombing senseless civilians with F-16s and helicopter gunships has the same structure and effect as more conventional nationalistic terror" (3).

As critical educators, we are faced with a new sense of urgency in our fight to create social justice on a global scale, establishing what Karl Marx called a "positive humanism." At a time when Marxist social theory seems destined for the political dustbin, it is needed more than ever to help us understand the forces and relations that now shape our national and international destinies. As Bertell Ollman (2001) opines,

> I think what Marxism is about is to avoid the temptation of taking a stand based solely on our emotions. Marxism encourages us not to moralize about good and evil and who is more good or evil when you are confronted with many people capable of such actions. Marxism encourages us to contextualize what happened and who is involved; of how this happened in our world today and how it fits into history, into time. When you do that you can't avoid dealing with and trying to make sense of the role that the US has played in its foreign policy and also in global capitalism. One must look at that and figure out ways of dealing with it so that we can handle not only September 11th but all of the September 11ths which are coming up ahead. (7)

One of the purposes of critical/revolutionary pedagogy is to work to bring about a global society where events of September 11 are less likely to occur. It does this through creating contexts in which revolutionary/transformative praxis can occur. Critical pedagogy is a politics of understanding, an act of knowing that attempts to situate everyday life in a larger geopolitical context, with the goal of fostering regional collective self-responsibility, large-scale ecumenism, and international worker solidarity. It will require the courage to examine social and political contradictions, even, and perhaps especially, those that govern mainstream U.S. social policies and practices. It also requires a reexamination of some of the failures of the Left.

In the face of such an intensification of global capitalist relations, rather than a shift in the nature of capital itself, we need to develop a critical pedagogy capable of engaging everyday life as lived in the midst of global capital's tendency toward empire, a pedagogy that we have called revolutionary critical pedagogy. The idea here is not to adapt students to globalization but to make them critically maladaptive so that they can become change agents in anticapitalist struggles. The revolutionary multicultural unity sought by proponents of critical pedagogy is unflaggingly opposed to its class-collaborationist counterpart represented by Bush, Powell, and Rice.

Without question, the attacks of September 11 have handed the capitalist ideological offensive and imperialism a major and unexpected victory. Parasitical capitalism under the banner of neoliberal globalization and spearheaded by the World Trade Organization, International Monetary Fund, and World Bank has been disastrous for the world's poor. The struggle ahead for leftist educators will be difficult, but there are some signs of hope. In her book *Students against Sweatshops*, Liza Featherstone (2002) writes,

> The triple extremities of war, terror, and recession could distract the public from capitalism's everyday inequities. On the other hand, they certainly dramatize the system's problems: Bush's tax breaks to corporations; the way every national burden, from economic slowdown to anthrax, is disproportionately shouldered by the working class. (104)

It is more likely now that people are beginning to question more seriously the present system. One encouraging development that we are witnessing is a progressive radicalization of youth. Featherstone (2002) reports that

> many activists say that the September 11 attacks have left people ever hungrier for forward-looking, optimistic social action. The global economic justice movement in particular may stand a better chance of being heard, at a time when Americans are suddenly looking at the world and wondering, "Why do 'they' hate us?" . . . For many, September 11 underscored the need to rethink America's role in the world, and to redress global economic inequality. (104–5)

The defeat of U.S. imperialism and the ongoing struggle against global capitalism will require teachers to join antiwar efforts and peace movements across the nation. Inaction on this front may lead to escalating acts of terrorism both here and in the "homeland" as well as throughout the world. Given the uncertainty that looms in our collective future, it is more important than ever that educators participate in popular social movements—regional, national, and international—to resist the military adventurism and Enronization of the global lifeworld fueled by U.S. imperialism. As Michael Parenti (2002) has eloquently expressed elsewhere, "Those who believe in democracy must be undeterred in their determination to educate, organize, and agitate, in any case, swimming against the tide is always preferable to being swept over the waterfall" (111). Critical revolutionary educators can be active participants in helping these social movements make connections among domestic and foreign policies and the history of global capitalism and the role of imperialist states. In this way, these new social movements can deepen their understanding of commitment to a socialist politics and participatory democracy. Ideally, the struggle for socialism will take place in an organizational collectivity grounded in a philosophy of liberation that participates both in the necessary theoretical labor required in advancing the dialectical relation between critical analysis and forms of organizational struggle and in imagining and developing noncapitalist futures (see *News and Letters*, 2004).

Educational progressivism has become metaphorically cordoned off from the wider world of social and political struggle. Like a Cold War apologist for capital, critical pedagogy behaves oddly whenever Marx is in frame, a fact that underlies its essentially reformist as opposed to revolutionary character. It also points to the fact that Marxist analysis remains an enduringly controversial critique of society that has not been rehabilitated in the eyes of the academy, by and large.

We can no longer take refuge in the *mundus imaginalis* of neoplatonic philosophy in which we can dream our world ever anew in the hyperspace of a consumerist utopia. We appear to have become incapable of imagining life or death outside capitalist terms of reference generated from an enchanted suburban mall set atop the Emerald City of a capitalist longing. Critical pedagogy cannot succeed armed only with its concatenations of analysis and argument; it must also advance a philosophy of praxis centered around a Marxist humanist pedagogy of negativity. Negativity—an ominous word in a culture of cheep thrills—should not be tarred as antisocial, pathological, or merely the opposite of "positive," as something that can't be productive for humanity. Negativity, in the dialectical sense that we are using the term, can lead to a new beginning.

Dialogical praxis and civil disobedience must be given pride of place in our revolutionary strategy as we acknowledge that classless society won't come about of its own accord. We cannot beckon it or plead with it to come forward but must compel it into being through our actions. As revolutionary consciousness gestates inside of us, we need to make ourselves porous to socialist possibilities. We are not about to discard Marxism as fortune-telling, as an act of academic scrying; rather, we attempt to bring it forward as a philosophy of praxis, one that helps to shape the world and our place within it. Neither are we prepared to crowbar Marxism into the contemporary setting since Marxism is fully present in the debates over capitalism even if in the field of education it is seen as critical pedagogy's poor relations. In this menagerie of capitalist contradictions that we call "civilization," we need to produce strategic filaments, connecting groups and communities, overcoming dualisms, and building revolutionary alliances in a massive popular front against globalized capital. Of course, programs such as the ecosocial Global Marshall Plan are welcomed, but it must be understood that they do not go far enough. We agree that a changeover to renewable energy can prevent conflicts for remaining world resources since the precondition for development, accompanied by the elimination of hunger and disease, is the realization of a constant supply of sustainable energy. Resource wars are the wars of the future, and it is clear that even Bush Jr. will not be able to capture all the rays of the sun. But on the other hand, such a program must be accompanied by a sustained commitment to anticapitalist struggle and socialist renewal—to the creation of a world able to reproduce itself in peace outside capitalist laws of value.

Socialist democracy is our founding axiom, the very condition of our praxis, since it is less a goal that can be fully achieved than it is a praxis that disrupts our silence, ruptures our political quiescence, and troubles our revolutionary entropy. We must reject the embourgeoisement of a critical pedagogy that defends itself from the poor as much as creates the conditions for their liberation. In so doing, we must not forget that the ruling elite possesses a pathological repugnance for equality and progress toward socialism and will not give up their enraptured state of wealth through rational argumentation alone or accept defeat by the sword of rhetoric. Even as we point out the egregious contradictions of capital and make our philosophical case for socialism, our province is to prepare our struggle for the outside world: on the picket lines, in the halls of justice, in the legislature, and in the streets.

References

Applebaum, M. 2003. Don't spare the brand. *Brandweek.* Lexis/Nexus, March 10.
Bales, K. 2000. Throwaway people. *Index on Censorship* 28(1): 36–45.
Bennett, W. 2002. *Why we fight: Moral clarity and the war on terrorism.* New York: Doubleday.

Boyle, F. 2001. Speech at Illinois Disciples. http://msanews.mynet?Scholars/Boyle/nowar.html (accessed May 15, 2002).

Canfield, C. 2003. Maine teachers warned on Iraq war talk. *The State,* February 28, www.thestate.com/mld/state/5282048.htm (accessed March 1, 2003).

Cockburn, A. 2002. The hog wallow. *The Nation* 275(5): 8.

Cockburn, A., and J. St. Clair. 1998. *Whiteout: The CIA, drugs, and the press.* London: Verso.

Dery, M. 1999. *The pyrotechnic insanitarium: American culture on the brink.* New York: Grove Press.

Dunayevskaya, R. 1991. *Rosa Luxemburg, women's liberation, and Marx's philosophy of liberation.* Champaign-Urbana: University of Illinois Press.

Engels, F. [1847] 1987. *The conditions of the working class in England.* London: Penguin Books.

Featherstone, L. 2002. *Students against sweatshops.* London: Verso.

Grey, B. 2000. Leaked CIA report says 50,000 sold into slavery in US every year. *World Socialist Web Site.* www.wsws.org/articles/2000/apr2000/slav-a03.shtml (accessed May 20, 2002).

Johnson, C. 2000. *Blowback: The costs and consequences of American empire.* New York: Owl Books.

Kameras, D. 1998. Bringing home child labor: What it takes to buy the products we buy. *America@work* 3(5): 12–16.

Kellner, D. 2001. *September 11, terror war, and blowback.* Unpublished manuscript.

Klein, N. 1999. *No logo: Taking aim at the brand bullies.* New York: Picador.

Kumamoto, B. 1993. The study of terrorism: An interdisciplinary approach for the classroom. *Social Studies Review* 33(1): 16–21.

Marable, M. 2001a. The failure of U.S. foreign policies. *Along the Color Line,* November 28. www.manningmarable.net. (accessed June 12, 2002).

———. 2001b. Terrorism and the struggle for peace. *Along the Color Lines,* October 25. www.manningmarable.net. (accessed June 15, 2002).

News and Letters. 2004. World crises and the search for alternatives to capitalism. *News and Letters* 49, no. 6 (July): 1, 5–8.

Niva, S. 2001. Addressing the sources of Middle Eastern violence against the United States. *Common Dreams News Center,* September 14. www.commondreams.org/views01/0914-04.htm (accessed June 1, 2002).

Ollman, B. 2001. *How to take an exam and remake the world.* Montreal: Black Rose Books.

Parenti, M. 2002. *The terrorism trap: September 11 and beyond.* San Francisco: City Lights Books.

Parks, J. B. 1997. This holiday season no sweat. *America@work* 2(10): 11–12.

Petras, J., and H. Veltmeyer. 2001. *Globalization unmasked: Imperialism in the 21st century.* Halifax: Fernwood Publishing.

Robinson, W. 2001. Social theory and globalization: The rise of a transnational state. *Theory and Society* 30: 157–200.

Said, E. 2001. Islam and the West are inadequate banners. *The Observer,* September 16. www.observer.co.uk/comment/story/0,6903,552764,00.html (accessed September 20, 2001).

Singer, D. 1999. *Whose millennium? Theirs or ours?* New York: Monthly Review Press.

Afterword

June 3, 2004
St. Petersburg, Russia

MANY LEFTIST EDUCATIONAL THINKERS OF THE DAY, not to mention the edu-cational mainstream, seem to think that capitalism is like a *dilemma* to which there is no solution. Capitalism has to be accepted, and human beings must learn to cope and live with it. Peter McLaren and Ramin Farahmandpur do not, however, belong to that celebrated league of educational scholars. As their *Teaching against Global Capitalism and the New Imperialism* demonstrates in its unique way, a dilemma is not the only possible way of characterizing cap-italism and its devastating impact on education and other life-sustaining prac-tices. In contrast to an unresolvable dilemma, McLaren and Farahmandpur in-stead conceptualize capitalism as a *problem* that can and must be solved. As they argue in their book, capitalism is a purely social and ideological construct, for its only essence is its own ideological structure. That structure and logic needs to be exposed and analyzed and then dismantled and destroyed.

Teaching against Global Capitalism and the New Imperialism is one of the few books that overtly uses a critique of political economy in the context of critical education. Moreover, McLaren and Farahmandpur are one of the few critical educational theorists and leading spokespersons among critical edu-cators who have the foresight, courage, and tenacity to apply persistently con-cepts like imperialism and class struggle in their analysis of globalization and new forms of imperialism. In their analysis and rhetoric, they combine two registers of scholarly writing, namely, those that combine political activism, civil disobedience, and revolutionary struggle with solid sociological analysis. What is especially remarkable in McLaren and Farahmandpur's work is that it is uncompromisingly Marxist; it stands alone in the field of critical educational studies. Certainly there have been numerous books on the topic of globalization and education in recent years but none that betray such a relentless drive to unpack capitalism's hydra-headed dimensions and pose socialism as an alternative.

The authors rank among the fiercest critics of U.S. imperialism in discussing not only education and its pitfalls but also other sociopolitical traumas of the current neoliberal era. They emphasize that the struggle against capitalist globalization and new incarnations of imperialism is not simply one among many other political fights but the primary struggle that strategically supersedes all others. McLaren and Farahmandpur are unequivocal in their assertion that it is capitalist social relations of production and its practices of valorization that put and keep people in a consumer nirvana of political quietude and that it is our subjectivity held hostage by capitalism that must be remade into a critical engine of revolutionary consciousness in order to change the world. It is precisely the question of class struggle that is too often missing from the otherwise sophisticated analysis of critical educators and political economists.

McLaren and Farahmandpur also put the question of class consciousness back on the agenda of critical educational theory. The question has to do, of course, with the role of culture and education in fostering working-class consciousness (without fetishizing it) and in catalyzing political organization, reflection, and action. In their analysis, not only is class antagonism still a valid category, but it becomes the cornerstone of critical educational analysis. By taking seriously the most important questions of critical education—those that deal with the political and economic conditions that make capitalism possible—McLaren and Farahmandpur force us to rethink the function, scope, and mode of present-day critical educational theory and praxis.

Some critics may claim that McLaren and Farahmandpur have fallen into the trap of socialist nostalgia similar to that of the *ulitsas* and *prospects* of St. Petersburg—still known to many as "Leningrad"—where Soviet kitsch from Red Army hats, bags, and collectibles to statues of the leaders of the October Revolution and CCCP are sold. Nothing, however, could be further from their politically accurate and intellectually timely project. Those critics who would decry McLaren and Farahmandpur's work as caught in the time warp of Cold War politics are often the very ones who do not want to recognize the totalizing and predatory nature of neoliberal capitalism. They prefer to live their lives in secluded college towns and judge the world by the parochial standards of their isolationism or the moral superiority of their hidebound lives.

It is these critics who remind me of Lenin's famous distinction between formal and actual freedom. In their numerous discourses and conversations and in their uses of various vocabularies, these pseudo-leftist thinkers exercise formal freedom, which is the freedom of choice *within* the shared coordinates of existing power relations. Not even in their dreams would they be willing to cross these limits of liberal discourse by stepping into the area of actual freedom and seriously questioning the very coordinates of the capitalist system. This "actual" questioning is exactly what Peter McLaren and Ramin Farahmandpur have done in their *Teaching against Global Capitalism and the New Imperialism*. By revisiting modes of critique often associated with the past, they have written a book that is ahead of the times.

Professor Juha Suoranta
University of Joensuu, Finland

Index

Abu Ghraib prison scandal, 14, 270
Abu-Manneh, Bashhir, 2, 3
"Academies of Travel & Tourism" (tourism industry training program), 202
advertising, corporate: growth of, 200–201; in schools, 165–72, 201–3
"affluenza," 215
Afghanistan, 259
Ahmad, Aijaz, 21, 75, 81–82, 87
Alamada, F., 27
Al-Amariyah prison, 270
alienation, 52, 180
Allawi, Iyad, 270
Allen, R. L., 209, 218
Allen, T. W., 107, 138–39
Allman, P., 27, 55–56, 121, 152, 185, 215, 216
al Qaeda network, 258–59
Alson, Allan, 272
Alter, J., 232
Alvarado, Elvia, 93
American Enterprise Institute, 205
American Express (finance company), 202
American Passage Media Corporation, 201–2

Amin, Samir, 69, 75, 84, 88, 91, 195, 220; imperialism, stages of, 41–42; Marxism, interpretation of, 79–80; on modernism, 62, 78; postmodernism, criticism of, 82, 85–86
Anderson, Perry, 74, 142
Angel Soft (toilet paper company), 171
Ansell, A. E., 133, 134
Antelo, E., 183
antiessentialism, 78–79, 93n4
antifoundationalism. *See* antiessentialism
anti-Semitism, 129
antiwar movement, 234, 251, 271–72
Anzaldúa, G., 112
Appelbaum, R. P., 40, 151, 163
Apple, Michael, 204
Applebaum, M., 272
The Apprentice (television show), 120–21
Aristide, Jean-Bertrand, 130
Arrighi, G., 128
Arroyo High School, 234
Ashcroft, John, 186–87
Azad, Bahman, 41, 45–46, 163

Bacon's Rebellion, 106
Bakst, Brian, 170
Baldwin, James, 141
Bales, Kevin, 263, 264
Banfield, G., 204–5
Bangladesh, 263
Barber, Bretton, 271
Baudrillard, Jean, 77–78, 80
Beatty, Jennifer, 203
Bello, V., 44
bellum justum, concept of, 42
Bennett, William, 134, 135, 231–32,
    269–70
Berger, Lisa, 228
Berliner, D. C., 205
Berman, M., 32
Bertsch, Charlie, 19
Biddle, B. J., 205
bin Laden, Osama, 258–59
Bloom, Allan, 136–37
Bloom, S., 251–52
blowback, 258–59
Blum, Bill, 3, 4
Boggs, C., 50, 80–81, 195
Bologh, Roslyn Wallach, 86
Bonacich, Edna, 40, 151, 163
"Book It" (reading program), 202
Books Not Bombs protests, 234
border pedagogy, 152
Borowski, John, 167
Bourdieu, Pierre, 183
boutique multiculturalism, 137
Bova, José, 187
Bozorgmehr, M., 144
Brandt, Deborah, 9
Brannon, L., 179
Brazil, 218
Brenner, R., 71–72, 197
Bretton Woods Conference (1944),
    68–69
Brown, B., 102
Buchanan, Pat, 132
Budgen, S., 197
Bumfights (Internet videos), 270
Burawoy, Michael, 217

Burger King (restaurant chain), 166, 202
Burns, R., 229
Bush, G. W., 14, 120, 192, 227–28;
    education policy, 205, 229–31;
    Middle East peace process and, 259;
    moral intelligence, lack of, 123–24;
    presidential appointment, 43;
    unilateralism of, 5, 268–69; youth
    opposition, galvanization of, 251
Butler, Judith, 26, 219
Butler-Wall, Brita, 272

California: cheap labor flow, regulation
    of, 144–45; education in, 159, 229,
    231; political initiatives, 132, 143–44;
    racism, 132
California Education Code, 159
Callinicos, Alex, 83, 193, 194, 221
Cámara, Helder, 192
Cameron, Ewen, 166
Cameron, Mike, 202–3
Campbell Soup Company, 203
Canada, 198–99
Canfield, C., 271
capacities, concept of, 60
Capital (Marx), 61
capital, types of, 172
capitalism: class inequality and, 181;
    democracy, relationship to, 19, 28, 42,
    62, 98–99, 121–22, 131, 142, 219–20;
    feudalism and slavery, comparison to,
    162; higher education, failure to
    critique, 7; identity politics and,
    24–26, 28–29, 173–75; Lenin's theory
    of, 40; liberal reform efforts, 248–49;
    Marxist criticism of, 15, 21, 23, 32,
    164–65; myth of success, 16–17;
    naturalized repression of, 193;
    postmodernism, failure to critique,
    17–19, 74, 81–82, 84, 219; structural
    contradictions, 44–47, 54, 80, 125–26;
    technology and, 44, 130; wealth,
    source of, 265–66. See also
    globalization; new imperialism
capitalism, global. See globalization

capitalist schooling, 51, 53, 76, 123, 131, 164. *See also* education
Cassy, John, 168
Center for a New American Dream, 200–201
Center for Commercial-Free Public Education, 202, 203
Center for the Study of Popular Economics, 194
Center X Forum (UCLA newsletter), 234
Central Intelligence Agency (CIA), 144; higher education and, 235–36; on slavery in the United States, 264; terrorism and, 258–59
Channel One, 167–68, 201
Chevron (oil company), 167
child labor, 263
child poverty, 8, 263
Children's Defense Fund, 215
China, 264
Chinchilla, N., 144
CIA. *See* Central Intelligence Agency
Cincinnati, race-based uprisings, 213
citizenship: within capitalist democracy, 179, 212; formal versus substantive, 274–75
citizenship, revolutionary, 212–13; civil commons and, 215–16; economic development and, 218
civil commons, value system of, 214–16
class: concept of, 173, 181; education and, 8, 9, 244; global formation of, 260; racism and, 139–40. *See also* capitalism, structural contradictions; identity politics; working class
class consciousness, 183
class struggle: human liberation and, 175–76; postmodernist discounting of, 83–89, 176–78
Clinton, Bill, 80, 133, 145, 205
The Closing of the American Mind (Bloom), 136–37
Cloud, Dana L., 174
CNN television, 269

Coca-Cola (soft drink company), 71, 166, 170, 202
Cockburn, A., 258–59, 267
Cole, M., 176, 179, 216; on marketization of education, 131, 168, 210, 211; postmodernism, criticism of, 30, 78
collective action, conditions for, 184
Collins, C., 122, 167
Collins, Susan, 271
Colombia, 263
commercialization, defined, 222n1
commodification, defined, 222n1
common culture, 134–37
communism, 125; U.S. policy against, 3–4
computer industry, 130
The Conditions of the Working Class in England (Engels), 264
conservative postmodernism, 80–81
consumption: cultural homogeneity and, 101–2; productive versus unproductive, 52
consumption capital, 172
contraband pedagogy, 91–92
corporate media, 10, 14, 155n1, 237, 269. *See also* television
corporate regime, underlying structure of, 214
Corporate Watch, 201
corporations, transnational: economic power of, 196; global economy, control over, 197–98; record profitability, 71; research centers, sponsors of, 165; states and, 71, 100, 122, 195; wealth depletion of developing nations, 163–64. *See also specific* corporations
Costilla, L. F. O., 212
Crapanzano, Vincent, 79
"Critical Literacy for Global Citizenship" (Farahmandpur and McLaren), 234
critical multiculturalism, 107–11, 114–15
critical pedagogy: class and, 8, 244; domestication of, 159–60, 218,

241–43; education reform and, 246;
empowerment of students, 53–56;
progressive education, comparison
to, 240; revamped approach,
principles of, 9; study of privatization
of education, 49–50; terrorism and,
273–75. *See also* education;
revolutionary critical pedagogy;
socialist schooling
Croteau, D., 24
Cruz, J., 115
Cuban, L., 205
cultural capital, 172
cultural homogeneity, consumption and,
101–2
cultural imperialism, 27
Cultural Literacy (Hirsch), 135–36
culture: defined, 108; globalization of, 76
Cunning Stunts (marketing company),
168

Dalla Costa, M., 99
Darder, A., 137–38
Davies, S., 102
Davis, A. Y., 108, 144
Dearborn High School, 271
debt bondage, 263
Defense, U.S. Department of: budget,
229; military recruitment, 5, 272–73
Dehli, Kari, 222n1
democracy: capitalism, relationship to,
19, 28, 42, 62, 98–99, 121–22, 131,
142, 219–20
democracy, radical, 173–74
demonstrations. *See* protests
deregulation, 262
Dery, Mark, 265
developing nations, wealth depletion
by transnational corporations,
163–64
Dial, David, 271
difference, right-wing versus liberal
understanding of, 133–34
Dinerstein, A., 40, 163, 212

Dirlik, Arif, 26
The Discontinuity of America
(Schlesinger), 103
Dlugin, Lee, 196
Dole Food Company, 169–70
downsizing, defined, 222n3
Doyle, Sara, 271
Dr. Pepper (soft drink company), 170
D'Souza, Dinish, 104
dual regime of accumulation, 45
Dunayevskaya, Raya, 257
Dunkin' Donuts (restaurant chain), 171

Eagleton, Terry, 15, 19, 32, 83
Ebert, Teresa, 17, 77, 80, 127–28, 244
Economic Policy Institute, 267
economic privilege. *See* class
The Economist, 44
education: bilingual, 103, 132;
California, 159, 229, 231; corporate
assault on, 49–50; corporate
management model, 199–200;
dropout rates, 131; homogeneity of,
102; JROTC programs, 272–73;
marketization of, 165–72, 201–3, 214,
222n1, 229–31; marketization of,
protests against, 202–3, 204;
Maryland, 229; military recruitment
and, 231, 272–73; multiculturalism
and, 135, 136; neoconservative
attacks on, 92, 103–4, 204–5, 209;
neoliberalism and, 171–72, 204;
paradox of, 172; racism and, 131,
132; reading programs, 230–31;
standardized testing, 204–6, 230;
underfunding of, 198–99, 229. *See
also* capitalist schooling; critical
pedagogy; socialist schooling
education, higher: access to, 9;
capitalism, failure to critique, 7;
Central Intelligence Agency and,
235–36; labor force and, 228–29;
marketization of, 235
education industry, 199–200, 201

Ehrenberg, J., 23
Ehrenreich, B., 80, 198
Eisner, Michael, 266
Elder, Larry, 234–35
Empire (Hardt and Negri), 1–2, 3
The End of Racism (D'Souza), 104
Energy, U.S. Department of, 229
Engels, Friedrich, 33, 61, 97, 102, 264; on
   common culture, 134–35; goal of
   socialism, 186
Enlightenment universalism, 24, 87, 149
equality, measure of social progress, 86
equality of opportunity, cost of, 194
Exxon (oil company), 167, 203

Falwell, Jerry, 92
Farahmandpur, R., 29, 152, 197, 210,
   216, 234; critical pedagogy,
   domestication of, 159, 241, 243; on
   revolutionary critical pedagogy, 180,
   181, 185
fascism, 5–6
Fattah, C., 229
FBI (Federal Bureau of Investigation),
   34n4
Featherstone, Liza, 276
Federal Bureau of Investigation (FBI),
   34n4
feminism, 25–26, 74–75, 85. *See also*
   identity politics
feudalism, 46, 162
Field Trip Factory (national education
   organization), 168
Fillmore High School, 234
Fischman, G., 179, 183
Fish, Stanley, 137
Flores, L. A., 110
Folbre, N., 194
Foothill Tech, 234
Fornäs, J., 77
Forrester, Viviane, 123
Foster, John Bellamy, 237, 250
Fox, M., 8–9
FOX television, 166, 232, 269

Fraser, N., 21
freedom, actual versus formal, 283
free market: defined, 196; value system
   of, 215–16
free-market democracy, 122–23
free speech zones, 168
Freire, Paulo, 17, 50, 53–54, 179, 217
Fukuyama, Francis, 101, 128

Gap (clothing company), 45
Gardels, N., 77
Gates, Bill, 194
Gee, J. P., 209
gender: class and, 85, 89. *See also*
   identity politics; women
General Mills (food company), 170
geopolitical correctness, 39
The German Ideology (Marx and Engels),
   134–35
Gibbs, David, 235, 236
Gibson, Katherine, 88–89
Gimenez, Martha E., 39–40, 75, 84, 85,
   113
Gindin, Sam, 60, 61, 213, 214
Gingrich, Newt, 205
Giri, A. K., 100
Giroux, Henry, 123, 178, 179; on
   government intolerance of protest,
   233, 234; on multiculturalism, 104,
   137; on neoliberalism, 171–72
Giuliani, Rudolph, 266
global capitalism. *See* globalization
globalization: defined, 195–96;
   beneficiaries, 120–21; benefits, myth
   of, 261; of culture, 76; economic
   consequences of, 120–21, 124, 194,
   262; ethical foundation, lack of, 72;
   ideology, manufacture of, 124–25; as
   imperialism, 39–41, 162–63, 262;
   internationalization, comparison to,
   259; labor force, exploitation of, 71;
   limits of, 98–101; political theory of,
   127–28; regulation of, 47, 71;
   resistance to, 101, 116–17; states as

agents of, 38–39, 57, 64–65n1, 163,
197; as transnationalism, 127. See also
capitalism; imperialism;
neoliberalism; new imperialism
Gordon, Linda, 134, 154
Graham, Julie, 88–89
Gramsci, Antonio, 17, 183
Grande, S. M. A., 152, 219
Green, A., 30, 74, 77, 232
Greider, William, 120
Grey, B., 264
Grundrisse (Marx), 146
Guppy, N., 102

Haiti, 265
Hall, Stuart, 115
Hamburger University, 202
Hamilton, C., 105, 144
Hardt, M., 1–2, 3, 41, 42, 197
Harris, J., 121
Harris, K., 109
Harvey, David, 61, 73
Hatcher, Richard, 181–82
Hawkes, D., 161
hegemony, trilateral transnational, 47–49
Heintz, J., 194
Hellman, C., 229
Helmore, E., 232
Helms, Jesse, 205
Hempel, J., 9
Hennessy, Rosemary, 221
Heritage Foundation, 205
Hershey Corporation, 166, 202, 203
Hickey, T., 29
higher education. See education, higher
Hightower, Jim, 187
Hill, Dave, 51, 176, 179, 216; on
education, 131, 210; education
reform proposal, 238–39;
postmodernism, criticism of, 30, 78
Hirsch, E. D., 135–36
historical materialism, 82–83
Holloway, John, 59, 245
Holst, J., 57, 58

homelessness, U.S., 266
Honduras, 265
Hopkins, T. K., 128
Hull, G., 209
Hussein, Saddam, 10, 237
hybridity. See multiculturalism

IBM, 264
identity politics: capitalism and, 24–26,
28–29, 173–75; collective action and,
184; criticism of, 153–54; Marxism
and, 84–85; neoliberalism and, 150.
See also class struggle;
postmodernism
Ignatiev, N., 107, 141–42
Imam, Hayat, 42, 160, 164
IMF (International Monetary Fund),
120, 196
immigration, U.S., 72; regulation of,
144–45
imperialism: Lenin's theory of, 2–3;
stages of, 41–42. See also
globalization; new imperialism
Indonesia, 124, 264
internationalization, 259
International Monetary Fund (IMF),
120, 196
Internet, 131
investment capital, 172
Iran–Iraq war, 236–37
Iraq war: Abu Ghraib prison scandal, 14,
270; protests against, 234, 271–72;
U.S. occupation, 4, 28, 49
Irving, David, 129
Israel, 259

James, J., 104
Japan, 124
Jarvis, Robert, 235, 236
JCPenney (clothing company), 264
Johns Hopkins Hospital, 267
Johnson, Chalmers, 258
Joines, Rick, 78
Jordan, J., 208

jus ad bellum, concept of, 42
Jusdanis, G., 101

Kading, Tristan, 168
Kagarlitsky, Boris, 60, 126, 155n2, 175, 194, 218; on democracy under capitalism, 219–20; on multiculturalism, 148–49, 150
Kameras, D., 263
Kautsky, Karl, 2
Keeley, Robin D. G., 17
Kellner, Douglas, 88
Kellogg's (food company), 166
Kenway, Jane, 26
Kenya, 263
Kilbourne, Jean, 201
Kincheloe, J., 27, 137, 143, 210
King, Rodney, 143–45
Kinsley, M., 232
Kissinger, Henry, 76
Klein, N., 45, 144, 203, 265
Knight, Phil, 266
Knoblauch, C. H., 179
knowledge, abstract versus practical, 181–82
Knowledge Universe (corporation), 166
Korea, 124
Korten, D. C., 69
Kovel, Joel, 113, 115
Kozol, Jonathan, 229
Krupskaya, N., 51
Kumamoto, Bob, 273–74

labor, value form of, 206–8
labor force: children, 263; globalization and, 71; heterogeneity of global, 73; higher education and, 228–29; prison, 264; women, 265
labor power, 206, 207, 247; price of, 146–47
Lacan, Jacques, 62
Laclau, Ernest, 24, 219
LaFeber, W., 152
language of critique, 257–58

Lankshear, C., 209
Larrain, J., 19
Larsen, Neil, 126
Lasn, Kalle, 166, 167, 196, 203
Lather, Patti, 25, 74–75, 177
Latin America: austerity programs, 128–29; financial crises, 124
Latinophobia, 132
Lauter, Paul, 8
Lee, Barbara, 267
Left, postmodernization of, 17. *See also* postmodernism
Legacy High School, 271
Lenin, V. I., 233, 234, 237, 238; capitalism, theory of, 40; on freedom, 283; imperialism, theory of, 2–3; on liberal democracy, 62–63
Leonard, John, 184
Leonardo, Z., 209, 218
liberal democracy, 62–63, 248–49
Libretti, T., 27
life capital, 60
Life in Schools (McLaren), 182
"Life of an Ant" (poster), 167
Lifetime Learning Systems, 202
Limbaugh, Rush, 103–4, 270
Lipstadt, Deborah, 129
Lockard, Joe, 19
Locke, John, 136–37
Lockery, T., 171
Long, Huey, 227
Los Angeles, 143–45
Los Angeles Times, 166
Loucky, J., 144
Löwy, Michael, 221
ludic postmodernism, 77
Lusane, C., 45
Luxemburg, Rosa, 162

MacDonald, Kevin, 129
Macedo, Donaldo, 132
MacMichael, D., 235, 236
MacWean, Arthur, 218
Malaysia, 124

Malik, K., 86, 149–50
Mall Academy, 171
Manifesto (Marx and Engels), 186
maquiladoras, 27, 265
Marable, Manning, 104, 105, 260, 261
marketization, forms of, 222n1
Martin, G., 251
Martin, Randy, 131
Martinot, S., 140
Marx, Karl, 33, 97, 220; alienation, four
    relations constituting, 52;
    capitalism, criticism of, 13, 15, 32,
    164–65; on common culture,
    134–35; diversity, belief in, 147; goal
    of socialism, 186; historical
    materialism, 82–83; labor, value of,
    146, 206; on money, 161; on social
    justice, 61; on technology, 44, 130;
    on universal ideology, 102; Weber,
    comparison to, 29
Marxism, 186; Amin's interpretation,
    79–80; attacks on, modern, 129;
    capitalism, criticism of, 14–15, 21,
    23, 32, 164–65; feminism and,
    25–26, 74–75; Holloway's
    interpretation of, 245; identity
    politics and, 84–85; multiculturalism
    and, 28; negativity, pedagogy of, 277;
    Ollman's interpretation, 275;
    postmodernist dismissal of, 19, 22,
    29–30, 77–78; poststructuralist
    dismissal of, 177; resurgence, 20,
    29–30; revolutionary critical
    pedagogy and, 277–78
Maryland, education in, 229
McCarthy, C., 110–11
McChesney, Robert, 16, 175
McDonald's (restaurant chain), 166–67,
    168, 187, 202
McGraw-Hill (publishing company), 167
McKay, Ian, 32
McLaren, P., 27, 29, 110, 210, 216, 234;
    on class struggle, 176; critical
    pedagogy, domestication of, 159,
    218, 241, 243; on multiculturalism,

108, 109, 115, 147, 152;
    postmodernism, criticism of, 21,
    30; public education, paradox of,
    172; on relationship of globalization
    and states, 197; on revolutionary
    critical pedagogy, 152, 178, 179, 180,
    181, 182, 183, 185; on whiteness, 32,
    105
"McLaw of value," 122
McMurtry, John, 16, 43–44, 60; on civil
    commons, 214–15, 216; on free-
    market democracy, 122–23; on public
    education, 198–200, 214; on
    transnational corporations, 197–98
McNally, David, 16–17, 188
McPhail, M. L., 110
McQueen, A., 130
media, corporate, 10, 14, 155n1, 237,
    269. *See also* television
Meese, Edwin, 205
Mell, Leonard, 86
mestizaje identity, 111–13. *See also*
    multiculturalism
Mészáros, István, 16, 52, 97, 99, 101, 180,
    196
Metcalf, S., 231
Milken, Michael, 165–66
Minkkinen, P., 47
modernism, 78
Monthly Review, 236
Moody, Kim, 57, 64n1, 69, 71, 72, 73, 90
Moonlight Bunny Ranch, 5
Moraga, Cherríe, 97
Morris-Suzuki, T., 152
Morton, D., 252
Mosley, Walter, 16
Mouffe, C., 24
Mouhibian, Alec, 235
multiculturalism, 26–29, 114, 143,
    151–52; education and, 135, 136;
    neoconservative attacks on, 102–4,
    136–37. *See also mestizaje* identity;
    racism
multiculturalism, critical, 107–11,
    114–15

multiculturalism, revolutionary, 147–49, 151–53
multinational corporations. *See* corporations, transnational

Nabisco (food company), 169
NAFTA. *See* North American Free Trade Agreement
National Security Act (1991), 235
A Nation at Risk, 204
nation-states. *See* states
NATO. *See* North Atlantic Treaty Organization
Neary, M., 206, 215
Negri, Antonio, 1–2, 3, 41, 42, 197
Negroponte, John, 267–68
neoconservatism: education, attacks on, 92, 103–4, 204–5, 209; multiculturalism, attacks on, 102–4, 136–37
neoliberalism: defined, 15–16; destructive power of, 69–70, 71–72, 101; education and, 171–72, 204; politics of, 150, 161–64; postmodernism and, 21, 85–86; resistance to, 133. *See also* globalization; New Right
Nestlé Company (food company), 170
neutrality, discourse of, 7
Nevins, Bill, 272
new imperialism, 8, 49, 163; defined, 40–41, 46; types of borders of, 10. *See also* capitalism; imperialism
new racism, 133–38
New Right: common culture and, 134–37; difference, celebration of, 133–34; personal responsibility rhetoric, 138; universalism of, 134–35. *See also* neoconservatism; neoliberalism; Right, radical
new teacher unionism, 208–12
New York University, 228–29
Niemark, M. K., 165
Nike Corporation, 202, 203, 265
Niva, Steve, 259

No Child Left Behind Act (2002), 194, 230–31, 272–73
nonclass process, 89
North American Free Trade Agreement (NAFTA), 198
North Atlantic Treaty Organization (NATO): U.S. control over, 195, 267
Noumoff, Sam J., 22–23
Nye, Joseph S., 235, 236

Oakes, J., 206
objectivity, discourse of, 7
O'Connor, James, 18
oligarchies. *See* corporations, transnational
Ollman, Bertell, 38, 54–55, 275
open universalism, 149
organic intellectuals, 183–84
Ortega, T., 129
Oscar Mayer, 170
Ostendorf, B., 98, 100
outsourcing, defined, 222n4
Ovando, C. J., 179

Panitch, Leo, 60, 61, 213, 214
Parenti, Michael, 72, 87, 173, 177, 220, 235, 277
Parks, J. B., 264, 265
Patriot Act (2001), 233
patriotism, right-wing construct of, 257
pedagogy, contraband, 91–92
peer reviewing, 208
Peery, N., 162
Pembroke Lakes Elementary School, 202
Penguin Books (publishing company), 129
Pepsi (soft drink company), 166, 170
Persuad, R. B., 45
Perucci, R., 172
Peterson, Bob, 136
Petras, James, 47–49, 127, 130, 261, 274–75
Philippines, 264
Phillips, A., 108

Pierre, R. E., 234
Pizza Hut (restaurant chain), 202
plantocracy, 139–40
Plawiuk, Eugene, 209
Poblete, J., 234
political dissent, post-9/11, 234
postmodernism: capitalism, failure to
    critique, 17–19, 74, 81–82, 84, 219;
    class struggle, discounting of, 83–89,
    176–78; indeterminacy of, 80–81;
    Marxism, dismissal of, 19, 22, 29–30,
    77–78; neoliberalism and, 21, 85–86;
    politics of, 22–24; radical democracy
    and, 173–74; radical Right, agent of,
    23, 30, 81; structural contradictions,
    20–21; successes, 17, 20, 74;
    universalism, suspicion of, 23–24, 78,
    149–50. *See also* identity politics
postmodernism, conservative, 80–81
postmodernism, ludic, 77
poststructuralism, dismissal of Marxism,
    177
potentials, concept of, 60
"pouring contracts," 170
prison labor, 264
privatization, 262; defined, 222n1, 223n5
progressive education, 240
proletariat, 185
Proposition 187 (California), 143–44
Proposition 227 (California), 144
protests: education, against
    marketization of, 202–3, 234;
    government intolerance of, 233–34;
    Iraq war, 234, 271–72; WTO, 130, 187
public education. *See* education
Puerto Rico, 27, 34n4, 273
Putaluma High School, 271–72

al Qaeda network, 258–59

racism, 213; anti-Semitism, 129; class
    and, 139–40; defined, 107; education
    and, 131, 132; neoconservatism and,
    104; social construct, 105–6. *See also*

identity politics; multiculturalism;
    whiteness
racism, institutional, 104–7
racism, new, 133–38
radical democracy, 173–74
Raduntz, Helen, 207
Raisons d'Agir (social movement), 183
Reagan, Ronald: anti-communist stance,
    3–4; education policy, 205;
    imperialist policies, 10; war criminal,
    10, 14, 260
Reaganism, 260
Red Cross, 270
Reed, A., 183, 184
Research Unit for Political Economy, 236
residualization, defined, 222n1
Resnick, S., 89, 99, 100
Revlon (cosmetics company), 167
revolutionary critical pedagogy, 7, 185,
    186, 241, 253–54; class structure
    and, 8, 244; goals of, 244, 276;
    Marxism and, 277–78; objectivity
    and neutrality discourse, 6–7;
    practice versus theory, 7–8. *See also*
    critical pedagogy; socialist
    schooling
revolutionary multiculturalism, 147–49,
    151–53
revolutionary working-class pedagogy,
    178–79, 180–84
Richardson, T., 219
Right. *See* neoconservatism; New Right
Right, radical: postmodernism as agent
    of, 23, 30, 81
Rikowski, Glen, 179, 187, 215, 216, 252;
    on education, 131, 210; on value of
    labor, 146–47, 206, 208
Rio Rancho New Mexico High School, 272
Robbins, Bruce, 149
Robertson, Pat, 92
Robinson, W., 116, 121, 259, 260
Roemer, John, 194
Rumsfeld, Donald, 14
RustOleum (paint company), 170

Sachs, Jeff, 248
Said, Edward, 275
Saldívar, José David, 111
Sandoval, C., 112–13
San Juan, E., Jr., 97, 174, 177–78
Santos, Boaventura de Sousa, 5
Sardar, Z., 81, 82
Sassen, S., 72–73
Savage, Michael, 270
Savage Inequalities (Kozol), 229
Schiller, N. G., 105
Schlesinger, A. M., Jr., 103
schools, work-site, 171
self-reflexivity, 110
Serra, S., 183
sexism. *See* identity politics;
    multiculturalism
Shacklock, G., 210, 211
Shell Oil (oil company), 167
Shivani, Anis, 5, 6
ShopRite (supermarket chain), 170
sign value, 76–77
Singer, Daniel, 216, 217, 266
Singh, A., 124
Sivanandan, A., 150
skills capital, 172
Skittles (candy company), 167
slavery, 263–65; capitalism, comparison
    to, 162; in the United States, 139–40,
    264
Sleeter, C. E., 137, 179
Smith, Adam, 123
Smith, Tony, 248, 249
Smyth, G., 210, 211
social capital, 172
socialism, 251–52
socialist morality, 213
socialist schooling, 51; social movements
    and, 55–57. *See also* critical
    pedagogy; education; revolutionary
    critical pedagogy
social justice, 61
social movements, 24–26; conditions for
    success of, 185; resistance to

globalization, 101, 116–17; socialist
    schooling and, 55–57
social movement unionism, 90
social world, dialectical understanding
    of, 54–56
"soft-radicalism," 7
Solís Jordán, Jose, 27, 34n4
Soros, George, 248
Spring, J., 164, 204, 205
Sri Lanka, 264
Stabile, Carol, 25, 76, 85
states: globalization, agents of, 38–39,
    57, 64–65n1, 163, 197; transnational
    corporations and, 71, 100, 122, 195
St. Clair, J., 259
Steinberg, S. R., 137, 143
Stiglitz, Joseph, 248
strong multiculturalism, 137
Students against Sweatshops
    (Featherstone), 276
Students United Against War, 234
subjectivity, registers of, 113–14
Sullivan, Charles, 169
SweeTart contest, 170–71

Taliban, 259
technology, 44, 130
Teeple, G., 161
television: *The Apprentice*, 120–21; child
    exposure to, 201; CNN, 269; FOX, 166,
    232, 269. *See also* media, corporate
"Ten Years Later" (Lather), 177
terrorism: CIA and, 258–59; critical
    pedagogy and, 273–75; right-wing
    construct of, 257; U.S. support of, 10,
    258–59, 260
Thailand, 263
Thandeka (theologian), 139
third way, 80
Thompson, Willie, 24, 126, 164–65
Tijuana Colonia Chilpancingo, 198
Time Warner AOL (communications
    company), 122
Tootsie Rolls, 167

Torres, R., 137–38
Toys Я Us (toy company), 264
"transnational capitalist clan," 121
transnational corporations. *See*
corporations, transnational
Trilateral Commission (1973), 123
Trotsky, L., 25
Trump, Donald, 120–21
truth, 80
TWA (airline), 264
Tyack, D., 205

underdetermination, 79
United Auto Workers, 229
United States: anti-communist policy,
3–4; crisis of legitimacy, 4; Defense,
Department of, 229, 272–73;
democracy, hypocrisy of, 27–28,
249–50; double-containment strategy,
3; economic power, 48; Energy,
Department of, 229; fascist
transformation, 5–6; global strategy,
195; homelessness in, 266;
immigration, 72, 144–45;
incarceration rate, 16, 270; informal
economy, 72–73; Iran–Iraq war,
complicity in, 236–37; labor force,
72–73; labor market, 44–45, 71;
market deregulation, 71–72; NATO,
control over, 195, 267; No Child Left
Behind Act (2002), 230–31, 272–73;
Patriot Act (2001), 233; slavery within,
139–40, 264; terrorism, support of, 10,
258–59, 260; wealth distribution, 44,
71, 126, 194, 266; white supremacy in,
107. *See also* Iraq war
universalism: of Enlightenment, 24, 87,
149; postmodernist suspicion of,
23–24, 78, 149–50
UN Security Council, 267
Unz, Ron, 132
use value, 77

value, labor theory of, 146–47
value, production of, 247
Veltmeyer, H., 261, 274–75

Victoria's Secret (clothing company), 264
Villenas, S., 219
Virginia, colonial, 139–40
Vrana, D., 166

"wage slaves," 125
Wainwright, Hilary, 23
Waldinger, R., 144
Wallerstein, I., 128
Wal-Mart (retail chain), 45
Washington consensus, 124
wealth accumulation credo, 160–61
wealth distribution, global, 8–9, 42, 72,
126, 164, 194, 266
wealth distribution, U.S., 44, 71, 126,
194, 266
Weber, Max, 29
Wendy's (restaurant chain), 166
Went, Robert, 58
white classism, 139
white identity, 141–42
whiteness: abolition, path to, 142–43;
concept of, 105–7; social function,
138–41. *See also* racism
Whiteout (Cockburn and St. Clair), 259
Whittle, Chris, 201
Why We Fight (Bennett), 232, 269–70
Wichterich, C., 45
Wilgoren, J., 145
Wilson, Peter, 132
Winant, H., 105
Witheford, N., 165
Wolff, R., 89
Wolin, Sheldon, 237
women: exploitation of, 265
Wood, E. M., 24, 46–47, 101, 176, 197
workers' centers, 151
Workers Party (Brazil), 218
working class, 129, 173–74; declassing
of, 216–17. *See also* class
working-class pedagogy, revolutionary,
178–79, 180–84
World Bank, 43, 120, 196, 211
World Trade Organization (WTO),
122, 128, 164; protests against, 130,

187; structural adjustment measures, 42

Wysong, E., 172

Yeskel, F., 122, 167
youth, progressive radicalization of, 251, 276

Zap Me! (marketing company), 167
Zavarzadeh, M., 30–31, 252
Žižek, Slavoj, 129, 138, 219, 249, 250; on class struggle, 176, 178; on Lenin, 62–64
Zukin, S., 71

Ramin Farahmandpur (l) and Peter McLaren (r). Courtesy of Laura Layera-McLaren

About the Authors

Peter McLaren is a professor in the Division of Urban Schooling, Graduate School of Education and Information Studies, University of California, Los Angeles. He is the author and editor of over forty books, three of which have won awards, and one, *Life in Schools*, which was recently chosen by an international committee of experts as one of the top twelve educational books worldwide in the field of educational policy. Forthcoming books include *Critical Theories, Radical Pedagogies, and Global Conflicts* (edited with Gustavo Fischman, Heinz Sunker, and Colin Lankshear); *Red Seminars*; and *Capitalists and Conquerors: Critical Pedagogy against Empire*. Professor McLaren lectures worldwide on the politics and pedagogy of liberation.

Ramin Farahmandpur is an assistant professor in the Department of Educational Policy, Foundations and Administrative Studies at Portland State University. His research in education encompasses globalization, imperialism, neoliberalism, Marxism, and critical pedagogy.